History
and Heartburn

History and Heartburn

The Saga of Australian Film
1896-1978

Eric Reade

Rutherford • Madison • Teaneck
Fairleigh Dickinson University Press

By the same author
Australian Silent Films
The Talkies Era
The Australian Screen

HISTORY AND HEARTBURN: The Saga of Australian Film 1896-1978
Copyright © 1979 by Eric Reade

First American edition 1981

Library of Congress catalogue card number:
L.C. 80-67410

Associated University Presses, Inc.
4 Cornwall Drive
East Brunswick, New Jersey 08816

ISBN 0-8386-3082-0
Printed in Hong Kong
by Colorcraft Ltd

This book is dedicated to my wife Christina who has given me love, devotion, assistance, and has endured the loneliness that only an author's wife can understand, when her husband is working on yet another book.

Acknowledgments

Grateful acknowledgment is made to the following, for permission to reproduce illustrations used in this book:
Film Australia: 5.24, 5.25, 5.26, 5.27. The National Library, Canberra: 1.16, 1.31, 2.20, 2.29, 3.17. R.P. Throssell: 1.16. R. Edwards: 1.24, 1.27, 1.36. H. Davidson: 1.34, 1.37, 1.39, 1.42, 2.30, 3.2. Young Historical Society: 1.40. L. 'Bunny' Bindley: 1.44. Margaret Veal: 2.22. C. Tingwell: 3.16. H. Malcolm: 3.17. B. Moran: 3.18, 3.19. Shell Company of Australia: 3.23, 3.24. M. Strizic: 4.9. V. Joyce: 5.9. G. Gray: 5.14. Jane Marston: 5.7. J. Duigan: 5.17. P. Carrette: 5.42. *Cinema Papers*: 5.45. Channel Nine, Sydney: 6.48. D. Parker: 6.52. Australian International Film Corporation: 6.58, 6.83. Julie Millowick: 6.63. Reg Grundy Productions: 6.65, 6.69. ABC Press, Amsterdam: 6.70. D. Kynoch: 6.71. Tasmanian Film Corporation: 6.91, 6.92. Rank Overseas Film Distributors: 3.5. J. Chatteris: 5.70. Australian Broadcasting Commission: 6.2. J. Nield: 6.10. A. Forbes: 6.22. Wim Cox: 6.39.

The following illustrations are from the private collection of Eric Reade and are reproduced with permission: 1.1, 1.2, 1.3, 1.5, 1.6, 1.7, 1.8, 1.9, 1.10, 1.11, 1.12, 1.13, 1.14, 1.15, 1.17, 1.18, 1.19, 1.20, 1.21, 1.22, 1.23, 1.25, 1.27, 1.28, 1.29, 1.30, 1.32, 1.33, 1.34, 1.35, 1.37, 1.38, 1.41, 1.43, 1.45, 1.47, 1.48, 1.49, 1.50, 2.1, 2.2, 2.3, 2.4, 2.5, 2.6, 2.7, 2.8, 2.9, 2.10, 2.11, 2.12, 2.13, 2.14, 2.15, 2.16, 2.17, 2.18, 2.19, 2.21, 2.23, 2.24, 2.25, 2.26, 2.27, 2.28, 2.31, 2.32, 2.33, 2.34, 2.35, 2.36, 3.1, 3.3, 3.4, 3.5, 3.6, 3.7, 3.8, 3.9, 3.10, 3.11, 3.12, 3.13, 3.14, 3.15, 3.20, 3.21, 3.22, 3.25, 3.26, 3.27, 3.28, 4.1, 4.2, 4.3, 4.4, 4.5, 4.6, 4.7, 4.8, 4.10, 4.11, 4.12, 4.13, 4.14, 5.1, 5.2, 5.3, 5.4, 5.5, 5.6, 5.8, 5.10, 5.11, 5.12, 5.13, 5.15, 5.16, 5.18, 5.19, 5.20, 5.21, 5.22, 5.23, 5.28, 5.29, 5.30, 5.31, 5.32, 5.33, 5.34, 5.35, 5.36, 5.37, 5.38, 5.39, 5.40, 5.41, 5.43, 5.44, 5.46, 5.47, 5.48, 5.49, 5.50, 5.51, 5.52, 5.53, 5.54, 5.55, 5.56, 5.57, 5.58, 5.59, 5.60, 5.61, 5.62, 5.63, 5.64, 5.65, 5.66, 5.67, 5.68, 5.69, 5.71, 5.72, 5.73, 5.74, 5.75, 5.76, 5.77, 5.78, 5.79, 5.80, 5.81, 5.82, 5.83, 6.1, 6.3, 6.4, 6.5, 6.6, 6.7, 6.8, 6.9, 6.11, 6.12, 6.13, 6.14, 6.15, 6.16, 6.17, 6.18, 6.19, 6.20, 6.21, 6.23, 6.24, 6.25, 6.26, 6.27, 6.28, 6.29, 6.30, 6.31, 6.32, 6.33, 6.34, 6.35, 6.36, 6.37, 6.38, 6.40, 6.41, 6.42, 6.43, 6.44, 6.45, 6.46, 6.47, 6.49, 6.51, 6.52, 6.53, 6.54, 6.55, 6.56, 6.57, 6.59, 6.60, 6.61, 6.62, 6.64, 6.66, 6.67, 6.68, 6.73, 6.74, 6.75, 6.76, 6.77, 6.79, 6.80, 6.81, 6.82, 6.84, 6.85, 6.86, 6.87, 6.88, 6.89, 6.90.

Editor's Note

Everyone who knew Eric Reade was saddened by his death in December 1978, while completing the final chapter of this book. *History and Heartburn* traces the entire growth and development of the Australiam film industry and includes reference to the 1978 annual industry awards but the author was not able to provide a conclusion to his remarkable historical research.

A brief final comment has been inserted which, it is hoped, provides some sense of the direction which the Australian Film industry finds itself taking.

CONTENTS

1
The Bright Flame

Out, out brief candle!
Life's but a walking shadow, a poor player,
That struts and frets his hour upon the stage
And then is heard no more.

Shakespeare — Macbeth

Like Shakespeare's candle, the Australian film industry had thrown light in a brilliance of entertainment, only to bow its flame to the winds of misadventure — some that it had caused itself; others that it was powerless to resist. It flickered, then went out, leaving spirals of smoke as mute witness of its existence. In the days of talking pictures, another match was used to peer into the yawning abyss that separated the silents from the talkies — but the second awakening produced only a sad epitaph of 'what might have been, if ...' Now the Australian candle has been relit for the third time. Is it an Olympic torch — a searing symbol, proud and fierce, that exists only for a limited period, then is extinguished? Or will it become another Flame of Memory proclaiming the glories of the past? Yet if we dared to hope, could it be ...?

In June 1977 Hector Crawford advised that the future of the Australian film industry was too clouded to determine whether it contained success or failure. He added that most actors still had to supplement their earnings by driving taxis or seeking other employment at night. Crawford should have some knowledge of the industry as he has been supplying features and series for radio and television for decades. (He even ventured into feature films with *The Box*.)

Yet is the scene more adequately described as confused rather than cloudy? We have many 'angry young men' taking over on the film front — ridiculing suggestions from past film makers, and regarding them as tattered remnants from a by-gone era. It is left to the serenely wise 'box office' to pass irrefutable judgement. The 'angry young men' may be blinded by the sheer brilliance of their own creations, but it is the theatre's cash box that makes out rejection slips. The only records such men have created are for short seasons.

It is the ardour of the unseasoned film maker that often results in an error of judgement in the selection of suitable screen material. Yet this is not the only disturbing factor. Just when the local film industry was revealing new vigour after dreary black and white television fare, the small screen gained a new dimension and interest with the introduction of colour. In the city picture houses, attendances fell away alarmingly. Even drive-ins, catering for the younger generation's demand for sex, horror and bikies, gave serious consideration to the land being worth more as real estate. (This was especially true in Sydney, where many outdoor theatres occupied very valuable land.)

Arty films are not the answer. Their appeal is limited even in an affluent and indigenously conscious society, which this country does not have.

In *Theatre Australia* (May 1977) Colin George, then overseas producer for the South Australian Theatre Company, summed up the situation by stating that 'Australia's worst enemies were other Australians'. As for the economy, everyone is well aware just how sick it was in 1978, and this too had an effect on film production. One of the things many Australians must realise is that we do produce films here, and quite often, damned good ones. Naturally we do make damned lousy ones too — but then so do England and America.

Unemployment reached staggering proportions in 1978, yet workers continuously agitated for more and more money — that could have counteracted any reason for box office fall off. In fact they would have kept the theatre cash register tinkling if patriotic enough to support local film production. Answers should be, but weren't forthcoming.

Now to the sobering part of that 'old hat' business. *Gone with the Wind*, although it premiered in 1939, was still good enough to enjoy very successful seasons throughout Australia as a 'rerun'. Is it the rare instance in the history of moving pictures? It does prove that film making was technically advanced enough then, to hold its own today. Almost forty years later in 1978 that same *Gone with the Wind* won the vote as the most popular film ever made in America, at a special function to honour the greatest pictures produced in that country.

An old dog may not learn new tricks, but the ones he did know were worthy of more than polite interest. As an old 'pro' stated recently, 'Why risk good money battling weather hazards on location, when rear projection could provide the same results, at a reduced cost. In addition you need only a small film crew for location shots. In this way you cut travelling expenses considerably in not having to provide transport for the cast. This provides a valuable lesson for even the most inspired of our younger film makers. Listen more. Protest less frequently about advice handed down from the older generation of feature film directors and producers. They were in the business too! Weigh up what you know and what you've heard — then use your common sense. The Australian film industry still requires worthwhile feature films, and directors like Peter Weir, Bruce Beresford and Phil Noyce have accepted the challenge!

Those older film history makers had their problems too — many had to make do with outdoor sets that were far from wind-resistant; to rely on make-shift cameras and lights; and to fight for their rights to be occupants of the Australian screens. All this was done without any financial or even moral support from the Federal Government. By noting such frustrations, Australians can not only have a new admiration for our pioneer film men, but can learn some of the pitfalls to be avoided from them. This should ensure stimulating achievement, and overseas recognition of our prowess in the formulative years ahead.

The First Films

Newhaven won the Melbourne Cup in 1896. Such a feat doesn't warrant the playing of 'Advance Australia Fair': many excellent horses have won the coveted trophy before and since — but the importance of that fact in this book is that the winner had made a significant contribution to the history of Australian films. A touch of irony was that it took a Frenchman, Marius Sestier, behind a Lumiere moving camera, to make that first film. Yet on 15 January 1898, Sestier's camera was offered for sale. Even he could see no future for Australia's infant industry. Worse was to follow. Australia (a country amazingly lax on the subject of preservation) allowed Marius Sestier to leave these shores with the negative of the Melbourne Cup film. It wasn't until the 1969 Melbourne Film Festival, that a copy was presented to the National Library, Canberra, from the Cinématheque Française.

The flame which flickered a little then, cast an even brighter light when an unexpected stimulus came from a most unlikely source — the Salvation Army in Melbourne. Joseph Perry of the Limelight Division, with the aid of another Lumiere moving camera, and a script from Commandant Herbert H. Booth, directed and photographed *Soldiers of the Cross*. It was first screened in the Melbourne Town Hall on 13 September 1900. With only one projector available, Perry had to resort to the use of slides to retain interest, while he threaded the second and succeeding reels.

Controversy has raged over the claim that this was the world's first full-length film. No matter in what category *Soldiers of the Cross* is eventually listed, no one can deny that it was a major contribution to the Australian film industry. The Salvation Army went on to make newsreels and travelogues,

1.1 *The Melbourne Cup of 1896 as photographed by Frenchman Marius Sestier. The hats of the women and men are worthy of note. The helmets of the policemen must have made them "the pride of the force".*

1.2 *Salvation Army City Temple — Bourke Street, Melbourne. At the back, Joseph Perry built his dark room for the development of religious and commercial moving film.*

along with religious subjects, as it saw a unique venue for spiritual promulgation in this new medium, as well as a source of revenue from theatres and government departments.

In 1901, Australia lost its second historic film, when Herbert Booth left the country with *Soldiers of the Cross*. He paid $600 for it — claimed to be one-half of the production cost. Unlike the Melbourne Cup film, Australia has been unable to trace *Soldiers* although the slides used in association with the showing have been recovered.

The Salvation Army continued with film making, and erected the first film studio in this country at Caulfield North in 1909. From its rafters came the drifting 'snowflakes' for scenes in *The Scottish Covenanters*. Also made in 1909 was *Heroes of the Cross* whose storyline bears a remarkable resemblance to *Soldiers of the Cross*.

But in 1910, a new and unimaginative Commissioner for the Army arrived, who did not view the advantages of film in the same light as his predecessors. Consequently he disbanded the Biorama Company and closed the studio — a severe blow to an industry that was showing lusty growth.

During the period that the Salvation Army was active, a ludicrous situation arose: one exhibitor was forced to become a film producer. Johnson & Gibson did not view their filmic adventure as a need to foster the new Australian film industry, but rather as an insurance against losses at the box office. The whole exercise was merely one of self-defence, when they encountered fierce competition from a 'live' show. Fame sometimes can be a most unexpected thing. Johnson & Gibson had built up a lucrative business

1.3 *"Soldiers Of The Cross" was screened in the Melbourne Town Hall on 13 September 1900. This still has been accepted as one from that Salvation Army production. However in 1976 Reg Perry stated that it was actually from "Heroes Of The Cross" made in 1909. The girl is claimed to be Vida Dutton. By 1909 the Army had erected a film studio on the southern side of Inkerman Road, just before Kooyong Road, journeying towards Caulfield.*

1.4 *Held by the National Library, this is reputedly part of the score from "Soldiers of the Cross". However a member of the Salvation Army Biorama Band at the time feels that it was written by Captain McAnally for "Heroes of the Cross" nine years later. It's a case of "Music, music, music" — but what's the score?*

as a film exchange in the Temperance Hall, Russell Street, Melbourne (approximately where the Total Theatre itself now stands). The pair also conducted successful open air and surburban hall circuits, exhibiting overseas shorts. It so happened that one night a 'flesh and blood' show interfered with their takings. That show depicted the exploits of the Kelly Gang.

The stage rights to the Kelly show were held by J. & N. Tait, who already had moved into the film business as exhibitors, screening a number of Johnson & Gibson releases. The Taits agreed that it was a capital idea to have the best of the stage and screen worlds. Consequently Johnson & Gibson produced the film version of *The Story of the Kelly Gang* for the Taits. This two-company combination eventually amalgamated.

Here too, the story of lost film has an infuriatingly familiar ring. But in 1975 an ardent South Australian film collector located eight short segments from *The Story of the Kelly Gang* (that was originally made for $800, and is estimated to net the handsome sum of $50000). In late 1977, approx 64 m (210 ft) of original camera negative film were discovered in an old tin trunk in Caulfield. On 14 February 1978 Ken Robb and avid film collector Harry Davidson both viewed the film in Melbourne, and through my book, *Australian Silent Films* they were able to identify the footage as part of Australia's first commercially produced feature film. Despite the age, the emulsion is well preserved — (see Pls). The backgrounds are more distinct than in those from one of the few remaining brochures. In 1975 a mere three seconds of screen time were all that existed of this film. Three years later, a further 210 feet were located. Who knows what the next few years may contribute to the total recovery of *The Story of the Kelly Gang* — 1906 style.

1.5 *Mrs Kelly turns the tables on the constable. (Note the shadows cast by the direct sunlight). This is another still from recently discovered footage of "The Story Of The Kelly Gang" of 1906.*

Johnson & Gibson cannot escape the condemnation of a film-going public; since that first film, the derring-do of the Kellys has been inflicted on a long-suffering public innumerable times, even as late as September 1977, when the Australian Broadcasting Commission telecast yet another version of the misdoings of the 'Bad Boys of Glenrowan'. To add insult to injury, the success of Ned in 1906 resulted in the first cycle of Australian films — bushranging.

The Bushrangers

The line-up began in 1910, with the roadside manners of John Vane, Captain Moonlight and Thunderbolt. The latter had previously failed as a play in provincial Queensland. Brisbane picture show proprietor R.F. Stephens recalls that *Thunderbolt* was written by Tom Cunningham, a touring performer, and had Andrew Kirk in the cast. Stephens met actor John Gavin who had been on tour in Queensland, and suggested that *Thunderbolt* could be a success as a film. When Gavin returned to Sydney, he convinced backers of its potential, and eventually appeared on the screen in the title role. As a film it was a success. (John Gavin died in 1938 after some four years of ill health.)

In 1911, the Australian screen offered two different versions of the Ben Hall story (one produced by and starring John Gavin), as well as the bushranging activities of Captain Midnight, Dan Morgan, Captain Starlight, Frank Gardiner and others. Yet in this particular year of the bushrangers, an important change took place that not only influenced this particular period, but would sour the whole of the ensuing silent film era.

1.7   *Ned Kelly (left) lines up with the rest of the gang for "The Story Of The Kelly Gang" screened in Melbourne in 1906.*

J. & N. Tait and Johnson & Gibson joined forces to form Amalgamated Pictures. This move soon made independent Australian exhibitors and film makers realise the utter frustration and sheer inability of competing with what soon became one of this country's first film monopolies. The only consolation at the time was that it was fully owned and controlled by Australians. Yet it was a development that would eventually prove to be a major disaster for the local industry.

Another group, Hoyts Pictures, had been formed in September 1909. It too was all Australian, and began activities in St George's Hall, Bourke Street, Melbourne. (This site later became Hoyts De Luxe and the Esquire — a historic theatre that was demolished in 1976 to accommodate an extension to a Coles store.) Although Hoyts confined their interests to the exhibiting side of films, this highlighted another monopoly that would have a detrimental effect on the Australian film front. Overseas vested interests later purchased a controlling interest in the Hoyts theatre chain that ensured priority for the Hollywood product.

In all fairness, however, Hoyts did screen Australian productions, both silents and talkies, and in the 1970s, they exhibited Roadshow releases. But Australia has had to take its place in the queue. Yet even in the 1970s, Australian productions are released at irregular intervals, when they come into open conflict with other Australian features, instead of competing with an overseas picture. Whether by design or coincidence, it turns out that way.

Amalgamated Pictures first created the illusion that they would give local production a gigantic boost, and in 1911 concentrated on screen versions of successful stage plays. This is a legacy from the silents that is still in evidence today. Just as radio writing differs from that for television, producers should remember that a stage play is compressed to meet the limitations imposed upon it, and even if extended beyond its boundaries for film purposes, is not generally suited for the screen. The camera can accommodate depth and width, and can extend far beyond the drawing room comedy and bedroom romps. Although I do not wish to extol the virtues of the bushranging epics, our early film makers had the right idea about outdoor action though much of this was due to lighting reasons.

During 1911, Amalgamated Pictures produced *Called Back, The Luck of Roaring Camp,* Charles Reade's *It is Never too Late to Mend* and *The Bells.* (The last named became a talkie in 1935 under the title of *The Burgomeister.* Directed by Harry Southwell and featuring music by Isador Goodman, it failed to gain a quota registration number under the New South Wales Quota Law that came into force in October 1935). Another notable entry for 1911 from Amalgamated Pictures was *The Mystery of a Hansom Cab* which was remade in 1925 by Arthur Shirley. Shirley was an Australian actor who had become a leading man in Hollywood, but returned to Australia in 1920 to make pictures in this country. He purchased a Rose Bay home, 'Ellerslie', and commenced producing the disastrous *The Throwback*. The film was never completed, and became the subject of a court case instigated by cameraman Ernest Higgins — one of the famous brothers: Arthur Higgins teamed with Raymond Longford; and Tasman Higgins became associated with Charles Chauvel's first talkie *In the Wake of the Bounty.* That film introduced

1.8   *Raymond Hollis Longford as a Stage actor in 1910. The same year he had appeared in the film "The Life And Adventures of John Vane, the Australian Bushranger."*

another famous face that would achieve stardom in Hollywood — that of Errol Flynn.

In 1912 Willard Johnson went to America as representative for Amalgamated Pictures and remained there in a similar capacity for Union Theatres. Johnson's departure heralded a new approach by Amalgamated, evidence of which was noticeable in the production schedule which revealed a marked decline in film making. Only two films carried the firm's banner — *Breaking the News* and *Rip Van Winkle* — both starring Arthur Styan who was seen the previous year in *The Bells*. The real significance of this slowdown was the marked change of policy — exhibiting rather than producing films. This was a definite green light for overseas producers.

Early Entrepreneurs

During the early portion of Australian film history there were three well-established film entrepreneurs — Charles Cosens Spencer, T.J. West and J.D. Williams. In their moments of individual glory, they did not realise that they would soon be eliminated by the simple means of a take-over. Undoubtedly the best showman of the three was Spencer, with West a close second. At the Lyceum Theatre, Sydney, Spencer billed 'Senora Spencer' as the only 'lady projectionist in the world'. J.D. Williams is best remembered today as the driving force behind the opening of Luna Park, Melbourne. Even the slogan 'Just for Fun' dates back to 12 December 1912, when this fun park was first opened.

Australia owes a debt of gratitude to Spencer for giving a new impetus to film production. At Rushcutters Bay, Sydney, in 1912, he erected a modern studio, combating the whims of nature that caused havoc in the open air studios. He did not have to contend with wind that damaged flimsy sets and rain that often ruined them. Instead he had everything under cover, with special glass from England to provide good lighting. The glass however did create problems, such as buckling the furniture and reducing make-up to coloured perspiration.

An even greater Spencer achievement was finding a director of sheer genius in Raymond Hollis Longford. Brilliant in his approach to film making, Longford was a man of clear vision, whose scripts for *The Sentimental Bloke* and *On Our Selection* revealed warmth, love, and an appreciation of his fellow men. In his time, Longford played many parts from seaman to stage actor, with service as a medical orderly in India thrown in for good measure. He was ahead of his time in the silents, yet amazingly enough, remained static and in time was passed by. By then he was a bitter, unwanted man who died almost unnoticed. 'High flies the lark at break of day' could well have been his epitaph.

In 1910, Longford appeared on the screen as an actor in *The Life and Adventures of John Vane, the Australian Bushranger*. The next year recorded his appearance in *Captain Midnight* and *Captain Starlight* — both directed for Spencer by Alfred Rolfe before he went across to the Australian Photoplay Company. It was Spencer who perceived qualities far beyond those of an actor in Longford; in 1911 Spencer selected him to direct *The Fatal Wedding*, *The Romance of Margaret Catchpole*, and *Sweet Nell of Old*

1.9 *Nellie Stewart, born in Woolloomooloo (Sydney) remained "Our Nell" to an adoring public for half-a-century. She first played "Sweet Nell Of Old Drury" on stage in 1902, and appeared in a film version in 1911. She is pictured here as Prince Charming for a pantomine.*

1.10 *Nellie Stewart, one of Australia's outstanding stage actresses in the film "Sweet Nell Of Old Drury" directed by Raymond Longford in 1911.*

Drury starring Nellie Stewart. Longford also appeared as an actor in the first two. This was the beginning of his long association with cameraman Arthur Higgins and actress Lottie Lyell — who became Australia's first film star.

Longford soon revealed that he had no intention of following current trends in Australian film making, but instead chose to break new ground. In 1913 he gave a superb demonstration of his amazing ability in *Australia Calls* — a story of a Japanese invasion of Australia which was a genuine fear that existed before the outbreak of World War I. Termed 'the Yellow Peril', this fear came perilously close to fact approximately thirty years later. *Australia Calls* starred William E. Hart, a pioneer Australian airman. At the time of shooting, there was only one aeroplane in Sydney, yet Longford was master of the situation. He made the solitary plane (with models to supplement his meagre 'air force') into an Australian fighter squadron going into attack. During the filming the American fleet conveniently visited this country, and Longford used it as a stand in for the Japanese navy. Inhabitants of Sydney's 'Chinatown' also had a field day portraying members of the invading force.

Then came another surprise move, and the second major set-back for the Australian film industry. Spencer's interests were taken over by Amalgamated Pictures and the showman returned overseas with the fortune he had made in a few short years on the local scene. Longford on the other hand, was 'short changed': his services were no longer required.

Shortly afterwards, Amalgamated absorbed West's and Williams. Amalgamated had overpowered likely competition, and acquired three chains of theatres throughout Australia. Union Theatres then came into the picture, taking over the Amalgamated monopoly, and going into only spasmodic production at Rushcutters Bay in the studio previously owned by Spencer. Australasian Films — a subsidiary of Union Theatres — later became Cinesound.

Token opposition in film production came from Fraser Films, Sydney, and Lincoln-Cass Productions, Melbourne. The former opened an office in Queen Street, Melbourne, occupying the premises of the Pathe Freres organisation which also had been acquired by Amalgamated Pictures.

Both Fraser Films and Lincoln-Cass provide interesting highlights. After his brilliant *Australia Calls,* Raymond Longford suddenly appeared on the credits for a Fraser film, as the director of an inconsequential comedy *Pommy, the Funny Little New Chum* or *Pommy Arrives in Australia.* Lottie Lyell was included in the cast. Whereas *Australia Calls* revealed the genius and vivid imagination of the director, the *Little Pommy* supplied an unbelievable contrast — a slapstick comedy combining of all things, cannibals and spiders, bathing girls and surf. In later years Longford must have wondered just who came first, he or Mack Sennett?

Lincoln-Cass, another independent production company, had many outstanding personalities associated with it: W.J. Lincoln who had adapted plays for the screen on behalf of Amalgamated Pictures; actor Godfrey Cass who had appeared opposite Louise Carbasse (later Louise Lovely) in films produced by Australian Life Biograph (another casualty of 1913); and photographer Maurice Bertel, who had been with Pathe Freres. A prominent performer for the company was Roy Redgrave (father of Sir Michael Redgrave). Unfortunately Lincoln-Cass was not issued with a survival kit.

Maurice Bertel, another Frenchman, was a man who had more faith in Australia than his fellow countryman Marius Sestier — and who remained here. He tried his luck on the Coolgardie goldfield, but had more success in 1909 when as a photographer for Pathe Freres, Melbourne, he made thirteen one-reelers for the Cole's Dramatic Company. These ranged from *The Cowboy's Romance* to *Buffalo Bill* — all completely foreign in title and content to the country in which they were made. In 1912 he was with Amalgamated Pictures, then followed Lincoln-Cass and J.C. Williamson Films, and finally he worked for Herschells. Two letters from W. Franklyn Barrett (a photographer and director) to Bertel provide interesting background stories to filming in those days. The first is on Pathe Freres letterhead. From Wanganui, New Zealand, on 30 June 1910, 'Frank' Barrett wrote:

By this mail I am forwarding a parcel of film for development. I cannot get a dark room here . . . . . the film will be slightly underexposed as there was bad light. I have tested each parcel, and I find that by forcing the development a little there is quite enough to make a good print.

I am leaving New Zealand for Australia on 8 July, and I can assure you I shall be glad to get back. In N.Z. the weather is something frightful — rain and floods everywhere.

Please do your best with these films for me. It is needless to ask that, for I know you always do — but the people of this town have paid the expenses of the trip, and I should like to have something to show them.

The above clearly indicates the standard of Bertel's work.

The second letter, (on Fraser Film Release and Photographic Co. Ltd. letterhead) from Hepworth-American Film Corp., New York, is dated 24 September 1914:

I know that you have joined the combine.*

You say that you understand I shall be back in Australia next year. I wish you meant it. There are so many things that I have to do — and the American 'hustlers' are the slowest things that I have ever encountered. My God — how they can talk. It is impossible to get a word in, even by turning it on edge, and you know I am a pretty good hand on the 'talk stakes' myself.

I have visited the Lubin and Biograph Studios. Undoubtedly, the Biograph is a magnificent plant. They use entirely artificial light. It has been quite an education to me. I go along as a 'mug' and they have told me how it is all done, and it has given me a lot of useful information. There may come a time when it will be useful.

This letter from Barrett is a most revealing document: Australia had been up with the leaders in the earliest days of film making, but by 1914 America, with its vast financial resources, had the technical edge. Sadly it makes one realise that the increased production during the war years merely provided a glimmer of false hope. And the use of the word 'combine' was an indication that even in those days, Australian film men recognised the existence of a cataclysmic monopoly.

The contribution to Australian photography by Maurice Bertel and the Higgins brothers has been acknowledged. But one of the outstanding yet seldom mentioned cine camera operators was Bert Ive. If the saying that journalists have printer's ink in their blood is true, then Ive would have elements of nitrate film in his. Born in Queensland, he died on 25 July 1939 at the age of 64. He began his career as a stage performer, but silent films became an obsession with him. By 1904 he was recognised as one of the best biograph operators in Queensland, and four years later held the reputation that the films he projected never broke, nor at any time was the screen image blurred. In 1909 Bert Ive's Electric Biograph was featured at the Woolloongabba Cricket Ground. In that same year, another well-known silent film identity, Edward Carroll, billed him as chief operator at the old Centennial Hall, Ann Street, Brisbane, for the screening of the Johnson-Jeffries fight. When Lord Kitchener arrived in Brisbane in 1910, Bert Ive switched from projector to camera to cover the event. Late the following year he was in Sydney as cameraman for a little known film, *Driving a Girl to*

1.11 *Bert Ive who became official cameraman for the Commonwealth Government, in 1913.*

* A press pass dated 2 September 1912 records the fact that Bertel was with Amalgamated Pictures which had absorbed Pathe Freres.

Destruction which was presented by the George Marlow 'brilliant dramatic combination' — Louise Hampton, Robert Inman, Nellie Ferguson, Ethel Buckley (with whom Inman appeared the same year in *The Luck of Roaring Camp* for Amalgamated Pictures) and John Cosgrove. Another film quickly followed — *The Angel of his Dreams*. This starred Ada Guilford (who later appeared in *The Mutiny of the Bounty*), H. Twitcham and J. Stanford.

The standard of the two productions (stated as being cinematographed by the Australian Picturized Drama Company, Adelphi Theatre) is best gauged by the contents of a letter from A.G. McGowan, King Street, Sydney on 13 March 1912.

> The great trouble in booking these two films, has been this. The photography is good — very good in fact — quite up to the imported stuff. But the acting — ugh — it is awful. These dramatic stars and "would be's" are no earthly good for picture work. They get an idea into their heads that they only have to say the lines, and that is all that is necessary. At the same time they will not be told what is necessary by someone who does understand the essential necessities of picture acting. Understand of course I am only repeating what picture people have told me.
>
> Another thing — it is no earthly use trying to book *The Angel of his Dreams* when there is no paper for it. You remember what a fuss Lloyd of Burwood kicked up, because he could not get any day bills. When I approach a man about it, the first thing he says is 'show me the hanger'. Then I have to admit that they are being printed. 'Very well,' he'll say 'I'll see you later when you have them.' That's the whole position in a nutshell.
>
> Mind you, there's business to be done on these pictures. I had a promise of $80 worth on *The Angel,* but it is off now as there are no day bills. If these pictures are to be hired out, you must have paper for your clients, to advertise them.

(This is not the only instance of a film maker being unaware that his job does not end on completion of the film. He has to 'sell it'. Fred Daniel had to face the same soul-destroying truth with *The Flying Doctor* some two decades later. Learning from past experience has never come easy to many Australian film producers.)

Bert Ive eventually was appointed by the Commonwealth Government to the Department of External Affairs on 27 May 1913, at a salary of $10 per week plus a travelling allowance of $1.25 per day when absent from Melbourne. Rail, coach and steamer transport were free. While still with the Commonwealth, Ive was cameraman for *The Bondage of the Bush* produced by Woods' Australian Films in 1916. Its stars were Charles Wood (who also directed), Wilton Power, Jeff Williams, Alfred Bristow and Gertrude Darley. At the naming of Canberra in 1913, Bert Ive was one of the cameramen who covered this historic occasion. (Raymond Longford also attended, but as a director.) Months later, Bert Ive was shooting film to publicise Australia at home and abroad. In 1915 he covered the departure of the first contingent of the AIF, travelling with the troopship to Albany, Western Australia. Bert Ive worked in the Cinema Branches of a number of Commonwealth departments, and at the time of his death, was with the film unit attached to the Department of Commerce, which became part of the Department of Information. Accordingly it can be claimed that Ive is in fact the father of the current Film Australia.

Lincoln-Cass Pty Ltd commenced feverish production in Melbourne in 1913 and made films at a rate that was staggering. The first was *The Sick Stockrider,* with the star, Roy Redgrave, reciting the poem during the actual screening. The story centred around memories of a dying stockman sitting in the rays of a waning sun, enjoying the fragrance of the golden wattle. Lincoln-Cass Films followed with *Moondyne* — recapturing the pioneering days of Western Australia. *The Remittance Man, Transported, The Road to Ruin, The Reprieve* and *The Crisis* were released in quick succession after *Moondyne.* Lincoln-Cass Films Pty Ltd dramatically ceased production in the same year in which it began so hopefully and promisingly.

The reason was available, if one searched in the right quarters. Many of the independent production houses were forced to close their doors because theatres were not available to show their films. Opposing forces — overseas and Australian — were baring their fangs. In Sydney, many of the Lincoln-Cass features were screened in such unlikely venues as the White City Stadium (under the auspices of 'Snowy' Baker, who later became a film star himself). Amalgamated Pictures, were, even at this stage, revealing the dangers associated with monopolistic control. No greater example of the evils of such a combine can be found than Raymond Longford, who for many desperate years fought the stranglehold that Amalgamated Pictures and later Union Theatres had on the industry — only in the end to be defeated on a technical knockout.

The War Years

In 1913 Longford moved to a new Sydney-based company, Commonwealth Films, to make *Neath Australian* [or *Austral*] *Skies* — a tale of the Queensland wilds. He returned to Fraser Films the following year for a far more ambitious project than *Pommy.* It was *The Silence of Dean Maitland.* During the initial screening a dramatic highlight was a close-up of the Dean (played by Harry Thomas) in the pulpit denouncing himself as a murderer. The theatre audience was startled when Thomas, from the stage, gave voice to the self-incrimination.

For the remainder of 1914, Longford's films drifted back to inconsequential ones: *The Swagman's Story, Taking his Chance* and *Trooper Campbell.* The last two were based on poems by Henry Lawson — but none set Sydney on fire. On 1 May 1915, although billed as a producer (?) for Fraser Films, Longford's stocks had reached an all-time low, and he had to resort to conducting a school for 'moving picture' actors at 321 Pitt Street, Sydney. In July, yet another Fraser film *Ma Hogan's New Boarder* did nothing to bolster Vockler, was best known for his Charlie Chaplin impersonations. A notable absentee from the picture was Lottie Lyell. Yet throughout it all, Raymond Longford remained a non-conformist. He did not ride the merry-go-round of patriotic films, which in 1915 included *The Fate of the Emden, A Hero of the Dardanelles, Will they never Come?* and *Within our Gates.*

In 1914 when supplies of overseas films looked like drying up due to World War I, the Australian film front was given a new lease of life. The industry put the bushranging cycle off the road, and embarked upon a programme of patriotic and heroic fare, glorifying the war effort. The Higgins

1.12 *Phil Gell was a police roundsman on a Sydney newspaper before he became publicity man for Spencer.*

brothers took full advantage of the new trend with *Australia's Response to the Empire's Call* and *It's a Long Way to Tipperary*. Another film, *Seadogs of Australia*, had to be withdrawn as it revealed too many details of Australia's flagship HMAS *Australia*. The war cycle continued to revolve merrily in 1916 with *Australia at War, Australia Prepared, Murphy of Anzac, If the Huns Came to Melbourne* and two versions of the execution of Nurse Edith Cavell — *The Martyrdom of Nurse Cavell* and *Edith Cavell* with a sequel to the latter production in *La Revanche*.

The guns-a-poppin' atmosphere must have proved indigestible to a man like Raymond Longford who had that spirit of inventiveness that the 'war cycle' smothered. This appears to provide the motive for Longford's departure to New Zealand to direct two films which would not only provide a marked contrast to the current productions from other Australian film makers, but would once again add lustre to his name. These 1916 productions were the romantic *A Maori Maid's Love* and the historic *The Mutiny of the Bounty*. The photographer for the latter was W. Franklyn Barrett.

Other film producers must have had similar thoughts to Longford's as the list for 1916 includes *The Life of Adam Lindsay Gordon* and two successful stage plays that became films — *Officer 666* with Fred Niblo (an American who later became a famous Hollywood director) and *Within the Law*, both from J.C. Williamson Films.

1.13 *"A Hero Of The Dardanelles" followed in the wake of such patriotic films as "It's A Long Way To Tipperary", "Seadogs of Australia" and "Will They Never Come?" With the supply of overseas films limited by the war, it was Australia's big chance to give new vigour to the local industry.*

1.14 *McNab uses an old trick of rattling chains to force a confession from Steve that he is an escaped convict. Thad McNab (Irve Hayman); Deidre (Alma Rock Phillips); Steve (Martyn Keith).*
This scene from "The Pioneers" comes through the courtesy of R.P. Throssell and the National Library, Canberra.)

Franklyn Barrett directed *A Blue Gum Romance* for Fraser Films in 1913, but did not figure prominently in technical credits until 1916 when he directed *The Pioneers*. This Nettheim-Barrett Production starred Charles Knight, Lily Rochfort, Fred St Clair, Winter Hall, Alma Rock Phillips and Martyn Keith. Based on the book by Katharine Susannah Prichard, photography and script were handled by Barrett.

A letter from Franklyn Barrett to Katherine Susannah Prichard dated 13 February 1916 reveals that he met with a lot of bad luck during production, and that the budget was exceeded by 50 per cent — the extra amount having exhausted the funds set aside for the picture.

We have not been able to do much in the way of publicity at the present time. As you are connected with journalism, you will know that 'pars' are controlled by the amount of advertising that goes to the paper. The producer as a rule is not the advertiser. The showman who runs the picture does that part. Consequently I have not been able to 'shoot any dope' through.

1.15 *The father demands an explanation of his son's debt to a man named McNab.*
From L. Charles Knight, Lily Rochfort, and Fred St. Clair. A scene from "The Pioneers" directed by Franklyn Barrett.

1.16 *From the Nettheim-Franklyn Barrett production of 1916 —*
"The Pioneers".
Davey: You're my sweetheart, aren't you Deidre?
Deidre: When you come back we'll be married.
Fred St. Clair as Davey; Alma Rock Phillips as Deidre.

This seems to be at variance with that written to Bert Ive concerning the two Adelphi Picture Dramas. Here, the producer expects the exhibitor to handle all publicity — an expectation that has caused the failure of many a production on some occasions, and added to the overall budget on others.

Franklyn Barrett's letter continues his original line of thought.

> May I ask you to carry out your offer of our last meeting, and give us a leg up by getting a few 'pars', as a preliminary. We have noticed that you have mentioned the picture on the several occasions that the papers have talked to you.

Concerning a later version of *The Pioneers*, Katharine Prichard on 7 March 1926 wrote to a Percy Hodder-Williams in London:

> I called on your agent while in Sydney to tell him that the presentation of the film of *The Pioneers* was due for the end of this month. This was the Raymond Longford version.
>
> I was not pleased with the dressing of May Cameron. It was out of period, not austere and quite without the romantic simplicity her dresses ought to have. I hope her pictures may be done again, but that may delay presentation a little.
>
> You will be interested to know that Australasian Films Ltd, bought out the Nettheim-Franklyn Barrett interest in the first film that was made, but they also unearthed a pirated version of the story under another name. The chase by Australasian Films after the old 'Pioneers' and the pirated version, is quite sensational. The cheque to me was for £250.

The following year, 1917, witnessed the abrupt phasing out of the war cycle. Only John F. Gavin's *The Murder of Captain Fryatt* was screened (with W. Franklyn Barrett again behind the camera). Yet the year proved to be one of unreality, directly traceable to the emergence of Beaumont Smith as a director. He began poking fun at the alleged (and later generally accepted) 'country oaf' with his *Hayseeds* series. He began with *Our Friends the Hayseeds* starring Roy Redgrave, and followed in the same twelve months with *The Hayseeds*

Come to Town and *The Hayseeds Backblocks Show*. Smith was shrewd enough to provide interstate backgrounds for the various adventures of the *Hayseeds*. In the cast of the second 'show' was Fred MacDonald who would later portray 'Dave' in the talkie version of *On Our Selection*.

But the 'who did it first' cycle was the most intriguing contribution to the Australian film front in 1917. It involved Raymond Longford and W. Franklyn Barrett, who along with Beaumont Smith, were to become the 'big three' directors of the silent era. Like Tom Cowan in the 1970s, Barrett was a good photographer, but less successful as a director. A photographer-director always has a restricted view of what goes on behind the scenes. In getting a well-balanced picture photographically, he often misses out on its dramatic counterbalance.

When Barrett issued *Australia's Peril*, it revealed a storyline very similar to that of *Australia Calls* which was directed by Longford in 1913. It provided another 'imaginary raid' on Australia, with our troops marching to defend Sydney. (Apparently Hart and his aeroplane weren't available at the time.)

The Post-war Period

An unbelievable coincidence followed when Barrett's *The Monk and the Woman*, starring English actor Percy Marmont, was shown in Sydney on 8 October 1917, while Longford's *The Church and the Woman* followed only five days later. Both were highly controversial — the former dealing with a monk who renounced his vow of celibacy because of his infatuation for 'the Woman' (Maude Fane).

The Church and the Woman had as its central character a priest who was tormented by what was revealed to him in the confessional. This occurred when a man confessed his guilt, and the priest became torn between his duty to his church and to his fellow men. The 'secret' revealed that another man had been convicted for a crime, and the priest could bring about his release by notifying the penal authorities of certain relevant facts. The film became so explosive that it was not screened in Melbourne until August 1921 (almost four years after its initial release).

1.17 *English actor Percy Marmont who appeared in "The Monk and The Woman", directed by W. Franklyn Barrett. In the same year — 1917 — Raymond Longford directed another controversial religious epic, "The Church And The Woman". Australia was running true to form with its "cycle system."*

'The Hayseeds' cycle was to continue, but the controversial 'church' theme died in the year of origin. Australia, realising that the 'green pastures' of home would soon wither under drought conditions imposed by hot winds from Hollywood, looked around desperately in 1918 for a stimulating new 'star' to promote a new cycle. The local film front was sure that it discovered the right answer in Reg 'Snowy' Baker as a 'super hero'. It was claimed that he out-stunted Douglas Fairbanks Snr (the swashbuckling devil-may-care of the American silent screen). Baker burst upon the screen in *The Enemy Within*. Although not really part of the 'war' cycle, it dealt with the activities of a German raider off the Australian coast. Enemy spies lurked in shadowy recesses; an attractive girl (Lily Molloy) had to be rescued from German agents; and Baker, a superb athlete, was called upon to climb down a cliff face, swaying giddily at the end of a rope, with spies using him for target practice, then (just for good measure) he had to dive into the surf at Bronte, and finally, in Tom Mix fashion, dispense with six 'heavies' in a single bout. His next film which followed quickly was *The Lure of the Bush*, in which Baker portrayed a 'dandy' jackeroo. He was held in contempt by the station hands until he rode the wildest brumby on the property to a standstill. A cattle stampede was another means of revealing 'Snowy' as a super hero.

Two actresses who were destined for Hollywood appeared in Australian films in 1918 — Renee Adoree in *500 Pounds Reward* and Sara Allgood in *Just Peggy*. The former appeared later in the silent *The Big Parade* in 1925, co-starring John Gilbert. Sara Allgood portrayed matronly roles in the talkies.

Beaumont Smith produced another 'backblocks' story in 1918, *The Hayseeds' Melbourne Cup*, that gave the capital of Victoria a chance to supply a background for another adventure of his farming family in caricature. Koala Films contributed their share to the 'bush' cycle with *The Waybacks from Dingo Flats*.

Beaumont Smith called a temporary halt to his *Hayseeds* series with the sensational *Satan in Sydney* that was really strong stuff in 1918. It dealt with opium dens and gambling halls. After only one day's showing at the Lyric Theatre, Sydney, the police demanded its withdrawal. (Years later Charles Chauvel realised the value of censorship controversy — and used it to his advantage.) *Satan in Sydney* made a much-publicised reappearance the following week at the Lyric, with the magical wording 'passed by the censor without alteration.' Six thousand people promptly attended the theatre every day to view the 'unabridged and positively sensational' production.

If 1918 did follow a cycle, it was slanted towards social problems. *Satan in Sydney* highlighted drugs and gambling. *A Coo-ee from Home* starring Gertrude Darley and the reliable Charles Villiers, pinpointed the stories of two men — one who trusted the woman he loved, the other, a social parasite who made mammon his god. The most significant film of the year, however was *The Woman Suffers*. Lottie Lyell was cast as an unmarried mother who was left 'holding the baby' while the father went on his merry way, footloose and fancy free. Not as sensational as *Satan in Sydney*, it was far more important in other departments of screen activity. It proclaimed that Raymond Longford had joined the Adelaide-based Southern Cross Feature Film Company — a production house that would provide him with the opportunity to inscribe his name on the roll of honour as one of the immortals of the Australian Film Industry. *The Woman Suffers* was premiered in Adelaide, capital of the state in which it was produced.

Also in 1918, Joseph Perry left Australia for Sourabaya as Eastern representative for Australasian Films. Perry was the man associated with the early Australian film productions, *Soldiers of the Cross* and *Heroes of the Cross*.

The year 1919 began disastrously for the film houses. Pneumonic influenza swept Australia. Mass innoculations were held in suburban public halls and schools of art. People were advised to wear masks in the street. Theatres closed in late January and re-opened in early March. However Sydney had a second closure — from early April until mid-May. It appeared that the year would provide the 'documentary' cycle. *Australia's Own* covered an Australian girl's adventures in what once had been German New Guinea. Then followed Captain Frank Hurley's *Australians in Palestine*. Yet another film was *Through Australian Wilds* with Francis Birtles (in some cities it was titled *With Birtles on the Tracks of Sir Ross Smith*).

Hurley's second documentary *In the Grip of the Polar Ice* was shown in November 1919, although it had been screened in England a few years earlier. The following month was highlighted by an amalgamation that took place between Australasian Films and Union Theatres on one part, and Electra Theatres incorporating J.C. Williamson Films on the other. The Australian film industry was now in the grip of an octopus whose origin was of this country's making. This combine proved that such power meant undoubted progress — but more in the manner of making money than in fostering a powerful local cinematographic production industry. In this year, Australasian Films' sole contribution to the Australian film front was the trite and unimpressive *Does the Jazz Lead to Destruction* directed by Fred Ward.

In 1919 Beaumont Smith left his *Hayseeds* in the hayshed, and concentrated on comedy and sporting themes. *Barry Butts In* starred English comedian Barry Lupino and attractive Australian actress Agnes Dobson. The plot involved a scene shifter who fell in love with a chorus girl. She inherits a fortune, is kidnapped, and he dashes to her rescue in a car, on a scooter, and finally by hansom cab. Smith's second feature, *Desert Gold* starred the racehorse of the same name, and human performers Bryce Rowe (previously in *A Coo-ee from Home*), Marie Ney and character actor John Cosgrove. Well-known jockeys and punters appeared in the big racecourse scenes.

Despite this activity, the year rightfully belongs to Raymond Longford. At long last, someone had listened to his plea to turn a much-hawked script into a film. That production would place him on a pinnacle that would never be attained by either Beaumont Smith or W. Franklyn Barrett. Almost sixty years later *The Sentimental Bloke* is still hailed as an immortal screen classic. Longford searched for and found the ideal lead in an ex-vaudeville star, Arthur Tauchert. Lottie Lyell was the perfect 'Doreen' and Gilbert Emery (who subsequently went to Hollywood) stepped from the Dennis verses themselves as 'Ginger Mick'.

As Sylvia Lawson wrote in *Nation Review* on 26 May 1977:

Longford used sets only. Many of the scenes were shot in the streets of Woolloomooloo — a location he preferred to the 'Little Lons' region of the poem. Where he did use them, they were right, capturing for instance in Ma's

1.18   *Raymond Longford was definitely at his peak with his silent film classic "The Sentimental Bloke" (1919). Arthur Tauchert (L) — "fag" and all — is seen in a street in Woolloomooloo.*

Langham
Mel.

1.20 *Agnes Dobson (R) recoils from "The Face" in the film "The Face At The Window". This still was taken after production had ceased for the day — and the fearsome face peered through curtains and not "the window".*

living room, the cluttered, struggling aspiration of the town's working class matron towards 'refinement'. On this level, the dreaded respectability is too petty to be a real threat to the 'Kid's' vitality.

Dennis did not so much provide a script for Longford as supply him with a fictional doorway into a social and national landscape which the audience already knew, but which had to be made intelligible on film, if it was to remain real to them. For all, Australian film had taken over where the story writers, balladists, and cartoonists of the great newspapers, had left off.

The verse titles in dazzingly elegant, long tailed art nouveau lettering are received as so many vivacious and characterful narrative links — but what counts as Longford's own, is a marriage of style to more substance than Dennis had comprehended.

When screened in England, a leading newspaper described *The Sentimental Bloke* as 'the greatest picture ever made' — an honour that a local director of the 1970s has yet to receive.

It seems ludicrous that this country could achieve such an international standard in 1919 — yet still be recovering fifty years later from the scars of the 1920s.

An English admirer of Arthur Tauchert addressed a fan letter to 'Dear Wonder Man' mentioning the screening at the 'Futurist' — Birmingham's 'most swagger picture house', where convulsive laughter had been heard continuously during the past six days (when the screening of *The Sentimental Bloke* had commenced.)

Less memorable films of 1919 included a screen version of the successful stage play *Struck Oil* starring Maggie Moore and H.R. Roberts (Maggie's second husband, her first was J.C. Williamson of theatre fame). Another was *The Face at the Window* produced by D. B. O'Connor and directed by Charles Villiers. It too had been a stage drama, and was presented in "five nerve thrilling reels". It was notable for three items: the second screen appearance in 1919 of the beautiful Agnes Dobson (she had appeared previously in *The Hayseeds' Backblocks Show* in 1917); the fact that this Australian version soon ran into trouble, when a British production of the same name was screened in Australia; and third, that stills for the indigenous film were taken after shooting ceased for the day. This is evident in one photograph that shows

1.19 *Opposite page: The very beautiful and talented Agnes Dobson who played important roles in "Barry Butts In" and "The Face At The Window" — both in 1919.*

The Face at the Window

Monsieur de Brison, the wealthy banker, is entertaining at his sumptuous home in Paris, when he receives word that the caretaker of his bank has been murdered and the contents of his private safe stolen. He sends for the greatest criminal detective in Paris, Paul Gouffet, and puts the case in his hands. From now on it is a duel of brains between the detective and "le Loup" (the Wolf), who always wears a hideous mask and utters a weird wolf-like howl before he enters the house of his victim. Monsieur de Brison himself falls before the dagger of "le Loup," and the whole community is at fever heat to ascertain the identity of the mysterious "face."

How this is eventually brought about and the criminal brought to justice is told in five sensational reels.

FEATURING

Lucio Delgrado	. . .	D. B. O'Connor
Paul Gouffet (Detective)	. .	Claud Turton
Lucien Cortier (Clerk at the Bank)		Gerald Harcourt
M. de Brison (a wealthy Banker) .		Collet Dobson
Barbelon (a criminal).	. .	Chas. Villiers
Marie de Brison	. .	Agnes Dobson

1.21   *The front and back pages of a handbill for the Australian film production "The Face At The Window." The story soon afterwards became the centre of a copyright wrangle.*

"the Face" *not* at the window, but leering at a frightened Agnes Dobson through curtains.

The overseas' picture drama of *The Face at the Window* was released through Williams (Australasia) Ltd, who issued the following warning:

> We have the exclusive rights in Australasia of F. Brook Warren's melodrama. It has come to our notice that another film of this title is being offered to exhibitors, who are warned that it is our intention to take proceedings against anyone violating our rights.

The Early Twenties

The 1920s were disastrous for the local film front. It has been stated that in 1914, approximately half of the screen productions seen by Australians were from America — and by 1923, the percentage had risen alarmingly to 94 per cent. The cultural colonisation of Australia had been accomplished by the United States without bloodshed. This passive conquest brought in its wake massive financial gain for America, thanks to Australian-owned chains of theatres conducted by Hoyts and Union Theatres. By 1921, for example, First National distributors were actually despatching Australian employees for training in Hollywood, with their money bags, so that they too could spread the American gospel of motion picture making. (A noteworthy example in the 1920s was Ken G. Hall — although he was to make a worthwhile contribution to Australia's early talkies era.) In the closing stages when Australia set up a pathetic Film Commission to inquire into the sick and sorry state of the local industry, a disillusioned Raymond Longford is credited with stating that this country could not blame America. It only did what Australia allowed it to do. America also tried to make inroads into the local scene when it tried to take a slice of the Australian production cake, even though it was noticeably smaller and less inviting in appearance. Those same Americans left hungry. Super hero 'Snowy' Baker began another form of American import, by stating in August 1919 that he had engaged American actor and director Wilfred Lucas to supervise his films. Keeping an eye on business, he commenced special classes for picture acting and joined forces with showman E. J. Carroll to form Carroll-Baker Productions. In April 1920, 'Palmerston', a twenty-eight-room house set in two hectares of land, complete with picturesque gardens and artificial lakes, was purchased, and our super hero had visions of becoming a movie mogul as well.

Overseas stars who came to our shores in the 1920s were Eva Novak, Yvonne Pavis and Brownie Vernon. In addition to Lucas, American directors Lawson Harris and Norman Dawn tried their luck. Only on the cinematographic side (with a few exceptions) was Australia well to the fore. Arthur Higgins, for one, was in great demand, not only by Raymond Longford, but Beaumont Smith and the American Lawson Harris.

But Hollywood productions were setting a standard that Australia, with its homespun style, could not match in such lavish spectacles as *Queen of Sheba, The Ten Commandments, Ben Hur, The Sheik* and *The Sea Hawk*. Stars too had the publicity experts and fan magazines to make them household names. (Charles 'Bud' Tingwell in 1977 pointed out that Australian film producers still lack an appreciation of how much a good public relations man can achieve.) Romantic Hollywood stars were Gloria Swanson, Ronald Colman (his brother Eric appeared in Australian talkies), Lillian Gish, John Barrymore and Ramon Novarro; swashbuckling heroes came in the form of Douglas Fairbanks Snr, John Gilbert and Milton Sills; and cowboys Tom Mix, Buck Jones, Hoot Gibson and Jack Hoxie rode as if they had been born to the saddle, and had grown up with a six gun. Finally, comedians of the calibre of Charles Chaplin, Buster Keaton, and Harold Lloyd, helped fill American banks with Australian currency.

In 1920, in Australia, the outback came in for its share of film fare. Far from making the farmer an object of fun and ridicule, it revealed the more demanding side of the land. Franklyn Barrett introduced *The Breaking of the Drought* (a copy of which was discovered as late as 1976 in a rusty can under a house in Hornsby, Sydney). This was the screen version of a successful stage play that Bland Holt gave Australian audiences earlier this century. Barrett's excellent photography revealed the effects of a pitiless sun upon a parched earth, of dams drying up, and sheep dying in their hundreds. Then came miraculous rain that restored life to the soil, and hope to the farmer. Despite the fact that this had all the earmarks of a story of the great outback, most of the plot dealt with the escapades of the playboy son of the farmer in the wicked city of Sydney. Naturally he fell victim to the wily schemes of a man and a 'woman of the world'.

Beaumont Smith, the only surviving Australian independent producer, and proprietor of his own production company, seemed to have forgotten 'the Hayseeds' and released *The Man from Snowy River*. Despite the excellence of *The Sentimental Bloke,* a film magazine of the day described the Beaumont Smith film as "the best Australian movie yet — scenically and in photographic and acting senses."

Yet today, the picture that has stood the test of time is *The Sentimental Bloke.* Smith's effort is not even a memory, despite the fact that it was billed as 'having a kick like a kangaroo', and as 'sunny as Queensland and as big as Australia'.

Raymond Longford's tribute to the man of the land in *On Our Selection* is another screen gem that is preserved by the National Library, Canberra. Far superior to *The Breaking of the Drought,* and even the talkie version of the happenings on the Rudd selection, Longford's script was sympathetic and at times, dramatic. It provided laughter with the Rudds, *not* at their expense, and vividly portrayed the high price for survival in a hostile bush. The highlight of *On Our Selection* was a raging bush fire, brilliantly filmed by Arthur Higgins. On the debit side, Percy Walshe's 'Dad' did wear an obviously fake beard — yet even Bert Bailey featured artificial facial growth until Ken G. Hall convinced him that a real beard would look more convincing for his appearance in the talking version of *On Our Selection.*

1.22   *From Dennis to Rudd! Raymond Longford felt the urge to film the work of Australian writers. His own screenplays even added lustre to the writings of both authors. The cast of "On Our Selection" (1920) are lined up in this "shot". (From L to R) — Olga Willard (Nell), Beatrice Esmond (Mum), Fred Coleman (Dan), Lottie Beaumont (Sarah), Arthur Wilson (Joe), Percy Walshe (Dad), Tal Ordell (Dave), Evelyn Johnson (Kate) and Arthur Greenaway (Sandy).*

Another Longford triumph in 1920 was a sequel to *The Sentimental Bloke*. Featuring the same three leads, the director felt that *Ginger Mick* was even better than its predecessor. (Up to now, no copy of the picture has been located.) It told of Ginger's experience as a soldier in World War I, and by means of flashbacks, the Bloke (Arthur Tauchert) and Doreen (Lottie Lyell) recall their associations with him. Gilbert Emery proved what a fine actor he really was, when after being wounded, he realises that death is only seconds away.

Newsreels and documentaries kept audiences up to the minute with the arrival of Sir Ross Smith on his prize-winning flight by plane from England — and of another visitor to Australia, His Royal Highness, the Prince of Wales.

In feature films, we journeyed back into the past to witness Ned Kelly take to the mountains once again. *The Kelly Gang* was the work of an overseas director, Harry Southwell, whose effort was as poor as that of the Tony Richardson fiasco of 1970. Shot in Melbourne, the now defunct Outer Circle Railway line in Kew was the stand-in for the Glenrowan train track. The

1.23   *A scene from "On Our Selection". Dave (Tal Ordell) centre, brings home his bride to the farm. But Dad feels that too much time has been wasted already on the "marryin' business". This Steele Rudd story was directed by Raymond Longford.*

1.24   *Godfrey Cass as "Ned Kelly" 1920 Style. The film — "The Kelly Gang" directed by*
Harry Southwell.
(Still supplied by Reg Edwards)

burning of the Glenrowan Hotel was staged at the back of a hall opposite
Pentridge Gaol. Godfrey Cass (real name Castieau) was the son of the
Governor of the Melbourne Gaol at the time the real Ned Kelly was hanged,
and by a quirk of fate, was cast as 'Ned'. It was Cass who made the dramatic
utterance, 'My God — I'm done — but I'll die like a Kelly.'

Southwell continued to make various versions of the Kelly story, despite
the fact that in one state or another, the picture was banned. The first instance
was the 1920 *Kelly Gang* that was not permitted to be screened in Adelaide.

Southwell made a second film in 1920 — *The Golden Flame* which was
retitled *The Hordern Mystery*. It was a weak and unimpressive film that did

nothing to enrich what was fast becoming an impoverished picture industry. Critics condemned the poor and jumbled plot, and indifferent acting. Yet the cast contained such well-known players as Godfrey Cass and Claud Turton (who had appeared in *The Face at the Window*).

The second bushranging epic was another remake — *Robbery Under Arms*. Directed by Kenneth Brampton, it drew attention to two members of the cast — Charles Chauvel and Roy Redgrave. It was Australian director Chauvel's first screen role, and English actor Redgrave's last. He died in Sydney two years later at the age of fifty, and was buried in South Head cemetery. Australian actress Tien Hogue also appeared in *Robbery Under Arms*. She had been seen in *Pommy Arrives in Australia* in 1913, and *Shepherd of the Southern Cross* opposite Arthur Shirley in 1914. Upon completion of *Robbery Under Arms* she left for America.

The second version was first screened on 2 October 1920 in Melbourne where the first version of the story had its premier on 2 November 1907. At that time J. & N. Tait had extended their activities to Queensland and on 3 December 1907 the Tait's screened it in the Shire Hall, Barcaldine. The biograph expert was Bert Ive (another familiar name) who was billed as being late of the Theatre Royal, Brisbane.

Arthur Shirley, mentioned previously, returned to Australia in 1920 after starring in Hollywood productions. He plunged into film making immediately with *The Throwback*. This was another case of a set-back for the local industry in the 1920s as it was never completed. Shirley had to wait another five years before success was his with *The Mystery of a Hansom Cab* — unfortunately yet another remake.

In 1920, United Theatres and Films Ltd was formed in Adelaide. This event is of no great historical significance beyond the fact that the managing director, A. C. Tinsdale, had been with Austral Photoplays in Melbourne. United Theatres acquired the assets, films and plant from Austral, plus its subsidiary company Kookaburra Film Exchange. Included in the take-over were the Austral films *A Romance of the Burke and Wills Expedition of 1860* (1918), *Hinemoa, The Laugh on Dad* and *Scars of Love* (1919) plus travelogues and featurettes. My visit to Adelaide in search of these films ended in a brick wall in the basement of 22 Waymouth Street, where United Theatres had offices; the premises were later occupied by Fox Films.

Super hero 'Snowy' Baker made three films in 1920 — *The Man from Kangaroo, Shadow of Lightning Ridge,* and *The Jackeroo of Coolabong.* Snowy's first larger than life hero was the Rev. Meeks — a fighting parson who also demonstrated his prowess in swimming, even to the naming of the various diving techniques. American Brownie Vernon was billed as "the girl with the sunny smile". Director Wilfred Lucas and Australian actor Charles Villiers were the heavies. This feature was well received. Baker portrayed a mysterious bushranger 'The Shadow' in his second epic. (With *The Kelly Gang* and *Robbery Under Arms* it would appear that the bushranging cycle was being revived in 1920.) During the action, 'the Shadow' single-handed took on some fifteen men, and in the free-for-all completely wrecked a bush pub.

It is difficult to ascertain whether the theme of *The Shadow of Lightning Ridge* was ill-timed, but the film undoubtedly contributed to the decline in popularity of 'Snowy' Baker which was clearly shown with his third and final production for 1920, *The Jackeroo of Coolabong* — box office takings gave it the 'Roman' sign. Screened in Sydney in October 1920, it waited six months for a Brisbane release and twelve months for a Melbourne showing. 'Snowy' played a man from Piccadilly (complete with monocle) who arrived at an outback station. The fun started when someone called him 'dear'. Arthur Tauchert as a villain did not have the same impact either as he did in *The Sentimental Bloke*. *The Jackeroo* buried the Australian super hero. In October 1920, Baker sailed for Hollywood, where he and his horse 'Boomerang' appeared in American outdoor films. His brother Frank Baker also took the Hollywood trail, and until his recent retirement, was a character actor. He often appeared in John Ford films. Bert Glennon, an American assistant director, returned to America with 'Snowy'. Following Baker's departure, E.J. & Dan Carroll merged with Southern Cross Feature Films to become Southern Cross Picture Productions. Two years later, this too ended in an unexpected and calamitous closure. The industry in 1921, still reeling from the disastrous blows of 1920, looked with envy at the American productions that were swamping the Australian screens. Yet how could Australia match the overseas product with such uninspired features as *Possum Paddock,* the first off the Australian production line for 1921? Despite this uninspired start, it was a most productive year, even though this country persisted with the *Possum Paddock, Dingo Flat* trend with such really dull titles as *A Girl of the Bush* from Franklyn Barrett and *Mated in the Wilds, Rudd's New Selection,* and *While the Billy Boils.* For good measure, the film scene really went bush for *The Gentleman Bushranger* — a hangover from the previous year. Just what was the aim in placing so much faith in 'the wild blue yonder'? Was Australia trying to place the accent on sentiment, or was it turning the 'Nelson eye' to the bill of fare from overseas? Even token opposition would have proved the point that Australians, noted for their fighting spirit in the Boer War and World War I, were still prepared to dig their toes in and get 'stoushin' mad' like 'The Bloke'.

Mated in the Wild took the audience back o' Bourke — to Central Australia to be exact. It was a film from a new company, Ramster Photoplays, and told the tearful tale of the hero dashing off on a motorbike, of all things, into the Simpson Desert or some similar arid region, after hearing the story second-hand that his girlfriend had become engaged to his rival. By some means best known to the director, P. J. Ramster, the villain wrecks the hero's motorbike, poisons the nearest waterhole, and generally behaves like an utter cad. Friendly Aborigines nurse the hero back to health. Meanwhile, the girlfriend, believing that her erstwhile lover has perished, demands to see his grave. Now you have the thrilling climax: the girl, her mother, and the villain — all mounted on motorbikes — going to wave their last farewell. Please put away the handkerchief. The hero and heroine are finally united, just before the fadeout.

Ramster in 1921 also provided such inconsequential screen material as *High Heels, Jasamine Freckel's Love Affair* (an Australian version of a Mack Sennett Mermaid comedy) and *Should Girls Kiss Soldiers?*. None made the box office till tinkle merrily.

W. Franklyn Barrett's *A Girl of the Bush* starred the attractive New

Zealand acress Vera James. Others in the cast were Stella Southern and James H. Martin. It followed the all-too-familiar pattern of buckjumping, sheep shearing and hostile blacks. The one notable feature of the picture was Barrett's camerawork.

Unfortunately Raymond Longford's *Rudd's New Selection* (part of which was filmed in the "Palmerston" studio previously occupied by 'Snowy' Baker) did not provide the marked contrast expected from this talented director. Longford was worthy of better things than further misadventures of the Steele Rudd family. *Smith's Weekly* did perceive merit in 'Dad's whiskers and Dave's gaucheries that were as mirth provoking as ever'. To be fair to Longford, *Rudd's New Selection* was proclaimed as the greatest attraction of the year when it was shown at the York Theatre in Adelaide in 1922. On opening night, the theatre was booked out by 7 o'clock.

In direct contrast to this 'bush merriment', Hollywood offered James M. Barrie's *The Little Minister, Jane Eyre, Under Two Flags,* Rudolph Valentino as *The Sheik*. Douglas Fairbanks Snr in *The Three Musketeers,* the talented juvenile Jackie Coogan was *Peck's Bad Boy* and Charles Chaplin was a member of *The Idle Class*. These few productions demonstrate the quality and variety that America was providing.

Back on the plains, Beaumont Smith chose Henry Lawson's tales around the camp fire, *While the Billy Boils*. The film invited audiences to 'Dip your pannikin deep — it's got the real Australian flavour'. The prologue featured the author himself. Lawson died the following year, and was buried in a grave once occupied by the poet Henry Kendall. It was business as usual when Smith provided *The Gentleman Bushranger*. A slight variation to the 'bail up' tradition was given in the opening by a fight in the rigging of a sailing ship en route to Australia. After the hero's arrival, the bushranging theme was true to form. A gold escort was waylaid, and the new migrant was accused of the robbery. He became 'the Gentleman Bushranger' complete with a price on his head, but the heroine, bless her, still believed in his innocence.

Yet Smith was to demonstrate his versatility in *The Betrayer*, his third feature for 1921. Partly filmed in New Zealand, and photographed by Lacey Percival, it starred Cyril Mackay, Stella Southern, John Cosgrove and Bernice Vere (who was seen in *The Jackeroo of Coolabong*.) Critics felt that the direction and photography were first rate, though the story was weak. A white man has an illicit love affair with a Maori princess. She dies giving birth to a daughter, who is raised by her grandfather, a Maori chief. The white man returns to New Zealand twenty years later. He is knocked unconscious by the chief, and dragged towards a boiling geyser. Then the Maori realises that a more fitting revenge would be to force the girl's father to take her back to Australia and introduce her to the society gatherings that were part of his current life-style. Stella Southern went back to New Zealand after this film to make another one, and did not return to the Australian screen for a number of years.

Although the *Life Story of John Lee — the Man they could not Hang* was a financial success in 1917, if greed wasn't the answer, it is hard to pinpoint any other reason for its remake in 1921 — and by the same producers, Haldane and Sterry. Its release in Sydney carried this sensational announcement:

For the first time in Australia!
A SPEAKING MOTION PICTURE.
At all sessions — Haldane & Sterry,
Brilliant dramatic actor orators
Tell the story while the film is
being screened.
Each character speaks the part.

Perhaps it was the appearance of two actors for the price of one that made such a startling difference. Yet this same 'speaking effect' was used previously in association with *For the Term of his Natural Life* and *The Silence of Dean Maitland.* Even the 1917 version of *The Man they could not Hang* had been given the oral treatment by either Frederick Haldane or Arthur Sterry.

Directed by Arthur W. Sterry, the 1921 remake was photographed by Tasman Higgins. It drew 36 000 people to its opening season. It did exceptionally good business later in Tasmania, and in 1922 J. R. Cameron saw the film's great potential, and smartly purchased the New South Wales country rights. Yet in December 1922 South Africa banned the picture on the grounds that it was not in the best interests of the country. (Apartheid wasn't mentioned once, which makes the reason hard to comprehend. This ban was yet another blow to the Australian silent film industry.) The story of *The Man they could not Hang* became a screen production for the third time, when it was issued as a 'talkie' in 1934, directed by Raymond Longford.

Longford's second film for 1921 was *The Blue Mountains Mystery.* A bigger and more elaborate production than *Rudd's New Selection,* it was another Southern Cross Picture Production. It revealed the real Raymond Longford and his ability to do full justice to a worthwhile story. It told of a murder that baffled the police, and of a mysterious society leader played by Marjorie Osborne. *Smith's Weekly* hailed it as Australia's most elaborate picture to date. Photography and direction were equal to 'the best imported stuff'. Acting was good, and scenery (of the Blue Mountains) was magnificent. Another critic classified it as 'the first real production to measure up to first class English and American standards'. *Everyone's* praised the excellent scenery and added 'it shows our producers to be capable of the best in film production *when given the opportunity*'. The Melbourne *Argus* felt that Marjorie Osborne was especially impressive and that the photography (by Arthur Higgins) was excellent.

Longford, with the impressive *The Sentimental Bloke* behind him, was making a desperate bid to demonstrate that the Australian director could hold his own in the world's best company, if afforded the opportunity. Perhaps Longford was the man who could have held the local industry together, ... but that had significant implications which will be unfolded shortly.

The Blue Mountains Mystery did record business. Eleven months after its Sydney premiere it was an outstanding success in Brisbane, and on 15 October 1923 it was being screened in Adelaide.

W. Franklyn Barrett let the Longford standard down with a resounding hollowness, when he stretched naivety to the point of incredibility in *Know thy Daughter*. The storyline was that of a married man who fell out of love with his wife, and in love with a beautiful girl who enters his life. Such a situation today is commonplace. But the climax reached the point of absurdity, when it was revealed that the young woman was his own daughter. Which raises one interesting question: where had she been all these years?

1.25   *Vera James (left) plays the role of an unmarried mother in the Franklyn Barrett film "Know Thy Child".*

The film front knows that backers are the life's blood of picture production. That is why failure is as fatal as a lack of donors at the blood bank. In 1921, however, there was a strange and unbelievable paradox. Commonwealth Pictures was formed by a group of businessmen intent on making quick profits — an unreal situation in the motion picture business. These men protected their investment by appointing an American director, John Wells; Wells had assisted Beaumont Smith the previous year with the direction of *The Man from Snowy River*. Brownie Vernon, another American, and leading lady for the now defunct Carroll-Baker productions, was added to the cast for good measure. Another association with Carroll-Baker is that interiors were shot at the Palmerston Studio. Male stars Raymond Lawrence and Robert Mackinnon received stiff competition from the racehorse star, Kennaquhair. It was a story of the Australian turf, with Randwick Racecourse providing a backdrop. When the jockey of Kennaquhair was prevented from riding, Brownie Vernon (as in the later American film *National Velvet*) did an Elizabeth Taylor act, and placed her feet in the stirrups. Even though *Silks and Saddles* was a success at the box office, and was sold for distribution in England, the financial returns were not prompt enough for the backers. Consequently, the company went into liquidation after only one film.

The other side of the coin relates to Bairnsdale, Victoria, businessmen who had backed *Strong is the Seed* in 1948. They are still waiting for a dividend from their investment, or even a sight of the film itself, for that matter. The picture was re-edited and released in non-city theatres in 1952 as *The Farrer Story*.

The final entry for 1921 — *Retribution* — is of interest mainly to Queenslanders. It is a film about which very little is known. Directed by Armand Lionello, it starred Thorene Adair as a female detective, who seeks to avenge the death of her father, a sapphire king. It highlighted the Anakie gem field, and used shots of well-known Boggo Road Gaol.

Unlike 1921, 1922 was a year of dismay and disaster. The genuine decline of the Australian film industry can be traced to it through the lamentable eclipse of Raymond Longford as a film director. The film front would be rejuvenated, but Longford did not possess the ability of the phoenix to take wing on rebirth. He had fought back after his services were not required by Amalgamated Pictures, and had directed some excellent features for various companies. Then Southern Cross Feature Films and Southern Cross Picture Productions had provided him with the opportunity to manifest his undoubted genius. That he was still at his peak was forcibly revealed in *The Blue Mountains Mystery*.

Despite its undeniable list of successes, Southern Cross ceased production with bewildering suddenness. It was a faith-shattering death blow to the industry. Totally unprepared for such a disaster, Raymond Longford looked helplessly at a now thoroughly confused film front — little realising that this was only the beginning of a calamitous year. Then Longford committed the cardinal sin of remaining in Australia. He still believed in the future of this country — a faith that was misplaced, as the ensuing years would prove. He was to learn that such confidence would not be matched by the local film makers' loyalty to him. It was to make him embittered and regretful.

E.J. & D. Carroll, after their second failure in two years, decided to leave the film making business. Even as showmen, they experienced the vice-like grip that the combines exercised over the picture houses themselves. As a specific example, for the Melbourne release of *The Blue Mountains Mystery* the Carrolls had to hire the Town Hall, despite the superior quality of the film itself. In 1926 it was revealed that E.J. & D. Carroll had lost $50000 in an endeavour to produce world-class pictures in Australia.

By eliminating Southern Cross, the Australian 'octopus' had itself squeezed the life out of film progress, and must accept full responsibility for the silencing of the Longford-Southern Cross combination — the only Australian production house that could compete with the American product, not with regard to budgets, but in its standard of quality. This was not an isolated case. A few years later, Charles Chauvel received the same treatment.

A letter from the Carrols stated that only unpatriotic people contended that it was impossible to produce pictures in Australia; the letter went on to include the following passage:

> *The Sentimental Bloke* (following outstanding praise at the London screenings) is to be shown in 5000 theatres in the USA. Our firm has either made, or been interested in the production of eight moving films. Seven of these have made a a profit. One will break even. Arrangements have been made for five out of the eight to be shown throughout the English-speaking world. The showing of one other, possibly two, is an absolute certainty. All these films, with the exception of one, were made without proper studio, lighting, equipment or efficient organisation. Now that we have all these vital factors, it is reasonable to think that we can produce better pictures than we have in the past.

Such illuminating facts only add to the confusion as to why the Australian film industry did disintegrate in 1922, if you eliminate the one blinding cause — the combines had the exhibition side of the picture neatly bottled up between four theatre walls.

Members of Parliament began agitating for a compulsory quota for Australian films in our screens. One producer added his voice to the outcry by advising that 'if conditions did not improve, Australian film production would die'. It was a prediction that would become an unpleasant fact.

While the industry was continuing to take stock of itself, W. Franklyn Barrett released *A Rough Passage* in 1922. The title was in keeping with the consternation on the film front, and became Barrett's obituary as far as film production was concerned. It was an unimpressive swan song for a man whose photography was well ahead of his ability as a director. *A Rough Passage* centred around a returned soldier, down on his luck, who took a job in a Sydney horse-training stable. The one bright spot was a donnybrook with racecourse crooks. It was a sub-standard film that did not receive a wide release. Ironically, Barrett joined the publicity branch of an American distribution company — a case of if you can't lick them, join them.

Another departure from the Australian scene was Charles Chauvel. After his appearance in *Robbery Under Arms*, he was appointed to the staff of Palmerston Studio by 'Snowy' Baker. With the eclipse of the Carroll-Baker Productions, Chauvel joined Barrett Films, and assisted in directing *A Rough*

Passage. On completion of the film, no doubt knowing in advance of Barrett's intentions, Chauvel headed for Hollywood in April 1922.

Four months later E.R. Jeffree and J.A. Bruce took over Palmerston and engaged P.J. Ramster to direct *A Triumph of Love*. Starring Jack Chalmers (a Coogee surf hero), it depicted castaways on a tropical island, where four desperate men wished to possess the same beautiful woman. This picture once again highlighted the plight of the independent producer who was unable to gain access to picture theatre screens which were controlled by the combines. As if the Australian film maker didn't have enough problems to overcome, without the film 'show windows' being declared out of bounds! *A Triumph of Love* had to wait until 1925 to obtain a metropolitan release — and then it was in Brisbane.

An unexpected arrival from America of director Lawson Harris and actress Yvonne Pavis brought high hopes of a much needed bolster for a flagging industry. Austral Super Films was formed, and the first production *A Daughter of Australia* went before the camera operated by Arthur Higgins. Even the title held promise — two Americans extolling the praise, and proud of the name of their adopted country. Yet the characters — 'Lanky Mag' in her pink gown, and shearers 'Squasky' Kelly and 'Spikey' McDonald did seem a little out of character when compared to, say 'Dave Rudd'. Australian audiences must have been a little dazed by press publicity such as

> Rather than laze in the lap of luxury, she chose to return to her native Australia.

With that as an opening gambit, the advertising settled shamelessly for sheer sentiment.

> But Fate dogs her mercilessly. The man whose love she had won, sought the vastness of the Australian bush, to forget the march of events, which in England had made him an outcast.

One could almost hear the strains of 'Advance Australia Fair' with this *pièce de résistance*.

> It was in an atmosphere of scented gums — an atmosphere charged with dramatic moments, that these two met again — a scene that will live forever in the memory of all who see this wonder picture.

In this year of meagre production, when neither Raymond Longford nor Beaumont Smith made a solitary contribution to the screen, it seems unbelievable that Austral Super Films immediately embarked on a second venture — *Circumstance*. Again starring Yvonne Pavis, *Circumstance* was the story of a girl who is financially insecure. She is befriended by a writer who pens a romantic novel based on her life. His cousin, a war hero, meets the girl and proposes. On her wedding night she confesses to her husband that after he had seduced her before leaving for war service, she gave birth to his child. One critic praised the clear photography of Arthur Higgins that 'did more to manifest the possibilities of successful production in Australia, than any of its predecessors'.

Such was the incongruous and unpredictable state of 1922 that *Circumstance* was the first picture screened. Initial showings were in Adelaide and Brisbane in September 1922, and Melbourne did not exhibit it until May 1923. Sydney ignored the film completely. *A Daughter of Australia* fared better in the Harbour City where it premiered in October 1922. Adelaide screened it one month later, but again Melbourne was lethargic, and waited until September 1923. The acceptance of these two films was not encouraging to a new and enthusiastic company, which (like Arthur Shirley) desired to make films in Australia for the world.

During such a precarious period when insecurity was rampant on the Australian film front, it would appear that the combines concentrated on promoting overseas productions more than on making even a token gesture to local pictures. While admitting that one of the monopolies did display a minor interest in one of the Austral Super Films, and the other did much the same for the second drama, the support given by the theatres was, to say the least, second grade. It was a searing indictment of the Australian combines concerned. Even more opprobrious and deplorable was that one of the parties controlled a film production company which was in no way adding to the Australian content. No doubt the climate was being conditioned for the time when 'what wasn't available, could not be screened'. In the closing years of the silent era, an effort was made by the same combine to get back into the Australian action ... but as was the case with the 1927 Royal Commission it proved to be too little, too late.

Yet another disheartening demonstration of the local scene in 1922 was given by the result of the formation of an independent company by Raymond Longford and Lottie Lyell — still displaying confidence in the future of the Australian film industry. By December 1922, they had completed *The Dinkum Bloke*. Far from receiving encouragement for this laudable venture, Longford was faced with the frustrating prospect of delayed release. Faced with the same situation as Austral, he too was to learn that producing a film was one thing — but having it screened was like matching a Clydesdale against a racehorse in a test of speed.

In sheer desperation, Longford accepted a position with the Commonwealth Government, and in 1923, with Arthur Higgins on camera, he directed a number of propaganda films touching on themes such as migration and dairying. He used film titles from his earlier productive years (which caused confusion later) but the contents were completely different. The four films he directed were *An Australian by Marriage, Australia Calls, Australia Land of Sunshine* and *Neath Australian Skies*.

Austral Super Films' third production *Sunshine Sally* gained the distinction of being the first Australian film screened in 1923. This time, Melbourne took premiere honours in January. This was in direct contrast to the sluggishness displayed towards the two previous films from Austral. Unfortunately a series of slow bookings followed — Perth in June; Adelaide in November; Brisbane did not screen it until August 1924; and once again Sydney displayed a lack of support for the Australian industry.

Yvonne Pavis was 'Sunshine Sally' who lived in Woolloomooloo. She was courted by a rabbit-o, and a bottle-o. For the right to claim Sally's hand, the pair agreed to a boxing match at the Stadium — winner take all.

Unknown to them, Sally had other ideas. F.W. Thring (later head of his own production company — Efftee) was then manager of the Paramount Theatre, Bourke Street, Melbourne. It was he who described *Sunshine Sally* in these praiseworthy terms: 'No matter what your previous opinion may be, we ask you to reserve your judgement on Australian pictures, till you see this real masterpiece'. But Yvonne Pavis and Lawson Harris, disappointed and disgusted with the lack of acceptance of their films and of their efforts to give an impetus to the local industry, turned their backs on Australia.

The year 1923 was an indecisive and crumbling one for the film industry: Australia seemed to lose interest both in the formulation of any set cycle, and in the production of films generally. On the other side of the Libran symbol, in 1923 Beaumont Smith tossed his lethargy aside and reverted to his moronic and rather irritating 'Hayseeds'. Probably he was following the adage of the vintage travelling theatre company that stipulated, 'When in doubt, perform "East Lynne".' Smith, in true showmanship fashion, merely substituted the pseudo Rudd character.

To everyone's horror and amazement, he put back the clock, not only by producing and directing *Townies and Hayseeds* (billed as the greatest Australian picture since *On Our Selection)*, but by journeying back in time to the stone age for *Prehistoric Hayseeds,* with Wup The Caveman, Mrs Wup, and all the little Wups. Sounds like the morning after 'Don's Party'.

Publicity for *Townies and Hayseeds* capitalised on a request for government protection for a deflated film industry by issuing this challenge to the general public: 'You wanted Australian pictures. Here they are.' With George Edwards as Thomas Townie of Toorak, and his children Miss Adelaide, Miss Brissy, Master Sydney, and Master Melbourne, *Townies and Hayseeds* dealt with the experience of the Townies in the country, and of Ma Hayseed's entry into Melbourne society. An interesting member of the cast was Lotus Thompson, the girl with the lovely legs. When she went to Hollywood (another loss to the local industry) she gained fame only as 'the legs' of leading ladies. In desperation she poured acid over them, to rid herself of her greatest liability.

The central theme of *Prehistoric Hayseeds* was the discovery of a genuine caveman and his family by a young student (Gordon Collingridge) who invites them to Sydney. Lotus Thompson again was in the cast, this time portraying the 'Golden Girl'.

Harry Southwell revived another link with the past when he reincarnated 'The Kelly Gang'. *When the Kellys Were Out* was a remake of his 1920 picture. Godfrey Cass retained his role as 'Ned' but the remainder of the cast was new, including Charles Villiers as 'Dan Kelly'. After the screening in Melbourne in July 1923, further bookings were not forthcoming until Perth screened it in August 1924. Brisbane was next on the list in October 1924. Sydney banned the film as the exploits of the Kelly Gang were frowned on in New South Wales. (The 1920 version *The Kelly Gang* suffered a similar fate in 1923, although it had been premiered in Sydney in February 1920.) Unfortunately Southwell did not profit from experience, and fell foul of the same autocracy with *When the Kellys Rode* in 1934. This production was banned under the provisions of the NSW Theatres and Public Halls Acts when Police Inspector Chaseling made a profound observation, with which others since have wholeheartedly agreed. He did not object to the story of Ned Kelly, but felt that it was time this particular bushranger was forgotten. (In 1977, yet another film was made, this time a tele-cine production, about the trial of Ned. It starred John Waters.)

The Returned Soldiers League viewed the deterioration of the local film industry with deep concern, and asked the Tariff Board to seriously consider limiting overseas films, by cutting the imports by half. The Federal minister, in reply, stated that he was loath to impose restrictions, and ended with the time-tattered cliché — any proposals for the encouragement of production of Australian films would receive consideration. It was a 'don't ring us — we'll ring you' attitude.

Two films with similar themes closed the entries for 1923 — *The Dingo* and *The Dinkum Bloke*. *The Dingo*, directed by Kenneth Brampton (who had acted in a similar capacity for *Robbery Under Arms*), was produced by another new mushroom company, British-Australian Photoplay Company. Filmed in the old Spencer Studio, Rushcutters Bay, the cast included George Edwards, beautiful Sybil Shirley, Godfrey Cass, Gordon Collingridge, and William Coulter (Uncle Jim in *The Sentimental Bloke*).

'The Dingo' (an insulting name in the Australian vocabulary) marries a girl who loves another man. Later he is gaoled, leaving an attractive daughter to fend for herself. On his release from prison 'the Dingo' searches for his child, and finds her living in the lap of luxury, with his arch enemy enjoying the role of a doting father. Once again, releases were in Dead March tempo — Sydney, June; Melbourne, November; Adelaide, February 1924.

The Longford-Lyell production *The Dinkum Bloke*, though ignored by Australian distributors, was considered worthy enough by Paramount Pictures to be released through them — a rare mark of distinction at that time for an Australian picture. (It was eventually released overseas; in England it was retitled *A Gentleman in Mufti*.) Directed by Raymond Longford, the cast of proven players contained Arthur Tauchert, Lottie Lyell, Lotus Thompson, Cecil Scott (who later played Tauchert's role in the talkie version of *The Sentimental Bloke*) and George Scott (previously in Longford's *Mutiny of the Bounty* portraying Captain Bligh).

Despite the time lapse in the release of *The Dinkum Bloke*, it enjoyed good seasons (mainly through Hoyts Theatres) due no doubt to its American associations. Sydney saw it in June, with a successful repeat season in December. Adelaide flocked to a screening in July; Brisbane and Melbourne saluted *The Dinkum Bloke* in August, and Perth in November.

Again promoting the father-daughter theme, the film revealed Arthur Tauchert as a Woolloomooloo wharfie who promised his dying wife that he would rear their child as a lady. To earn additional income he sang in the streets. Ultimately his daughter enters society (a great personal achievement in the twenties), only to provide a number of awkward and embarrassing situations for the father, including the stigma of class distinction a carry-over from Edwardian days, when the position meant more than the man. It was a more credible plot than that of *The Dingo* — but Longford's succeeding pictures as an independent producer never realised the same degree of fulfilment as *The Dinkum Bloke*.

The Mid-twenties: Distribution Problems

Longford's next production in 1924, *Fisher's Ghost,* was based on a Campbelltown (Sydney) legend. It centred around a settler named Farley who saw a ghost on the bridge spanning the Bunburry-Curran Creek. The spectre drifted away, and disappeared over a spot where the body of Fisher was later exhumed. He had been murdered. This Longford-Lyell production received a belated Sydney release in October 1924 — too late to prevent the company from going into liquidation the previous June. It was a humiliating situation for a man who had contributed so much to the stature of Australian film making and who tried to stabilise it through his own heroic efforts when it tottered. It was cruel — almost to the point of being unjust — that *Fisher's Ghost* was screened in Brisbane in December 1924 in two different theatres and was revived there in August 1928. Adelaide showed it in February 1925 and Perth in March 1926. But no independent producer can afford to keep his studio doors open with such lengthy periods between screenings of his films.

The third independent production, *The Bushwackers*, was treated even more harshly by exhibitors, yet rather ironically it enjoyed a three-theatre simultaneous release at its first screening in Sydney in July 1925. In that same year Lottie Lyell died from tuberculosis — another bitter blow for Longford.

The Bushwackers was billed as an Australian masterpiece. Following the tracks of the 'Hayseeds' outback (where all similarity ceased), it centred around a character who has since disappeared from the Australian highway — the swaggie or sundowner. Combining such diversified views as Sydney harbour and the Blue Mountains, the film related the adventures of two mates on the 'wallaby', portrayed by Rawdon Blandford and Eddie O'Reilly. They walk along hot dusty roads from farm to farm, until gold prospecting becomes an obsession. One of them falls over a cliff and is believed dead. The other marries the missing man's wife. Life has a tranquil air until the 'dead' man stands on the doorstep.

Exhibition of Australian films remained a problem for independent producers for many years. It was a cause of constant irritation that gave rise to a depressing aura of frustration. This in turn acted as a deterrent to a great deal of progress that could have been made, if local films had received the right type of encouragement from exhibitors. This sorry state of affairs was not confined solely to the silent era.

Critics too have added their own brand of thoughtlessness to a situation fraught with contentious implications. Again, Longford serves as the ideal example, where critics lost sight of the old Australian tradition (possibly excluding pub brawls) — 'never kick a man when he's down'. When Longford's *The Sentimental Bloke* had a triumphant return season in Melbourne in August 1923, enthusiastic audiences greeted it with the same warmth displayed on its first release. It was left to one critic to rub salt into the director's deeply engraved wounds:

'The Bloke' makes a perennial appeal to Australian audiences. The regret is that Raymond Longford has not seen fit to produce another picture to equal his great achievement.

Hopes ran high in 1924, but results were neither memorable nor commendable. Beaumont Smith sprang some surprises by turning his back on 'the Hayseeds' until the talkies arrived. Instead he made two films starring Arthur Tauchert, and a comedy featuring the monocled comedian, Claude Dampier. Three pictures in one year was really assembly-line production. Smith followed a pattern set by Raymond Longford in *The Dinkum Bloke*, even using Arthur Tauchert and Lotus Thompson. (In Smith's defence it must be admitted that he also used the girl with the magnificent legs in his 'Hayseeds' features in 1923.) *The Digger Earl* was Bill Jones, a Dinkum Digger in France. He goes to the assistance of a wounded mate only to fall foul of an officer for doing so. He promptly deserts. The wounded mate — the Earl of Margate — contacts the military authorities and clears Bill's name. The Digger returns to Sydney in style — in the Earl's yacht — and is persuaded to become the 'Digger Earl' for a few sensational weeks.

Beaumont Smith's second film for 1924 recalls how often Henry Lawson has provided the basic storyline for a screen production. 'Joe Wilson and his Mates' became *Joe*. (The same story was later refilmed as *The Union Buries Its Dead* in the Cecil Holmes' epic *Three in One* that won Festival awards, but received only one commercial showing in its entirety in a capital city.) On

1.26   *"Joe" — a 1924 production from Beaumont Smith — was photographed by Lacey Percival. The lead was Arthur Tauchert (right).*

the screen it was hard to find any similarity between the written and film version *Joe*. Again with Arthur Tauchert in the lead, it had Marie Lorraine in the supporting cast. In 1926 Marie would star in *Those who Love* produced by the McDonagh Sisters and directed by P.J. Ramster.

In *Joe*, a country girl working in a Sydney store realises that her lover is losing interest in her. To retain his love she borrows a frock from her employer's stock and spends a night of 'exotic joy in dancing'. A match thrown by a jealous woman sets her dress alight. She cannot return it to the store, nor can she afford to pay for it. She waits in dread of tomorrow when she will be branded a thief.

P.J. Ramster (mentioned above in association with *Those who Love*) continued to make his low key films. He directed the far from noteworthy *Tale of a Shirt* in 1922, and the following year, *Should a Doctor Tell?* This was no masterpiece according to *Smith's Weekly* — yet according to the same publication, it did demonstrate how fast the standard of Australian films was improving: 'We get better results pro rata than some of the million dollar productions'.

Should a Doctor Tell? dealt with a vital theme — whether a doctor should remain silent when he knows a patient should not marry. Fred Oppey portrayed the doctor, Stirling Worth. The picture did exceptionally good business in Adelaide where more than 24000 people saw it in one week.

Ramster's contribution to 1924 was *The Rev. Dell's Secret*, a film with many interesting associations. In the cast was Lyn Salter, cousin of Melbourne film critic Denbeigh Salter. The cameraman, Jack Fletcher, had spent some time in America with the Charles Ray Company. Billed as even greater than *The Silence of Dean Maitland*, the central character, Rev. Dell, was a well-known figure in every hovel and lane in the underworld. A scintillating example of the intriguing dialogue: 'You call yourself her father, yet you debase your soul, by parading her in this den of iniquity.' Even better was the high-pressured advertising that provided this immortal passage to the press: 'In the underworld, he [Rev. Dell] had seen the girl forced to reveal herself in scanty costume. Why did he question her parentage? — What secret did he hide in his heart?'

Australasian Films caused surprise when they announced big plans for future production. The company had remained lethargic during a period when it could have supplied stability and enthusiastic support for the local film front. However in November 1924 it publicly stated that a strong effort would be made to produce pictures in Australia of a quality that would justify inclusion in programmes generally.

Independent producers in the past had made films that warranted a place on the local screen, but they could not gain access to the theatres. Australasian Films were in a more favourable position: they had Union Theatres behind them, which meant the difference between success and financial failure. Ken G. Hall, although he did contribute more than his share to the success of early Australian talkies, was in the same happy position since Cinesound was a subsidiary of Greater Union Theatres.

However in July 1924, Australasian Films had already started the production line with *Dope* — a film directed by Dunstan Webb. As a standard bearer it was no shot in the arm for the industry, and after its initial

Sydney release, it waited until January 1925 for a further metropolitan release which was in Brisbane at the Majestic which did not normally function as a first-release theatre. If *Dope* had been made by an independent producer, its chance of success would have been remote. But in this case, a king could do no wrong.

The story of opium smuggling in Australia (hence the title), it had a deck hand on a pearling lugger as a central character. In a brawl on Thursday Island, he thinks that he killed a man. Years later — now a successful business man — he still remains haunted by the memory of the 'dead' man.

In August Louise Lovely (previously known in early Australian silents as Louise Carbasse) returned from Hollywood where she had starred in a number of pictures. Her aim was to use her charm and give her assistance and experience to making Australian films for the world. (How often have Australians heard this now rather hackneyed ambition voiced?) Annette Kellerman also returned. A famous Australian swimmer who had made the one-piece bathing suit popular, she was another local girl who had made good in Hollywood. Her visit here was not to make films; rather her aim was a personal one — to promote her film *Venus of the Seven Seas*. The picture blurb proclaimed it to be 'filmed in local waters', which was misleading, as it was financed and 'shot' in New Zealand. Its only Australian association was that it was released through the Beaumont Smith organisation.

In the meantime, Louise Lovely, enthusiastic over the scenic attractions that Australia offered, entered into an arrangement with Stuart F. Doyle of Union Theatres, to tour each state in search of likely screen actresses and locations. Consequently, in September 1924, Melbourne began its search for 'Victoria's prettiest flapper'.

The search for Australia's most beautiful girls, judged on their photogenic qualities in filmed sequences, went on in every capital city. An added attraction was the personal appearance of Louise Lovely and Wilton Welch, in a novel motion picture act, *A Day at the Studio*.

When addressing members of the 'Millions Club' in Sydney on 9 September, Louise Lovely stated that it was possible to establish the motion picture industry in Australia on a profitable basis.

It would be necessary in the first instance, to import experienced men from other countries, as heads of departments. Without the supervision of experts, it would be difficult to compete with those who had been operating in the industry for years.

Miss Lovely went on to describe how snow scenes were filmed in America. But fifteen years earlier (1909) in Australia, Joseph Perry already had achieved this effect in a studio for *The Scottish Covenanters*. He used tiny strips of paper that fell like snowflakes when released from the rafters. He did not have to resort to kapok, electric fans, and glistening salt on the floor.

By November 1924, Australasian Films had engaged an American producer, F. Stuart Whyte. He too availed himself of the opportunity of making a 'personal appearance', and was not hesitant in giving Australians the benefit of his vast knowledge and experience: 'Providing pictures were produced on a safe economical basis, there was every possibility of success.' (Those who grew up with television in this country can remember similar occasions when Canadians and Americans came out to teach us the finer points of television. The author vividly recalls how one Canadian rang him to ask how he tackled a certain problem.) After the familiar cliché about our magnificent climate and scenery, Whyte aired his dislike for legitimate actors: 'I am far more interested in the fresh talent that Louise Lovely is discovering.' Stuart Whyte emphasised the practical impossibility of manufacturing pictures on the extravagant scale of America and concluded: 'A masterpiece does not evolve through a producer waving a magic wand. Picture production means months of organisation. It is not a business for amateurs.'

A Daughter of the East — a Roy Darling Production, had Charles Villiers prominent in the cast. It was released one month prior to Mr Whyte's analysis of the state of the Australian film industry. It claimed to be about a previously untold episode in the Gallipoli campaign which involved an Englishman who was born in the Dardanelles and who was still a resident there in the early stages of World War I. The Allies were supposed to have received great assistance from information supplied by the Englishman. (As the Gallipoli campaign, although a symbol of heroism for the Anzacs, represented a total disaster in the annals of the war this 'untold' episode provides a bewildering puzzle: how much did the information assist the Allied cause?)

How McDougal Topped the Score is a little-known film that was photographed in the Melbourne suburb of Ashburton and in the nearby Dandenong Ranges. Like the pelican in the recent film *Storm Boy*, one of the attractions of *McDougal* was not human: an intelligent dog appropriately named 'Pincher'. During a cricket match between Piper's Flat and Molonglo, McDougal takes a vicious swipe at the ball. Pincher seizes the ball in flight and runs off, chased by the fielding side, whilst McDougal keeps on running between the wickets. He not only 'tops the score', but wins the game. *How McDougal Topped the Score,* an unpretentious but enjoyable film based on a humorous poem by Thomas E. Spencer, received only one metropolitan screening, in Adelaide at two theatres: one in November, the other in December.

The Australian National Films' production *The Price* was another that did not receive a wide release, as it was only shown in the smaller theatres such as the Piccadilly, Sydney, in October 1924, and the Elite, a Brisbane 'flea pit' early in 1925. With direction credited to Dunstan Webb, it did nothing to improve his standing after his unsuccessful *Dope*. In *The Price* a banker's son becomes a jockey, but after a severe illness, his services are no longer required in racing circles. With the last of his savings he purchases a horse that he had ridden to victory some years previously, but that is now destined for the glue factory. With his once famous mount for company, he takes up residence in an old stable.

There were a number of successful documentaries in 1924. Francis Birtle's *Australia's Lonely Lands* competed with two Papuan travelogues — Captain Frank Hurley's *In the Paradise of Unknown Papua* and J.E. Ward's opposing camera views in *Death Devils in a Papuan Paradise.*

Beaumont Smith closed the entries for 1924 with a comedy, but thankfully not in the *Hayseeds* tradition. *Hullo Marmaduke* was the tale of a remittance man who remained in Australia because he had to. Then he made good because he wanted to. Finally he carried on like a mother hen because a girl loved him. The film starred Claude Dampier (known on stage as the silly ass with the toothy grin) who played a role similar to that of Ralph Lynn in the early British talkies such as *Rookery Nook*. In Perth the following year (1925) *Hullo Marmaduke* not only received praise, but the whole industry was lauded.

> There are those that tell you that good motion pictures cannot be made in Australia, but they are constantly being made. Beaumont Smith is plugging away with two pictures a year. Union Theatres are making their first.* Pyramid Pictures are working on one, and Louise Lovely Productions have started. Australian films are being made as far as limited resources will permit, and all motion picture theatres worthy of the name, are screening them today.

Despite this rosy picture painted by J.C. Williamson Films, who still controlled theatres in Western Australia, many Australian producers felt that they were not getting a fair deal from exhibitors in the eastern states, and made their feelings known to the Minister of Trade and Customs. Yet the President of the Federated Picture Showmen's Association (W.J. Howe) denied there was any combine. And the suggestion that extra taxation be placed upon the industry to spoon-feed unskilled producers merely implied that picture producers would spring up solely for the sake of the subsidy, he stated. Two phrases in the statement require close scrutiny — combine, and unskilled producers. Raymond Longford went bankrupt because his independent productions were not given the 'ready' support to keep his finances buoyant. And he was no 'unskilled director'. His list of successes proved that point. As to the non-existence of a combine — just who did Mr Howe think he was convincing?

Opposition would be voiced again when a quota system for Australian films was advocated — or any similar suggestion was made to ensure the survival of the industry. In fact the only loyalty that many Australian showmen had was to their own pockets. The 1927 Royal Commission would supply ample evidence to that effect.

In a statement by the Federated Picture Showmen's Association, Beaumont Smith received special mention as the ideal producer in their eyes. He went about his business in a practical manner, and produced Australian pictures at a profit. Yet after his second Claude Dampier film (screened in 1925), he too departed from the scene.

Pyramid Pictures made two features — a remake of *The Mystery of a Hansom Cab* and *The Sealed Room*. Then Arthur Shirley, who headed the company, left Australia in a huff, taking to Rhodesia the signboard proclaiming that his films were 'Made In Australia'. He would paint out the word 'Australia' and substitute 'Rhodesia'.

Then there was Louise Lovely who made only one picture drama, *Jewelled Nights*. Surely if everything was above board as Picture Showmen claimed, why was the casualty list so high — and why did it include Beaumont Smith who was credited by them 'with knowing his way around'?

*This is incorrect. Smith made two films in 1923, and three in 1924. Union Theatres already had started production in 1924 with *Dope* — an Australasian Film.

Union Theatres, through Australasian Films, made an inauspicious re-entry into the Australian film field with the unexciting and unsuccessful *Dope*. Australasian Films first tried Dunstan Webb as the director for *Dope* in 1924, but for their 1925 production *Painted Daughters*, they appointed the highly publicised American F. Stuart Whyte, to call the shots. *Painted Daughters* starred Zara Clinton and Rawdon Blandford and it was felt that the theme (following the fortunes of the original sextet from *Floradora*) was charged with sentiment. The production revealed the touch of a trained American hand, but despite 'the noteworthy direction', the loudly acclaimed Whyte silently disappeared from the film scene, as did many of the lovelies from the Louise Lovely auditions who were featured. Whyte is credited with having commenced direction of *Sunrise* (released in 1926), but it is also claimed that Raymond Longford completed the work.

At this stage the Australian film industry did not appear to be headed in any apparent direction. If there was an existing pattern, Australasian Films seemed to dictate the course. The only non-conformist was Ken G. Hall, later to become a successful Cinesound director. During this period he was National Publicity Director for Union Theatres and Australasian Films.

Australasian Films, on the surface at least, settled their long-standing difference with the one man of any standing as a director in this country — Raymond Longford. As a token of their goodwill they acquired the rights to the Longford-Lyell Production *The Bushwackers*. Longford experienced a sense of satisfaction and security when he directed three films for the company in 1926, and completed *Sunrise* which F. Stuart Whyte had commenced. In addition he had his fourth independent production, *Peter Vernon's Silence*, screened.

Painted Daughters made the Sydney screen in May 1925; then followed Adelaide in July; Melbourne in August; and Brisbane in October. This proved that an Australian film could command attention when an outlet was available — and Union Theatres could clear the screens for their own product. Orrie Perry, Joseph's son, and then manager of the Lyric-Wintergarden, Sydney, claimed that he had to engage extra staff to handle the crowds who wanted to see *Painted Daughters*. The manager of the Sydney Lyceum enthused over the unprecedented demand to see the picture, even though one day's attendance had been low because of a severe storm. (Both theatres naturally enough were controlled by Union Theatres.) If these reactions were typical of the film's appeal, why did F. Stuart Whyte depart after all the flag waving for his arrival? He didn't even wait to see the 'sunrise' on his second project.

The remake of the 1911 Amalgamated Picture *The Mystery of a Hansom Cab* assembled a fine cast with Arthur Shirley as the accused murderer; Grace Glover, his fianceé; Godfrey Cass; Cora Warner (outstanding as the gin-sodden Mother Guttersnipe); and Isa Crossley (the child actress in *The Scottish Covenanters* and later a member of Pat Hanna's touring stage company 'Diggers'.) The film elicited the statement that 'Australian pictures had come of age, and were here to stay'. The period was not specified!

In 1926 on behalf of Pyramid Pictures Arthur Shirley advised that 'Australian films at long last, had come into their own with the triumph of *The Mystery of a Hansom Cab* and *The Sealed Room*.' The years were 1925 and 1926 respectively. Shirley was the writer, director and star of *The Sealed Room*. His acting role was that of an officer in the Flying Corps who is blinded while perfecting an invention. He is a witness to a murder committed by foreign agents. The sightless man meets the sister of the murder victim — but she has lost her memory. The hero regains his sight and a romance develops. During their honeymoon in the Blue Mountains, the film builds to an exciting climax.

Again the uncertainty of the local industry manifested itself, and Shirley departed, yet another director-producer with two recent outstanding successes to his name who left the country savage and disgruntled.

The second Claude Dampier comedy and the last silent film produced by Beaumont Smith, *The Adventures of Algy*, made its screen debut in Sydney in June 1925. If further proof was really necessary as to the actual position on the Australian film front — this was it. Shirley could possibly be dismissed as a comparative newcomer (even though he had been prominent in earlier indigenous productions), but when Beaumont Smith left it placed an entirely new complexion on the case. He had been on the scene before the 1920s and had not only remained fiercely independent, but had been extremely successful. Now it was a case of how long it would take the industry to die.

The Adventures of Algy made extensive use of New Zealand locations. Algy (complete with monocle, tall hat and spats) is a misplaced person in the land of hot lakes, geysers, and attractive Maori women. To everyone's amazement, Algy strikes it rich by discovering oil on what was proclaimed worthless land. He completely outflanks the villains who knew of the oil deposits, but were only offering 'peanuts' for the property.

When Smith, like Algy, packed his bags for New Zealand, it was to become managing director of J.C. Williamson Films in that country.

Bound to Win was a surprise entry in 1925 though there is reason to believe that it was made six years earlier. It seems that Brisbane was its only metropolitan release. It starred such unbelievable players as the notorious Mebourne criminal 'Squizzy' Taylor (who was shot in 1927) and his girl friend Ida 'Babe' Pender. Squizzy apparently saw in the film a way to whitewash his image. He was depicted as a genuine sportsman — and tried to bolster this impression by riding a horse over hurdles at Flemington. Despite the fact that, on hearing of its production, the Victorian Government promptly banned it, Squizzy found the ways and means of completing the picture. But how did he arrange distribution, and through one of the Union Theatres in the bargain?

The 1925 release *The Bushwackers* was another film that carried a verse from Henry Lawson — this time from 'Out Back'. The quotation ended 'they carry their swags out back.' As it was released by Union Theatres, picture house doors opened magically. It obtained a double release in Sydney at the Lyric Wintergarden and Lyceum on 25 July (an honour bestowed upon *Painted Daughters* two months earlier). Then followed three different theatres in Adelaide in September; Melbourne in October; and Brisbane in December 1925. Longford was learning the hard way that the only way to survive was by learning how to polish boots.

After all the departures from the film scene, E.J. & D. Carroll sprang a bewildering surprise when Dan, at a luncheon given by the Lord Mayor of

Sydney in the Sydney Town Hall, stated that he was leaving for America on 16 September 1925, to ascertain whether Australian films were a viable proposition in the USA. This was totally unexpected news as the Carrolls had lost heavily in film making, and when everyone seemed to be deserting the industry, they were re-entering it. They attributed their previous failure to a slump in motion picture production at the time. Since then the Carrolls had become involved in theatre management. Consequently they were assured of release dates for productions in which they had a financial interest. This solution to exhibition problems only provided further proof that the independent producer was at the mercy of theatre management.

Unfortunately, the Carroll's trip proved a waste of time and money. America was on the verge of the talking picture era, when scores of its own expensively produced silent films would gather dust on the shelves, or have musical backgrounds hastily added to reap some return from pictures that had become out-dated practically overnight. But one must admire the Carrolls. They backed their faith in Australian films, not only by providing theatres in which to screen them, but with their own finance.

They even imported an American director, Phil K. Walsh, for their latest production, *Around the Boree Log.* Based on the popular poems by John O'Brien (who stated that this work was nothing but a collection of 'jingles'), the film premiered in 1925. Molly O'Donohoe was 'Laughing Mary'.

One reputable critic classified *Around the Boree Log* as the most lovable picture that ever graced the screen. It told of the simple man and woman direct in the ways of living and loving. 'Even an amazing cobweb glistening with dew has been included by an artistic and poetic director.'

Nothing further was heard of Phil K. Walsh until 1928, when a group of business men in Young, NSW financed the film project *The Birth of White Australia*, part of which was devoted to the infamous Lambing Flat Gold Riots. Unfortunately for Walsh, the production was not successful, and enjoyed only one brief season in Young itself.

Out of the cartoon strip and on to the screen, was the achievement of the red-headed freckle-faced terror of the neighbourhood — Ginger Meggs. Directed by E.J. Ward for First National Films, *The Terrible Twins* burst into life on the screen in July 1925 at Sydney's Haymarket Theatre. Ginger somehow retained a fascination for youngsters — and many adults too — and as late as 1978, a Sydney newspaper re-introduced this young ruffian in shades of brilliant red.

It would be pleasing to state that 1925 ended on a bright and sparkling note with *Jewelled Nights*, starring Louise Lovely. Directed by Wilton Welch, and featuring outstanding photography and scenery, the film was equal to anything from America in every department. Despite the star's previous tie-in with Union Theatres, the picture was released in October through Hoyts De Luxe, Melbourne. The film actually opened in that city with Louise Lovely playing a social butterfly, who is on her way to be married. Dressed as a bride she descends an elaborate stairway. (The staircase, with its mounted statue at the base, was once the pride and joy of the Princess Theatre, Melbourne.)

1.27 *Opposite page: A unique still of Louise Lovely dressed as a man for her role in "Jewelled Nights" (1925). Photography was by Tasman Higgins with Wally Sully on second camera. (Still supplied by Reg Edwards)*

Miss Lovely disappears before the actual ceremony, and disguised as a boy arrives at an osmiridium mining camp in Savage River, Tasmania.

High hopes were held for this film complete with an international star, but theatre managers did not form the expected queue to handle its exhibition. After the premiere, Brisbane screened it four months later; two of Sydney's lesser theatres billed it in early 1926, and West's Olympia, in Adelaide followed in May 1926. Exit Miss Lovely and any future plans she may have had.

(In 1977 a frenzied search was instigated by the National Library to locate a copy of *Jewelled Nights* in Tasmania. To that date the only film of Louise Lovely's that the Library held was a copy of an old Hollywood picture *The Heart of the North.)*

1926

No jubilant bonfires were lit on the Australian film front in 1926 either! Charles Chauvel arrived back in Australia, and set about making two 'meat pie' westerns in Queensland, in the 'Snowy' Baker tradition. Chauvel was to remain essentially an outdoor man of action. He did not enjoy making 'studio style' pictures that isolated him from the Australian scenery he admired and appreciated.

1.28   *A rare and unique photograph — Marsden Hassall as the lead in "Moth Of Moonbi" — directed by Charles Chauvel in 1926. This "still" is badly marked and needed a lot of retouching even to get it to this stage.*

Chauvel's first 1926 film, *The Moth of Moonbi*, was his own adaptation of a poem by Ethel M. Forest, 'The Wild Moth'. First shown in the then beautiful Wintergarden Theatre, Brisbane (now a flea market) on 25 January, the photography was handled by Al Burne who had left the Sydney scene in sheer disgust. Using the Hotel Cecil, George Street, Brisbane, and the Newmarket salesyards (now gone) for location shots, plus the wooded hills of the cattle country near Warwick as a backdrop, *The Moth of Moonbi* was not a success story for Chauvel. Doris Ashwin played the daughter of a station overseer who inherits $1000 and sets out for the bright lights of the city to wine, dine and make merry. After meeting many insidious males, she returns to the station and the jackeroo who loves her (a role played by Marsden Hassall). The usual cattle duffing was to the fore, with Charles O'Mara and Arthur Tauchert as the 'bodgers from the backblocks'.

The main location for Chauvel's second 1926 production, *Greenhide*, was the Dawson Valley. Starring Bruce Gordon and Elsie Sylvaney (later Elsa Chauvel), the story different only slightly from that of *Moth of Moonbi*. On this occasion, the daughter of a station owner becomes bored with city life, and sets off for her father's property in a rebellious frame of mind. The cattle duffers this time were played by one-time Queensland boxing champion Frank Thorn and by Arthur Greenup. A stirring chase on horseback by the strong man of the story, 'Greenhide', provides part of the action. The studio location was a large allotment behind Oxford House, Ann Street, Brisbane, on which was built an outdoor stage measuring 18 x 8 m. Mirrors, reflectors, and a bright sun supplied all the lighting for so-called 'interiors'. This film was first screened in Brisbane in His Majesty's Theatre on 20 November 1926.

It has been stated repeatedly that the independent producer had a hard road to traverse. Charles and Elsa Chauvel found that it was extremely difficult to have productions screened as the metropolitan theatres in general were controlled by the combines that the distribution companies claimed did

1.29   *This time Arthur Tauchert (R) is a cattle duffer in Charles Chauvel's first film "The Moth Of Moonbi", for which the interiors were especially built. His companion in crime is Charles O'Mara.*

not exist. Even country theatres were tied up through a 'block booking' system that provided showmen with a minimal opportunity to present Australian films, even if they felt a strong desire to do so. As Elsa Chauvel described the situation, after this continuous kicking of dust uphill, they took their films to America — but the talkies had arrived before them.

Making allowances for the extravagant presentation of American films (including expensive stage prologues arranged by the city theatres themselves), the prime reason for the failure of Australian silent pictures was a lack of theatres to screen the product. Admittedly, there were some very bad Australian silent films — but not every American picture was a box office success either. But like the corner grocery store that was to suffer the same fate later, independent operations did not receive the right assistance at the right time, and were not backed by the general public's willingness to support their efforts. The combines, wiped out the independence of silent film makers like the supermarkets of later years decimated small family grocers.

Today the film industry may be displaying signs of healthy growth, but like the Australian silent film industry and the early talkies, it will soon reveal the damaging effects of malnutrition if it is not nurtured and allowed to develop along carefully planned lines. A guiding hand is required, that is not restrictive, and encouragement from enlightened critics should be forth-coming. Finally, Australian productions should be made welcome by exhibitors who do not demand a prohibitive and exorbitant share of the box office takings. (These charges are dealt with in detail in a later chapter.)

On 27 March 1926 an unheralded film, *The Tenth Straw* left by the exit door of the Empress Theatre, Sydney, as unobtrusively as it made its entrance. With an unknown director, Robert McAnderson, and an equally unfamiliar star, Ernest Lauri, it was billed as 'Australia's greatest picture' — a sequel to *The Fatal Wedding* (directed by Raymond Longford in 1911). The claim does not appear to have been substantiated by either the box office, or the general public. At a time when reputable companies and directors were in despair at the state of the industry, it is a puzzle how this film came to be made, let alone screened. The blurb for *The Tenth Straw* seems to have transposed from a novel by Ethel M. Dell:

> It was her wedding morn. The sunbeams fell, but seemed to fade in falling. Next came the peal of the penitentiary bell ... each note bringing forth a sound of sorrow that seemed to sear her soul. She had never doubted — just lived for the day — the little chapel with its chiming bells — then someone whispered — but her hungry heart could not believe.

P.J. Ramster was still active in 1926, writing and directing, and must have felt a 'Leap Year' itch when he presented Sydneysiders with the film *Should a Girl Propose?*. It too had a limited showing, yet Mr Ramster managed to keep going when other Australian directors gave Australian films away. Starring Cecil Pawley and Thelma Newling, it proved to be more than a romantic interlude: there was a runaway car with a frightened child aboard; a struggle for life in an angry sea; and a daring 'Snowy' Baker rescue by rope from a dizzy cliff ledge. It was premiered at Sydney's Piccadilly Theatre on 24 April 1926.

This was the year that Captain Frank Hurley made a dramatic change — startlingly altering his pattern from documentary to a drama that was also in the 'girly' tradition — *The Jungle Woman*. Backed by Sir Oswald Stoll of the British-based Stoll Film Company, Hurley was to have filmed *The Jungle Woman* in Papua, but as photography was forbidden in the area, he switched to Dutch New Guinea. For lighting he used the old outdoor technique of taking the roof off a shed or building, and replacing it with light calico stretched over the rafters to filter the sun through. In this picture, Grace Savieri, mentioned earlier, played a native girl. However the leads were English.

The search for a goldmine leads to the capture of the white party by natives. The intruders are sentenced to death. Very conveniently, the chief becomes ill, and the execution is postponed in the hope that one of the prisoners can save his life. One white man escapes, and the other is befriended by a native girl, who assists him to gain his freedom. Flying foxes, unfriendly pythons, and frenzied pursuit by the natives gave a Tarzan touch to the climax. It opened to a two theatre simultaneous screening on 22 May at the Haymarket and Lyceum Theatres, Sydney.

The same two theatres featured Hurley's second film *Hound of the Deep* on 6 November 1926. This time, the backcloth was Thursday Island, with pearling luggers in the foreground. (Hurley was to go back to the same location for the 1938 Cinesound production, *Lovers and Luggers* for which he captured many magnificent shots on film. Both films repeated the same event — the cutting of the hero's air supply line, while under water. No doubt if the idea was good enough for *Hound of the Deep* it was worth repeating in *Lovers and Luggers*.)

Critics did not receive *Hound of the Deep* as enthusiastically as *The Jungle Woman*. In fact, the acting and storyline were considered rather crude,

1.30 *Australian actress Grace Savieri played a native girl in the Captain Frank Hurley production "The Jungle Woman". The location was the then Dutch New Guinea. Grace Savieri also appeared in "Mystery Of A Hansom Cab".*

and the picture was padded out with unnecessary detail. In the plot to inherit a vast estate under the terms of his uncle's will, the hero must match a world famous pearl discovered by the deceased. Like W. Franklyn Barrett, Hurley was an excellent photographer, but as a director ...?

The year 1926 was to reveal both sides of the coin. In *Everyone's* on 23 June, it was stated that the pressure of business had prevented the Federal Government from considering the Senate's request for an increased duty on foreign films. A codicil revealed doubt as to whether the House of Representatives would take any positive action. The recommendation concluded: 'it behoves showmen and others to see that no effort is spared to point out to Federal Members, the iniquities of this additional impost'. The butter was showing on both sides of the bread, and *Everyone's* did appear to be on the side of the showmen. Despite earlier declarations, the statement does reveal that the Commonwealth Government had no interest in the future of Australian films nor did showmen display any inclination to screen the local product. This gives a ring of truth to Chauvel's findings.

The reverse side of the coin revealed that Australasian Films was going to activate local production. It purchased a Bondi skating rink in 1925 and a new studio was erected and modern equipment installed to the value of £100 000. (Later this became Cinesound Studio 1.) Was the giant really awake at last, and in an endeavour to offset its previous neglect, would it give the industry a much-needed boost?

Raymond Longford, although working on limited budgets, applied himself to the task of directing films with a newly found zest and zeal. His first, a remake of the 1916 film *The Pioneers,* was shown at Sydney's Haymarket and Lyceum Theatres on 5 June 1926. Photography by Arthur Higgins was brilliant, and the settings compared more than favourably with those in American productions. One critic felt that Mr Longford tried to bring too much story into the picture when, after two hours of screening, new issues were still arising. 'If cut, this would stand as a landmark in the history of Australian films.' William Thornton and Virginia Beresford portrayed Scottish immigrants who adopt the daughter of an ex-convict. Years later the girl experiences unexpected problems when her real father is accused of cattle duffing.

It was an excellent start, and Longford looked forward with confidence to a future filled with promise. He had heard along the grape vine that a 'super' production was just around the corner. His hopes soared.

The second film, *Tall Timber,* often credits Dunstan Webb with the direction. This is debatable. Webb as a director hadn't been very successful with *Dope* — and both Ken G. Hall and the *Sydney Morning Herald* credit Longford as being the director. In fact, the paper considered that Longford's captions were the weakest part of the film. They contained too much Australian slang. (Perhaps this criticism is not warranted as the script was by Dunstan Webb.) The story unfolded with a wealthy young man (Eden Landeryou) giving a party at a cabaret. Police raid the premises, but the party-giver escapes. The father, unhappy with his son's behaviour, gives him a cheque for £200, and tells him not to return until he is a real man. He goes to the tall timber country of northern New South Wales, where he finds romance, and experiences the dangers of 'logging'.

Then Raymond Longford received an unexpected jolt. The £100000 remake of *For the Term of his Natural Life* was not given to him to direct, but instead a visiting American, Norman Dawn. The American invasion took place in mid-1926, with the arrival of the actress Eva Novak, and actor George Fisher.

Now came the second mix-up involving Longford. The film was *Sunrise*, and although the first part of the direction is credited to F. Stuart Whyte, with Raymond Longford completing the picture, a third member of the American invasion team is mentioned — cameraman Len Roos. This raises another interesting question. Where exactly was Whyte between *Painted Daughters* and *Sunrise* — and as Longford had been appointed director in between those pictures, was Whyte still around at the time Roos was behind camera? In addition, was Whyte responsible for the merry mix-up surrounding the appointment of Norman Dawn?

In *Sunrise,* the manager of Mount Sunrise mine returns from a visit to the city, and to the surprise of the local inhabitants, is accompanied by his bride. The villain (Dunstan Webb) covets the young wife, and she falls from a cliff while trying to elude him. The widower seeks solace with the mine-owner's daughter. The heavy still tries to cause trouble, but a twist is given to the climax, when the hero rescues the villain. *Sunrise* opened its season in Sydney on 16 October 1926 and was praised for both acting and photography, with outdoor scenery providing an outstanding highlight. Zara Clinton (from *Painted Daughters)* and Robert Travers played leading roles.

The last of the independent productions under the Longford-Lyell banner was released by Paramount Pictures once again. With Arthur Higgins on camera and with Longford as director, *Peter Vernon's Silence* was excellent from a scenic point of view, but weak in storyline, although written by Longford. Some of the best snow scenes ever presented in an Australian production only confused the final assessment of the film. Peter and Phillip Vernon, station owners, were both in love with Marie, the daughter of a neighbouring squatter. Phillip becomes engaged to her, then murders her father. Peter, out of love for Marie, states that he is the murderer, and is sentenced to prison. Phillip and Marie marry but he becomes ill, and confesses his guilt on his death bed. Peter derives little satisfaction from his brother's admission, as he has already served his full sentence. The stars were Rawdon Blandford, Walter Hunt and Loretta May.

The embittered Raymond Longford saw his final production for Australasian Films, *Hills of Hate*, screened in Sydney on 27 November 1926. His reign and his raised hopes had been short-lived. Based on a novel by E.V. Timms, the stars of *Hills of Hate* were Gordon Collingridge and Dorothy Gordon (who returned after ten years in Hollywood). Later, Dorothy became better known as radio personality 'Andrea'. In America she had been a stuntwoman, and had played minor roles — in Wallace Reid's last film, and in one starring a youthful William Boyd, whose later role as 'Hopalong Cassidy' was to make him better known. In addition, Dorothy Gordon was an assistant to Cecil B. DeMille on the set of *The Ten Commandments.* When Australasian Films thought she knew everything about film making, she let the 'big wigs' go on thinking just that.

Hills of Hate, another low budget film, was shot in the Bondi Junction studio and at Dungog. In the story Dorothy Gordon is abducted by a half-caste ex-shearer, played by Big Bill Wilson. For dramatic effect, the rape scene was enacted on a rocky outcrop. The actress was terrified of heights, and after being hauled into position by block and tackle, had to struggle with Wilson after he had ripped off half her skirt. She was so frightened that she, metaphorically speaking, was quite prepared to allow the rape to actually take place. Yet the advertising billed it as a 'feud born in the peace of the New England district.'

In her autobiography, 'Andrea' claimed that *Hills of Hate* was no world-beater. Rather critically she pointed out that Union Theatres only 'put peanuts' into film making, and she believed that this was the wrong approach. She was of the opinion that you had to spend money to make money.

Hills of Hate was a good exit line for Raymond Longford from Australasian Films. In desperation he appealed to Queensland exhibitors to finance him on yet another remake of *Robbery Under Arms*. The reply was sympathetic — but no guarantees were forthcoming. In sheer desperation Raymond Longford left Australia to seek fresh encouragement and inspiration in picture making overseas. *Robbery Under Arms* was to remain an obsession for Longford, and when he returned in the talkies era he still cherished plans for committing the story to film. Ken G. Hall inherited the same desire, but *Robbery Under Arms* wasn't remade until 1957, and then by a British company.

Two films in 1926 that did not take Australia by storm were *Down Under* and *Key of Fate*. *Down Under* was directed by Harry Southwell for the little known Anglo-Australian Films. After his clash with the New South Wales authorities over his *Ned Kelly* productions, Southwell went to Perth, intending to make that city the film capital of Australia. (Similar views were held 1974-78.)

The Perth cast included Nancy Mills, sister of Beryl Mills, the then current Miss Australia. Director Harry Southwell played the leading role of a drifter. However, the photographers Lacey Percival and Cliff Thomas were from Sydney. *Down Under* was set in England and Australia — and was described as a conventional melodrama. (The difference between straight melodrama and the conventional style was never fully explained.) But casserole-style, *Down Under* did include everything from a cattle muster and a corroboree to a trotting meeting. The *West Australian* after a preview reached the conclusion that 'when the film reaches London, it may undergo finishing touches'. It was felt that many of the scenes could be shortened, as the film had a tendency to drag. The final outcome of the film remains a complete mystery.

The John F. Gavin 'quickie', *Keys of Fate* was made in seven weeks. It was photographed by Arthur Higgins, and was projected in the cameraman's house in Randwick. After that private preview *Key of Fate* does not appear to have opened any doors.

Another 1926 production to fall by the wayside was *Northbound Ltd*, directed by the youthful Victorian, George Palmer. The previous year he had directed and produced *The Mail Robbery* which he had hawked around country towns in Victoria and New South Wales.

There was another mild film invasion in November 1926, when Juchau

Productions was formed with American principals — director, cameraman, scenario writer, editor, technical director and assistant director. Only the cinematographer Jack Bruce and director C.J. Sharpe appear to have achieved anything at all. Their only film effort, *The Menace* in 1928, fizzled after the preview.

The final production for 1926 — *Those who Love* — was from the McDonagh sisters, with P.J. Ramster as director. The story was trite, but the McDonagh sisters stated that Australian films in those days made us out to be a lot of 'bushwackers' with a Dad and Dave image and they wanted to get away from this. They are 'off beam' with such a statement as Longford's work alone used many themes far removed from the 'down on the farm' atmosphere.

Few critics were impressed with the photography in *Those who Love* which wasn't up to American standards, and the theme itself was unoriginal. One of the camera operators was Jack Bruce. Jack Fletcher, who had spent time in America, was the other. Fletcher would again be associated with Ramster and the McDonagh Sisters on *Far Paradise*.

In the story, Barry Manion, with a social background, befriends a penniless girl, Lola. She is frightened of storms, and during a fierce one, the pair find romance. Lola runs away when warned off by the Manion family solicitor. Barry indulges in drinking bouts, while Lola becomes a nursing aide. After an accident while working as a wharfie, Barry is nursed back to good health by Lola. The parents become reconciled to Barry's ultimate fate after Lola confesses that Barry's infant son was born after their forced separation. Barry (portrayed by William G. Carter) and Lola (Marie Lorraine) were supported by Robert Purdie and Kate Trefle. *Those who Love* premiered at the Sydney Haymarket Theatre on 11 December 1926, but had to wait twelve months for a screening in Adelaide.

It has been stated that the Governor of New South Wales cried at the preview. Was it the story, or the future of the Australian film industry that worried him?

A preview of things to come was given in 1926, when De Forest Phono Films were demonstrated in Sydney. In May 1926, Australians viewed them as a novelty, nothing more. It served as a definite warning that silent films were doomed, yet Australia blissfully went on trying to make 'silents' golden. Wally Sully was the first Australian cameraman to use the 'sound' camera: he recorded for De Forest the speech by the Duke of York when he arrived in this country in 1927, to officially open Canberra. The Sydney Lyceum screened this memorable and historic event. The inevitable talkies had struck their first blow.

In Australia, 1927 provided two conflicting items of news concerning the local film front — the outstanding success, at least from the viewpoint of the audience, of *For the Term of his Natural Life*, and the Royal Commission, whose purpose was to investigate the real state of the industry, which many interpreted as looking closely at the reasons for the failure of so many local productions. Such hopes (like the eventual findings) were an anti-climax, being unrealistic and utterly futile. Even the advent of the 'talkies' was either unheeded or unnoticed by the Commission and the verdict was obsolete before the results were announced.

COYLE · ORDELL PRODUCTION

featuring
POP
ORDELL

The Kid Stakes

SYD NICHOLLS CARTOON CREATIONS
BROUGHT TO LIFE ON THE SCREEN

FATTY FINN AND HIS **GANG**

FOR THE FIRST TIME ON THE SCREEN
A GENUINE GOAT RACE

THE LAUGH OF THE YEAR

THIS IS NOT A CARTOON FILM

ROTARY PRESS LTD - 904 DUNDAS ST, SYDNEY

1.31   *The creator of Fatty Finn as mentioned in this film poster, was Syd Nicholls. He fell to his death from a Kings Cross building on 3 June 1977 at the age of 81. (The goat race mentioned was filmed in Rockhampton, Queensland.)*

'Kid Stakes' could apply to the findings of the Commission, but was in fact a Coyle-Ordell film production. Commercially screened in Brisbane on 9 June 1927, *The Kid Stakes* was written and directed by Tal Ordell and photographed by the reliable Arthur Higgins. This production was described by Sylvia Lawson in *Nation Review* on 26 May 1977 as follows:

> Probably the Australian screen's final splendid moment — a movie made from a long-running comic strip (Fatty Finn and His Gang), it told of slum kids and a billy-goat race. It all happened with unforced hilarity, and without heroics out in the run-down streets behind the wharves (it was made in the Woolloomooloo-Potts Point area) with kids and cops acting as easily as the billy-goat himself — an outstanding piece of neo realism, nearly 20 years before the term was invented. By the time *The Kid Stakes* was on view, the fabric was being pulled apart, or to fray irremediably.

For the billy-goat race staged in Rockhampton on Saturday morning 5 February 1927, sixty goats arrived, and a crowd of 6000 witnessed the running of the Billy Goat Derby. Tal Ordell played a radio commentator who described the race. One of the players, Joyce Hazeldean, once played in a film with the boy wonder Jackie Coogan.

All in all, 1927 was an unrewarding year. *Environment* was directed in Melbourne by Vaughan C. Marshall, and screened in that city on 23 July at the Palace Theatre. It was not well received, and supplied no answers for a tottering industry. Described as 'photography generally good — acting uniformly expressionless', it starred Beth D'Arvall as a model who indiscreetly reveals three inches of knee while posing. She married — yet only hours after the ceremony her 'husband's love turned to hate, when he realised that she was the type of woman who couldn't be insulted'. Now comes the real drama — or does it? Two young policemen wander into a strange house and shoot a marauder. They leave the body there, while they notify General Blamey (who at the time was Victoria Police Commissioner). As the people in the next room (?) didn't hear the shot, Blamey decides to take no further action. (As one critic so aptly wrote, 'This is just a sample of the fustian of the plot.')

An Australasian Films' Production was shown at the Melbourne Majestic Theatre on 10 December 1927. (Originally the Majestic had been built by Amalgamated Pictures, but it became part of the Union Theatres deal.) The film was *Melbourne's Wonderful Tramways*, depicting forty years of progress in the tramways, and in the rapid development of Melbourne itself.

The big film for 1927 was undoubtedly *For the Term of his Natural Life* complete with a funereal dirge for a theme song. This $120 000 picture enjoyed sensational seasons throughout Australia. The premiere at the Theatre Royal, Newcastle, on 20 June 1927, was followed by the Sydney showing, five days later. There it remained for eleven weeks. Following a rewarding season at the Crystal Palace, it enjoyed a billing at the Lyric Wintergarden in September. In July 1927, *For the Term of his Natural Life* was screened in Brisbane and Adelaide; in Perth and Fremantle in August; and on 8 October, it recorded seven weeks' run in Melbourne.

Although the Port Arthur convict settlement site was used extensively,

1.32   *A scene from "For The Term Of His Natural Life" after an escaped convict from Port Arthur is re-captured. Gabbett (Arthur McLaglan) is seated. On his left is Arthur Tauchert as Warder Troke. Behind is Dunstan Webb portraying Captain Frere, and on the right, Carlton Stuart as Commandant Burgess. Included in the caption is the statement that Norman Dawn is adapting the novel for the screen. This bears out Andrea's remarks in the text.*

1.33   *The famous "glass shot" used for the film "For for Term of his Natural Life". Across the strip of water, is the ruins of the penal settlement of Port Arthur. Bert Cross is behind the camera on the first platform, and "shoots" through a pane of glass on which was painted the "missing portion" of the ruins. This "restored" the building to its "original appearance" without any costly re-building.*

additional scenes were shot outside Sydney Harbour, and at Dundas, NSW, as well as the Bondi studios. The star, Eva Novak, stated that it was a fictional story — but was it? Author Marcus Clarke spent considerable time researching in the Launceston Museum, in which there is a mask worn by a certain Rufus Dawes (the name of the hero of the book).

The photographers were American Len Roos, Australians Bert Cross and W. (Bill) Trerise — the last named deputising for Loos for ten days when Loos injured an ankle during the shooting of a dockside scene. The cast was also impressive — Eva Novak, George Fisher, Dunstan Webb, Arthur Tauchert, Arthur McLaglen (brother of Hollywood film star Victor McLaglen), Katherine Dawn, child actress Beryl Gow, Mayne Lynton, and Marion Marcus Clarke (daughter of the author).

An interesting part of a critique of the production was that director Norman Dawn was compared to Raymond Longford: 'A distinct advantage on any Australian film yet, with the exception of *The Sentimental Bloke*, with the latter being produced on a much more modest budget.' The script too came in for caustic comment: 'Against inspiring and natural scenery, and a truly skilful way in which the director has dealt with some of the characters, there must be balanced, a crudely written scenario and a multitude of weak captions.' Dorothy Gordon (from *Hills of Hate*) and Victor Longford (son of Raymond) adapted the film play from the novel — but this was a cause of bitter scorn from Andrea in her autobiography. She called the film a screaming flop, and stated that Dawn didn't use the script submitted, but his own. Andrea became so infuriated that she demanded the withdrawal of her name from the credits.

Actors who received special praise were George Fisher as the convict Rufus Dawes (who was sentenced to penal servitude for life for a crime committed by his twin); Mayne Lynton as the Rev. North; and Arthur McLaglen as the escaped prisoner Gabbett, who turned cannibal and killed and devoured his fellow escapees.

Following his work in *For the Term of his Natural Life*, Len Roos made life exceedingly hard for Australian film historians. He made a one-act comedy drama for T.J. Gorgan who ran the Grafton, Casino, and Lismore film circuit. Made in 1927, it was titled *The Adventures of Dot*. On the original list of Australian Feature Films issued by the National Library, Canberra, in September 1965, this production was credited as being a 1930 feature. Then in a supplementary list, the year was shown as 1927 — and carried the following caption 'actually a short'. However a full-length version was filmed after that date, and from information to hand, was shot in various areas with local casts. One of *The Adventures of Dot* was shot in Colac, Victoria in late 1932 by Community Films. It was directed by J.M. St Ledger. The amazing fact is that it was a silent film at a time when Australia was producing 'talkies'.

To end the year on a hopeless note, the Royal Commission must stand as one of the greatest examples of a very expensive waste of time. It heard conflicting reports, its findings were ignored (with one possible exception), and overall it stands as a colossal monolith bearing the inscription 'Dedicated to one of the dead wonders of the Australian Film Industry'.

The Late Twenties — A Royal Commission

It began when a Select Committee in 1927 brought pressure to bear on the Federal Government, after three different groups demanded positive action. The complaints were received from:

1. Empire loyalists who wanted protection for British films in Australia. (It's a pity a similar group wasn't formed in the 1930s for protection of the Australian film in England, when Australian films were classified as 'foreign'.) It should be kept in mind that duty of 1½d. per foot was payable in Australia on all film imported from overseas foreign countries, yet England was charged only 1d. per foot. At this time England was charging 5d. per foot on imported film to protect its own film industry.

2. Australian film makers — the Motion Picture Producers' Association — opposing the power of the Exhibitors' Combine. 'Block booking' of American films made it practically impossible for Australian films made by independent producers to get releases on reasonable terms. This group agitated for a 'quota system' to protect the local film industry. (American distributors were responsible for 'block booking' by baiting picture show proprietors with a lavish display, then forcing them to sign contracts not only for the 'spectacular' productions but for the acceptance of 'junk' as part of the agreement. The expensive features on the whole were outstanding, but America did make scores of inferior films as well. The enforcement of the screening of the imported rubbish deprived better Australian films.)

3. Women's organisations — campaigning for increased film censorship, especially of overseas pictures.

The Royal Commission on the moving picture industry was convened on 2 June 1927 in Melbourne, and after visiting the various capital cities, concluded its hearing in Sydney on 2 February, 1928.

One of the bitterest attacks on the combines came from Raymond Longford. As an independent producer, he knew the problems attached to obtaining film releases. Some of his pictures had been refused a first release in capital city theatres, and on one occasion, after criticism from him, certain distribution houses threatened to discontinue supplies to small exhibitors who showed Longford's films. One vitriolic outburst was saved for Australasian Films, and American director Norman Dawn, whom Longford claimed was a cameraman, not a director, and was not well known. (Some critics have blamed Longford's outburst on his blinding hatred for Australasian Films — but one must admit that he was handed a raw deal on a very dirty platter. However in Dawn's case he did allow his feelings to prejudice his better judgement. Dawn was a pioneer cinematographer, widely honoured for the introduction of 'special effects'. One example was the 'glass shot' used by Bert Cross for the filming of the main prison block at Port Arthur. Placing the glass close to the camera while filming a scene some distance away, it was possible to 'reconstruct' the complete prison building from the standing ruins. The 'missing' portions clearly visible in the existing structure were painted on the glass, and giving it the right perspective, the screen revealed the building in its entirety. Added to that ability, Dawn did direct 'action' films.)

John F. Gavin was a keen supporter of the 'quota system'. Having played 300 roles during the eight years in Hollywood, and scores of parts in Australian films before that, as a producer of some twenty-six features, he felt in a position to speak with authority. 'We have the talent, and just as many brains as the Americans,' he stated, and urged that a 20 per cent quota be imposed.

C. J. Sharp, who arrived from America to form Juchau Productions and who was managing director of Commonwealth Film Laboratories, at the time of the Commission, felt that production in Australia must be commenced on a small scale. This would allow those engaged in the industry to acquire the technical knowledge of America. If a quota was established, it would be necessary to have an Appeals Board to assure exhibitors that the pictures they were compelled to screen conformed to a proper standard.

Another American, Frederick Phillips, managing director of Phillips Film Productions (a company set up to make a series of films starring Eva Novak), was of the opinion that films with international appeal could be produced in Australia for the world market, at a cost not exceeding $20000. He considered it a good idea for the government to spend up to $500000 in establishing national studios. These could be rented to producers. Biased opposition to this suggestion came from a number of factions, including, strangely enough, a number of Australians.

William W. Bellion, secretary of the Motion Picture Exhibitors' Association of Western Australia, expressed the view that as an individual proprietor, he had screened a number of Australian pictures, and they had not been up to standard. In fact, Australian films did not draw at all. Stories were only occasionally good, the acting was crude, while the photography was open to criticism. (Mr Bellion's remarks cannot go unchallenged. Australian pictures on a number of occasions had been responsible for record takings and attendances in Western Australia. As to the standard of photography, that is one department of the industry that has always been outstanding, from the Higgins Brothers and W. Franklyn Barrett in the silents, through George Heath, Captain Frank Hurley, Carl Kayser, and Noel Monkman in the earlier talkies, to Russell Boyd, John McLean, youthful Ian Baker, Don McAlpine, Vince Monton and many others in the 1970s.)

A managing director of Hoyts Theatres (Australian-owned at the time) felt that with a few exceptions, Australian pictures were the worst produced in any country. Companies did not even know how to 'cut' a film. To pay for itself, a film must have an international market and contain international appeal. He did agree that America should be compelled to pay a percentage of Australian film hire to aid Australian production. (In 1927 Australia spent about $1600000 on American film imports.) He added that such a levy should be controlled by the companies involved and not by means of legislation. He was against the quota system: 'When pictures are produced that are worth screening, they will be shown, even in America.' (?) He was against having American actors establishing the industry. American technical staff were of greater importance. (In the past, both American actors and technicians had arrived — but did not make any marked impression upon the progress of the industry.)

Some 250 people contributed their opinions that were duly recorded in the pallid pages of the report by the Royal Commission. Yet the summing up on 25 April 1928 was unreal and unbelievable. Anzac Day was well chosen. On one hand it commemorated the deaths of those killed in battle, but in 1928, the Royal Commission sentenced the Australian film industry to an inglorious demise.

The Commission stated:

1. It was unable to discover any evidence in substantiation of the allegation of some witnesses, that the American picture industry had a stranglehold on the Australian counterpart. (Such a finding is sheer fantasy!)

2. Few of the attempts to produce pictures in Australia had been successful. (That was a statement — not a solution.)

3. One witness (Arthur Whitford, proprietor of *Everyone's*) had offered $200000 towards the cost of a national moving picture studio, if the Commonwealth Government contributed a similar sum. The plan was not recommended.

A lot of balderdash covered such comments as — money for 1250 Australian pictures, representing an investment of $50 million, had been provided by Australian capital without the assistance of overseas investment; Australia, with its excellent and varied climate, its extended range of scenic beauties, its geographical situation, was especially suited for production of outdoor moving pictures. (These were well-known facts before the Commission sat — but what was really required was a screen to display such scenery — and protection from a government that was interested in having the home product screened. Financial assistance could come from levies on imported film.)

A statement of the obvious was that unlimited scope offered by the established industry in the United States made it unlikely that talented Australians who had gone to America would be prepared to return unless every encouragement and assistance were given officially to make production in the Commonwealth possible. (Here the role of the Commission should have been to suggest ways that this could be achieved.) The report went on to state that recent Australian films had been made at a cost between $60000-$100000 *(For the Term of his Natural Life* cost $120000), but they must be of a standard to ensure acceptance overseas. Evidence also revealed that there was a dearth of suitable Australian stories for filming, and the Commission considered that some encouragement should be given to induce Australian writers to contribute stories suitable for screen adaptation.

Even in the Commission's recommendations there were no startling revelations or incentives:

1. A Board of Censors to be established consisting of two men and one woman.

2. The limiting of exhibitor-distributor contracts to 12 months, with an inclusion of a rejection clause of 5 per cent in all contracts. (This did not in any way interfere with the system of "block booking" which still kept Australian films off the screen.)

3. The establishment of an Empire (*not* Australian) quota of 5 per cent for

the first year commencing 1 January 1929; 10 per cent the second year; 15 per cent the third year.

4. Increase in tariff on foreign film from 1½d. to 2d. per foot. (Once again British productions scored.)

5. A system of Awards of Merit was advocated, such as an award each year for the best films produced in Australia. The films would have to build up national sentiment, contain high moral standards, and humour. Propaganda that would prejudice relations with other countries should not be countenanced. (Note how this clause adversely affected *The Devil's Playground* in 1930.) The first award should be $10 000; the second, $5 000; the third, $3 000.

6. For the best film scenario written by a resident of Australia, $1 000; with another $1 000 for the best scenario containing Australian sentiment.

For the independent film makers, the whole inquiry was an utter farce. The recommendations favoured a quota for British films only. This kept many local studio doors firmly closed. Despite the Commission's findings, many of its recommendations would require ratification by the states, and the transfer of state rights to the Commonwealth. This damned the whole concept from the outset. Even when the report was issued, it was already in past tense. Talkies and the depression were looming formidably in the foreground.

Perhaps the greatest achievement of the Royal Commission reflects no glory upon its findings. This was the provision of an unquestionable manifesto for the complete annihilation of Raymond Hollis Longford as an independent film producer. He asked for hope and a helping hand. Both were denied him. Longford may have been too outspoken for his own good — but in the days of the Australian silent film, his is the one name that stands out with distinction. Where the combines destroyed, Longford created masterpieces.

The year 1928 was to witness a frenzy of production that contained only the minutest degree of actual achievement. Yet it did provide one man with an opportunity to direct, a position he would carry with distinction in the early talkies — Ken G. Hall. Even then it came about through a colossal blunder made by the American company for which he worked, when it purchased a German film *Unsere Emden*.

Eva Novak had arrived back in Sydney in April 1927, to take up residence in Australia, under contract to Phillips Film Productions. (Like Anne Baxter of more recent times, her residence would be short and not very sweet.) Another American arrival in the same year was American film director Scott Dunlap, who would call the shots for Miss Novak's new picture *The Romance of Runnibede* — another Steele Rudd story. Later in 1927, Dunlap left for America to purchase complete studio equipment, including the latest form of studio lighting. While in the States, Dunlap was to arrange for the American release of all films starring Eva Novak. Phillips Productions also arranged for Hollywood photographer Dal Clausen to film their productions. (There you have it — an American company, American star, American director, American photographer, American lighting.) According to many appearing before the Commission, this was what this country needed. But instead of meeting with outstanding success — the company went insolvent.

1.34   *Eva Novak the American actress, after her appearance in "For The Term of His Natural Life", made an unsuccessful attempt to sponsor films produced in Australia. "The Romance of Runnibede" was the beginning and the end of such a project. Here Eva Novak appears with Queensland aborigines in this scene from the film. However, many of the leading aboriginal roles were portrayed by white actors.*

1.35   *This demonstrates a warning Australia did not heed. Wally Sully centre stands behind the camera, to film and record the speech made by H.R.H. Duke of York on his arrival in Sydney in 1927. However only a few theatres were equipped to show De Forest Phono Films — the forerunner of the talkies.*

Despite the activity of 1928, the year made one point clear — silents were doomed, thanks to Warner Brothers, and a certain Mr Al Jolson, who sang the praises of 'Mammy' on some new fangled mechanical contrivance called 'talkies'. Yet 1928 opened hopefully enough for Australia, on 9 January, at the Brisbane Wintergarden Theatre, with *The Romance of Runnibede*. Directed by Scott Dunlap, it was photographed by, strangely enough, Len Roos (not Dal Clausen). Starring Eva Novak, Viriginia Ainsworth, Gordon Collingridge and Dunstan Webb, one of the locations was the Barambah Aboriginal Settlement near Murgon, Queensland.

The story was of the daughter of a Queensland station owner, and a tribe of 'uncivilised' Aborigines who took up residence close to the property. The blacks believed that the girl was their queen who had returned in a different guise. This belief was fostered by an outlawed 'ochre' man who had taken refuge with the tribe to avoid capture by the Queensland police.

The Melbourne *Argus* felt that the scenes and incidents of native life provided a colourful background. (This was one of the highlights of the original Rudd story.) Scenery was typical of the back country, and the photography was good — helped by our own bright sunlight that needs no Kliegs. According to *The Life and Times of Steele Rudd* by his son Eric D. Davis, it was revealed that Brisbane in particular felt that the film did not do justice to the book, nor was it an accurate picture of the Australian way of life. It was too American.

Phillips Productions had trouble finding theatres to screen the film, and met strong opposition from the powerful film combines that controlled theatres and film distribution. (Yet the findings of the Royal Commission issued in that same year of 1928 denied the claims that such a 'stranglehold' existed.) Even Steele Rudd protested loudly about American interests holding the local film industry to ransom. Yet in the beginning Rudd had been so enthusiastic over the Phillips' venture that he had written a second story for the screen. The unexpected bankruptcy of the company terminated his fanciful dreams. To this day Rudd's son does not know what happened to that unfilmed script.

Phillips Productions however revealed that the failure was not due to lack of enthusiasm — only of theatre screens. William R. Reed, production manager, and cameraman Dal Clausen embarked upon a promotional venture in provincial New South Wales. With a script by Jack McLaughlin, they made a three-reeler at the Capitol Theatre, Tamworth, appropriately titled *Tam of Tamworth*. With a local cast, they added dramatic interest to the story with a spectacular fire sequence (which of course involved the local fire brigade. St Ledger used the same technique later when filming the various versions of *The Adventures of Dot*). *Tam* was screened on 5 February 1928, in the theatre in which it was produced. The same unit made *Olive of Orange, Priscilla of Parkes* and others — covering an area that ran from Grafton to Wollongong. However, on the collapse of the company Eva Novak and William R. Reed were granted the American rights to *The Romance of Runnibede* in lieu of salary.

The first and last Juchau Film swept across the screen like a spasm of nausea. At a trade screening in the Prince Edward Theatre on 2 February 1928, critics saw little to excite them. In fact *The Menace* did not warrant screen space. 'Unhealthy sensationalism is the keynote. *The Menace* is drug traffic — and the first scenes show the trade being purveyed in a back alley.' The critique made references to restless, violent acting; weak captions; and an undramatic scenario (again mainly the work of Americans). The lead was Virginia Ainsworth, a promising American operatic and dramatic screen star. She was cast as Frinzi, at one-time a member of a criminal gang in Chinatown. Then apparently she turned over a new leaf, and made a pact with the police to track down the 'brains' of the drug ring. Virginia Ainsworth (who had appeared a month earlier in *The Romance of Runnibede*) had as her co-star William G. Carter who was in the 1926 production *Those Who Love*.

Another 'private screening only', again at Sydney's Prince Edward Theatre (this time on 4 October 1928) was *The Russell Affair*. In this, Juliette De La Ruze, a twenty-four year old New Zealander, ably demonstrated how to lose a $6000 inheritance in one romantic yet unrewarding gesture — making a film. She wrote the story, headed her own production company, chose the Australasian Films' studio to realise her ambition, and selected P. J. Ramster to direct it. The cast included Jessica Harcourt (mentioned later in *The Adorable Outcast*), Gaston Mervale (once a director for Australian Life Biograph) and Arthur McLaglen (Gabbett in *For the Term of his Natural Life*). The cameraman was one of the best — W. Trerise. The finished product received scant notice, and the arrival of the 'talkies' destroyed any chance that *The Russell Affair* may have had.

An addition to the list of non-starters was the first release from a Melbourne-based company, Koala Films — *The Rushing Tide*. Written and directed by Gerald M. Hayle, with photography by Tasman Higgins, it starred Beth D'Arvall (last mentioned in association with *Environment*) Norman Lee, Godfrey Cass (of *The Kelly Gang* fame) and Iris Roderick. It was announced that it would be available for early release — but there appeared to be no takers.

Caught in the Net, the second film from Melbourne, this time directed by Vaughan C. Marshall, fared a little better than *The Menace, The Russell Affair* and *The Rushing Tide*. It did have a limited season after its premiere in Adelaide on 29 October. Its stars were Zillah Bateman, John Mayer and Charles Brown. If it contained any noteworthy feature, this could be covered by the claim that Australia's best-known members of society appeared. A beauty parade could be thrown in for good measure, even though Mack Sennett had leant on it very heavily, a decade or more previously. Naturally there was the rescue of the heroine by the hero at Portsea — a popular Victorian seaside resort.

Tanami and *The Unsleeping Eye,* two pseudo-dramatic travelogues produced by a Scottish Company, Seven Seas Screen Productions, were directed by Alexander Macdonald. Wendy Osborne starred in both. Australia took little or no interest in the features, but English critics slated *The Unsleeping Eye:* 'Alexander Macdonald attempts to combine drama with travel interest, and is only moderately successful. The story is unreal, and the scenery (New Guinea) is the ordinary jungle type that could just as easily have been made in Africa or the West Indies. The savages take the acting honours.' Australian cameraman Wally Sully filmed *The Unsleeping Eye* and combined

1.36   *A scene from "The Rushing Tide" directed by Gerald M. Hayle. Beth D'Arvall is in the centre.*
(Still supplied by Reg Edwards.)

1.37   *John Gavin (L) in his own production "Trooper O'Brien".*
(Still by courtesy of Harry Davidson.)

with Lacey Percival on *Tanami* — a tale of an alleged romance and adventure in North Queensland.

The list of 'short runs' continued with monotonous regularity. *The Grey Glove,* released through J. C. Williamson Films, was directed by Dunstan Webb who claimed to have acted in a similar capacity on *Tall Timber.* The cast was a mixture of known and unknown players — Aubrey Kelner, Val Lassau, Charles O'Mara (the cattle duffer in *The Moth of Moonbi*), Claud Turton (seen in *The Face at the Window*), George Ames, and James Alexander (lead in *The Price).* Based on a story by E.V. Timms, *The Grey Glove* was screened in smaller theatres — Adelaide on 16 July 1928, Melbourne on 25 August. The story was of an amateur detective (Aubrey Kelner) who vowed to unmask a criminal who always left a grey glove behind, mockingly, after every crime he committed. Chinese opium dens, a willing free-for-all, and a spirited chase were some of the ingredients that did not seem to mix successfully on the screen.

Trooper O'Brien, directed by John F. Gavin (a familiar name in Australian 'silents' prior to and during the war years) was another film that did not fare well on the local screens. *Trooper* had its main screening in Sydney on 13 October. It recorded the sacrifices made by a provincial policeman in New South Wales, as well as telling of the romance of two Aborigines, and of the problems experienced by a mother and daughter 'outback'. The photography and scenery were praised, but too much action was crammed into one film. An unwieldy cast of twenty proved too difficult a task for the director to handle successfully. Well-known Melbourne film collector, Harry Davidson, expressed the opinion that it seemed to be a positive blending of two films, utilising the excess footage of a picture Gavin had directed previously, with additional fresh material.

On the same 13 October, but with greater impact, was the premiere of *Odds On.* With top flight cameraman Arthur Higgins taking on additional duties as director, this is claimed to be Australia's first 'quickie'. Yet it was a runaway success. Following the Sydney showing, *Odds On* was seen in Melbourne and enjoyed two separate seasons in Adelaide. Beauty winner Phyllis Gibbs, Check Hayes (as a jockey suspended for misconduct), Arthur Tauchert (a racecourse urger) and seasoned veteran John Faulkner were in the cast. A surprise appearance was that of Stella Southern (who was in two 1921 productions, *The Betrayer* and *A Girl of the Bush).* Leading racehorses of the day — Limerick, Winalot, and Statesman — figured prominently. *Smith's Weekly* made this assessment:

> No Australian picture yet produced, has offered the interest provided by *Odds On.* In casting, acting, and production generally, this is well above the average of overseas movies — and the story is brought with exceptional neatness, to a magnificently thrilling race climax, and a clever surprise finish. Choosing a subject that is effective yet simple, producer Arthur Higgins has given us the ultimate aim of all movies — excellent entertainment.

Here was a paradox indeed. A quickie had succeeded when other self-styled superior productions had failed miserably. The word 'failure' continued to hover over the scene like a ravenous bird of prey, waiting to pick the bones of an ailing industry.

One film which did not progress beyond its short premiere season on 5

September 1928, was *The Birth of White Australia* directed by American Phil K. Walsh. The theatre was the Strand in Young. It too has passed into oblivion, and stands today as an auction room for used furniture.

Despite an exciting still in the advertisement which depicted troops departing from Victoria Barracks, Sydney, to quell the Lambing Flat Riots of 1861 — and the recreation in the film of the blood-thirsty white miners driving the Chinese from the gold fields — *The Birth of White Australia* remains yet another Australian production that was seen by so few, and almost forgotten by most.

Now to some of the better remembered films of 1928. The first was *The Adorable Outcast* produced by Australasian Films, and directed by Norman Dawn — with Australians Arthur Higgins and William Trerise on camera. Shot in Fiji, and screened in the United States as *Blackbirds of Fiji*, it used the Polynesian culture as an effective backdrop. It told of a white girl kidnapped by natives and reared as one of them. Central characters were a gold prospector and the girl Luya, who lived half the time with the natives, and the remainder with the small white community. Compton Coutts, playing the beachcomber guardian of Luya (Edith Roberts) looked incongruous in a dilapidated bowler hat and a monocle. Missionaries and unscrupulous blackbirders flit in and out of the story like mosquitoes, and there is a fierce fight between the whites and islanders. A typical disregard for authenticity came in the grand Hollywood manner, when Tivoli chorus girls portrayed sensuous South Sea beauties. Edmund Burns was the hero; Katherine Dawn, a missionary; the villain was in the capable hands of Hollywood heavy Walter Long and Australians John Gavin and Arthur Tauchert. Jessica Harcourt and Arthur McLaglen also appeared.

The Adorable Outcast opened at Brisbane's Wintergarden Theatre on 2 July 1928, then went to Melbourne and Adelaide, before Sydney. One critic considered the story rather trivial, and thought that Dawn's work had only average merit and appeal. On the other hand, the camerawork of the two Australians was highly praised, with much of it 'exceedingly beautiful'. Many recent historians have praised the work of Norman Dawn, but Ken G. Hall in his recent autobiography stated that *The Adorable Outcast* flopped badly.

Even W. A. Gibson, a director of Union Theatres, and one time pioneer film maker, stated in 1929 that a great deal of money had been spent on *The Adorable Outcast* and *For the Term of his Natural Life*, but returns had not been favourable: 'Much better pictures would have to be made, to be successful overseas.'

Yet it does not take a long memory to recall that Union Theatres and Australasian Films hired this Hollywood director, Norman Dawn, American cameraman Len Roos, and leading American players such as Eva Novak, because they had no confidence in their Australian counterparts. In addition, the American director had the benefit of Klieg lights that were especially imported. Now comes the poser. With allegedly advanced American picture-making aids, and Americans to use them, why weren't better results achieved? Were the wrong people chosen, or was it that America had more money to throw around, and more film to waste in the process? Lurking in the background like a grim-faced gargoyle are the familiar features of Raymond Longford. You can almost hear him whispering, 'I told you so!'

1.38 *Nell Ferguson in "Trooper O'Brien." She appeared later in the Cinesound Production "It Isn't Done" opposite Cecil Kellaway.*

1.39 *Gordon Collingridge and Merle Ridgeway in "Trooper O'Brien" released in 1928. It was directed by John F. Gavin. (The grain is on the film itself).*
Still by courtesy of Harry Davidson.

1.40   *The not so infrequent "stoush" outside a Lambing Flat "groghouse".*
Another still from "White Australia Policy" by courtesy Young Historical Society.

1.41   *Clash between foot police and miners in Lambing Flat as depicted in the silent film*
made in Young, "Birth of White Australia."

The McDonagh Sisters were back in the film news in 1928 with *Far Paradise,* with Marie Lorraine, Gaston Mervale, Paul Longuet, Arthur McLaglen and John Faulkner. Premiered at the Sydney Regent Theatre on 14 July, it was directed by Paulette McDonagh in conjunction with P.J. Ramster, and photographed by Jack Fletcher. It was yet another romance — the theme was considered 'good, plausible, and sentimental'. Some of the actors were considered too self-conscious, leaning far too heavily upon stage technique. *Far Paradise* was the last Australian silent film to be shown in Adelaide.

The closing entry for 1928 is *The Exploits of the Emden* — a First National Film release. It was first screened at the Victoria Branch of the Navy League on 7 July, and shown commercially at Sydney's Prince Edward Theatre on 22 September 1928. (The theatre was part of the E. J. & D. Carroll picture house chain.) On the souvenir programme (priced 6d.) is a drawing of the HMAS *Sydney* with guns blazing, while in the background is the familiar figure of a helmeted Britannia with her Union Jack shield. The caption read *The Exploits of the Emden* and her ultimate destruction by HMAS *Sydney*. (This took place off Cocos Islands in November 1914.) A reviewer of the film supplies all the salient facts:

> The greater part of the film was prepared under the auspices of the German Admiralty — but a considerable section was produced in Australia by Ken Hall. One depicts affairs aboard the *Emden* — the other on the HMAS *Sydney*, prior to and during the engagement off Cocos Island. Hall has woven it into a smoothly flowing and homogeneous narrative, so that if the dual authority were not acknowledged in a caption, one would have thought it the work of a single production authority. Valuable as an official record, yet by no means cold and colorless.

1.42   *1915 featured "How We Fought The Emden" and "How We Beat The Emden". This still, however is from "The Exploits Of The Emden" (1928). Originally a German production, it gave Ken G. Hall his first film assignment — directing the re-shooting of the Australian segment. This shows the H.M.A.S. "Sydney" preparing for action. (Still by courtesy of Harry Davidson.)*

A newspaper feature writer opened 1929 with this solemn and profound statement, 'Talkies are here to stay.' That same 1929 blasted the screen with all the loud discord of a discotheque. The final *coup de grâce* had been delivered by the Americans — and their films were virtually the sole occupants of the Australian screen. Today the United States may condemn the Australian accent, but the grating dialects of those from the Bronx, the hills of Kentucky, and from the 'li'l ole South, ah do declare' should have carried English sub-titles. The King's English not only was fractured — it was mutilated. No wonder stage actors suddenly were in demand.

On the other hand Australian silents offered only token resistance. They were embarrassing and archaic on a screen that had developed a voice overnight. People flocked to see *The Singing Fool* (starring Al Jolson), *The Broadway Melody* (Charles King, Anita Page, Bessie Love) and *The Canary Murder Case* (with the sauve ex-villain William Powell).

In the midst of all this bewildering confusion, Walter Marks, chairman of the Royal Commission, arrived back in Sydney, blithely stating that there was a big market in London and Canada for Australian films of merit. He could have placed films like *For the Term of his Natural Life* and *The Adorable Outcast* within an hour of his arrival in London, with a cinema circuit of 200 theatres. Then came the punch line: 'I have yet to discover any serious attempt to market first-class Australian films in England.'

Later, Mr Marks advised that the Federal Government had adopted all fifty recommendations from the Commission (for what they were worth) but one constitutional stalemate existed. It was necessary for each state to pass a Short Bill transferring its rights to the Commonwealth for film production, distribution and exhibition. Yet on 26 April 1929, not one state had agreed to the transfer of those controls.

A small theatre, the Central Hall in Little Collins Street, Melbourne, screened two silent Australian documentaries in 1929 — *In New Guinea Wilds* on 1 June, and *Coorab in the Isle of Ghosts* three weeks later. The former which was photographed by William J. Jackson for Oriental and Oceanic Pictures, covered pearl diving, cocoa growing, and the making of sago. Locations were New Guinea, New Britain and New Ireland. *Coorab in the Isle of Ghosts* dealt with the life-span of 'Coorab' from a small boy, through his initiation ceremonies, to an old man. Shot in the Northern Territory, the photography was commenced by Francis Birtles, but completed by Torrance MacLaren.

Thanks to the assistance of L. V. 'Bunny' Bindley, the year 1929 concluded on a very satisfying, if not exhilarating note. The dream of this researcher was rewardingly fulfilled when I was able to unravel a mystery that has provided genuine frustration in recording the progress of the Australian film industry. *The Devil's Playground* (not to be confused with the Australian production in the 1970s nor the American version in the 1930s starring Richard Dix) and *Trobriana* were two titles that remained hidden behind a veil of uncertainty, without any apparent means of penetration. Now the full story can be told for the first time — starting with the statement that *The Devil's Playground* and *Trobriana* are one and the same film.

The original title was *Pearl of the Pacific* (as stated in The *Sydney Sun* on 27 June and 1 August 1928). The title was changed to *Trobriana* (recorded in

Film Weekly 25 October; *The Sydney Mail,* 7 November; and *Australian Sporting and Dramatic News,* 15 December 1928, as well as *Film Weekly* and *Movie Maker,* January 1929). Finally it became *The Devil's Playground.* This Fineart Film, produced by Jack R. Allan, was written and directed by Victor A. Bindley. Photography was handled by Jack Bruce of Commonwealth Film Laboratories, although ex-Frenchman Henri Mallard also claims he was on camera as well. (In the credits Mallard held the position of technical director.) The cast included Elza Stenning (now Elza Jacoby), John Haddock, Joseph Potter, J. R. Allan, Joe Davis and Burton Crocker.

Briefly, the story centred around a stand-over man, Bull Morgan, who always had his own way — by using a bull whip. The heroine incurs his displeasure and he gives her the full 'treatment'. The hero goes to her assistance, and receives the bull whip lash across the face. However after Bull is vanquished, a passionate love scene ensues. Meanwhile a South Sea Island chief, unhappy with the 'white invasion' of his domain by missionaries and traders, calls upon the spirits of his ancestors for guidance. The natives finally attack the white residents and set fire to a number of huts. The British marines arrive, and the riot is quelled after many natives have been killed.

Strangely enough, the first screening of this film did not take place until 18 November 1966 in St Mark's Hall, Avalon, NSW. But therein lies another story to be told later. The director, Victor Bindley, was a stage and film identity who had been with J. C. Williamson as a lighting and set designer. Later he was manager of the Civic and Mayfair Theatres, Sydney. He took his role as a film director very seriously, even wearing a cap and carrying a megaphone. When he moved to Broken Hill, he continued to take an interest in theatre management — when one of his 'halls' was declared black for industrial reasons, he promptly hired another hall and staged a 'live' musical

1.43 *The film that has caused so many headaches for researchers. Originally titled "Pearl Of The Pacific", it became "Trobriana", and finally "The Devil's Playground". It has now been finally established that "Trobriana" and "The Devil's Playground" are one and the same film.*

1.44 *Joseph Potter as the villain "Bull Morgan" uses a bull whip on the planter's daughter (Elza Stenning) whilst the hero (John Haddock) nurses his wounds. A scene from "The Devil's Playground". Stills by courtesy of L. "Bunny" Bindley.*

play. He was technical director for Charles Chauvel's production of *Heritage* (screened in 1935) and in 1938 directed *Safety First* for the New South Wales Road Safety Council. He later became producer and set designer for a number of amateur musical societies which attained a high degree of professionalism. In July 1959 his production of *Oklahoma* for the Bathurst Musical and Dramatic Society included Monte Miller in the cast, as 'Jud Fry'. Miller today is better known as a Melbourne television writer. Victor Bindley is credited with being the first to recognise the potential talent of June Bronhill, who as June Gough, appeared in a stage production which he directed in Broken Hill. He died in Broken Hill on 14 September 1963.

There are further surprising developments that are centred around *The Devil's Playground* which will be revealed in the following chapter; strangely enough, these developments are related to Australia's early talkies era.

1.45 *A black and white impression of Mr. Victor A. Bindley. The well-known and popular Manager of The Civic and Mayfair Theatres.*

1.46 *The lover's united. Note the whip scar on John Haddock's face. The torn dress of Elza Stenning was a "daring" piece of filmcraft in 1929. "The Devil's Playground" was directed by Victor A. Bindley.*

1.47 *Bobby Jackson (played by Stanley Murdoch) returns from schooling in Sydney, to be welcomed by storekeeper (Joe Davis) and Bobby's father (J.R. Allan) in "The Devil's Playground". Various tradenames are well displayed.*

1.48 *"The natives" ready to attack. Local lifesavers were recruited for the roles in "The Devil's Playground".*

1.49   *This scene of British marines firing on natives was the main reason for "The Devil's Playground" being banned. It was felt that such an enactment would offend British viewers.*

1.50   *The design for a set for the stage production of "Oklahoma" as planned by former silent film producer Victor Bindley.*

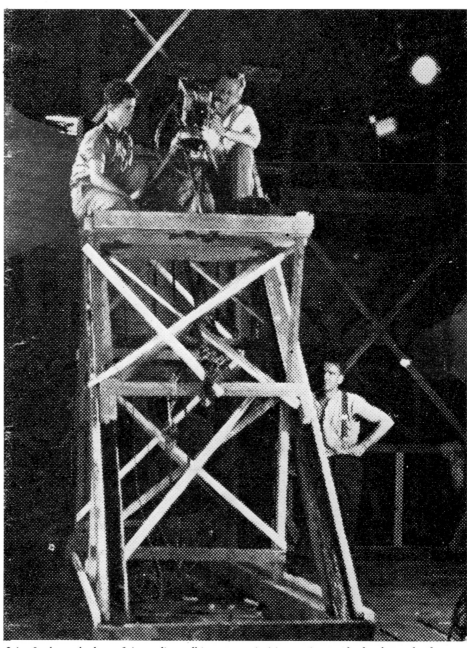

2.1   *In the early days of Australian talkies, very primitive equipment had to be evolved as a substitute for more sophisticated facilities. Today, audiences are familiar with "crane" shots. But in the Australasian Films' Studio, Bondi, this bulky wooden platform was used for "overhead" work. It was lowered by rope on heavily greased runners. Behind the camera is Wally Sully. He is assisted by Syd Whiteley.*

2
A Time of Speaking

> There is a time of speaking,
> And a time of being still.

William Caxton

Under the Klieg lights, Australia's time of speaking began in 1929, but a new chain of success snapped rather suddenly in 1940 under the impact of the war. The talkies found Australia a far different place than it was at the beginning of silent films. World War II halted the industry where World War I had helped it. The reason was simple enough: at the end of the Depression the initiative and ambitious drive of our pioneer film makers were lacking and Australia seemed prepared to drag her heels in the dust of past achievement.

Initially, newsreels such as Movietone coupled with realistic sound covered such sporting events as the Melbourne Cup; prominent visitors were interviewed and the Australian Prime Minister J. Scullin used this medium to introduce his new cabinet. In the Columbia Gramophone Studio, Sydney, fourteen year old pianist Nancy Weir was filmed and recorded for the second time on 15 January 1930. Yet one wonders whether Movietone's symbol — a Laughing Jackass — was 'giving the bird' to Australia's lack of fight in coming to grips with the talkies! To prove the point, Raymond Longford arrived back in Australia, still keen to direct *Robbery Under Arms* — this time as a talking picture. A British company had guaranteed $60 000 if Australian backers found another $24 000. There were no takers. 'Talkies' it seemed were a dirty 'seven-letter' word. On Friday 7 February 1930, Sydney's *Evening News* carried this sensational banner headline:

CENSOR BOARD BANS EXPORT OF FIRST AUSTRALIAN TALKIE!
NO REASON
ARBITRARY ACTION CAUSES STIR

It may come as a surprise to many film historians that the film was *The Devil's Playground*. Victor Bindley with realistic foresight had counted on the impact that talkies would have, and had made a 'sound on disc' as well as a silent version of the picture.

An even greater blow to the industry as a whole was that the British rights had been sold in advance to an American distribution house. Chief censor W. Creswell O'Reilly stated that he took action under regulations. Yet there was no precedent for the ban. All copies, it seems, were destroyed with the exception of one silent copy that turned up mysteriously years later. The regulations as mentioned by O'Reilly were printed in the *Evening News*. No Australian production could be exported if it:

1. Is blasphemous, indecent, or obscene.
2. Is likely to be injurious to security, or to encourage or invite to crime.
3. Is likely to be offensive to any friendly nation.
4. Is likely to be offensive to the people of the British Empire. [Detrimental connotations for the British?]
5. Depicts any matter, the exhibition of which is undesirable in the public interest or likely to prove detrimental or prejudicial to the Commonwealth of Australia.

Many years later Henri Mallard suggested two likely reasons for the banning of *The Devil's Playground*.

a. Native girls rushing down the beach, throwing off their grass skirts and diving into the water. [Those native girls were 'white' in black tights. In addition it was a long shot.]

b. British marines shooting at natives. [This could have offended the English code of honour — and all that! Besides a British soldier never fired upon natives in anger. It just wasn't cricket.] The 'natives' were lifesavers, 'blackened' for the film.

In 1930 the Australian film industry had another formidable enemy — the Depression.

The only boost to come out of the Royal Commission was the Commonwealth Film Contest that closed on 31 March 1930. Only four films were received for judging — *Fellers; The Cheaters; Tiger Island* and *The Nation of Tomorrow*. None was considered worthy of either first or second prize, but *Fellers* received the third place award of $3000. Mr A.B. Faye, on behalf of the producers Artaus Ltd, bitterly criticised the decision, claiming that according to the scale of points awarded *Fellers* was entitled to second prize.

The film was screened for the press on 23 May 1930, but reports were acrid and aculeate. The story of the Australian Light Horse in Palestine was labelled 'absurd and trivial'. Arthur Higgins, the director of the silent portion, supplied the film's one saving grace — a mass grouping of horsemen in the desert during the action scene, with vistas of cloud above.

On 5 September 1930, Arthur Tauchert, star of *Fellers* voiced his disgust at the lack of interest shown by Australians in the picture. To that time *Fellers* had had an indifferent season.

> The standard may not be equal to the best, but it held its own on an average level. It represented a struggling young industry that appeared to have earned contempt, for no apparent reason. At present only one company was at work in NSW making a picture.

This clearly demonstrates the state of the film industry in 1930, but it does not justify the term 'young'. It was struggling — there's no argument on that score — but was young only in terms of 'talking pictures'.

The McDonagh film *The Cheaters* tried its luck at the Roxy Theatre, Sydney on 1 June 1930, but was as badly mauled as *Fellers*. It wasn't as interesting as *Far Paradise,* and the captions contained too many Americanisms such as 'Big Boy'. It suffered from a badly told story, and towards the end absurdities sprang up in battalions. The piece of dialogue that brought the picture to a close was in the sentimental style of outworn melodrama. The acting headed by Marie Lorraine was weak. The only items to receive any praise were the settings.

The Cheaters was originally listed by the National Library and *Film Weekly* as a 1926 production with sound dubbed later. However, Graham Shirley, a fellow film historian, has kindly provided the following information:

> According to Neville Macken, the film's financial backer, it was decided in late 1929, just before *The Cheaters* had been completed as a silent film, to add two 'sound on disc' sequences to comply with entry conditions set down by the Commonwealth Government's Film Competition.
>
> With a camera inside a glass-windowed box at the Vocalion studio in Melbourne, two scenes were recorded — one a breakfast conversation with Leal Douglas; the other, a song at the piano featuring Marie Lorraine and Paul Longuet. It was billed as 'The first Australian talking picture.'*
>
> Macken recalled later that the appalling standard of the Vocalion disc recording turned the screening into a farce. No adequate sound control existed, and when Leal Douglas tapped his egg for breakfast, it sounded like 'The Anvil Chorus'. The audience was hysterical.
>
> Later in *Everyone's* it was written that the McDonagh Sisters' attempts hadn't been matched by the technical sophistication in sound recording.

Graham Shirley advised that according to Paulette McDonagh, it was decided to dispose of the sound sequences and release *The Cheaters* in its original concept — a silent film. Unfortunately the picture did not meet with any success.

Captain Frank Hurley's documentary *Southward Ho! With Mawson* with synchronised sound effects was Australia's only feature-length contribution to 1930. This came out in Sydney in August.

Out of the swirling mists of confusion there finally emerged F. W. Thring, a man of vision, complete with the confidence to put Australia back in the film business. The managing director of Hoyts Theatres, he disposed of the bulk of his holdings to Fox Film Corporation of America in order to obtain the capital to make pictures. It was a great pity that Australian control, even of a combine, should pass into the hands of America, but for what it was worth literally, Thring obtained a guarantee that Hoyts would screen Efftee films. At least Thring felt that he was beating the bugbear of the Australian independent producers before him by having the means of exhibition assured before production commenced.

In September 1930, still very much a man of action, F. W. Thring secured a lease on His Majesty's Theatre, Melbourne, as his future studio. Portion of the theatre had been destroyed by fire the previous year but the stage itself remained intact.

* Very obviously incorrect.

The Era of 'Firsts'

Around this time everything was being labelled 'a first'. On 15 October 1930 the Auditorium in Melbourne, showed the Commonwealth Government's *This is Australia* ... a two-reeler depicting a journey from Perth to Queensland. The commentary was recorded by the Commonwealth's Swanston Street Studio, Melbourne, under the 'sound on disc' principle. Billed as 'The first official Australian talking film released for exhibition' it was compiled by Bert Ive, Reg Pearse, and Cyril Bradstreet. Another 'first', *This is Sydney* was screened six months earlier than *This is Australia* and was billed as Australia's first all-talking travelogue. It was shown at the Prince Edward Theatre, Sydney on 9 April 1930.

Then to the State Theatre, Sydney on 27 March 1931, came *That's Cricket*. This Union Theatre's two-reeler was recorded at Cinesound and was directed by Ken G. Hall. It presented W. M. Woodfall, Australian captain; Don Bradman, the wonder boy; Billy Ponsford, the stylist; Stan McCabe, the young white hope, W. A. Oldfield, the master wicket keeper; Clarrie Grimmett, the googly king and Allan Kippax, the Test hero. It too carried a 'first' tag — 'this country's first real talkie.'

Nineteen thirty-one was dominated by three important happenings: F. W. Thring was an aggressive film producer; Dick Harwood took line honours in the talkie production race; and Norman Dawn was deflated on the Australian scene.

In January Tom Holt (father of the late Prime Minister Harold Holt), general manager for Efftee Films, arrived back in Australia with $50 000 worth of sound equipment. With him was American D. J. Bloomberg to install it, and well-known cameraman Arthur Higgins and sound engineer Alan Mill were there as well.

Union Theatres advised that Australasian Films would use an Australian recording system that was devoid of all background noises. It had been perfected by Arthur Smith. The St Kilda studio would have sound stages constructed, and a truck would be fitted out to commence making a special weekly sound gazette in Victoria. A. R. Harwood provided the Palace Theatre, Melbourne on 21 August 1931 with the first complete programme of Australian talkies — *Isle of Intrigue* and *Spur of the Moment*.

Made in Australia by Australians with Australian equipment these A. R. Harwood Talkie Productions were produced at the Harwood Studio, West Melbourne. Releases however were mainly confined to second-rate theatres, and today hold little more than interest value.

Isle of Intrigue was the better film, and contained more action. Mysterious robberies on pearling luggers were investigated by the son of the owner of the pearling fleet. The cast included Norman Shepherd, Dorothy Stanward and D'Arcy Kelway. *Spur of the Moment* had a visiting Scotland Yard detective solving a puzzling murder in a Collins Street building. One atmospheric shot was the mobile pie stall that was once part of Melbourne's after-dark social life. The script by Betty M. Davies was based upon her quarter-hour radio play broadcast through the Australian Broadcasting Commission. Betty Davies was to become even better known as Betty Roland who wrote the three-act play 'A Touch of Silk' and the novel *Beyond Capricorn*. The photographers were Les McCallum and Ed Wintle; and

Frank King and J. Watson Gunner handled the sound. Leading players were Syd Hollister, James Alexander and Beatrice Touzeou, with Eddie Balmer (a Melbourne radio announcer) portraying a derelict.

Critics felt that both pictures showed encouraging signs of progress, but would have been more acceptable if the producers had taken advantage of Australian scenery. They found no fault with the acting, and felt that the lighting was generally good.

On 6 November 1931 F. W. Thring premiered the Efftee programme *Diggers* and *A Co-respondent's Course*. Arthur Higgins photographed both features.

Today, many do not appreciate an exaggerated style of humour delivered in a lazy drawl, but *Diggers* did liberate laughter and made the box office tills tinkle merrily. With George Moon, Pat Hanna portrayed a Digger not overfond of discipline who enjoyed rum that was questionably obtained from the quartermaster's stores. The film was successful in Sydney, Brisbane and Melbourne, and drew good crowds in other capital cities.

2.2   *Much confusion has arisen as to whether Joe Valli was in "Diggers". This still reveals that he did actually appear (in a minor role). He is seated centre, wearing a tam o'shanter. At the same table is George Moon. Pat Hanna is at the table on the right, and the girl is Eugenie Prescott.*

One critic wrote:

> Though much had been expected, the excellence of the first Efftee productions surprised a most enthusiastic audience.' Another reported that, 'in recording, lighting and photography, *Diggers* is faultless. It deserves wide popularity for its excellent fun, its spirited action, and its entire freedom from false sentiment. *A Co-respondent's Course,* the support, is a farce of matrimonial tangles. It too is marked by good technical work.

Sydney enthusiastically praised Eugenie Prescott, and described her as 'as lovely as any in Hollywood'. Cecil Scott (the lead in *The Sentimental Bloke*) was also in *Digger*. *A Co-respondent's Course* featured Donalda Warne, John D'Arcy, Patricia Minchin, Norman Lee, George Moon and Adele Inman.

Thring, described by Noel Monkman as a man 'whose big body was matched by his courage, vision, and ambition' proved to be an aggressive film maker when he ran into trouble with *The Haunted Barn*. Censors banned it as 'too frightening for young people'. He appealed against the ruling and stated that if his application failed, he would consider suspending his feature film production in Australia. Thring won his appeal, but *The Haunted Barn* only warranted billing as a support to *Diggers* in its second Melbourne season at Hoyts Theatre De Luxe, then at the Sydney Lyceum on 12 December. *The Haunted Barn* was the least impressive of Thring's features of 1931. The consensus of the critics was that the mystery surrounding the original ban was greater than the one unfolded on the screen.

2.3 *Phil Smith in "The Haunted Barn" one of the earlier Efftee Films.*

The final entry for 1931 is Norman Dawn's inglorious attempt to make an all-talking, all-singing film in Australia. According to Graham Shirley:

> *Talkie Mad* was the shooting title for what became *Showgirl's Luck*. Production began in April 1930 and the shooting itself seems to have been completed by September. However problems with the sound delayed its release. It was premiered on 2 December 1931 at the Lawson Theatre, Redfern (Sydney). *Showgirl's Luck* was released in England through Universal Pictures in June 1933. British film magazines gave the film poor reviews.

Ken G. Hall in *The Australasian Cinema* on 6 October 1977 penned the following:

> Norman Dawn arrived from Hollywood with a sound engineer Jack 'Skipper' Pratt, and a half-baked disc outfit that was to say the least, primitive. They made *Showgirl's Luck* at the Lapstone Hotel, but never did get it properly into sync, and received no more than token release. It was pretty bad. So was the sound.

2.4 *Arthur Tauchert in a more debonair role in "Talkie Mad" — later titled "Showgirl's Luck". Susan Denis is the girl in the apron. The director of this production, Norman Dawn, had replaced Raymond Longford as director for Australasian Films, when "For The Term Of His Natural Life" was in the planning stage. Arthur Tauchert had been given his first screen success by Longford.*

Norman Dawn, the man who first arrived in Australia to a fanfare of trumpets, left to a mere whimper from a toy saxophone.

Exit Norman Dawn — enter Raymond Longford. The two names became tangled together because of the debacle over *For the Term of his Natural Life*. On October 1931, F. W. Thring announced with a great deal of satisfaction and pleasure that he had engaged Longford as an assistant director. Yet Longford's period of employment by Efftee must have provided moments of embarrassment on many occasions.

Meanwhile, F. W. Thring, always eager to add variety to his programming, saw some of Noel Monkman's 'nature study' work in Fox Movietone and asked the photographer to work for him. Monkman flatly refused (even though Frank Thring Jnr. once described him as 'one of father's photographers'). Instead, Monkman went into partnership with F. W. to form Australian Educational Films Pty Ltd, with each holding 50 per cent of the shares. The only provision was that the cutting and editing were to be handled by Efftee. They agreed to produce a series of shorts centred around the Barrier Reef.

Monkman attacked the work with zest, and forwarded material regularly. However he began to worry when he never received any notification in return as to how the work was progressing. Finally, Noel and Kitty Monkman went to Melbourne to learn first hand the reason for the breakdown in communication. They soon ascertained that those associated with the editing and cutting were not naturalists. At that point, Monkman took over. As well as handling the photography, he also did the editing and supplied the commentary for the five Barrier Reef shorts he had previously submitted. When Thring went on a sales promotion tour to London, the five Monkman shorts went with him.

In Kitty Monkman's book *Over and Under the Great Barrier Reef* she recalls a news item in a Sydney newspaper stating that the English censor objected to the scene in one of the featurettes of the turtle laying her eggs

2.5 *Underwater photographer and film director — Noel Monkman.*

This gave one of the cartoonists a good idea, and a cartoon appeared in a newspaper showing a stork carrying a napkin containing a baby turtle in its beak. Underneath read 'Can it be that the English still believe the stork brings baby turtles?'

The Barrier Reef series was to reach a degree of excellence that was the equal of any that the world could produce. When at first Sydney showmen did not accept the series, Thring unleashed a fury of indignation reminiscent of the time when he battled with the censors over *The Haunted Barn*.

1932: Tentative Success for the Talkies

Efftee Films in 1932 was to have Hoyts De Luxe Theatre, Melbourne, as its showcase. The first release was *The Sentimental Bloke* on 26 March and *His Royal Highness* on 29 October.

The Bloke was directed by F. W. Thring but when compared to Longford's silent masterpiece it was unsubtle and artificial. Even the script by C. J. Dennis himself was not the equal of Longford's. Neither was it as financially successful as the latter. Using its original setting around Little Lons instead of Woolloomooloo did not prove a bonus, and in the two-up sequence, it was impossible to top Tauchert's performance. (How Longford as assistant director must have writhed over it all.) Cecil Scott, Ray Fisher, and Tal Ordell headed the list of players. Critics praised the high technical and production standards as well as the sound and Arthur Higgins' camera work. Sydney observed that the 'photography and technical work was carried out with the utmost skill' — a statement that damns the film with faint praise. But one critic wrote:

> It is surprising that Mr Thring did not take the opportunity to speed up the action by filming *The Bloke's* fight with the swindlers. It is described second-hand, by eye witnesses — and the audience is left to imagine an encounter that certainly would have been exploited to the full by an American producer.

His Royal Highness was the first screened at the Regent Theatre, South Yarra (a Melbourne suburb) on 26 August, 1932, (although its city release was on 29 October). This burlesque operetta told the improbable story of George Wallace an Australian 'rough diamond' who was proclaimed king of a small duchy totally committed to insurrection. George was assisted in his antics by John Dobbie, Marshall Crosby, Frank Tarrant, and Donalda Warne. Many of the sequences were extremely humorous — especially those when Wallace as king, plays poker with his liveried servants, and demands the royal prerogative of winning every hand! In addition music by Alaric Howitt was very tuneful. Today some film historians describe the production as crude, yet while doubting Thring's artistic ability, they did admire his skill as a producer.

Once again Melbourne and Sydney were poles apart in their opinions.

> Melbourne: Elaborate and spectacular, with the handling of large crowds, a triumph for the director. The music was well done, and in both solos and choruses, the voices were of a much higher quality than those of overseas musical films.

Sydney: People with simple minds and undeveloped tastes may enjoy this film, but others are likely to find it a bore. As to Mr Thring's direction, it is some years behind the times compared to English and American standards. It is irritating to think that a film with crude characters, will be shown abroad as representative of Australian production.

2.6 *George Wallace has his usual foot trouble, this time in "His Royal Highness".*

The interesting part of the Melbourne comment is how Thring handled large crowds. This is one department in which so few directors reveal proficiency, even up to and including the eventful 1970s.

A solid fact in Thring's favour that made him such a force in the industry is that he knew film and every aspect of exploitation. He knew what has become such a shock to many producers; that he would have to be his own salesman, and in this field he was dynamic. On 23 August 1932, F. W. Thring packed his bags for England, taking copies of *Diggers*; *The Sentimental Bloke*; *His Royal Highness*; *Harmony Row*; (released in Australia in 1933), *The Haunted Barn*; *A Co-respondent's Course*; a George Wallace short *Oh what a Night; The Barrier Reef* series, and nine other featurettes. He expected to be overseas for about six months. Even with his departure, the Efftee Studio did not remain idle, as was the case, years later at Cinesound, when Ken Hall went to Hollywood. Pat Hanna moved in to produce and direct *Diggers in Blighty*.

In England F.W. Thring not only sold every film, but created a record into the bargain. His was the first occasion on which the entire output of an Australian film production house had been accepted, and in addition, contracts drawn up for future productions. As a smack in the eye for some critics, *His Royal Highness* was shown in England under the title of *His Loyal Highness.*

Years later, in 1967, the *Sydney Cinema Journal* felt that *His Royal Highness* — Frank Thring's little shown show — stood the test of time very well. Some of George Wallace's improvised dialogue was 'hilarious, and completely off the cuff'.

The long awaited *On Our Selection* was eventually screened commercially at Brisbane's Majestic Theatre on 6 August 1932. This Ken G. Hall effort provided a major surprise. Was it necessary to resurrect the Dad and Dave characters with the Steele Rudd type of *gauche* humour? This was better suited to the silents than the more sophisticated talkies. Even Longford's script resisted the impulse to make them 'simple-minded' bushies. Instead he concentrated on their trials, their doggedness, and their spontaneous family humour, all of which did not make them objects of ridicule.

Yet in all fairness, Hall did prove that he was a shrewd assessor (or at least Stuart F. Doyle was) of what the public needed, and despite the fact that Longford's *On Our Selection* was a much better production, the talkie version of *On Our Selection,* made on a budget of $12 000, proved to be no slouch at the box office, returning $120 000 in Australia alone. Bert Bailey, Fred MacDonald, Alfreda Bevan and Dick Fair played Dad, Dave, Mum and Sandy. Here's what Melbourne and Sydney had to say:

2.8 *The lively barn dance in "On Our Selection" — an Australasian Films production, that was part of the take-over by Cinesound. Ken G. Hall was the director. Fred MacDonald as "Dave" is at the head of the male dancers (R).*

> Melbourne: The comedy tends to farce and converts drama into melodrama. There are a few minor faults such as length and camera consciousness. Essentially an outdoor picture, the opening shots are a splendid challenge to the ancient slander that Australian birds are songless.
>
> Sydney: Australian Films and Ken Hall are to be congratulated on the splendid way they produced Australia's first big national talkie. F.W. Thring's *The Sentimental Bloke* had been a disappointment to those who had gone to see it, hoping that it would abound in typical and natural Australian atmosphere. But no allowances need be made for *On Our Selection.* In vitality, in picturesqueness, in originality (?) and above all, in the superb beauty of the camera work, the film can stand comparison with the finest products of Hollywood and Elstree. There are flaws. Some parts have been a little over-acted, and there is an elocutionary flavour in the love scenes. A special word of praise for Wally Sully and his supervision of the photography.

Ken Hall appears to have had a devoted attachment to the Rudd family. He released *Grandad Rudd* in 1935; *Dad and Dave come to Town,* 1938; and *Dad Rudd M. P.,* 1940. In fact his talkie productions opened and closed for Greater Union Theatres, with the doings of the Rudds.

'Stone the bloomin' crows — has it gotta be fair dinkum?'

You wouldn't believe it — Beaumont Smith was back in Sydney — and so were *The Hayseeds.* Whether it was the influence of *On Our Selection,* or the fact that Smith somehow went back to his spin off of Steele Rudd — they were back on the screen, and talking too, at Sydney's Civic Theatre on 9

2.7 *An unusual photograph of George Wallace who began film work with Efftee.*

December 1932. There appears to be some doubts as to the 'real' director of *The Hayseeds* — some crediting Beaumont Smith with it. Yet at a gathering in the Rushcutters Bay Studio on 22 July, Beaumont Smith was named as producer, and it was he who stated that Raymond Longford would direct it. Then on 7 August, the newly soundproofed studio to be known as Cinesound Studio No. 2 was officially opened. After the speeches, nine powerful lamps were switched on, and the boom swung into position for a short scene from *The Hayseeds* — a Beaumont Smith production directed by Raymond Longford.

Later, in the same studio a ballet was filmed from above, weaving floral patterns (Hollywood style) that would be interpolated into musical sequences with a score by F. Morton Chappell who performed a similar task for *The Squatter's Daughter.*

On the credit side of *The Hayseeds* was the music and the acting of Cecil Kellaway as 'Dad Hayseed' and Molly Raynor as 'Pansy Ryan'. On the debit side, John Moore, Arthur Clarke, and Shirley Dale spoke a genteel type of Oxford English; the antiquated sentimental and stilted dialogue was not appreciated, with the plot developing into an injudicious echo of some of the earlier films, not happily chosen in the first place.

Nineteen thirty-two ended on a peculiar note with the making of a silent film in Colac, *The Adventures of Dot* that has been already discussed. The production of this picture as a silent proved a money spinner for the director J.M. St Ledger. It provided a type of community involvement with the schools, the local fire brigade, and the Shire Council, as 'Dot' was a schoolteacher, and her two suitors were interested in civic affairs. A fire conveniently involved the fire brigade. In this way every citizen of the town was either in it, or had relatives who had a 'film star' in the family. Result — packed houses.

Film collector Harry Davidson knows that *Dot* was produced in a number of towns such as Maryborough (Vic) and Glenelg (SA). He has seen a further *Adventure of Dot* from Glenelg, produced as late as 1937 under the same director, J.M. St Ledger.

Efftee and Cinesound: The Get Up and Go Spirit

On 11 February 1933 another Australian programme was featured at Hoyts De Luxe Theatre, Melbourne. This was *Harmony Row* from Efftee, and *Diggers in Blighty,* A Pat Hanna Production, filmed in the Efftee Studio. The sound in *Harmony Row* was better, but the indoor photography could have been improved upon. Even Sydney felt that *Harmony Row* was the first really successful picture that Efftee had produced.

> *The Sentimental Bloke* was an unconvincing attempt to be very Australian. *His Royal Highness* was an Australian cum Hollywood effort. But in *Harmony Row* it had been realised that the play was the thing. Wallace has improved enormously since *His Royal Highness*, and now could be compared with the best overseas comedians.

2.9   *The typical "Digger" has been portrayed on the Australian screen on numerous occasions, yet it took Pat Hanna (a former New Zealander) to depict the genuine "Anzac" of World War I both with his concert party and his films in the early talkies era.*

Here's to every
Digger who wore
the old Slouch

Pat

Pat Hanna had argued with Thring over the placement of the three segments in *Diggers*, believing that the poignant 'Mademoiselle From Armentiéres' sequence should have been in the centre and not at the end where Thring had placed it. He now decided to make all future films through his own production company. He began with *Diggers in Blighty,* a story of Blighty and the handing out of misleading information to German spies, starring Pat Hanna, Joe Valli, George Moon, Norman French and John D'Arcy.

2.10   *Probably the last cartoon Pat Hanna ever did. He was taken to hospital before he could complete the glass and the Author's name. He died on 24 October 1973. Pat Hanna made three films — "Diggers" (1931), "Diggers In Blighty" (1933), and "Waltzing Matilda" (1933).*

Pat did not fare well with the critics. Melbourne critics felt that the production could have been improved with stronger lighting and more freedom and variation in the composition of the scenes. Sydney critics were caustic: 'The direction is antiquated and unsatisfactory. Story and continuity are extremely weak. Some genuinely amusing moments however, were discovered towards the end. Directors must realise that actors need direction. Merely to turn them loose in a drove across the studio floor, is fatal.'

Charles Chauvel's first talking picture *In the Wake of the Bounty* was screened in Sydney on 15 March 1933. Chauvel with this film established a pattern that would draw attention to his current production — a joust with the censors. It had begun in September 1932, when the censor seized film shot by Tasman Higgins in Tahiti and Pitcairn Island. In October Chauvel was allowed access to the film to edit it, and re-submit it before the production was screened. Early in 1933, three cuts were ordered in the Tahitian sequences, and one from the dramatic portion filmed in Australia.

Chauvel contended that the deletion of these scenes would affect the dramatic quality of the film, and applied to the Commonwealth Appeals Board for a review of the Film Censor's directive. The Board passed every portion of the film with the exception of some sequences of a native dance.

Chauvel did the F. W. Thring act, and went directly to the Minister for Customs. He left with the threat, 'if the Minister fails to reverse the decision

2.11   *Charles Chauvel in his production "In The Wake Of The Bounty" introduced a certain Errol Flynn as Fletcher Christian. In this way, Australia gave Hollywood yet another star. A similar case, but to a lesser degree, was that of Mary Maguire.*

of the Appeals Board, the film will not be shown in Australia.' This leaves us with one cynical observation: Was the film really worth the fuss?

Critics praised the photography of the documentary part of the film that followed the course of the *Bounty* from Tahiti to Pitcairn Island where the vessel was eventually scuttled. The studio scenes, however, were the least convincing aspects of the film. Lighting was defective; make-up indifferent; and acting stilted. The only convincing players were Mayne Lynton as Captain Bligh, and John Warwick as a member of the ship's company. A certain Errol Flynn as Fletcher Christian in his first screen role did not receive a mention.

Ken Hall's first film for Cinesound was *The Squatter's Daughter*. It would appear that the 'country' theme had retained its appeal for him. This too was a remake of a silent, originally written by Bert Bailey ('Dad of *On Our Selection*) and Edmund Duggan. A new scenario was prepared by E.V. Timms and Gayne Dexter. Captain Frank Hurley and George Malcolm handled the cameras. The cast was headed by Jocelyn Howarth, Grant Lyndsay (Dick Fair), John Warwick, and Fred MacDonald ('Dave' of *On Our Selection*.)

Critics liked the scenery, photography, and casting. One said that the camera and not the microphone was the prime factor in picture making. A Sydney reviewer supplied this poetic description:

> It contains some of the loveliest photography yet seen on the screen. Frank Hurley has seized on everyday life of a sheep station, and brought forth from it an extraordinary expressiveness. It is a rare delight to watch sheep moving to and fro, amid an aura of mellow sunshine. When remarkable pictures of a raging bushfire are introduced, the general tone of the screen changes from black and white to a dull reddish brown, as soon as the flames begin to dart among the trees. Realism is accentuated by roaring and crackling sounds.

2.12 *Attractive Australian countryside photographed so well by Captain Frank Hurley, can become a blazing inferno as revealed in the film.*

Despite the undoubted 'get up and go' spirit at Cinesound, the Australian film front still had a 'bits and pieces' approach with no apparent pattern in sight.

The McDonagh Sisters' *Two Minutes Silence* directed by Paulette McDonagh was screened commercially in Canberra on 18 October 1933. The enthusiasm engendered by *The Squatter's Daughter* did not flow on to *Silence*. The film opens in London as Big Ben is about to boom 11 o'clock on Armistice Day. The two minutes' silence stirs memories of the First World War in four people: a charlady (Ethel Gabriel); Denise an orphaned French girl (Marie Lorraine); a Digger (Leo Granklyn) and a butler.

'On the stage', wrote one critic, 'it received a great deal of praise, but on the screen it is flat and devoid of real dramatic content — even making allowances for cramped studio space. It lacked camera angles and changes of depth to add variety. Various newsreels have been interpolated to add any atmosphere that the film contains.'

In Canberra, one significant observation was that it demonstrated Australians could do something better than caricature their farming community (an obvious fillip at *On Our Selection* and *The Hayseeds*).

On 16 June 1933 H. Bowden, the New York and London representative for J. C. Williamson Ltd censored Cinesound's *On Our Selection*,* and condemned films that depicted Australians as foolish and simple-minded. 'Is it little wonder that many British people think that we are vulgar, and that such films are a fair sample of Australian mentality.'

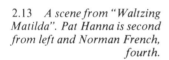

2.13   *A scene from "Waltzing Matilda". Pat Hanna is second from left and Norman French, fourth.*

To rub salt into the wound, Pat Hanna's second independent production was *Waltzing Matilda,* which was shown at Hoyts Theatre De Luxe in Melbourne on 2 December. In this Pat Hanna and Norman French have a

heavy night in Melbourne and become involved in a brawl. Next morning they learn that a policeman has been savagely attacked and that French is wanted for questioning. The pair leave rather hurriedly for Banjarra Station, where the overseer is Joe Valli. French becomes romantically involved with Dorothy Parnham, and then to his surprise hears that he is heir to a fortune. Pat and Norman in the end actually thrash the thugs who attacked the policeman. It was considered a distinct improvement on *Diggers in Blighty* and showed that Pat Hanna had gained stature as a director. But this same film produced yet another casualty of the talkies. Pat Hanna ceased making pictures.

2.14   *John Longden and Charlotte Francis (as the seductress Alma Lee) in the then controversial "The Silence Of Dean Maitland", directed by Ken G. Hall for Cinesound.*

1934: A Bleak Year

Although Ken G. Hall was rapidly becoming one of Australia's best directors, and certainly the most prolific, 1934 was not a good year for him. *Cinesound Varieties* screened in Sydney on 1 June, and *Strike Me Lucky* premiered in Sydney on 16 November, were two disasters. *Cinesound Varieties,* an hour-long musical had nothing to recommend it. In *Strike Me Lucky,* Roy Rene ('Mo') tried very hard, but lacked the rapport with a live audience. The only item of interest was to see Roy Rene with a genuine beard, instead of a painted one. Like Bert Bailey, Ken Hall had insisted that 'Mo' grow the genuine facial adornment.

By way of a complete change came Hall's remake of *The Silence of Dean Maitland,* shown in Sydney on 25 May 1934. A clergyman (John Longden) allows his best friend to be imprisoned for a crime committed by Maitland himself. Years later he meets the now embittered friend, and no longer able to suppress his guilty conscience, Dean Maitland confesses his crime from the pulpit.

Prior to the shooting of the picture, Cinesound took over Melbourne's *Herald Newsreel* including the services of journalist Tom Gurr as editor and a cumbersome, silent film De Brie camera enclosed in a huge metal blimp. Using the camera, Hall could photograph a scene in *The Silence of Dean Maitland* reasonably close to the microphone, and achieve a smooth dolly shot. This addition to the studio equipment aided the director immensely.

Like Chauvel, Hall ran into censor trouble with three scenes. One was Alma Lee in a state of undress. The second — a skilfully handled but passionate interlude between John Longden and Alma (Charlotte Francis). The third — and the only one that could have been edited without any serious loss to the storyline, was a village oaf sniggering at Alma Lee bathing. One Melbourne critic penned the following memorable lines:

> When the history of Australian picture making is written, after due credit is given to the gallant pioneers, it will be said that the story really begins with *The Silence of Dean Maitland.*

(In the 1970s, a similar statement was made. The only alteration to the above was to substitute *Sunday too Far Away* for *The Silence of Dean Maitland.)*

---

*   Note: Australasian Films made *On Our Selection* as already stated but the Cinesound tag came about when it took over Australasian Films before the picture's release.

2.15 *"A Ticket In Tatts" was
George Wallace's third full length
feature for Efftee. Made in 1934,
the supporting cast contained
Campbell Copelin, Guy Hastings,
John Dobbie and Marie La Varre.*

F.W. Thring was perhaps more progressive in his thinking than Ken Hall yet did not meet with the same success. His first film in 1934 was *A Ticket in Tatts* starring George Wallace. It opened in Fairfield (a Melbourne suburb) on 6 January, with its city release one week later at Hoyts Theatre De Luxe. (Like the Civic in Sydney, the De Luxe acted as the Melbourne showcase for Australian productions.) Part of the authentic background for *A Ticket in Tatts* was Flemington on Oaks Day, 1933. However the 'punters' (such as George Wallace and John Dobbie) stood behind a picket fence in the Efftee studio, and were photographed as they watched the progress of a man off camera walking across the floor with a raised broom handle.

The treatment of the Melbourne Cup sequence received praise, but critics thought the talent of Campbell Copelin and Thelma Scott as the lovers, and Harold B. Meade as the owner of the Melbourne Cup winner was wasted. The storyline itself was dated, and the picture wasn't as well received as *Harmony Row*. George Wallace did everything expected of him — he fell off horses, tripped over his feet, and pulled down shelves of groceries. And he won $20 on the Cup and married the maid.

Efftee's second production in 1934, *Clara Gibbings* was similar to *Two Minutes Silence* in one aspect in that it was a successful stage play which failed on the screen. Even the talents of Dorothy Brunton, Guy Hastings, Marshall Crosby and Harold B. Meade could not combat an immobile camera. This complete lack of action tended to overload the film with far too much dialogue which imparted a stiffness to the production. It was released at Melbourne's Mayfair Theatre on 13 October but did not have a Sydney release. 'One saving grace', wrote a critic, 'is that it provided relief from Steele Rudd.' Despite the shortcomings of *Clara Gibbings*, the Commonwealth Films Awards on 7 March 1935, awarded it three prizes out of eleven entries. Top Award went to Chauvel's *Heritage* with Cinesound's *The Silence of Dean Maitland* in second place.

F.W. Thring closed his new Wattle Path Studio in St Kilda in 1934 — which was another disaster for Australian production. George Wallace transferred to Cinesound. Disaster followed catastrophe — the Australian film industry, endeavouring to get on its feet for a second time, stumbled then faltered in its stride. The first cataclysm was *The Man they could not Hang*, a remake of a remake about John Lee. Premiered in Sydney on 1 June (15 days before the disastrous *Cinesound Varieties*) the picture was written off in the following manner:

> Once more Australian production has reached for dramatic material from the dead and vanished past. The language is far-off and unreal. The one bright spot is the acting of Ron Roberts as John Lee.

Made on a shoe-string budget, the camera very seldom used a close-up. The actor came into frame immediately, and establishment shots were merely blow-ups of postcards. The fire scene was rehearsed without flares or smoke pots, and on the shooting schedule was placed at the end of the day's 'takes' so that the smoke would clear from the studio in time for the following day's scenes.

The real tragedy was that the director was Raymond Longford. From this film onwards his career went into decline. He was afterwards seen only in small and undistinguished film roles.

2.16 *Dorothy Brunton and Harold B. Meade in "Clara Gibbings".*

2.17 *Frank Harvey and Guy Hastings in "Streets Of London".*

The 'dig up the past' cycle continued. Closely on the heels of *The Man* and *Cinesound Varieties* came another calamity *When the Kellys Rode Again*. Once again Harry Southwell was the man responsible for shaking the rust off the Kelly armour. As usual, NSW banned it. (Harry it seemed would never learn.) Photographed by Tasman Higgins (who was also behind camera for the 1923 version *When the Kellys were Out)* it was premiered at the Brisbane Wintergarden on 23 June. The picture set out to make the bushranger an almost lovable person. Sixteen days later W. Creswell O'Reilly passed the picture for export and general exhibition in Victoria after cuts were made.

Melbourne considered it unconvincing and laughable: 'It is time producers forgot about Ned Kelly and *The Man they could not Hang.*'

Southwell must have dispensed with the services of a scriptwriter, especially during the 'shoot out' at Glenrowan. The schoolmaster waved a lantern to save a train load of troopers, then magically it was daylight when the hotel was stormed. The hotel was set alight in darkness, yet the duel between Kelly (Hay Simpson) and Sergeant Steele (George Randall) was in the sunlight. It took the Kellys only one week to repack their saddle bags and ride out of Melbourne again.

After scraping the bottom of the story barrel, 1934 came up with a minor aeroplane cycle. It began with A.R. (Dick) Harwood's *Secret of the Skies* shown simultaneously in Sydney at the Australian and Arcadia Theatres on 31 March. This was based on the disappearance of the 'Southern Cloud' on a flight from Sydney to Melbourne. In the picture, the plane was the 'Golden Eagle' that had a forced landing in the Victorian Ranges. The pilot was well portrayed by John D'Arcy, and the actual crash was cleverly staged with dramatic intensity. In fact the sequences in the cockpit prior to the disaster were extremely well handled. The film's main fault was that the remaining passengers on the aircraft lacked colour and interest, but Harwood managed to capture the remoteness of the stranded passengers and the hopelessness of their position.

At the Liberty Theatre, Sydney, on 10 August, was *The Old Bus*, a Jack Percival Jnr. production. The purpose was to relate the history of flight in Australia with an emphasis on the historic trip of 'The Southern Cross' across the Pacific. Sir Charles Kingsford Smith's name figured prominently — but the film did not add laurels to Australian film production. On the contrary, it was dubbed an 'ugly hotch-potch'.

The third in the aeroplane cycle, *Splendid Fellows*, highlighted the Centenary Air Race from London to Melbourne. Directed and produced by Beaumont Smith, it was screened in Sydney on 17 November 1934. It was a bewildering change from *The Hayseeds*. Newspapers admired Smith's idea of being very modern by showing the arrival of the fliers, and the Duke of Gloucester's progress through the streets of Melbourne. Then came the big crunch:

> The plot and dialogue are crude — the character drawing somewhat childish. Technically, Beaumont Smith has everything to learn about production. Eric Coleman is the only one who adapts his voice to the requirements of studio recording.

2.18   *Another location shot for "Sheepmates" based on the book by William Hatfield.*

2.19   *Campbell Copelin and Harold B. Meade in the uncompleted Efftee film "Sheepmates".*

After *Splendid Fellows*, Beaumont Smith once again packed his bags and
departed. Already the fatality rate was increasing in alarming proportions on
the local film front.

A Troubled Year

Nineteen thirty-four had far more controversies than the Kellys, the Rudds,
and the John Lees put together.

These began early in the year with the announcement that a second
inquiry into the film industry on behalf of New South Wales would be
conducted by F.W. Marks, who was at the head of the vainglorious 1927
Royal Commission. Almost immediately a 'quota system' was mooted. It was
pointed out that this requirement had saved the British industry and would be
the salvation of local production. It was stated that Australia was in a
healthier position than England before the introduction of the quota with
four Australian studios: Filmcraft, Cinesound, Commonwealth Film
Laboratory, and Australian Film Laboratory all better equipped than
England's studios and all technically able to produce films of a high standard.
In addition, the quota would assure that new theatres built with foreign
capital would be compelled to show a number of Australian films. The
Victorian government was to be approached to seek its co-operation in
passing uniform legislation.

The inquiry came as a surprise since it had been as late as August 1933
that a delegation from the Australian Natives Association, Melbourne, had
requested the Chief Secretary to ensure that the Commonwealth Government
be empowered by the states to control the film industry and prevent foreign
distributors from imposing unreasonable and harsh contracts upon
exhibitors. The Chief Secretary had replied that he was strongly opposed to
transferring powers to the Federal Government, as it lacked the facilities
possessed by the states for the enforcement of laws.

By the end of January 1934, several Federal ministers thought along
similar lines to the ANA, and began agitating for Federal control of films. In
February 1934, Stuart F. Doyle, managing director of Cinesound (apparently
as a piece of public relations to show how well his company was doing
without a quota system) stated that *On Our Selection* had taken $92000 and
The Squatter's Daughter, $24000 to date, and was expected to take an
additional $26000. A genuine surprise was that the strongly criticised *The
Hayseeds* which had cost $12000 to make, was estimated to earn at least
$40000 in Australia and New Zealand.

F.W. Thring had also displayed supreme optimism when he announced
that his highly successful Australian musical stage romance *Collit's Inn*
would be made into a film late in 1934. Another book purchased by Efftee
was William Hatfield's *Ginger Murdoch*. Efftee's *Sheepmates* was also
nearing completion in the Wattle Path Studios. (Unfortunately all three
projects never reached fruition.) On the heels of this announcement came the
Thring bombshell: Efftee Film Studios would close. Thring had been unable
to secure a release in Sydney for Noel Monkman's *People of the Ponds,
Catching Crocodiles* and *Nature's Little Jokes* — all of which had met with

outstanding success in Melbourne and had been purchased for screening in America and England.

One Sydney paper looked upon Thring's threat with alarm.

> The Australian film industry looked to two large organisations — Efftee and Cinesound — for future development. The rights and the wrongs of this declaration must be argued in another place. The fact to be faced is that he intended to close down at the very time the film industry seemed to be entering a period of significant expansion.

The film inquiry continued to create a potent witch's brew. Pat Hanna gave evidence that Australian producers had been forced to accept terms that would kill the Australian industry if they were allowed to continue. A protest was lodged by the Melbourne Branch of the Cinematograph Exhibitors Association when a proposal was put forward by the Victorian Talking Picture Producers' Association (comprising Efftee, Pat Hanna Productions, A.R. Harwood's Centenary Films and Charles Chauvel's Expeditionary Films) to extend the existing film quota legislation to include Australian feature films. At that time, the exhibitors in Victoria had to include 610 metres of British film in every programme — of which 305 metres must be Australian. The Producers Association asked for a quota of 5 per cent of Australian feature films.

Chauvel continued to fight for the cause of Australian films and spoke out strongly in favour of Australian pictures being able to secure an unrestricted market in this country. A quota would not only preserve and foster the spadework done during the past few years, but would encourage investment of the necessary capital into film making for the erection of studios, the advancement in technical efficiency, and the release of a better product. Yet the Melbourne branch of the Cinematograph Exhibitors' Association felt that the present quota system was quite satisfactory, and that the requested quota was inadvisable as it would lead to ill-managed companies making trashy films.

Breakthrough

Rather amazingly, Greater Union Theatres and Hoyts were more interested in F.W. Thring's outburst, and entered into a lease on the old Tivoli Theatre in Sydney. This made part of Thring's dream come true, because it provided him with a long desired outlet for 'live' production in the Harbour City. On 22 June 1934, with all the tinsel and flag waving at a showman's right hand, he staged *Collit's Inn.*

Following in the wake of F.W. Thring's big theatrical breakthrough, came the F.W. Marks report. It recommended a five year quota system for Australian films. A further recommendation was that before the quota law expired consideration should be given to the advisability of extending it. Marks urged that quota legislation contemplated by New South Wales should be submitted to other states in an endeavour to obtain uniform legislation throughout Australia. At the end of July 1934, the NSW Cabinet approved of Marks' recommendations. The Chief Secretary was instructed to draft the necessary Bill and to confer with the Victorian Government about uniformity of legislation.

Anticipating the enforcement of a quota law, Cinesound built up an organisation capable of large-scale production. At this time the Bondi Studio was in continuous production and the Rushcutters Bay premises was providing studio space for independent productions.

F.W. Thring became enthusiastic and announced that Efftee would embark upon an important programme of expansion. This included a three-year plan for production in which film directors, technicians and actors would be brought from overseas. Being a man of initiative, he advised that he would tour England and America for the required talent.

Set-Backs

But like the words of a certain song, Australian production didn't know that the cards were stacked already. A bed of roses can produce its own thorns.

At the formal opening of new extensions on 19 October, Stuart F. Doyle stated that Cinesound now employed 144 people on a permanent basis, and 450 as intermittent workers. Despite this situation, independent producers were still worried over the wording of the impending quota law. On 28 November, at a meeting of these independent producers, chaired by Raymond Longford it was anticipated that great pressure would be exerted to obstruct the passage of the legislation.

The NSW Talking Picture Producers' Association, convened by Noel Monkman, also expressed concern. If clauses in the proposed Bill were deleted, the legislation would be nullified. Any law passed should be along the lines of the British Cinematograph Films Act which placed the British industry in the position that it occupied at the time. Monkman advised that Efftee had closed down following the attitude of the Victorian Government in rejecting quota legislation, and that the excellent Wattle Path studio was now a skating rink. This announcement wasn't misplaced. According to *Over and Under the Great Barrier Reef* by Kitty Monkman (Cairns Post, 1975):

> Noel Monkman ceased making nature films to help in the fight for the quota. Block booking tactics were still being employed by American and British film distributors. This meant that as payment had to be made twelve months in advance, an Australian exhibitor wishing to screen a local production, would have to discard an American or British film for which he had already paid, in order to make room for the indigenous product.

Noel wrote regularly pointing out this iniquity, but only *Everyone's* remained sympathetic. Eventually Gayne Dexter, realising the consequences, ran a Monkman article. Immediately American distribution companies withdrew their advertising. That act of loyalty to Australian films cost Dexter his job.

One of the big Sydney dailies was next to be bearded by Monkman. He breezed into the editor's office unannounced and demanded the reason for his letters not being published. The editor, taken aback, went with him to the paper's film department. When they arrived, Monkman was introduced to the man in charge of the division. Noel Monkman stated: 'Don't you think this is significant and proves my point? Here I am, an Australian film producer, and your Mr — has never met me, let alone wished to know my views on the right of the Australian film producers to have their films screened in their own country.'

The editor issued instructions to print every letter that Noel submitted alongside the film department's comments.

After a great deal of lobbying and circularising of Members of Parliament a conference was conducted in the Chief Secretary's office. Noel Monkman attended. In an attempt to discredit the man from the Barrier Reef, one of the Australian managers of an American distributing company said, 'If you were to turn Mr Monkman upside down, you would not shake sixpence from his pocket.'

'You are right,' replied Noel. 'And I will tell you why. It is because of you — and you — and you,' stabbing his finger and pointing to each of the Australian managers of the various American distributing companies. 'You are only glorified office boys for your American masters, and just obey instructions to crush Australian film production wherever possible, and so keep Australian films from Australian screens.'

Nineteen thirty-four ended on an unbelievable note of despair. Ken G. Hall decided to take a trip to Hollywood. The Bondi studio was closed and the staff paid off. Now both Cinesound and Efftee were inoperative. Meanwhile the Films Quota Bill was having a stormy passage through Parliament. Overseas vested interests would walk the corridors of Parliament House rather than take a stroll along Pitt Street.

Downhill

Nineteen thirty-five was a very poor year for Australian films. *Grandad Rudd* already has been discussed and Harry Southwell made another abortive attempt to gain recognition by remaking the hoary old stage classic *The Bells* under the title of *The Burgomeister*. (This had been a silent in 1911 in the days of Amalgamated Pictures.) Using an excellent cameraman, George Heath and interpolating music by Isador Goodman, Harry appeared as Mattias the innkeeper, and Stan Tolhurst was the wealthy Jew.

The Burgomeister never went beyond the preview on 29 September 1935. It was then taken over by an American company. By 30 December it was still awaiting a release. Finally the picture was refused a Quota Registration number by the Board which had been set up under the NSW Quota Act to review all Australian films. The Board's role was to ensure that a set standard of quality was maintained so that the film stood a reasonable chance for release abroad. The Board's banning of *The Burgomeister* was used to good purpose by those opposing the Quota Law.

The only worthwhile film for the year was Charles Chauvel's *Heritage* which was named best film in the Commonwealth Film Awards that year. *Heritage* was an ambitious project — a family saga which covered Australia's pioneering days and went as far as the 1930s. The film proved Chauvel was an intelligent and progressive pictorial artist. One of the big scenes was the arrival of the bride ship, with a youthful Peggy (later Mary) Maguire as an Irish lass seeking a husband in a new land. The crossing of the Blue Mountains, the Macquarie regime, and other important historical happenings were faithfully reproduced. The film's major weakness was the leading male star, Franklyn Bennett, who neither looked like nor suggested the ruggedness and strength of a nation builder.

However the growth of the Australian film industry was another matter altogether. Enemies of the Quota Law were carefully planting seeds of doubt as to whether Australian could meet the requirements specified. But Noel Monkman continued to do battle:

> Encouragement has been sadly lacking owing to insidious propaganda over many years, that has been circulated by parties who are not desirous of seeing a film industry established in this country. Low grade films from overseas have been accepted and shown without comment, but an Australian picture receives severe criticism.

Finally on 28 September 1935, the New South Wales Quota Act was officially proclaimed and came into force in October.

New Techniques, Poor Stories

On 7 February 1936, F.W. Thring arrived in Sydney to transfer his activities to that city. He linked up with Mastercraft Film Corporation whose new studios were being built. He hoped to commence film production in early April with *Collit's Inn*. Thring stated that Sydney was the coming Hollywood of Australia. Melbourne was far too conservative. He had intended shooting a new George Wallace film, *Ginger Murdoch,* at his Wattle Path Studio, but lack of action on the Victorian Government's part had made him choose Sydney. He would leave for Hollywood on 4 March to engage directors and players. Raymond Longford was left in charge of the new Efftee production centre.

The first Australian production for the year was Cinesound's *Thoroughbred* at the Sydney Mayfair Theatre on 9 May. Based on the career of Australia's famous racehorse Phar Lap, it had scenes from Flemington and Randwick Racetracks woven into the story. During the actual production Hall introduced something new to Australian film making: rear projection, an innovation he had studied in America. By this means action and authenticity would add a new dimension and depth to Cinesound features. Helen Twelvetrees, the 'star' of the film, came to Australia after the running of the Melbourne Cup but through rear projection she was actually there. A camera sled towed behind a car was employed to obtain the low angles of the galloping hooves of the horses.

Hall had contracted Seward, the American scenario writer to write the script for *Thoroughbred*. But what Hall didn't know was that the script was very similar to *Broadway Bill*, an American film starring Warner Baxter which was released in 1934. Crowds flocked to see *Thoroughbred* but critics remained less than charitable.

> Although written by Seward, the plot is difficult to follow; characters are ill-defined; and it is best to draw the veil over the humorousness of the dialogue. The most successful part of the film is the climax filmed by George Heath, where the favourite is shot from the Flemington grandstand during the running of the Melbourne Cup. Helen Twelvetrees is suave, crisp, and

competent; John Longden, sincere and effective, although he doesn't have the meaty role of a Dean Maitland. Frank Leighton does well in a thankless, colourless, and rather muddied role. [So much for the work of a Hollywood film writer.]

When the horse was shot in the race, Lance Skulthorpe doubled for the jockey and took a genuine spill.

On 18 July Cinesound's 'world standard' production *Thoroughbred* became a mere dray-horse at the hands of English censors. Scenes to be deleted were buckjumping sequences, the rescue of a horse from a blazing stable, and the reduction of the falling of the racehorse to a momentary flash.

Ken Hall was incensed: 'The contention that scenes suggesting cruelty to horses, hurt me deeply. It shows how little the English censor knows of Australian horsemanship. Backjumping scenes are common to any station in Australia where horses are broken in. As to the fire scene — no horse was ever near the blaze. The impression gained was achieved with "rear projection". The fall at the finish was simply a photographic record of an actual happening that could have occurred in England's own Grand National. If it had taken place in an English race it would be shown in British newsreels.'

Edmond Seward's second script for Cinesound was based on a story by Dorothy Cottrell. *Orphan of the Wilderness,* screened at Sydney's Lyceum Theatre on 17 December, was in some respects Ken G. Hall's most charming film. It was seen at Adelaide's Mayfair on 23 December, and Brisbane's Regent Theatre on 31 December 1936. Featuring Australian animals in a bushsetting built in the Cinesound Studio by that superb scenic artist J. Alan Kenyon, 'shooting' required infinite patience both on the part of director Ken Hall, and cameraman George Heath. A big red kangaroo, a koala, a dingo a small joey — the real star of the picture — and a frog in a small pool covered with water lilies, became familiar sights to the production crew. When the joey grew up and became a boxing kangaroo, the mood of the film changed to that of a scathing indictment on the behaviour and cruelty of man towards

2.20   *Brian Abbot, the ill-fated hero of "Orphan Of The Wilderness", directed by Ken G. Hall for Cinesound. This was one of the most time-consuming films of Hall's career. A big hit in 1936, "Orphan" was badly mauled by the English censor. Abbot was lost at sea, between Lord Howe Island and Sydney, late in the year of the film's release.*

2.21   *Sylvia Kellaway and Gwen Munro in circus gear for Cinesound's "Orphan Of The Wilderness."*

animals. The bush scenes were entrancing and at times, poetically beautiful — but when man interrupted the serenity of the setting, the film became less interesting and at times, tedious.

Marginal Successes

National Productions, Pagewood, supplied two features in 1936; *The Flying Doctor* on 18 September, and *Rangle River*, on 19 December. Charles Farrell and Victor Jory, two fading Hollywood stars were featured.

Frederick Daniell, General Manager of National Productions, discovered a startling truth, a truth that even today, some four decades later producers have not heeded. Daniell entered into financial discussions with Gaumont British covering costing, etc. without realising that part of the deal was that he had to meet exploitation charges, for which he had not budgeted. He did not foresee being called upon to actually become a persuasive salesman as well as a film maker. Fred Daniell personally took *The Flying Doctor* to England, and despite assurances and promises, the picture received only secondary release. Daniell stated later, 'I don't think anyone can succeed in making films in Australia on a shoe-string. There must be a positive approach to production and distribution. Australian films have fallen down in the past, because the manager of the production unit has had to be executive in charge of distribution at the same time. The point is, both aspects cannot be wedded successfully.'

Directed by Englishman Miles Mander *The Flying Doctor* was excellent in landscapes, cutting and continuity, even though shots of Bondi and the Harbour Bridge were superfluous. But the story itself was pitifully weak. Charles Farrell was a carefree vagabond who arrived at a sheep station in the Blue Mountains area. He fell in love with the owner's daughter (Mary Maguire). After marrying her, for obscure reasons best known to himself, he hightailed it for Sydney. There he met a flying doctor (James Raglan) and made the acquaintance of an unhappily married woman (Margaret Vyner) whose pompous husband was Eric Coleman.

The Flying Doctor was not handled gently by critics, yet the film did well at the box office, and was awarded a Certificate of Merit at the International Film Exhibition in September 1937.

Rangle River was made by National in association with Columbia Pictures. Brilliant camerawork by Errol Hinds and Damien Parer was the genuine highlight. Zane Grey (supposedly in Australia at the time) is credited with having written the story, but another account claims American director Clarence Badger contacted Charles Chauvel for a script. In *Rangle River* the critics were more interested in how the scenery around Gloucester would impress Hollywood as being something new and unique in backgrounds. The acting did gain plaudits. Victor Jory was sincere and convincing; English Robert Coote had a freshness that made even unpromising lines and situations appear humorous; Australian leading lady Margaret Dare possessed charm and grace of movement; Cecil Perry was a capable villain; and silent film star George Bryant gave a neat character study as an old inhabitant of the cattle country. It was really a 'meat pie' Western with floods. In one scene Robert Coote climbed upon a log in a swollen stream and dubbed it the Queen Mary.

2.22   *Hollywood film star Charles Farrell star of the Australian production "The Flying Doctor".*
(Still by courtesy of Margaret Veal)

2.23 *Margaret Dare and Victor Jory in "Rangle River" a Columbia Picture made in the National Pagewood Studio.*

It was Jory who suggested that Coote go to Hollywood.

Charles Chauvel's contribution to 1936 was *Uncivilised*. Premiered in Sydney's Embassy on 25 September, it was screened at Brisbane's Regent on 9 October. The story was that of Hoey, a white man who was chief of an Aboriginal tribe. Sydney hears of Hoey, and a young author (Margot Rhys) is sent to cover the event. She meets a mysterious Afghan (Ashton Jarry) who is a disguised detective seeking opium smugglers. A half-caste (Marcelle Marnay) tries to steal the white leader's hoard of rubies. During a savage tribal fight, the village is set alight. Chauvel had his usual brush with the censor — two scenes had to be deleted before the picture was passed for export. One was Margot Rhys swimming nude in a bush pool; the other, the strangling of an Aborigine. Critics felt that the bathing scene was handled with taste and discretion, and as for the strangling, 'far more grim and harassing episodes from Hollywood had been allowed on local screens'. But the film was criticised for uneven acting, for import Dennis Hoey being too mature for the role, and for the photography of Tasman Higgins and Jack Fletcher which was said to be a little too dark.

The Barrier Reef production *White Death* starring Zane Grey, the writer of Westerns who tried hard to look every inch a deep sea fisherman, was screened at St James Theatre, Brisbane, on 23 October, followed by the Sydney showing at the Mayfair, 6 November. Despite the hoo-ha and handclapping from trade papers, the film was merely another chase, this time on water. Brave Zane went in search of the legendary Shark 'White Death' that frequented the North Queensland waters. Drama — Zane Grey style — is charitably best left in the realm of forgotten things.

In the final analysis 1936 proved that Australian films would not be noted for their scenarios. However the results of a poll conducted by the Film Critics Guild of Australia voted *Orphan of the Wilderness* as best film of the year, with *Rangle River* second and *Uncivilised* third. Later, in 1937 Charles Chauvel advised that *Uncivilised* had been extensively booked in the United

2.24 *"Uncivilised" — an
Expeditionary Films Production
directed by Charles Chauvel, with
Dennis Hoey, Margot Rhys,
Marcelle Marnay, Ashton Jarry.*

States. Costing $34000 to produce, it enjoyed one of the most important successes of any Australian film in America. (Which proves that Australian productions did make the American screens in the past.)

More Problems

On 19 June 1936, F.W. Thring returned from America, and was immediately placed in a Melbourne hospital where he died on 1 July. This was an irreplacable loss to the industry. A man of drive and initiative, a power dynamo with ambitious plans for Australian films, Thring left behind a void that the local film front could not camouflage.

Even worse was the fate of Raymond Longford at Hunter's Hill studio. After Thring's death National Productions purchased the building and equipment, and Longford had many talks with Fred Daniell about his future. 'My one regret,' recalled Daniell, 'is that such plans fell through.' It seemed Longford was a born loser.

Quota Battle

The film industry continued to count its losses. Peggy (Mary) Maguire signed a seven-year contract with Warner Brothers, and left for Hollywood. In June 1937 Mary's first 'B' grade picture was announced — *That Man's here Again.* The caption read, 'Mary's nuts about Hugh . . . and you'll be nuts about Mary.' It was not a promising start as the Hugh referred to was the 'woo-woo' comic Hugh Herbert. One Australian publication wrote, 'no matter what you thought of Mary in Australian pictures she's a sensation in her first Hollywood role.'

Another loss occurred in October 1936 when Brian Abbot (*Orphan of the Wilderness*) and Leslie Hay Simpson (*When the Kellys Rode*) left Lord Howe Island in a 5 metre skiff *Mystery Star* for Sydney. Both had appeared in *Mystery Island.* They were never sighted again. A further departure, silent and this time unlamented, was American screen writer Edmond Seward, who couldn't even set nitrate film alight.

It was in 1936 that the Quota Law had more than teething trouble. In

May, the Legislative Assembly raised the question as to how the word 'acquire' could be interpreted. This was the one word that would eventually destroy the effectiveness of the whole Act. Noel Monkman had fought very hard to prevent any alteration to the British Act on which it was patterned, and did warn their opponents of the system were lobbying to undermine the efficiency of the proposed Act.

At the time American distributors were assuming that they were only compelled to 'acquire' not less than 5 per cent of Australian films *if* such was available on the open market.

The Chief Secretary was then asked:

Does the word 'acquire' in the Act mean that American film distributors must obtain their Quota requirements even if they had to go into picture production to obtain them?

The Chief Secretary replied:

The word had its definite meaning in Law and if exhibitors were unable to comply with it, they were required to apply for exemption. Applications would be considered on their merits.

Already the Law was revealing structural weaknesses even if the Chief Secretary was loath to admit the fact.

The cat-and-mouse game continued. On 1 December 1936, the Chief Secretary reminded film distributors that six out of thirteen companies registered under the Cinematograph Film Quota Act had not complied with the provisions of the Law. Failure to do so would be regarded as a serious contravention of the Law.

It was in the closing stages of 1936 that the *Sydney Morning Herald* took a serious look at the Film Quota situation. It stated that already a great majority of the film trade looked upon the Act as a dead letter. After January 1937 the government would have to consider its next move. The weakness of the Act hinged on the word 'acquire'. In the beginning it was intended that the Americans would have to finance production of Australian films if none could be purchased on the open market. But in a court of law 'acquire' may not be deemed applicable to production at all.

All the excitement attached to the new deal under the Quota Act, disappeared in 1937. National Studios ceased production; Efftee Films came to an abrupt halt after Thring's death; and Charles Chauvel cooled his heels. In 1937 the industry became fully aware that the Quota Act wasn't specific enough; the government wasn't strong enough; and overseas interests gleefully predicted the failure of Australian films. They used *The Burgomeister* incident to advantage by insinuating that the backers' money was no longer safe. Finally satisfied as to their own impregnability overseas interests threw their trump card on the table. Their film supplies would be withheld from NSW if the government tried to enforce the Law. It was effective blackmail and revealed the ruthlessness of the crowing enemy.

The government revealed unbelievable timidity on 29 January 1937 by declaring its lack of intention to introduce legislation to compel film distribution houses to participate in film production in Australia. Nor would prosecutions be launched against those that had not fulfilled their quota requirements.

The final film entry is *The Avenger*. On 23 December 1937 *The Film Weekly* mentioned a preview, and the fact that the production was to be distributed by Atlas Films. Dick Harwood was the director, and Arthur and Tasman Higgins were responsible for some excellent photography. A reformed young crook (Douglas Stuart) is given a job in a factory owned by Raymond Longford. Former partners-in-crime (John Fernside and George Lloyd) seek the reformed crook's assistance to rob the pay clerk of the factory. The hold-up is foiled, and the would-be hold-up men are sent to prison. On their release, one crook tries to have his ex-friend framed for murder.

On 30 March 1938 *The Avenger* was sold to Columbia Pictures for distribution in the United Kingdom, and carries the dubious distinction of being the last Australian Quota Film admitted under the old Film Law in England.

On 17 December, Motion Picture Producers in Sydney again appeared hopeful, when the State Government passed the Films and Theatre Bill. Ken G. Hall felt that the important feature of the legislation was the reciprocity clause that opened an overseas market for Australian films. The present Act appeared to be more realistic in its approach, as it presented an opportunity for local producers to meet quota requirements. The previous Bill had called for more films than production facilities were capable of handling. Yet once again it would prove to be nothing more than a case of wishful thinking.

Charles Chauvel agreed that the 3 per cent Quota was not biting off more than the local industry could chew. Another important provision was the inducement for American companies to acquire Australian pictures for distribution overseas. Frederick Daniell of National Productions observed that the old Quota Act had fallen short of supporting the industry by the ambiguity of the word 'acquire'. The new Legislation placed the position beyond doubt. Yet the real assessment of the fact merely amounted to another desperate attempt by the befuddled and embarrassed NSW Government to right its own ineptitude. Cynically one could add 'that's what nothing's all about'.

After the hoopla manipulations of the government, England in 1938 did the 'European Common Market Act' on Australia by passing the Cinematograph Films Bill on 25 February. It excluded the rights of all films produced in the Dominions to be counted for Quota purposes in the United Kingdom. Explanations were offered, but it was felt rightly or wrongly, that the real purpose was to force Australians to grant Britain a film quota, despite the fact that English productions were granted a special privilege by admitting them duty free into this country, while foreign films were charged 8d. per foot. (This time there was no outcry from Empire loyalists as in 1927. Perhaps all things were equal when only Australia was on the receiving end.) The outcome of the new NSW Quota Bill wasn't given any future when Stuart F. Doyle returned from a trip to the United States. He felt it extremely unlikely that American distributors would comply with the stipulations of the amended Quota Act.

Only Cinesound remained the fortress of Australian production, and gave

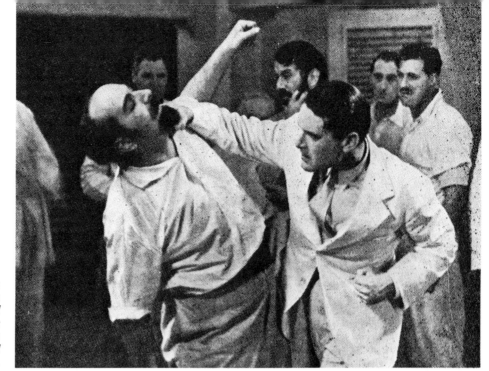

2.25 *Lloyd Hughes tries Ron Whelan's chin for size in Cinesound's "Lovers and Luggers". In those days, it was the villain who wore a beard. The 1970s gave the idea quite a novel twist.*

this country a really good boost for 1938 with *Lovers and Luggers* that opened at Brisbane Tivoli Theatre on 31 December 1937. In fact this picture altered the theatre's normal policy of a weekly change of programme to that of a fortnight's season due to the overwhelming response from the public. With yet another of Hollywood's fading stars in the lead role, Lloyd Hughes was given excellent support by James Raglan as an artist. Shirley Ann Richards supplied the romantic interest, and Ron Whelan was the villain. One critic wrote that Hall had shown an even sounder grip of film technique. Yet another gave this description:

2.26 *A window setting, supposedly in "Australia" House, that was featured in the Cinesound film "Lovers And Luggers". This too was the work of J. Alan Kenyon.*

> *Lovers And Luggers* clearly shows that Australia has definitely arrived as a film producing country with vast possibilities. So great is the stride forward that Ken G. Hall's previous productions in retrospect are a little amateurish by comparison.

Although George Heath handled most of the photography, Captain Frank Hurley's lensing of the pearl luggers under full sail near Thursday Island plus the sheer beauty of the tropics received unstinted praise.

An about face came on 5 March when the government declared its determination to enforce the Film Quota Act. The government looked forward with confidence to distributors showing support for the Act in the proper manner. At this point theatre roofs came toppling inwards. The Motion Picture Distributors of Australia declared they were considering a complete withdrawal of their pictures from NSW and probably Australia. Such action would take place at the end of the year as a direct result of the State Government's attempts to force American companies to comply with the film quota. The MPD pointed out that this was not to be considered blackmail or a threat. (Exactly how it was to be classified, was not stated.) The MPD would find it cheaper to sacrifice profits in this country in lieu of spending money on production.

American and British companies mounted the band wagon and stated openly that they could not be forced to make films in Australia. The most they could be compelled to do was buy whatever Australian pictures appeared on the market. (Neither the 1936 or 1937 productions by Australia could hope to fulfil the required quota.)

If ever F.W. Thring was missed, it was at this crucial point. He could have started his own productions, called upon Raymond Longford and Noel Monkman for assistance, and with the necessary persuasion National Productions could have pulled their weight. And he was big enough to tell the Americans to go to hell.

Independent Productions

Cinesound was the only studio in continuous production, yet in 1937 it made only three films — *It isn't Done,* screened at the Embassy Theatre, Sydney, March 1937; *Tall Timbers,* Tivoli, Brisbane, and *Lovers and Luggers,* Tivoli, Brisbane, December 1937.

By now Ken G. Hall was gaining stature as a director, and for those days, inventive effects such as a timber drive in a studio became a Hall trademark. His one weakness was his failure to select a good story. Even in *Tall Timbers* the screenplay by Frank Harvey based on a story by Captain Frank Burley, received a mixed reception. But with a special effects director like the talented J. Alan Kenyon, Hall had it made in that department.

Melbourne critics noted a chronic weakness in the dialogue. Another wrote that the film stopped short of a really rip-roaring finish by not keeping the hero in the hut until the last minute. As he was right in the path of falling timber, suspense was lost by having him (Frank Leighton) escape so swiftly and easily through a window.

Hall admitted later that critics were a little cool on the storyline — but due credit must be given to him. Acting honours went to Frank Leighton, Harvey Adams as the timber contractor, and Campbell Copelin and Frank Harvey as the villains of the piece.

Three minor independent productions completed the output for 1937. All three were originally screened in Sydney. *Mystery Island* was the first on 6

March. Its greatest appeal was the magnificent scenery of Lord Howe Island, and the staging of a shipwreck in a raging storm. (It seems a little eerie to recall that the male lead, Brian Abbot, was lost at sea after the picture was completed. A major fault was the poor soundtrack. The story itself presented good dramatic possibilities with a murderer and a detective in the list of survivors, but the suspense was lacking. Jean Laidley, the leading actress, was credited with a good speaking voice — but that alone does not save a film.)

On 4 June, Stuart F. Doyle announced his resignation as managing director of Greater Union Theatres. Shortly afterwards Norman B. Rydge was appointed to succeed him. To put it bluntly, Rydge was a bookkeeper, not a creative genius. As Greater Union was in financial difficulties, Rydge was called upon to balance the ledger.

The parade of independent productions continued on 24 September with *Phantom Gold*. This was to introduce a new name to motion pictures — Rupert Kathner. He was to hold the dubious reputation of never making a first class film, yet his whole soul was in moving pictures. He was a very good artist — yet he preferred to direct features and documentaries. A Kathner-Tolhurst Production, *Phantom Gold* starred Stan Tolhurst as Harry Lasseter, who in 1930 set out to find a gold reef, but only succeeded in creating a legend. The picture was produced in 'voice over' style, but the script wasn't terse and tense enough to match the gaunt pictorial record. Even the dramatic realism was missing from the agony and despair of Lasseter's suffering, before his unfortunate death.

Cinesound remained in the film news in January 1938 when *On Our Selection* once again drew packed houses at Sydney's Lyceum Theatre. This was the fifth time that the rural romp played seasons in the Harbour City's metropolitan area. Often the Lyceum had to turn away business, and request police assistance to control the crowds. Despite the fact that in 1938 *On Our Selection* was considered a box office freak, the Commonwealth Censor, W. Cresswell O'Reilly reported that he would not pass any more pictures of the type featuring the Rudd family. In that same January theatres were forced to close because of a wide-spread epidemic of paralysis throughout Australia, causing an extensive death toll.

Disappointments

If a high peak of optimism ever disappeared under a wave of disappointment and uncertainty such a happening can be headed '1938'. Cinesound must have had some premonition of the ultimate end of the second phase on Australian film making and embarked upon a programme of desperate production. Never again would Cinesound work at the same tempo, and never again would Ken Hall be able to demonstrate his extreme versatility.

Cinesound hit the February jackpot with *A Nation is Born* screened at Sydney's Prince Edward Theatre on 12 February 1938. This semi-documentary, directed and photographed by Captain Frank Hurley, combined views of Sydney with mining at Broken Hill; revealed Farrer experimenting with wheat, and the dreams of Macarthur and Marsden envisaging great progress in wool growing. Special highlights were scenes from

The Squatter's Daughter and *Orphan of the Wilderness.* Unfortunately it suffered from a wordy and laboured commentary by Harry Dearth.

Yet another big film success for Ken Hall was *The Broken Melody* premiered at the Sydney Embassy on 17 June. The plot centred around a 'vagabond musician' (Lloyd Hughes) who had been disowned by a wealthy father, and forced to play a violin on street corners. He became a celebrated composer and violinist, and married an opera singer, who too had to walk along the hard road to success. The climax was an operatic sequence composed by Alfred Hill and performed on an elaborate tiered set devised by J. Alan Kenyon.

The critics of the day were loud in their praise of *The Broken Melody* declaring that Ken Hall had not only done a good thing for Cinesound, but for the Australian Film Industry in general — which at the time was wholly based in Sydney.

2.27   *Broken Melody.*

2.28   *A mid-shot of the stage setting for "The Broken Melody". Lionello Cecil and Diana du Cane are the two singers holding hands. See the still of the scaffolding supporting this enormous opera setting.*

Hall's next film did not receive the same praise. It was another unfortunate excursion into the realm of comedy. This picture entitled *Let George Do It* heralded George Wallace's first appearance under the Cinesound banner. In this film George, tired of life, arranges for a crook to murder him. When he inherits a fortune he tries to call the deal off, but the would-be killer believes in sticking to his end of the bargain. There is a slapstick speedboat chase across Sydney Harbour with Wallace trying to evade the criminal and his cohorts. Narrowly missing ferries and every known form of water transport, he cuts a sculling shell in half with the crew still rowing as both parts sink. The film received such write-ups as, 'one can scarcely call George Wallace a subtle comedian. His humour is derived from the lusty exuberance of vaudeville.' It was premiered at the Brisbane Tivoli Theatre on 17 June 1938, with the Sydney showing at the Capitol on 15 July.

In 1968, when some fifty five minutes of *Let George Do It* was screened as a tribute to Ken G. Hall, people who had never seen or heard of George Wallace were helpless with mirth.

The final Cinesound offering for the year provided another chance to meet the family that Ken Hall fussed over like a Dutch uncle ... the Rudds. Down they came to Sydney and the Capitol Theatre on 30 September, with their baggage labelled *Dad And Dave come to Town*. In August 1939 Adolf Zukor, chairman of the board of Paramount Pictures paid a special visit to Cinesound, to state that on his journey to Australia on the *Mariposa* he saw *Dad And Dave come to Town*. He met Bert Bailey, then working on his new feature *Dad Rudd MP* and Zukor was pleased to visit the studio where such a good film was made on an extremely modest budget.

Only two independent productions made the screen in 1938 — the more important being *Typhoon Treasure* directed by Noel Monkman, who previously made *The Barrier Reef* series. Originally billed as 'Queensland's own adventure-teeming photoplay' it was considered to be no celluloid masterpiece. Yet there was plenty of action, no glaring production faults and fairly average quality acting. Underwater scenes off Green Island were filmed by Noel Monkman. *Typhoon Treasure* had its world premiere at St James Theatre, Brisbane on 23 September 1938. The season was only one week. The Sydney showing was at the Cameo and Civic Theatres on 28 October.

2.29   *Noel Monkman's 'Typhoon Treasure'.*

2.30   *Campbell Copelin and Gwen Munro in "Typhoon Treasure", directed by Noel Monkman. (1938) (Still by courtesy of Harry Davidson.)*

Melbourne had closed down its film industry completely by 1938, and A.R. Harwood had to direct his *Show Business* in the National Studios, Pagewood. Once again Arthur Higgins was on camera. Like *The Avenger* this film achieved little distinction in Australia, and does not appear to have gone beyond its preview at the Village Theatre, Toorak (Melbourne) on 7 August. In *Show Business* an adventuress Nina Bellamy (Joyce Hunt) uses the love letters of two brothers (John Barrington and Jimmy McMahon) to force money out of their wealthy father (Guy Hastings) to back her in a show. Meanwhile brother Bill wishes to produce a stage show starring Joan Leslie (Charmaine Ross) and the other brother Wally plans to direct a film. Nina resorts to blackmail but her plans are thwarted by her husband (Fred Tupper). 'Dick' Harwood used an identical plot later in *Night Club*. In *Show Business* Jimmy Coates and his band supplied the music, and Barbara James was a featured singer.

In a recent publication listing Australian Films, *Below the Surface* directed by Rupert Kathner is shown as a 1938 feature. Actually intended to be a full-length picture, a letter from the *Newcastle Morning Herald* dated 15 July 1968 provided the following information:

2.31   *Director Dick Harwood greets the then 3AW radio personality, Fred Tupper at the Pagewood Studios, Sydney, prior to the shooting of "Show Business" Fred died 15.3.76.*

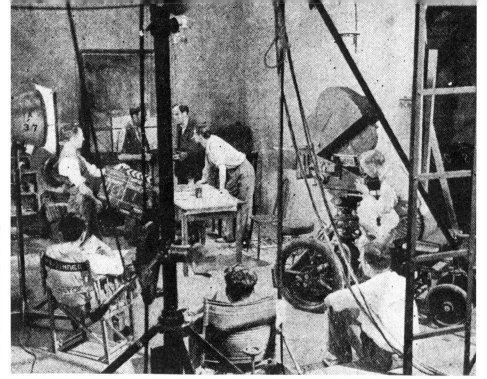

2.32 *"Below The Surface" being shot in the National Studios, Pagewood. Rupert Kathner is director, and George Hughes in charge of production. It was advertised as a coming release by the Cameo Theatre. This was never completed, but Kathner did use some of the "Below The Surface" sequences covering coal mining in Newcastle in his "Australia Today" series.*

We checked on your inquiry re *Below the Surface.* I am advised that the film was made in Pagewood Studios, but the production company went into liquidation, and it was not completed.

However Kathner appears to have retained some of the footage shot in Newcastle concerning coal mining, for on 9 September 1938 at the News Luxe Theatre, Sydney (a newsreel theatre) the first programme of *Australia Today* was screened. Patterned on the American *March of Time,* it was an Enterprise Films release directed by Kathner. One item was on drug smuggling in Australia, another — a very significant entry — devoted itself to the situation in the coal industry. This section was titled *Below the Surface,* and covered coal mining in Newcastle.

By 8 December 1968, the NSW Government was prepared to implement desperate measures to save face and to boost local production. Under a new Bill, the Treasurer had the power to guarantee local production, the necessary financial backing should it be required, until such times as a market was obtained. The following day the Chief Secretary explained the statement in greater detail. The government would guarantee bank overdrafts of local

2.33 *A youthful Peter Finch and the charming young singer Jean Hatton in "Mr Chedworth Steps Out", Cecil Kellaway's second starring vehicle for Cinesound.*

2.34 *Cecil Kellaway counts his unexpected windfall, little realizing that the money is counterfeit. This currency supplies the main theme of "Mr Chedworth Steps Out" — a Cinesound Production.*

producers where warranted. To further encourage local film makers, the government would allow an exhibitor to include for quota purposes, fifty-two issues of an Australian Gazette during any year as one Australian Quota film.

Nineteen thirty-nine opened promisingly enough with *Mr Chedworth Steps Out*. The world premiere of this film starring Cecil Kellaway was held at the Strand Theatre, Hobart on 17 February, followed by the Brisbane showing at the Wintergarden Theatre one week later. Sydneysiders saw it at the Lyceum on 8 April. A topline cast included James Raglan, Rita Pauncefort, Jean Hatton, Peter Finch and Sidney Wheeler. Charmaine Ross (from *Show Business*) played a minor role. Based on a novel by Francis M. Howard, with excellent direction from Ken G. Hall and superb backdrops by J. Alan Kenyon, *Mr Chedworth* had everything in its favour to ensure success.

Kellaway portrayed a mild-mannered, but hen-pecked clerk, who finds a large sum of money, little realising that it was counterfeit. He decides to live life to the full, but runs foul of the gang searching for the lost money; is questioned by a Commonwealth official on the track of the counterfeiters; and still has to cope with the selfishness of a demanding family. Jean Hatton's clear, flute-like voice was heard to advantage, with Hamilton Webber supplying first-class musical backing.

Cinesound's second production was another comedy with music. Shown in Sydney at the Capitol Theatre on 22 September, *Gone to the Dogs* starred George Wallace. The comedian demonstrated his versatility by being one of the writers of the screenplay, and composing one of the songs. In this film George accidently discovers a substance which is supposed to assist greyhounds to run faster. Wallace also finds time to participate in a full-scale production number, elude dog-racing crooks, and have hysterics in a haunted house.

2.35 *Musical comedy star Lois Green and George Wallace are certainly not studying a guide to form in "Gone To The Dogs".*

The final offering from Cinesound was yet another comedy with music titled *Coming Up Smiling* or in some quarters *Ants in his Pants* but like *Strike Me Lucky,* it didn't make it. Ken G. Hall this time does not have to accept responsiblilty as director, although he did write the original story under a pseudonym (John Addison Chandler) and did act as producer. The film starred Will Mahoney and it was directed by an import, William Freshman, who promptly left Australia on completion of the picture.

Extras in the film were two people who would become well known later — Chips Rafferty and Charles Bud Tingwell (then a schoolboy). Evie Hayes, Shirley Ann Richards, Guy Hastings and Lou Vernon were additional members of the cast.

Screened at the Capitol Theatre on 29 December 1939, the critics left little to smile about down Cinesound way:

Cinesound do not seem to make the most of comedians. It happened with Mo, George Wallace, and now Will Mahony. William Freshman wrote the screenplay and directed the picture, but production remains an average Cinesound sample. The most invigorating acting comes from Evie Hayes. Although her part is the sketchiest, she speaks and sings in a way that makes it mean something. Others who do well are Jean Hatton (whose light soprano voice records exquisitely for the screen) and Alec Kellaway.

The only independent production for 1939 was *Seven Little Australians* directed by yet another import, Arthur Collins. This Ethel Turner story did not raise the same enthusiasm as the ABC television production of three decades later. It was screened at the Sydney Lyceum Theatre on 18 December.

The demise of the Australian film in the 1930s witnessed the pathetic disintegration of the once highly respected Raymond Longford. Rupert Kathner, working on his *Australia Today* series, decided to include *The Albury Pyjama Girl Mystery*. Despite a warning not to proceed with the project, Kathner issued it on 18 August 1939 at the Sydney Capitol and newsreel theatrettes. As the coroner, Longford received no mention in the credits. Another brief and thankless role followed in *The Power and the Glory* in 1941, when he appeared mid-shot as a Nazi admiral.

War and Collapse

In February 1939, the English Board of Trade announced that it was considering an amendment to the British Quota Act to give Australian films the benefit of the local distributors' quota. However the matter would not receive the attention of Parliament until the autumn sitting. Even the gleam of a promise was to have no effect upon the ailing local industry — and the second failure was inevitable.

In actual fact, the reprieve had to be shelved for a much more important issue — another bloody war. With this war came the total collapse on the Australian film front. Cinesound, whose total output for 1939 was only three films, faded out.

2.36 *Will Mahoney, Jean Hatton, and Sidney Wheeler (in the caravan) in the Cinesound Production "Come Up Smiling" or "Ants in His Pants". The old "Rugby" car adds more than a touch of interest to the "still".*

3
Transition

Men must endure
Their going hence, even as their coming hither;

Shakespeare — King Lear

The Lean Years

By 30 December 1939, agreements had been signed between the NSW Government and three production houses — Argosy, Cinesound and Famous Feature Films, assuring financial backing for four proposed productions. This might have been interpreted as some measure of success for the NSW Government in their desire to promote local features. On 12 March 1940 the documents were tabled in Parliament.

Cinesound was the first to honour the agreement with *Dad Rudd MP* at the Brisbane Wintergarden and Sydney Capitol and Lyceum on 14 June. Bert Bailey, Fred MacDonald, Alec Kellaway, Connie Martyn, and Grant Taylor were included in the cast. The picture was not greeted with any great enthusiasm. One of the highlights was when Dad's political rival stole a march by booking all available halls. Dad reacted to this chicanery by bringing beautiful mannequins from Sydney, to entice the crowd away from his opponent's rally.

On 27 June 1940 a loud clatter came from Eric Porter's cartoon *Adolf in Plunderland* that was announced for an early release. A burlesque on *Alice in Wonderland* it revealed Adolf Hitler as a little boy picking petals off a daisy. As he threw each petal over his shoulder, it turned into a swastika that fell with a loud metallic clang. It was the same day that Ken G. Hall delivered a thunderbolt. Cinesound would cease the production of feature films. There was an ironic twist to this decision. Australian Films (later Cinesound) had entered the talkies with the successful *On Our Selection* and closed, feature-wise, with the lukewarm production *Dad Rudd MP*.

Film activity slowed to a crawl until 13 September when at the Sydney Capitol, Rupert Kathner of all people provided Australia with its first World

War II theme, *Wings of Destiny* starring Jim McMahon, George Lloyd and Marshall Crosby. The film highlighted a fifth columnist attempt to secure Australia's vast wolfram supplies for our enemy's needs. Billed as 'Australia's first great outdoor epic, set in the grim deserts of Central Australia', the film never fulfilled its promise. Yet the story was imaginative and the outdoor photography was praiseworthy. The faults were in the limited movement of the camera in the 'interiors', and failure to sustain dramatic tension.

The next film — another war theme — took Australia and the world by storm. Charles Chauvel who had been comparatively quiet after completion of *Uncivilised* made a triumphant come-back with *Forty Thousand Horsemen*. Chauvel had taken this picture to America before screening it in Australia. He felt certain that he would be able to open up a new market at a time when local production was threatened with extinction.

3.1 *Making the various headgear for the Charles Chauvel feature "Forty Thousand Horsemen".*

Yet it wouldn't be a Chauvel film without a word from the censor. Cuts were ordered in scenes of the famous charge by the Australian Light Horse at Beersheba. The love scene between Betty Bryant and Grant Taylor in a desert hut was frowned upon; and an Eastern dance scene was far too seductive. The Commonwealth Film Censor's decision was upheld by the Appeals Censor but the NSW Chief Secretary's Department passed the picture for exhibition in that state without cuts. Finally on 21 December 1940, the censor allowed the 'charge' scenes to remain, but the seduction scene during a sandstorm, and a *café chantant* sequence in Cairo featuring 'Eastern' dancers were again banned.

Unexpectedly the Minister For Customs handed Charles Chauvel a Christmas bonus on Christmas Eve when he allowed *Forty Thousand*

Horsemen to be screened overseas uncensored. In his opinion the love scene had been filmed artistically and in good taste, and the famous charge was magnificent and thrilling. His only reservation was that the dancing scenes could have been 'less enticing'.

With a fanfare of trumpets, this $60 000 production opened at Sydney's Mayfair Theatre on Boxing Day 1940. By today's standards, the action sequences still stand as the best ever filmed in Australia. The dialogue unfortunately cannot be judged by the same yardstick. It is stiff and unreal. Even the cooee from the horsemen — then a familiar Australian call, now sounds like an echo from some forgotten age. In the 'charge' scenes, a great deal of credit must go to such brilliant cameramen as George Heath, Frank Hurley, Tasman Higgins and John Howes. Every movement of horse and rider, from sliding down sand dunes to leaping over enemy fortifications, was splendidly captured on film. Charles Chauvel was aided by two excellent art directors from Cinesound — Eric Thompson and J. Alan Kenyon. Kenyon created a complete Arabian village for the sand hills between Cronulla and Kurnell, and tall palm trees were duplicated to implant in the barren soil.

It was refreshing to see the excellent reviews, followed by record seasons in Australia and overseas. Chauvel's timing had been perfect.

> The famous charge is as dynamic in its dramatic realism — and the sustained battle action is as imaginative as any Hollywood or English production. The fierce hand-to-hand combat is something that has to be seen before it can be fully appreciated.

Charles Chauvel would never equal his *Forty Thousand Horsemen* — an outstandingly successful Australian production that hit the financial jackpot.

Argosy Films was the last company to honour the agreement with the NSW Government and supplied two films, *The Power and the Glory* and *That Certain Something*. After the release of the two features, Argosy Films like Cinesound, closed down.

The Power and the Glory went to the Sydney Mayfair Theatre on 4 April 1941. This film combined exciting entertainment, with good technical skill and superb photography by the old master, Arthur Higgins. The aerial scenes were described as having a quiet realism. (Aerial photography was by George Malcolm and Bert Nicholas.) The RAAF was used for the flying sequences — but later in the war, the Wirraways featured in a disastrous sequel that was real. These outmoded machines were all that Australia possessed for the defence of Darwin, and young airmen were blasted from the skies, or destroyed before they could take off from the ground, by the vastly superior Japanese Zeros. The second Argosy Film *That Certain Something* was billed at the Mayfair, on 22 May. Originally designed on the lines of a Clara Bow picture that had been directed by American Clarence Badger — Argosy tried to repeat its success in an Australian setting, using the same director. Unlike Badger's previous Australian assignment, *Rangle River,* it failed dismally. Technically the production was first class, but the storyline was weak. It told of a demure girl (Megan Edwards) who wins a screen role after overcoming the prejudices of a producer (Lou Vernon) and stiff opposition from a glamorous rival (Thelma Grigg). Howard Carven was the poster artist hero, and Ronald Morse a pseudo French producer. The camera work was flat.

The War Years

In 1941 Rupert Kathner remained productive and on 21 November had *Racing Luck* at the Sydney Haymarket Theatre. Made with a maximum of expense, it lacked story and direction. However Darby Munro, the jockey, publicly stated that it was the best Australian picture he had ever seen. Raymond Longford's last screen appearance was in *Racing Luck*. It was a swan song unworthy of Australia's greatest silent film director

Although the war virtually killed the Australian film industry, in photography at least, this country held its own. Damien Parer took his camera to the Owen Stanley Ranges for his *Kokoda Front Line,* a record of steaming jungles, bitter fighting and of wounded Australians being carried over tortuous trails and precipitous paths. It won for Parer and Cinesound America's first Academy Award for an Australian production.

Nineteen forty-two provided a co-production *A Yank in Australia* from Austral-American Productions. Directed by Alfred Goulding, it starred Al Thomas, Gus and Kitty Bluett. As a film it was worthy of even less attention than *Racing Luck,* and had one charity showing in Brisbane in 1944. Nineteen forty-three fared even worse — a complete blank.

3.2   *A rare photograph of director Rupert Kathner, with actor George Lloyd on the set of "Racing Luck". In this film silent film director Raymond Longford played his last "bit" role in talkies. (Photo by courtesy of Harry Davidson)*

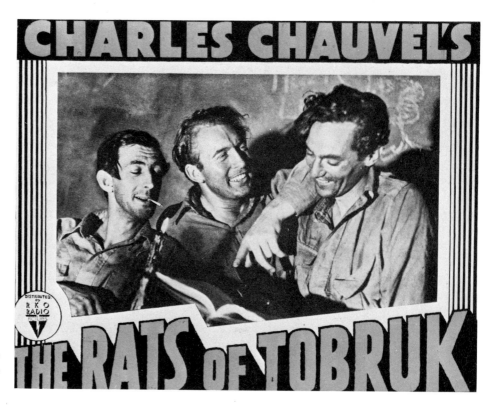

3.3 *Chips Rafferty, Grant Taylor, and Peter Finch in a light-hearted moment at Tobruk.*

Nineteen forty four provided one film that had a reasonable release — *Rats of Tobruk*. Directed by Charles Chauvel it was an unworthy successor to *Forty Thousand Horseman*. Yet most of the cast were excellent performers — Grant Taylor, Chips Rafferty and Peter Finch as 'Rats' and Mary Gay, a nurse. On the other hand, capable comedians Joe Valli and George Wallace were given such poor material, that they were humourless and embarrassing. It was only in the action sequences that Chauvel recaptured some of the magic of his previous success.

One critic summed up the picture in this cynical fashion:

> We know that Taylor, Rafferty and Finch are going somewhere, when the camera opens up with them droving in Queensland. But their arrival in Tobruk deserves a better fate, historically.

The years dragged on. In 1945 came another Austral-American production with direction credited to Hartney J. Arthur. *Red Sky in the Morning* does not appear to have been screened under that title. It was acquired by Arrow Films, re-edited, re-titled and released in suburban theatres in NSW and Victoria as *Escape at Dawn*.

Australian film makers received a severe jolt when the overseas invasion began — headed by Ealing Studios that eventually took over the National Productions' Studio at Pagewood. From then until the end of 1961, English and American companies made a total of eighteen films. Australia during the same period, equalled the total, but some were never screened, and others had only minimal releases. This foreign incursion added few riches to the local film front. Australia gained nothing and learnt precious little. One lesson provided by this period that Australia still has not heeded is that co-productions are lethal where this country is concerned.

Ealing Productions

Ealing's curtain raiser and most successful picture was *The Overlanders*. Directed by Harry Watt, and screened at the Sydney Lyceum on 27

September 1946, it won for the director a Jackeroo Award from the Royal Empire Society. Handled in semi-documentary style, it related the trials of a cattle drive from the Kimberleys to Queensland during a threatened Japanese invasion. Fording swollen streams, a cattle stampede, and animals falling over the edge of a cliff on a narrow mountain pass were just a few of the hardships depicted. *The Overlanders* was superbly photographed by Osmond Borrodaile, and the leading role of a rugged boss drover was ideal for Chips Rafferty. Excellent support was given by John Nugent Hayward, John Fernside, and Jean Blue.

Eureka Stockade — another Ealing production screened at the Sydney Lyceum on the 6 May 1949. This film revealed that Harry Watt wasn't so successful in the field of straight drama. Scenes like the attack on the Stockade by the militia, stuntman Jim Gray posing as a miner being thrown down a mine shaft; and the fire at Bentley's 'Eureka Hotel' were well-staged and cleverly photographed by Australian George Heath. Yet the production itself was uneven, and Chips Rafferty as Peter Lalor wasn't convincing. The best actors were Peter Finch in the minor role of John Humffray of the Ballarat Reform League, and Jack Fegan as the agitating Irish miner Timothy Hayes. English members of the cast were Gordon Jackson and Jane Barrett.

Chips Rafferty provided a better character study in the next Ealing picture *Bitter Springs*. Ralph Smart was the director this time, and camera work was handled by Australians George Heath and Ross Wood. First shown in London in July 1950, it had its Australian release on 25 August. Once again the venue was the Sydney Lyceum. Rafferty played the strong-willed head of the family that took up a holding claimed by a tribe of Aborigines. The family used firearms to keep them at bay. Michael Pate as a Northern Territory policeman warned the white settlers of the dangers attached to their continuous occupation of the land. Like *Eureka Stockade, Bitter Springs*

3.4 *Charles Bud Tingwell (R) about to land an old fashioned punch to the jaw of Gordon Jackson. Jean Blue is in the centre, and Chips Rafferty in the background. A scene from "Bitter Springs" shot in South Australia.*

lacked dramatic tension and was dismissed as a 'refreshing and pleasant trifle'. English comedian Tommy Trinder as a 'new chum' was included solely for laughs that were few and far between. Other cast members were Gordon Jackson, Charles Bud Tingwell, Nonnie Peifer, Jean Blue, and child star Nicky Yardley.

The Shiralee directed by Leslie Norman was the next film off the Ealing production line. This was first shown in London on 11 July 1957, followed by its screening in Scone, NSW on 17 August, and Sydney's St James Theatre, 22 August. The English were certainly not revealing to the Australians the art of successful film making. *The Shiralee* suffered from patchy photography, unconvincing characterisations, and very dull interior settings. In it, Peter Finch leaves his faithless wife in Sydney and goes on the track taking his daughter — not out of love, but out of spite. The girl eventually wins her father's affection after she narrowly misses death. He wins a divorce and is given custody of the child, but not before he is beaten up by the thugs who are employed by his ex-wife's lover. Finch isn't brutal enough in the earlier scenes but overall handles his role competently. It is young Dana Wilson as his daughter who steals the show. Elizabeth Sellers portrays the wife, and Sidney James and Tessie O'Shea (two English performers) are a friendly, outback couple.

However, these Ealing productions were to prove only one point — they provided work for Australian actors and technicians — but contributed precious little to the progress of the local industry itself.

By 1960 Ealing Studios were in full retreat. They had arrived in Australia to build up Pagewood Studio to the extent of $200 000, but prior to the release of *The Siege of Pinchgut* they packed their cameras and equipment worth $80 000 in sawdust and despatched the lot to England. Pagewood had once again become a 'white elephant'.

Ealing's swan song, *The Siege of Pinchgut* was premiered at Sydney's Embassy Theatre on 3 March 1960. Ironically enough it was directed by Harry Watt who fourteen years previously had commenced Ealing production in Australia with *The Overlanders.*Overseas artists dominated the cast — Heather Sears, Aldo Ray, Victor Maddern, Neil McCallum, Carlo Justini and Barbara Mullins. The Australians in minor roles were Gerry Duggan (as the caretaker of Fort Denison — 'Pinchgut'), and Grant Taylor and Deryck Barnes (as policemen).

English Productions

Perhaps one of the most delightful films made by England in Australia was *Bush Christmas*. It was produced and directed by Ralph Smart for Gaumont British Children's Entertainment Films. This time a great deal of credit must go to Australia in cameraman George Heath and cast members Chips Rafferty, John Fernside and Stan Tolhurst (as three horse thieves) and the junior brigade of Nicky Yardley (who stole the show), Helen Grieve, Michael Yardley and Aboriginal Neza Saunders. With a maximum of action, a minimum of dialogue, and the magnificent scenery of the Blue Mountains as a backdrop, it followed the adventures of the children trailing horse thieves. It was featured at Sydney's Embassy Theatre on 19 December 1947.

3.5 *Neza Saunders (L) and Nicky Yardley standing, watching the horse thieves, in the charming English-produced children's film "Bush Christmas". (1947)*

Wherever she Goes, produced by Fauna Films and directed by Michael Gordon, was first screened in London on 28 January 1951, but did not reach the Sydney Lyceum until 30 May 1952. Dealing with the early life of Australian concert painist Eileen Joyce, critics summed the film up in three words: 'lack of showmanship'. It was felt that it had little to recommend it beyond Suzanne Barrett's performance as the child and the playing of the soundtrack by Eileen Joyce herself. The supporting cast contained Nigel Lovell, Muriel Steinbeck, and Clem Dawe.

Robbery Under Arms, screened at Bourke and Port Augusta on 4 December 1957, and Sydney's State Theatre on 12 December, was a J. Arthur Rank Organisation production which wasn't worth the time that went into making it. Any resemblance to the original story by Rolf Boldrewood was purely coincidental. Directed by Jack Lee, the opening was uninspired and only the colour cameras saved it from being a complete disaster. Peter Finch, much more at home as Captain Starlight, the gentleman bushranger, than in *The Shiralee,* completely overshadowed the remainder of the cast, making the story of Dick and Jim Marston a mere side issue. The brothers were portrayed by Ronald Lewis and David McCallum. Jill Ireland was the gentle bride and Maureen Swanson was the fiery mistress of Ronald Lewis. Only the scenery of the superb locations chosen gave *Robbery Under Arms* any real distinction.

The final English effort — and a very feeble one — was *The Bungala Boys* made by Jimar Pictures for the Children's Film Foundation. Directed by Jim Jeffrey, this 'quickie' was expertly photographed by Australian Carl Kayser ... even though the cameraman had to film outdoors in continuous rain. The story in a nutshell was that of two brothers who formed a surf club for a Sydney beach that hadn't been previously patrolled by lifesavers. Leonard Teale who appeared in the film stated that Jeffrey expected five young actors without previous experience to row a surf boat out to sea. This sequence had to be filmed many times, as some were washed overboard during a heavy swell, and others voluntarily abandoned the boat when the sea became too rough. The catch to *The Bungala Boys* was that the voices were dubbed in England and Leonard Teale was shocked to hear that he had acquired a high-pitched Cockney accent. It was premiered in England on 2 December 1961.

America Steps In

The American invasion provided a very mixed bag — some films were good; others were utter trash. Columbia Pictures led the 'Yankee Doodle' run in 1946 in a praiseworthy style with *Smithy.* Australian and ex-Cinesound director Ken G. Hall was responsible for the bouquets bestowed upon the picture as he had gathered around him cameraman George Heath, scenic artist J. Alan Kenyon (whose reproduction of a room in Buckingham Palace was a masterpiece), and used such players as Ron Randell, Charles 'Bud' Tingwell, Muriel Steinbeck, John Tate, Joy Nicholls and John Dease. As a bonus he had Federal politician W.M. Hughes and flier P.G. Taylor in this picture. Smithy traces the life of Sir Charles Kingsford Smith from World War I, to his disappearance over the Bay of Bengal. It was hailed as the best feature film yet made in Australia and was exhibited at Sydney's State Theatre on 27 June 1946.

If *Smithy* was the best American-financed film made in Australia, *The Kangaroo Kid* was the worst. Produced by Allied Australian Films — a joint USA-Australian venture — and directed by Lesley Selander, it was nothing more than a snail-paced 'meat pie' Western. Embassy Pictures were associated with this film, but in essence it was more an American feature than Australian right through to the leading roles. This co-production put yet another local film maker out of business. With Americans Jock O'Mahoney, Veda Ann Borg, Douglas Dumbrille and Martha Hyer as leads, the token performances by Australians Grant Taylor, Guy Doleman, Alec Kellaway and Jack Fegan did nothing to enhance the value of the film. On camera, proven Australian cinematographers Harry Malcolm and Bren Brown were camera operator and assistant cameraman respectively. It came to the Sydney Victory Theatre, 2 March 1951.

Twentieth Century Fox, already holding a major share in Hoyts, turned its covetous eyes towards the film production aspect in this country. Lewis Milestone and prized technicolour cameras were despatched to Australia to make *Kangaroo.* Milestone took a horrified look at the script and advised his

3.6   Charles Bud Tingwell (L) in his first speaking role in "Smithy". He is wearing his own service uniform.

3.7   Ron Randell and W.M. (Billy) Hughes (a former Prime Minister) in "Smithy". This was handled by former Cinesound director Ken G. Hall for Columbia Pictures.

bosses to have it deodorised. He looked around the countryside, and found a far more interesting story that portrayed Australia with more sincerity than the screenplay he had read. The director was impolitely informed to shut up or pack up. Looking as his bank balance, Milestone whipped through *Kangaroo* as if making a 'quickie' sequel to *The Kangaroo Kid*.

This $500 000 production stands as a monolith to moneyed mutilation. It was premiered at New York's Roxy Theatre on 16 May 1952 to a blurb of publicity that was unbelievable rubbish: 'The wild Aborigines of Australia dance a blood-tingling corroboree'; 'see animals extinct everywhere else for 60 million years'; 'see the land that time forgot'. Despite such 'time capsule' superlatives, *Kangaroo* was to be cited as a reason why American companies did not make films in Australia. No mention was made of a superficial and threadbare script, nor of Milestone's protests about it.

The now defunct Melbourne *Argus* awarded the booby prize to Maureen O'Hara and Peter Lawford in a review of the best and worst films of 1952. *Kangaroo* was described as the film 'we expected so much from, and received so little in return.' Just how un-Australian *Kangaroo* really was is left to a scene where a well-dressed man handed his luggage to a hotel porter and asked him to mind his 'swag'. Two episodes of the picture that supposedly depicted life on an outback cattle station (or should it be ranch?) is a savage fight with stockwhips between Richard Boone and Peter Lawford, and a windmill going berserk in a windstorm. But those Twentieth Century boys gave *Kangaroo* the Hollywood razzamatazz by holding the Australian premiere simultaneously in Brisbane, Canberra, Melbourne, Adelaide, and Port Augusta on 4 June 1952.

Twentieth Century Fox financed two moderately budgeted films later in *Smiley* and *Smiley gets a Gun* — and amazingly enough these were far more successful than the vastly over-rated *Kangaroo*. Both were produced and directed by Englishmen Anthony Kimmins. When *Smiley* opened at the Sydney Mayfair Theatre on 6 December 1956, it was received with genuine

3.8 *Jock Levy, Grant Taylor, Jack Fegan, and John Tate in a prelude to a brawl in "Smiley" — a 20th Century Fox release.*

3.9 *Charles Bud Tingwell as the schoolteacher in "Smiley" directed by Anthony Kimmins. On the receiving end is Colin Petersen.*

affection. Described as a fresh, engaging and beautifully directed film it had an added attraction — a theme song 'A Little Boy called Smiley' sung on the soundtrack by Australian zither player, Shirley Abicair. Set in a typical outback town with its red dust-prone street lined with peppercorn and chestnut trees, there was the usual hotel, general store, the corrugated house rooves, and the inevitable police station.

Smiley (Colin Peterson) a small, barefoot boy, strives desperately to save enough money to purchase a bicycle. However everything goes wrong. In a mud fight with the schoolmaster's son he smashes a church window. Away go his savings. His father (Reginald Lye) locates Smiley's second hoard and uses it for drink. The boy angrily seizes a cricket bat and accidently hits his father on the head. He rushes out of the house firmly believing that he has killed his parent. He runs straight into the police sergeant (Chips Rafferty) who questions him regarding a package that he delivered to an Aboriginal camp. It is thought to contain opium. Smiley runs away and is found by a boundary rider (Guy Doleman). The opium pedler is finally arrested and Smiley purchases his bike. Bruce Archer was Smiley's friend, Sir Ralph Richardson the bush parson, John McCallum the suave villain, and Charles Bud Tingwell, the headmaster. *Smiley* was one of the happy memories of a period when the Australian film front had little to boast about.

The sequel *Smiley gets a Gun* was the big attraction at Sydney's Esquire Theatre on 18 December 1958. There were a few changes. This time Keith Calvert was *Smiley* and Australian Ross Wood replaced Ted Scaife as director of photography, although he had been camera operator on the original *Smiley*. Smiley this time is promised a pea rifle if he can keep out of trouble for a month. He tries hard enough, but is blamed for a goat being in church, a bushfire and the theft of the local witch's hoard of gold. There were some delightful characters in the picture — Dame Sybil Thorndike as the witch, Chips Rafferty again as the police sergeant, Leonard Teale, and an outstanding portrayal by Ruth Cracknell as the village organist who fancied herself a queen of song, and a censor of public morals.

In 1959 two American films *Summer of the Seventeenth Doll* and *On the Beach* were of great interest to Australians generally. The former was based on a stage play by Ray Lawler; the latter on a novel by Nevil Shute. Both originally had one thing in common — they were set in Melbourne. However the Hecht-Hill-Lancaster production *Summer of the Seventeenth Doll* had its location switched to Sydney. Probably director Leslie Norman thought it more interesting to have views of the Harbour Bridge etc. than the sleezy hovels of Carlton.

When the play *Summer of the Seventeenth Doll* was a huge success in London, America paid $250000 for the film rights. However, when it failed on Broadway, John Mills and Anne Baxter were named as replacements for Burt Lancaster and Rita Hayworth, who originally were to appear in the picture. The world premiere was held at Sydney's Century Theatre, on 2 December 1959. Additional overseas stars were Ernest Borgnine and Angela Lansbury. Australians in the cast were Ethel Gabriel who gave an outstanding performance, Vincent Ball, Janette Craig, Deryck Barnes, Dana Wilson (child star of *The Shiralee*), Al Thomas and Frank Wilson.

Critics were unimpressed. The views of Bondi, the Harbour Bridge and

Luna Park were scenically superior to the musty atmosphere and shabbiness of Carlton, but the whole atmosphere of the play was missing because of the change in locale. The cane cutters lusty arrival in the city at the end of the working season, their thirst for women and grog, and their empty promises, drifted into nothing more than a fleeting romance against a scenic background. The bitter-sweet mood of another doll, another visit, and the dreary passage of the years extending from that first exciting physical encounter was lost in the play's transfer to the screen.

On the Beach was premiered in eighteen major cities throughout the world (including Sydney and Melbourne) on 17 December 1959. Described by the official Soviet News Agency *Tass* as 'the film that relates a story that never occurred and must never occur', this Stanley Kramer production was far more successful than *Summer of the Seventeenth Doll*. However, author Nevil Shute was so dissatisfied with the treatment of his story, that he refused to attend the premiere.

A surprisingly good performance was given by ex-dancer Fred Astaire, as a racing car driver who participates in the Australian Grand Prix, where contestants show an utter disregard for life, as the end of the world isn't far away. On the other hand Ava Gardner as an Australian girl was hopelessly miscast.

More American Productions

The Sundowners directed by Fred Zinnemann was filmed in Australia and based on a book by Jon Cleary. Capturing more of the genuine atmosphere of this country than most of the other overseas films produced here, it was premiered at the Radio City Cinema, New York on 8 December 1960 to an audience of 6000 people. It was nominated as one of the ten best American films of 1960, and Robert Mitchum was listed as the best actor. It did not reach

3.10 Anne Baxter (the barmaid) and Ernest Borgnine (the cane cutter) are the "seasonal" lovers in "Summer Of The Seventeenth Doll' directed by Leslie Norman. The change in location from Melbourne to Sydney was not hailed with delight.

3.11 Anne Baxter, Ernest Borgnine, and Australian Ethel Gabriel in "Summer Of The Seventeenth Doll" released through United Artists.

3.12 Gregory Peck, and Ava Gardner (badly miscast as an Australian girl) in "On The Beach". Frankston on the Mornington Peninsula and Williamstown, a Melbourne suburb, were used extensively for location shots.

3.13 Fred Astaire, Gregory Peck and Ava Gardner in "On The Beach" directed by Stanley Kramer. Astaire, usually a song-and-dance man played an excellent dramatic role as a racing-car enthusiast.

the Embassy, Sydney or Athenaeum until 30 November 1961, almost twelve months after the original American screening.

It was a rambling story in which nothing eventuated, although scenes of beer swilling, sheep shearing contests and two-up contained gems of drama and comedy. A spectacular bush fire provided realistic elements of despair and heroism. Robert Mitchum portrayed an itinerant drover and Deborah Kerr played his wife, with Michael Anderson Jnr as the son. Peter Ustinov and Glynis Johns were in supporting roles. Australians in the cast were Jack Fegan (who fought Mitchum in the picture), Leonard Teale, Gwen Plumb, and author Jon Cleary.

Shadow of the Boomerang was made in Australia to lend support to Billy Graham's evangelistic campaign. With two Americans, Dick Jones and Georgia Lee in the main roles, it was released at the Liberty Theatre, Sydney on 17 August 1961. Its central theme is racial tolerance. The story is simple: a young American and his sister, by some means known only to the scriptwriter, run an Australian cattle station. The brother's racial prejudice causes confrontation with the Aborigines. Jimmy Little is an Aboriginal stockman; Vaughan Tracey, a flying doctor; and Margaret Hathaway a nursing sister. Technical assistance is supplied by Cinesound. It was an unpretentious film that rated no great enthusiasm or criticism.

3.14   Peter Ustinov, Robert Mitchum, Deborah Kerr and Michael Anderson Junr (dressed as a jockey) in Warner Bros. "The Sundowners". The race sequences were under the supervision of the Australian jockey, the late Neville Selwood.

Australian Efforts

There was little of merit to warrant unstinted praise for Australian films. Some productions were poor, many mediocre, while others held some promise for the future. New film makers arrived overnight and hurried off into oblivion soon afterwards. It was a desperate time when men strove, often unsuccessfully, to do something about the whole sorry state of the local industry.

Eric Porter, better known for his cartoon work, made one of his few excursions into film drama with *A Son is Born*. Directed and produced by him, possibly the picture's greatest claim to fame is that it was shot in one of the world's smallest studios (about 17 m by 11 m). A woman (Muriel Steinbeck) leaves her child (Peter Dunstan) and a thoroughly unpleasant husband (Peter Finch) after many years of sheer frustration. She marries John McCallum (who had to age some twenty years to play the role). Ron Randell portrays the grown-up son who is just as despicable as his father.

One critic felt that the film had a character of its own, with location shots providing a realism that was effective. Seen at Sydney's Victory Theatre on 20 September 1946, it did not enjoy a twenty-one weeks' season like *The Overlanders* that was released in Sydney one week later.

In 1947, the newly established National Film Board under Stanley Hawes began to demonstrate that Australia, in the documentary field at least, could throw down the gauntlet. This fact was revealed in a thoroughly convincing manner with the notable *School in the Mail Box*. Happily for the industry, the National Film Board (later the Commonwealth Film Unit and ultimately Film Australia) proved that it had the talent and ability to remain on the scene.

A far different picture is painted for the feature film side of the industry. Embassy Pictures was yet another Australian independent production company that arrived without a fanfare of trumpets and disappeared one year later, just as quietly. Their first picture, *Always another Dawn* directed by T. O. McCreadie, was the main attraction at Sydney's Embassy Theatre on 24 September 1948. Starring Charles Bud Tingwell, Guy Doleman, Betty McDowell and Queenie Ashton, this war-time story had realistic battle scenes featuring units of the Royal Australian Navy, and provided an insight into naval procedure at Flinders Naval Depot. First class camera work by Harry

3.15   *Queenie Ashton as the mother, and Charles Bud Tingwell as her son who work a small farm in New South Wales. At the outbreak of World War 2, the son follows the tradition set by his father (who had been a naval officer) and enlists as a naval rating. The film — "Always Another Dawn" — 1948.*

3.16   *Charles Bud Tingwell and Margo Lee in "Into The Straight". Director T.O. McCreadie is bottom R. Cameraman Harry Malcolm is partly obscured. (Still by courtesy of Charles Tingwell).*

3.17 *A Randwick racecourse sequence in "Into The Straight". Jockey George Moore is on Horse Number 2, and Harry Malcolm is behind camera. (Still by courtesy of National Library and Harry Malcolm.)*

3.18 *A young Michael Pate studying his lines for one of the "Sons Of Matthew". (Still by courtesy Bruce Moran.)*

Malcolm deserves special mention, however the handling of its rather tragic story was unimpressive.

On 15 July 1949, Embassy's second feature *Into the Straight* had its premiere at Perth's Theatre Royal. Directed by T. O. McCreadie, Charles Bud Tingwell once more headed the cast. Other players were Muriel Steinbeck, George Randall and Nonie Peifer. The storyline of *Into the Straight* followed a sporting family that cherished a lifelong ambition to own a horse that had won the Melbourne Cup. Authentic background atmosphere was obtained at the St Aubin's Stud, Scone (NSW), while excitement was captured at Randwick and Flemington.

Perth turned it into a gala occasion with searchlights and a band. The road in front of the theatre was cleared and the guests arrived in formal attire. *Into the Straight* had a three weeks' season, then transferred to the Princess Theatre, Fremantle. The amazing thing was that attendance figures for the opening days eclipsed those of *The Overlanders* which had until that time held the record for the Theatre Royal. Despite the warmth of the Western Australian reception, Embassy Pictures decided to call it a day.

At the St James Theatre (now the Palace) in Melbourne on 28 September 1949 was an MGM Silver Anniversary Picture, *The Inlanders*. This very interesting documentary was produced by Kingcroft Productions for the Australian Inland Missions. Special music was composed by Australian John Antill. Inland padre 'Skipper' Partridge was the key figure that linked sequences in Broken Hill, Birdsville, Alice Springs and Tarcoola.

The most important Australian entry in 1949 was *Sons of Matthew*. It carried the name of one director who had remained on the local scene — Charles Chauvel. The picture was advertised as being too big for one theatre so it enjoyed the unique experience on 16 December of opening at two Sydney theatres simultaneously, the Lyceum and Victory. In this picture, Michael Pate played his first important role, having had a bit part as an Arab in *Forty Thousand Horsemen*. He was cast as the eldest of the O'Riordan boys, with Tommy Burns, Ken Wayne, John Ewart and John Unicomb as the four brothers. John O'Malley was the rugged Irish father and Thelma Scott his Devonshire wife. Jack Fegan played the uncle and Wendy Gibb was the romantic temptress, Cathie. On camera were Bert Nicholas and Carl Kayser (who did such brilliant work later for *Jedda*). The sheer magic of the camerawork revealed the harshness of drought; the frightening devastation of fire; the grandeur and enthralling beauty of rolling clouds over the Lamington Plateau and McPherson Range... that rocky magnificence of land that the

rugged O'Riordans claimed for their own. All this made viewing a memorable experience. And who can forget the flippant, lively lilt of 'The Goanna Song' by Rod Mansfield, which heralded the appearance of the sons of the soil? One critic was not impressed: 'It began with the ambition of being a large-scale family drama, then faded into a triangle between two brothers and a girl.' Viewed later on television in April 1969, it is hard to justify this critic's comments. There was a quiet sincerity about the acting, and an undoubted enthusiasm on the part of the players. Thelma Scott was outstanding as she efficiently spanned the years from youth to middle age, with dignity and charm.

The critic's reference to a family saga drifting into a romantic triangle is sheer rot. The sons set off to carve a future for themselves, leaving their parents and their home in which they knew both tragedy and security. When the situation finally arises where two brothers fall in love with the same girl, the inevitable triangle must and does develop.

From success to failure! Arthur Collins, the American director who had introduced *Seven Little Australians* (1939) came up with *Strong is the Seed*. It's only release under that title was at the Majestic Theatre, Adelaide on 4 March 1949. (Even today there are businessmen in Bairnsdale, Victoria, who wonder whatever happened to the money they invested in this picture.) Based on the life of William Farrer, the great Australian who did so much for the wheat industry of this country, it was filmed by Ross Wood and starred Guy Doleman in the leading role. Lloyd Lamble was cast as his friend. It was purchased by Ray Films, cut from 2195 m to 1829 m and re-titled *The Farrer Story*. This abridged edition was released in the United Kingdom by Monarch Film Corporation. Later, a further 244 m were deleted and it was released in Australian country towns in October 1952.

Unfortunately calamity reigned throughout 1951 and 1952. Rupert Kathner and *The Glenrowan Affair* headed the list. Portion of the filming took place in the new Sydney Studio of Commonwealth Film Laboratories, Turrella, with Harry Malcolm on camera. It was screened at Sydney's Capitol Theatre on 17 August 1951. It was the same old Ned Kelly saga with a new twist. About the time the film was being made, a man claiming to be Dan Kelly was making headline news. That's right! In *The Glenrowan Affair* Dan Kelly escaped from the blazing hotel. Bob Chitty, ex-Melbourne footballer was Ned, and it was said later that if the picture had been billed as a comedy it would have done better business. Kathner himself played Aaron Sherritt, John Fernside was Father Gibney, and Stan Tolhurst, a blacksmith. Charles Bud Tingwell was narrator.

Renewed Effort: A Struggling Industry

On 21 September, the Commonwealth Government Jubilee Feature Film Contest (probably with the disastrous *The Glenrowan Affair* in mind), tried desperately to bolster a very flabby film industry. The conditions of entry were that it must be of at least one hour's duration and shot mainly in Australia. It had to be screened in this country at any time between 1 January 1901 and 15 November 1951. On 20 January 1952, the judges announced a special award for *Mike and Stefani*. Yet this film did not comply with at least two rules of the contest: it was not 'mainly shot in Australia' it was photographed in Europe; and it had not been screened in this country during the dates stated, instead, its first commercial screening was on 4 October 1953 at the Village Theatre, Watson's Bay, (Sydney) which at the time specialised in Continental films.

Mike and Stefani related the experiences of two Lithuanian displaced persons who decide to settle in Australia. The film was described as slow-moving, but one review stated that 'the way is still wide open for a good Australian film maker to search into the absorbing drama of human conflicts, hopes, and doubts, locked in the heart of every new Australian'.

On the day following the announcement of the Jubilee Film Awards, Chips Rafferty expressed positive views on one of the disturbing factors that had led to the decline of Australian film production.

> The Capital Issues Board has cut the throat of the industry by classifying film making as non-essential, and refusing capital to be raised for the local film producers.

Chips had hoped to make *The Green Opal* at Pagewood. A group of businessmen were prepared to back the film for world distribution. In addition thirteen three-reeler television featurettes were planned. When permission was requested to raise $240000, the Capital Issues Board rejected the application. Ken G. Hall backed Rafferty's statement by advising that it was planned to make *Robbery Under Arms* at the Pagewood studio. Two-thirds of the capital to make it had been guaranteed, but once again the Capital Issues Board had refused permission to raise the balance.

The next year, 1952, showed no signs of improvement. In fact it was disastrous. Producer David Bilcock Snr lost heavily and eventually his second feature *2000 Weeks* put him out of business. A. R. Harwood directed *Night Club* for Cambridge Film Productions, Box Hill (Melbourne). *Night Club* was Dick Harwood's last picture, and had only minor releases after its preview in December 1952 in Coburg (Melbourne). Photographer was Len Heitman, and music was composed by Geoff Kitchen. Stars were English comedian Joey Porter, Joan Bilceaux, singer Colin Crane, Joff Ellen (who later appeared in Melbourne television) and Frank Holbrook. The script was closely patterned on *Show Business* (1938) and opened on the usual angle — a

3.20 *Joan Bilceaux and Frank Holbrook.*

playboy, son of a wealthy grazier, becomes infatuated with a night club singer who, of course, is looking for a backer for a new show. The father, acting on advice from a show business friend, packs his son off to a country town. There, the playboy meets an old time vaudeville comedian who is producing a local revue. He backs the show, but when his ex-girlfriend learns that she is not included, she threatens to cause trouble. The comedian, however, recognises the night club singer as his wife who had deserted him many years previously.

Low-Budget Films

When Ealing left Australia, the Pagewood Studio was taken over by Associated TV Pty Ltd. Cameraman George Heath who had been so successful on English productions, and former Commonwealth Film Unit director Lee Robinson teamed with Chips Rafferty to make a series of low-budget films designed solely as supporting features.

The first Platypus Film was *The Phantom Stockman*. Although it contained some fisticuffs and a little gunplay, it lacked the action of even the average American cowboy film. But this 'meat pie' Western did return a handsome profit to the company. Chips Rafferty, displaying a great sense of salesmanship, pre-sold this $20 000 production to India, Pakistan, Burma, and Ceylon for $2 000. Then in Hollywood, while appearing in *Desert Rats*, Chips sold the American rights for $70 000. He added another $15 000 for the British rights. By that time Platypus was already $67 000 in the black. Australian takings were an added bonus.

The Phantom Stockman took twenty-six days to shoot in the hills around Alice Springs. In the cast were Jeanette Elphick (later Victoria Shaw), Guy Doleman, Max Orbiston, and Aboriginal painter Albert Namatjira. The story evolved around a wanderer, 'The Sundowner' (Chips Rafferty) who helps solve the murder of a station owner, and puts down a gang of cattle duffers. It was premiered at the Brisbane Tivoli Theatre on 4 June 1953.

The following year Platypus became Southern International (an unfortunate move for Chips Rafferty) and went to Thursday Island to make *King of the Coral Sea.* On 17 July 1954, it was premiered on the Island in an open air theatre. Underwater sequences were shot at Green Island by Noel Monkman, with the balance of the photography in the capable hands of Ross Wood. Rafferty as a pearler, discovers the body of a man in the ocean off Thursday Island. The dead man is an investigator following a lead concerning illegal smuggling of people into Australia through the Island. Rod Taylor, looking suave behind a moustache, is Rafferty's assistant. Charles Bud Tingwell is the owner of the pearling company who arrives in Thursday Island and falls in love with Ilma Adey. In the climax, Reginald Lye is unmasked as the leader of the smuggling organisation.

3.22   *Underwater cameraman Noel Monkman, Charles 'Bud' Tingwell, and Chips Rafferty during the filming of "King Of The Coral Sea".*

Four days after the release of *King of the Coral Sea,* a special editorial in *The Sydney Morning Herald* bemoaned the fact that the feature film side of the Australian industry was almost dormant, yet this country was actually producing some of the best documentaries in the world.

To prove the point *Back of Beyond* (a classic documentary) won the

3.21   *Opposite page: Jeanette Elphick and Chips Rafferty as the mysterious "Sundowner" in "The Phantom Stockman". The film was photographed in the Northern Territory by George Heath.*

3.23   *The mailman's truck approaching Birdsville — the end of the run.
Two native women and their children are waiting to greet him. Still from
the Shell film unit's "The Back of Beyond". Released in 1954, this multi-
award winning documentary was directed by John Heyer.*

3.24   *Mintulee of Thurabee better known in the Birdsville Track area as
Old Joe the Rainmaker, going through his rainmaking ceremony. In his
hand is a bunch of eagle hawk feathers. "Back Of Beyond" a Shell film
unit production was directed by John Heyer.*

Grand Prix at the annual International Documentary Film Festival in
Venice. It depicted a journey over the 483 km mail track from Maree in South
Australia, to Birdsville in Queensland. Ross Wood took photographic
honours, with superb direction from John Heyer, who was then with the Shell
Film Unit. Ross recalled that they lived in the desert for three months and ate
sand most of the time.

The feature film *Long John Silver* had its world premiere at Sydney's
Plaza Theatre on 16 December 1954. Produced by Treasure Island Pictures,
directed by Byron Haskin, and photographed by Ross Wood, this has been
classified as an Australian picture for a number of good reasons. It began
when American producer Joseph Kauffman wanted an English-speaking
country in which he could produce low-budget films. Along with American
director Byron Haskin, he chose Australia. Backed partly by American
finance, but mostly by collateral guaranteed by the Commonwealth Bank,
they commenced with a budget of $476000, but spent nearly $1 million on a
feature and twenty-six half-hour TV episodes. At that point the Commonwealth Bank stepped in and took over.* Part of the company's financial
problems was that one American banker reneged.

* *Cinema Papers* March 1975.

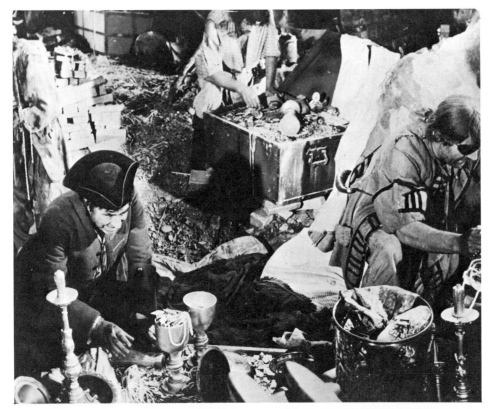

3.25 *Robert Newton as "Long John Silver" (left of photograph) shows pleasure and greed after discovering a treasure trove.*

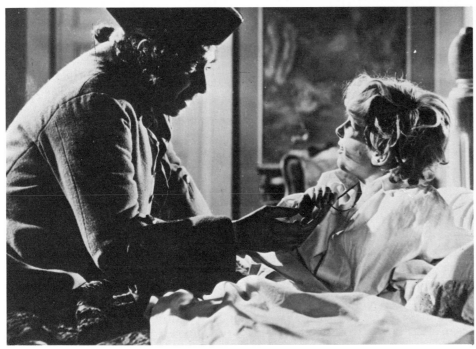

3.26 *Robert Newton as "Long John" is very interested in the locket that Kit Taylor is wearing.*

Haskin made the understatement of the year when he explained that *Long John Silver* wasn't a good feature. One English critic summed it up as: 'Robert Newton would appear to have told the cameraman, "Don't shoot until you see the whites of my eyes".' Remembering Newton's fondness for the bottle at the time, that would have been a very hard mission to accomplish. The TV shows, however, fared better and Leonard Teale who appeared in some of the twenty-six episodes, feels that they were ahead of their time. Photographed in colour they were filmed in the Pagewood Studios.

Cecil Holmes entered the low-budget area in 1955 with an Associated TV Production *Captain Thunderbolt* which was later released through Ray

Films. Interiors were shot in Pagewood and in a woolshed in Pyrmont. It had been completed some years previously, but did not obtain an initial release until 22 June 1955, and then only in the Capitol Theatre, Armidale (NSW). It was later screened in Sydney at the Lyric Theatre and was booked by Hoyts for their country circuit.

Two outstanding Australian cameramen of the period were undoubtedly Ross Wood and Carl Kayser. Kayser's work received accolades for *Jedda*. This film was edited in London, and although it was not the financial success it deserved to be; it is remembered today with a nostalgic wistfulness because it was Charles Chauvel's last feature film. Unfortunately it was not his greatest. First screened in Australia in the Star Theatre, Darwin, on 3 January 1955, *Jedda* captured the audiences' interest and retained it. It was the first film to show the centre of Australia in colour, and it showed the brilliance of the cool blue water and stark red cliffs of the outback. There were some magnificent long shots of Jedda and the warrior Marbuck on the crags above a glittering river.

Among critics there was the general impression that *Jedda* was technically perfect, but dramatically unsound. Darwin felt that 'it will probably prove to be the best advertisement Australia has had, since the discovery of the platypus.' Sydney regarded it as 'the most original and beautiful film to come out of Australia.' Wason Byers (a genuine Northern Territory station owner) who was cast as the tough, two-fisted boss drover, refused to attend the premiere when he learnt that his slow, deep, outback drawl had been replaced on the soundtrack.

Robert Tudawali played the Aborigine Marbuck who desires then wills the young Aboriginal girl, Jedda, to his camp fire. In one scene Jedda (Ngarla Kunoth) who has been reared by white foster parents (George Simpson-Lyttle and Betty Sutor), is seated at the piano when she looks at Aboriginal weapons, and hears the overpowering throb of the didgeridoo and the clack of music sticks. Marbuck is willing Jedda to his camp fire. She goes. At first the handsome warrior fascinates her, but his innate cruelty turns admiration into repugnance. Jedda's original lover, a half-caste stockman, accompanied by other Aborigines, sets out in pursuit. One man is taken by a crocodile in a muddy creek, another is killed by Marbuck. In a cave in the cliffs, Marbuck rapes Jedda — a scene handled with great finesse and delicacy by director and actors. Paul Reynell as the half-caste lover is too much a stage actor with a cultivated accent, which weakens the film considerably. Although slow moving at times, Chauvel's direction is most effective near the climax when Marbuck, outlawed by his tribe, slowly goes insane after the old men have pointed the bone, and sung the warrior to his death. In this sequence Robert Tudawali, an untrained actor, gives a superb performance.

After 1959, when Chauvel died, it appeared that all film records of *Jedda* had disappeared. However in 1972 Elsa Chauvel located in England the only existing copy. This was a black and white tri-separation print from which, by processing in combination with colour filters, *Jedda* was restored to its original brilliance. Ray Edmondson of the National Library and Colorfilm Laboratories, Sydney, reconstituted the film. *Jedda* was re-screened at the Boulevarde 'Blue' Cinema, Canberra, on 19 September 1974.

Feature Films Take a Down-Turn

With Chauvel's withdrawal from feature film making, the Australian film industry plummeted. At the time there was no talented director to replace him. The industry had to wait a decade and a half for a Peter Weir. Southern International made four films — none with distinction and mostly with limited returns. *Walk into Paradise* was released in 1956; *The Restless and the Damned,* a 1959 picture, was ignored completely; and in 1960 they released *Dust in the Sun* and *The Stowaway.* After this, like many other Australian companies, Southern International went out of business. Again here is an example of the dangers and pitfalls of co-production: Southern International had linked with a French production house, and made pictures that would cause even a skunk to retreat. Perhaps Chips Rafferty and Lee Robinson did have the right idea when they formed Platypus: modestly made pictures backed with good salesmanship did make money; more ambitious films cost the company money.

Walk into Paradise became the object of designated opposites, when it was re-titled *Walk into Hell* for TV screenings in America and Australia some years later. First shown at Sydney's St James Theatre on 24 October 1956, *Walk into Paradise* was the best of the co-productions, and Carl Kayser's photography was highly commended by the Cannes Film Festival Committee. The combination of Kayser and Australian actors Chips Rafferty and Reginald Lye provided the only highlights of the film. Reginald Lye who seldom gave a poor performance, was in complete character as a ragged prospector.

Set in New Guinea's swampy lowlands and magnificent highlands, it followed the journey of a patrol officer (Chips Rafferty) into Paradise Valley to prepare an air strip for geologists in search of oil. The massed tribes performed, completely oblivious to the camera, and the final 'sing-sing' on the grassy plains with blue-hazed mountains in the background was stirring and spectacular. The romance between two French players, Francoise Christophe and Pierre Cressoy, was very artificial. Francoise herself never once looked professional enough to be a doctor.

The Restless and the Damned with Americans Edmond O'Brien and Richard Basehart and Australians Reginald Lye and Nigel Lovell was a complete fiasco. It was never released in Australia, and must have placed a terrific strain upon the finances of Southern International. Now arises a cynical touch of black humour. The French version directed by Yves Allegret, with a dubbed soundtrack, believe it or not, was screened in America as *The Ambitious One* in 1959, and in 1964 on television as *The Climbers.*

In 1960 Southern International had two belated releases — *The Stowaway* a co-production, and their own feature *Dust in the Sun.* Both were exhibited at Sydney's Capital Theatre — the former on 27 May, the latter on 12 August. The main attraction of *The Stowaway* was the artistry displayed by Desmond Dickinson in capturing the natural beauty of Tahiti in colour. The plot centred around an inquiry agent (Reginald Lye) endeavouring to trace some mysterious Frenchman. For some reason best known to the French mystery writer Georges Simenon, the inquiry agent is pursued by another Frenchman (played by Italian Serge Reggiani) and an

English confidence man (Roger Livesey). Martine Carol was *The Stowaway* who fell in love with a ship's officer (Karl-Heinz Boehm). No doubt a large slice of the mystery was the inclusion of Arletty in the cast who made a brief and not very noteworthy appearance in a night club.

Before stifling a yawn, let's see whether *Dust in the Sun* offers more excitement!

Based on Jon Cleary's book *Justin Bayard*, the film was shot around Alice Springs. Once again Carl Kayser was able to reveal what a masterful cameraman he was, and how colourful the centre of Australia could be on film. Yet even with a good Australian story to work upon, Lee Robinson committed an unpardonable error. With the wide open spaces to call upon, he ignored the scenery and concentrated on the human drama at the station which he handled with a complete lack of finesse. Yet he had a Northern Territory policeman (Ken Wayne); an Aboriginal murderer (Robert Tudawali); the Kapunda tribe tracking the killer to prescribe their own type of justice; the murder of the English wife of the station owner (Jill Adams) by a half-caste stockman (Henry Murdock); the escape of both murderers; and a chase by both the Aborigines and the policeman. With all that going for him, Lee Robinson still failed to make an interesting film.

Following the collapse of Southern International, Australia drifted into a listless period of inactivity.

Doldrums For Independents

In 1956 Australia was represented at the Karlovy-Vary Film Festival, Czechoslovakia, and the Edinburgh Festival with *Three in One* an Australian Tradition Film directed by Cecil Holmes. The film was awarded a major prize in Czechoslovakia, and was written up favourably in *The London Times* on 20 September 1956, after the Scottish festival. *Three in One* included a story called 'A Load of Wood' by Frank Hardy and 'The Union Buries its Dead' by Lawson. Leonard Teale starred in 'A Load of Wood'. The story is set in Jindabyne in the Depression. It is winter and there is a severe shortage of wood. A militant labourer (Levy) talks his more timid friend (Teale) into cutting down a tree in a nearby paddock owned by a mean farmer. His idea is to distribute the wood among the poorer people in the district. The pair acquire a truck, and set out for the spot at the dead of night. (This is where Ross Wood's camera ability and Holmes' direction must receive full credit. With the aid of back lighting, an enormous shadow is seen on the wall of a building. Then as an anti-climax a small truck emerges.) The chopping of the wood causes the barking of the farmer's dog. They hastily load the truck, and climb aboard. The engine refuses to start, and in sheer desperation, the load of wood is pushed to the brink of a hill. As it commences its downhill run, the engine coughs then starts. The labourer gives away the wood, leaving his own woodshed empty. Exteriors were shot at Windsor (NSW) in approximately one week and interiors at Pagewood took only a few days. Despite overseas honours, *Three in One* was given the cold shoulder by Australian distributors, and had one short season at the Rex Theatre (later the Town Theatre) in Fortitude Valley, Brisbane on 21 June 1957.

3.27   "The Load Of Wood"
sequence in "Three in One" set in
the depression days. Leonard
Teale (far R) is one involved in
sawing down a farmer's tree
during the night, to obtain wood
for the town's people.

Joe Wilson's Mates which is included in the *Three in One* production was based on Lawson's story 'The Union Buries its Dead'. In this film a body is found near a creek, and a union card is discovered in the clothing. Blokes from a nearby pub decided to give him a decent burial because he was a union man. The day is very hot, and at every pub along the way, more followers drop off, until at the edge of town only four pall bearers are left. As the filming progressed, everyone realised that the best actors had been included in the 'drop-outs'. That was how Alexander Archdale appeared in a much more important role as a Shakespearean actor, and the Bushwackers Band were included to perform. With these additions, the story slowly drifted away from the original Lawsonian concept.

3.28   A stark shot from "The
Union Buries its Dead" in the
Cecil Holmes production "Three
In One".

Once again, Ross Wood's photography is magnificent. One memorable shot was taken from the interior of the horse-drawn hearse showing the line of mourners — and another, the hearse and mourners are outlined against the skyline as they climb the hill to the cemetery. Charles Tasman, the driver of the hearse, was in his sixties at the time, and knew little about horses. Coming down the hill he turned the team to provide an additional shot for Ross Wood, but overturned the vehicle, injuring his back. Another notable member of the cast was Reginald Lye.

Joe Wilson's Mates, was purchased by Hoyts and released as a featurette. It was the predominating shades of the Comintern that frightened local film men. With the disaster of *Three in One* backers beat a hurried retreat like two-up players during a police raid. For years afterwards, independent production became dirty words in the Australian businessman's vocabulary.

Holmes who had produced *Three in One* and *Joe Wilson's Mates* selected another film which seems to be completely out of character with the other two. This was *The City* and it is difficult to comprehend why he chose to produce it. Starring Joan Lander, Brian Vicary, Gordon Glenwright and Betty Lucas, it was a dull story of an engaged couple being unable to obtain a house. They quarrel and part. The idea of mateship is stretched beyond the point of credulity when the man's workmates promise to help raise the money to build a home. The lovers are then re-united.

Promoter Lee Gordon entered the ranks of 'one shot' producers in 1959 — and not very successfully — with *Rock 'n' Roll*. Lee Robinson late of Southern International, was director. Those trying to 'out shout' the band were Fabian, Col Joye, Johnny O'Keefe and Johnny Reb. After a very brief season in a large NSW provincial city, it was hastily withdrawn when Twentieth Century Fox threatened legal action because Fabian was under contract to them at the time.

The 1950s closed on a note of despair, but no one realised that the next decade would lay the foundations for an unbelievable revival.

4
The Industry Stirs Again

No life that breathes with human breath
Has ever truly long'd for death.

Tennyson

The sleeping film industry tossed restlessly and although new life was not yet apparent, there was a stirring of fresh hope. But even the sixties had trouble at the barrier and got off to a bad start.

In nineteen sixty-one Tas-American TV Corporation Ltd produced *Port of Escape.* Directed by John Calvert, and starring Calvert and Philippine singer Pilita Corrales, this stands as a good example of how to lose money without even trying. Calvert had 'honey tongued' a number of Tasmanian investors into backing him in this film venture. When the backers started to ask leading questions as to the progress of the film, Calvert disappeared with all 'evidence'. Today it is debatable as to whether the production was ever completed, but one positive fact still remains — The Tasmanian 'angels' like the Bairnsdale backers of *Strong is the Seed* are still waiting, rather disconsolately, for any returns for their investment.

When 1962 arrived, the bookies wouldn't even quote odds as to a positive revival of the Australian Film Industry. Many awkward questions were being asked repeatedly in Federal Parliament. Yet when the Vincent Report arrived in that same year, it was not debated in Parliamentary circles. Consequently its recommendations were as helpful to a flat industry as was the New South Wales Quota Act, regardless of the fact that it did contain a request for support for local television, and the making of feature films.

During the period 1962-67 the feature film industry was so badly mauled that the urgent need for the services of an undertaker was apparent. In 1962 only one feature film was produced — and that one was for children. *They Found a Cave,* a Vistatone-Island Production, was the attraction at the now demolished Grosvenor Theatre, Melbourne, on 21 December. The timing was just right for the Christmas holidays. Directed by Andrew Steane, it was filmed in colour in Tasmania. A simple and delightful tale, it involved five youngsters (four of them being new arrivals from England) who found adventure on a farm. The children were able to foil the efforts of an adult couple who were intending to rob their aunt, while she was in hospital. Larry Adler, the well-known American harmonica player, supplied the music, and Beryl Meekin headed the cast.

The lean years became downright emaciated, and it wasn't until 1965 that the industry gave another flicker of life. *Clay* directed by Giorgio Mangiamele had its world premiere at the Cannes Film Festival in May. In September it was screened at the Commonwealth Film Festival in London, and later won a Silver Award in Australia. It had a commercial showing at the Palais Theatre, St Kilda (Melbourne) on 25 August 1966.

As a cameraman, Mangiamele was dramatically impressive, especially when he turned his camera on rural settings that stood out starkly in deeply etched black and white. The acting was not of such a high standard. George Dixon played an escaped murderer who sought sanctuary in the artists' colony of Montselvat (Victoria) and Janine Lebedew was the girl who fell in love with him. The main fault with this production was that it was slow moving. An additional handicap for Mangiamele at least was that he tried to do too much, from writing, through to producing and editing.

Nineteen sixty six provided nothing more substantial than a children's fantasy and a pseudo Italian's adventures delivered in pure 'Strine'. Both held moments of interest, but neither provided the necessary fillip for the industry.

Funny Things Happen Down Under was from Pacific Films that had previously concentrated on children's series for television, including the various adventures of *The Terrible Ten*. A special Christmas attraction at Melbourne's Princess Theatre, it opened on 26 December 1966. Directed by Joe McCormick and photographed by Roger Mirams and Dennis Trewin, it had music by Vern Moore performed by the Horrie Dargie Quintet. The story concentrated on sheep that grew multi-coloured wool that was sought by buyers from all over the world, whether they obtained it by fair or foul means. A member of the cast would later become a super-star overseas — Olivia Newton John. The kids at least enjoyed it.

4.1 *International woolbuyers in the Pacific Film "Funny Things Happen Down Under". Frank Rich portrays a Scotsman; Kurt Beimel a Continental buyer; William Hodge as a North of England wool man.*

Another feature tried to retain the atmosphere of funny things happening down under by coming up with *They're a Weird Mob*. On 27 August 1966 there was a simultaneous inter-city screening at the Sydney State Theatre, and Melbourne's Forum. At the Forum it ran for a record forty-one weeks. But the producers pulled a switch. They selected a real Italian, Walter Chiari, to play John O'Grady's fictional Italian, Nino Culotta. An English producer-director Michael Powell, an English director of photography, an English screen writer Richard Imrie, and English-Australian finance from J. C. Williamson did little more for the Australian film industry than to provide work for Australian actors at a time when work was hard to obtain. Yet it did not revive the picture-making business. Even its substantial profits in Australia were devoured by heavy losses overseas.

4.2   In "They're A Weird Mob" Walter Chiari as "Nino Culotta" tries his hand at rolling his own. John Meillon, as his tutor, is not quite sure that Nino has followed instructions.

Australia continued to stagnate, and in 1967 produced *Journey out of Darkness* and a 16 mm production called *Pudding Thieves*. *Journey out of Darkness* at Sydney's State Theatre on 15 December, was an Australian-American Picture Production directed by Australian expatriate James Trainor. Like *Jedda* this picture seized upon Central Australia for its background. The marked difference between the two films was that Andrew Fraser on camera was no Carl Kayser. The key characters were an inexperienced Northern Territory policeman (played by American Konrad Matthaei, who also showed his inexperience before camera) and an educated Aboriginal tracker Jubbal (Ed Devereaux with a 'mammy' face.) Following a fierce tribal duel, Arunta law style, the two men set out to bring the victor to trial — as the white man's law demands. Surprises never ended in this film. Kamahl (born of Sri Lankan parents in Kuala Lumpur) was the surviving Aboriginal duellist. The three remain at the Arunta camp overnight, where the bone is pointed at Jubbal. (It's a pity it wasn't pointed at the picture at the same time.) Ronald Morse as a typical outback police sergeant, suggested the film's theme — the stupidity of dispensing British justice too readily to the Aborigines. Critics regarded the direction as 'sloppy'. Bronwyn Binns the film editor would like to forget that she was ever associated with the feature; she spent such a great deal of unrewarding time on *Journey out of Darkness*.

4.3   Slim de Grey, Walter Chiari, John Meillon and Ed Devereaux in "They're A Weird Mob" — the film that did well in Australia, but was not favorably received overseas.

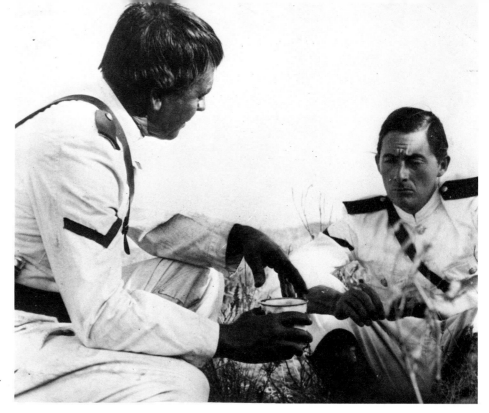

4.4 *Ed Devereaux as a black tracker, and Konrad Matthaei as the unseasoned Northern Territory policeman in "Journey Out Of Darkness" — an Australian-American Picture of 1967.*

The Pudding Thieves from Brian Davies was a better constructed film than *Journey out of Darkness*. It related to the plight of a photographer who turns to pornography to make 'quick money' only to despise himself for his greed. George Dixon from *Clay* played the leading role. It was a 'Festival' film more than a commercial proposition, and was programmed with *The Restless Years* directed by James Wilson, at the Palais Theatre, St Kilda on 17 September 1967.

Meanwhile the late Sir Robert Menzies had given a sigh of relief and left the Vincent Report and its implications as to the fate of the Australian Film Industry, if its recommendations were not heeded, to his successor, Harold Holt. Holt as well as going all the way with L.B.J., thought that Australian culture should be encouraged a little more than it had been in the past. In November 1967 he announced the establishment of the Australian Council of the Arts, whose work was centred more upon opera, drama, and ballet than on making films. However one stipulation was that the Council was to advise the government on grants for film making for television, with the emphasis upon educational and cultural pursuits.

1968: An Opening Up

In this year the sediment was being stirred from the bottom of the bowl. *Movie News* later described 1968 as the year when Australia turned the corner, and opened up the film front. Overall, it was a restless and unsatisfying period when agitation was rife and technical equipment was hopefully taken out of its mothballs.

An ironical touch to 1968 was that Raymond Longford's fifty year old *The Sentimental Bloke* was voted Number One film at the World Film Festival, Uruguay. This picture had been selected by Charles Gilbert of the National Library, following a request from the Festival Committee, to send a film representative of this country's film style. It was a belated tribute to Raymond Hollis Longford who died on 2 April 1959 — a bitter and frustrated eighty year old. The sea had first called him, and the sea witnessed his demise as a patrolman on Sydney's waterfront.

One false lead in 1968 was a proposal to set up a National Film School at the Prahran Technical College in Melbourne. On 20 April 1968, Colin Bennett in *The Age* described the proposal as the first in the Southern Hemisphere, if not the first English-speaking film school on a national scale in the world.

> Preliminary proposals provide for two sound stages each about 30 m square, and two projection rooms each seating 150 people ... sound studios, studios for animation, titling and special effects, editing rooms, library and archives, tutorial rooms, a processing laboratory, workshops, dressing and wardrobe rooms ... to provide adequate facilities for low to medium budget, feature film production.
>
> The whole idea is breath-taking — a major breakthrough in the cause of an Australian feature film industry. For those who — noting such famous school academies as Lodz in Poland — have long pressed for a full-scale school in this country ... the school is a vital first step towards a renaissance of our cinema.
>
> The Commonwealth Film Unit (Film Australia) and other units, mainly in television, do provide sound technical training; also Swinburne Tech has already instituted a film course on a small scale. But Australia has nothing that can adequately train our feature directors and writers of the future.
>
> The eventual benefits to be derived from a national school are incalculable at this stage. If the Commonwealth would only follow this proposal through by adding a public fund designed to subsidise features, nothing could hold Australia back. Within a few years she would be showing her face on the screens of her own and other countries, in dynamic feature films which might well become the envy of the world.

The Prahran School did not materialise, but Mr Bennett's hopes were realised a few short years later — in Sydney.

In 1968 two young film makers — both with a future — were harnessing their undeveloped skills. The first was Antony Ginnane who on 19 February was a member of the Melbourne University Film Society Production Group. He was busily engaged with *We are None of us Perfect.* (This feature receives attention in Chapter 5.) Nine years later, Ginnane became Executive Director of Australian International Film Corporation. The second man, Nigel Buesst, was on camera for the Ginnane feature, and has since become a film maker in his own right as well as a teacher of film at the same Swinburne College that Colin Bennett mentioned. Swinburne College remained in the news, and on 2 May 1968 young producer-director-cameraman Ian Baker, made a short called *Clever Dick* on Port Melbourne beach.

4.5 *Elinor Wilson who appeared in the featurette "Hey Al Baby". Directed by David Minter, it was screened commercially in 1969.*

It is worth recalling that the Melbourne University Film Society Production Group included in its completed projects for 1968 *Hey Al Baby* directed by David Minter. This thirty-five minute romp centred around a young man continuously making 'wise cracks' to conceal his loneliness. Suddenly he is plunged into a lost weekend where he is surrounded by a houseful of girls. The cast included Alan Finney, Chrissi Loh, and Chris Maudson. (Alan recalls that Chrissi Loh was killed, rather tragically, during the filming.) *Hey Al Baby* and Nigel Buesst's *Squizzy Taylor* (a documentary on the life of the notorious criminal) were screened commercially at the Carlton Theatre, Melbourne, on 28 April 1969.

4.6   *Christina O'Brien and Rory Hume in the Arkaba Film Production "Time In Summer". This feature was produced in Adelaide.*

The Australian feature film *Time in Summer* was, according to producer-photographer Ian Davidson, made for 'Continental' tastes, but proved to be little more than another 'Festival' film. Made in South Australia, and directed by Ludwik Dutkiewiez, it carried a sensational long shot (for 1968 at least) of Christina O'Brien walking nude along the foreshores of Victor Harbour. In ponderous style it told of a girl's reaction to her first romance during a beach holiday in summer. It went off on a pseudo-intellectual tangent to introduce mental impressions of the girl's brother at a party. Premiered at the Adelaide Festival of Arts on 17 March 1968, it was featured at the Berlin Film Festival in the same year.

A television special *The World of the Seekers* was later released as a colour film, and was a school holiday special at the Australia Cinema, Melbourne, on 13 May 1968. Directed by Rod Kinnear (who was in the late 1970s associated with the direction of the Ray Lawler trilogy for TV) and produced by Ajax Films and the National 9 Television Network, it starred the then world famous singing group 'The Seekers' (in which Judith Durham was a member). Edward Hepple appeared, with the narration being handled by Tony Charlton.

Japanese Hit Town

It was in 1968 that another minor invasion occurred: the Japanese came to the local film front with a 'meat pie' Western called *The Drifting Avenger*. They used Australian equipment and facilities for the shooting and used locations near Tamworth. Familiar situations ranged from stage coach journeys to the big 'shoot out'. The Japanese were the 'goodies'. *The Drifting Avenger* used the facilities of Supreme Films and the services of Australian players Judith Roberts (who required the protection of Ken Takakura), Reg Gorman and Ken Goodlet. It never reached the Australian theatre screens but was seen on local TV in 1972.

The second Japanese feature to be produced in Australia was *The Blazing Continent*. A Tokyo artist comes to this country seeking his ex-girlfriend. Just to make things interesting, she has fallen in love with an Australian. The awkward triangle is conveniently solved by having the girl killed in a motor accident. The artist wanders off into the Australian outback, nearly dies from thirst, and returns to his own country — no doubt to become a salesman for collapsible canvas waterbags.

From out of the blue, there appeared what seemed to be a major breakthrough, only to end dismally as another example of the pitfalls of co-production. Like Southern International, Australia once again, was the loser. Reginald Goldsworthy and the American-based Commonwealth United Corporation formed Goldsworthy Productions, to make feature films in Australia. Mostly however, it provided work for American players and scriptwriters with an ex-American as director.

Yet it can truthfully be stated that 1968 stirred up a lot of dust from volumes containing past promises and hopes. (Sir) John Gorton, yielding to increasing pressure from all sides, carried out Harold Holt's promise and set up the Australia Council for the Arts, under Dr H.C. Coombs. Ken Hall in his autobiography *Directed by Ken G. Hall* considered this a sincere but unprofessional appointment. His reason is that Coombs was an economist not a film maker, and the Committee, he announced later, was loaded with academics. Council members were nominated in June 1968. The first meeting was held the following month, and the Film and Television Committee that included Phillip Adams and Barry Jones first assembled in November 1968.*

But what a hornet's nest was stirred up by these announcements! The first stirring came by way of Roland Beckett, president of the Producers and Directors Guild of Australia. This organisation and others tried to make the government aware of the dust-concealed 1935 New South Wales Cinematograph Act which had not been repealed. This called for a 2½ per cent quota of screening time of Australian films in the cinemas in NSW. The reason advanced for the lack of enforcement was that the Theatres and Films Commission had felt that it was not the Commission's policy to force compliance, and the exhibitors for their part, conveniently looked the other way.

NSW Chief Secretary Willis, in reply to inquiries, stated that the Commission had made a recommendation that registered distributors be reminded of their requirements, and that the government expected them to fulfil their quotas of Australian films, so that exhibitors could meet their obligations under the Act.

As Australia imported about 400 films a year at that time, the required 2½ per cent represented ten films. Again, the quota system never took off — but thankfully Australian films did.

One of the opponents of any type of aid for the film industry was Nigel Dick (then general manager of GTV 9, Melbourne). In late 1968 he stated

* Read John Gorton's speech 2 December 1969 at the AFI Awards.

that a subsidy was not the answer to establishing a film industry. He maintained that a producer would not work as hard on a subsidy basis, and that the standard would not be as high as that of an independent operator. He declared that subsidy glorified mediocrity.

Renaissance of Australian Film

Nineteen sixty-nine was of paramount importance to the renaissance of the Australian film industry. The bearing this year had on future development cannot be stressed enough. It contained the embryo of a long-cherished dream. There were times when goals were perhaps a little illusory, but nevertheless the nucleus of an Australian film explosion was undoubtedly there. This explosion would startle many Australians and make people overseas fully aware that we did possess a film industry after all.

The first blast off in 1969 was not successful in certain areas, and the film that was hoped would provide the major thrust was a dud. It provided the type of anti-climax that became a disastrous somersault. A few overseas companies tried to mount the band wagon only to learn that their product was off-key.

The Piccadilly Theatre in Perth took line honours however, with the first Australian production for 1969. It was *You Can't See 'Round Corners* screened on 17 January. It was made by ATN Channel 7, Sydney. One critic wrote that it was based on 'Jon Cleary's contrived little tale with stock characterisations.' In many ways it was a brutal movie: the dominating mood was harshness and violence. Yet it was a bonus film based on the very successful TV series of the same name. Made for $100 000 it was a smash hit in Perth, and did record business in Sydney. It was the story of a born loser (Ken Shorter) who was an SP bookie before his military call-up. He became a deserter, and after his girlfriend (Rowena Wallace) would have nothing to do with him, he picked up a Kings Cross 'call girl' (Carmen Duncan). Slim de Grey (from *They're a Weird Mob*) and Lyndall Barbour were other members of the cast. The director was David Cahill.

4.7 *Rowena Wallace bends over Ken Shorter, who in "You Can't See 'Round Corners" is hurt in a fight. Note the clapper board recording the scene number.*

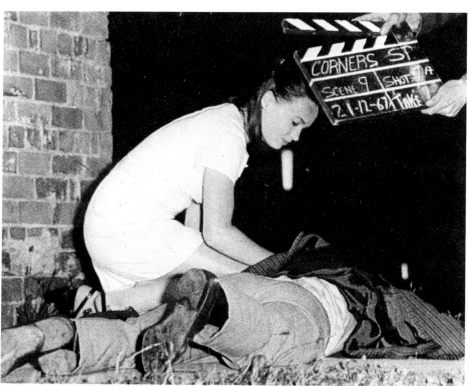

4.8   *Helen Mirren as the model who poses for an artist (James Mason) whose brush no longer works magic on the canvas. "Age Of Consent" directed by Michael Powell, was screened in 1969.*

Meanwhile Michael Pate had returned from Hollywood and set about arranging a project that had interested him for years; the converting of a Norman Lindsay novel into a film. The result was *Age of Consent,* the premiere performance of which was given at the Brisbane Wintergarden Theatre on 27 March 1969. Possibly the only benefit that Australia gained from this picture was that Pate remained in this country. It was produced by two Englishmen, Michael Powell (previously in Australia for *They're a Weird Mob*) and James Mason. Both had additional interests in the production, the former as director, the latter as 'star'. The only touch of local colour and talent was the scenery of Dunk Island; the associate producer (Michael Pate); the scripter (Peter Yeldham); and supporting players (Neva Carr Glyn, Harold Hopkins, and Michael Boddy.) *Age of Consent* was the story of a famous artist (James Mason) who no longer had magic in his brush. He returns to a small island off the coast of Queensland and meets a teenage girl (Helen Mirren). He paints her in the nude. The girl's drink-swilling grandmother (Neva Carr Glyn) sees evil in the teenager modelling for the artist, and demands money to remain silent. The grandmother plunges to her death from the top of a cliff and a Professor Higgins-Eliza Doolittle relationship develops between the artist and the girl. Then he begins to realise that she is more than a model, she is a woman. James Mason gave a masterly performance, and Neva Carr Glyn was superb. Helen Mirren on the other hand was perhaps too well educated in her speech, but she did possess vitality and beauty.

Even with the arrival of *Age of Consent* Australia was not quite satisfied and still waited for the production that would give real meaning to the rebirth of the Australian film industry. Australia sat up expectantly and said, 'This is it!' when the much publicised *2000 Weeks.* came to the Melbourne Forum screen on 28 March. Directed by Tim Burstall it arrived with a fanfare of trumpets, and left by the back entrance eleven days later without a whimper. From there it became a 'Festival' film and was shown at the Sydney Film Festival, on 8 June; and during the following month at the Moscow Film Festival.

4.9 *Director Tim Burstall (left) on the set of "2000 Weeks" an Eltham-Senior Films Production. Harold Koch is camera operator; and in the background, Robin Copping, Noel Ardern, and Ron Johansen.*

Tim Burstall did not claim to be a 'method' director, but his approach to *2000 Weeks* did reveal a recognisable influence. When he won a Harkness Scholarship he studied at the Actors' Studio in America conducted by Lee Strasberg* whose best known student was Marilyn Monroe.

At the time he was directing *2000 Weeks* Tim Burstall stated rather bluntly that he wasn't going for 'the narrow minded, nationalistic stick-in-the mud thing'. He felt the need for Australians to be Australian, even though ours was an urban Western culture that was little different, but just as good as any other.

One critic wrote:

> *2000 Weeks* could have been our best film to date, were it not for the abominable dialogue. The film is a useful experience for Tim Burstall and Patrick Ryan (Eltham Films) and Senior Films.

Another saw it as technically the most professional film yet made in Australia, but noted that the characters were dangerously thin, if not cardboard. The big weakness this critic said, was the Burstall-Ryan script. As the 'film that might have been' it missed out badly.

In July 1968 *2000 Weeks* had been described as a $100000 gamble. That gamble proved disastrous for David Bilcock Snr, chairman of Senior Films. In 1952 he had formed Cambridge Film Productions in Box Hill, Melbourne, and after eight years, set up Senior Films with studios that were alleged to be the best in Victoria. One of his cherished dreams was the production of an Australian feature film. It had to have a theme that was purely local (like life in urban Melbourne), yet relevant the world over. Having failed at Cambridge with *Night Club,* he had the courage to try a second time. Unfortunately *2000 Weeks* cost him his business, and today David Bilcock is an independent producer of documentaries. He made the engrossing documentary *The Foundations Belong to the Incas* which is a one-man show. This was screened on ABV 2 Melbourne on 1 January 1978. The pity is that such an informative, imaginative, and well-produced film was delegated to an afternoon spot — and without prior publicity.

*The Constantin Stanislavsky method of acting was brought to the U.S.A. by Moscow Arts Theatre actors, where it was taught to such people as Stella Adler, Lee Strasberg, and Harold Clurman. The last two with Cheryl Crawford, gave new vitality to the American theatre, with the Group Theatre, Elia Kazan, Cheryl Crawford, and director Robert Lewis. Names emerging from this group were Marlon Brando, Paul Newman, Shelley Winters, Eli Wallach, Ben Gazzara and Joanne Woodward.

4.10, 4.11   *Mark McManus and Jeanie Drynan in a scene from "2000 Weeks". Directed by Tim Burstall, this failed at the box office.*

Boost to Industry

It was on 26 May 1969 that Dr H. C. Coombs, chairman of the Australian Council of the Arts, announced a plan to give Australia's film and television industry a boost.

The scheme covered the formation of:
1. A National Film and Television School.
2. A film and television fund.
3. An overseas film and television marketing board.
4. An experimental fund for low-budget productions, and a television outlet for experimental films and programmes.

The report stressed that films and television were powerful influences on Australia's national character. Yet relatively little of our dramatic television, and virtually none of the feature films screened in our cinemas were of local origin.

Coombs recommended that an interim film school receive immediate attention to form a staff of creative personnel — writers, directors and editors — for all branches of the industry.

Although Colin Bennett acclaimed the idea of a Film and Television School, over the years there had been many opposed to the idea. Ken G. Hall cited it as a cart before the horse attitude, and doubted whether any inquiry was held as to whether such a school was necessary. He also doubted that Australia could afford the luxury of such an institution. Another vital factor was whether a limited industry could absorb the output of students who still had to gain some professionalism.

Terry Bourke in late 1974 also entered the arena. He was firmly convinced that there was no substitute for actual experience in feature film making. By that he didn't mean knowing how a camera works; how to thread film into it; and what to shoot.

> I refer to working on films that are being made. I believe that a person shut up in a classroom cannot learn how to make pictures. The real way is to be there when films are being produced. I think the government should adopt a more practical way of training students by assigning them to films being made by Peter Weir, Tim Burstall, Bruce Beresford or Michael Thornhill. In this way students can work as trainee cameramen, directors, and editors, and get the feel of film making. They can learn about pressure, deadlines, schedules, and trying to chase the sun and the clouds, on exterior shooting. In the classroom, people may be able to lecture on film making; to nominate the right books to read; and to study techniques used in various pictures. But if Australia must retain a film school, why not use it as a central base from which trainees can be allocated to the film companies making features at the time. The main thing I feel is adapting themselves to working on a feature, rather than making some experimental film or going out and shooting 'self expressive' material. Let them learn things; see things; discover how a team works as a unit. Trainees will soon find that a certain amount of 'know how' of doing things, will rub off on them.

This was the same Terry Bourke — the lad from Bairnsdale, Victoria — who had journeyed to Asia to make films, and in 1968 was begged by one critic to come home — Australia needed him. Terry arrived in Australia in August

4.12   *David Bilcock Snr. and Patrick Ryan, co-producers of the Senior-Eltham film "2000 Weeks". David Bilcock has since remarked that he wished the film had lived up to its title, and ran for 2,000 Weeks so that he could have recouped some of the costs.*

1969. His film *Sampan* was featured at the Adelaide Festival of Arts in the same month. When he learnt that 23 m had been cut from the most essential part of his picture, he stated that the censor should play Ned Kelly, as he had acted like some type of bushranger: 'They are only men holding scissors. They know nothing about the technicalities of a film,' Bourke said.

However British film director John Boulting had his own views on film making in Australia. He stated at a seminar at the National University Canberra on 29 May 1969: 'Film is not only an art, but an industry.' The purpose of this seminar was to seek support for the performing arts in Australia. Mr Boulting could see no hope for films in Australia. He advised that the standard of present studios and facilities may be good enough to produce the occasional modest film, but that this country could never make competitive films for export: 'Although Australia could be one of the major powers within twenty-five years, the world at present knows nothing about it.'

On the same panel was Lionel Harris who was in Australia for Veric International-British Lion films, and the making of *Mr Burke and Mr Wills,* which was never produced. Mr Harris felt that if all the studio facilities in Australia were assembled in one place, they would constitute no more than one studio. He also said that the moment more than one feature was in production, difficulties would arise. He agreed that some feature films were being produced but pointed out that they were mostly on location. Harris felt certain that if the government provided assistance for film makers, investors would not be far behind.

More Co-operatives; More Flops

The first Goldsworthy Production *It Takes all Kinds* took a bow at the State Theatre, Sydney on 12 June 1969.

4.13 "It akes All Kinds" — the first of the Goldsworthy-C.U.C joint productions that had a very short life. In this still are Americans Vera Miles and Robert Lansing.

Robert Lansing is a merchant seaman, who is knocked out in a brawl and regains consciousness in the apartment of a mysterious blonde (Vera Miles). She threatens to turn him over to the police for killing a man in a fight unless he assists her in stealing valuable art treasures. The robbery involves him with a wealthy industrialist (Barry Sullivan), a 'fence' (Sid Melton) and a young insurance agent (Penny Sugg).

The director, Eddie Davis; the director of photography, Mick Bornemann; and the leads were all American. Australia's main contribution to the picture included assistant director Warwick Freeman, and minor cast members Penny Sugg, Reg Gorman, Ted Hepple, and Alan Bickford. Even the script was from the good old US of A. It was summed up succinctly as 'production, direction and cutting are efficient. There is non-stop action coupled with unpretentious sets and sensible camera work. Nothing in the film makes it notable. Nothing detracts from it as a fair average movie.'

The only things this co-operative deal sparked were a lot of fat promises that weren't worth the hot air in which they were packed. Maurice Silverstein and his wife (ex-Australian film actress Betty Bryant), arrived 'jet packaged' from America, and descended upon the Goldsworthy lot. Friend Maurice viewed rushes of the third production *That Girl from Peking*, nodded his head in approval, and as head of Commonwealth United Corporation, unctuously announced that instead of the hitherto modest $400 000 productions, they would jointly make two $1 million epics a year. He smiled benignly. 'Australia is booming and is about to rate a big spot on the world maps in capital letters.'

Australia might have been booming, but CUC 'went bust' the following year, and Goldsworthy Productions became the first casualty in the revival of Australian film making. Yet the lesson has never been heeded. Even as late as 1977, the Australian Broadcasting Commission in its co-productive telefeature deal had to call a halt halfway through the project. Australia neither learns nor gains anything in this way — and only provides the means for making films 'on the cheap' for overseas companies.

Experimentals

Skippy, a very popular TV series that sold well overseas had a feature film 'spin off' called *The Intruders.* Unlike *Skippy,* a Fauna Production, *The Intruders* was labelled a Woomera Film. The director was Lee Robinson; the photographer, Peter Menzies, with underwater sequences handled by Ron Taylor. Ed Devereaux, Tony Bonner, Lisa Goddard, John Unicomb, Jack Hume, Jeanie Drynan and Ron Graham who made up the cast were not called upon to display any great histrionic ability. The basic motive of this adventure story was to provide Christmas fare for the children. The uncomplicated plot told of abalone divers at Mallacoota being hired in an illegal bid to salvage gold bullion. The season for *The Intruders* began in Brisbane at Hoyts Town Theatre on 11 December 1969; Hoyts Palace Theatre, Sydney, 12 December; the Paris Theatre, Melbourne, 17 December.

Jack and Jill — A Postscript is an unusual film in a number of ways. It began as a 'Festival' film but picked up commercial bookings later. It was an experimental feature from a two-man team in Melbourne — Phillip Adams (who gained prominence later as a film producer and a newspaper article writer who enjoys 'rubbishing' the Establishment) and Brian Robinson (head of the Swinburne Film and TV Course).

Jack and Jill cannot be classified as a 'great film', but its approach was different. It was a modern love story between a kindergarten teacher and a tow truck driver and bikie. Here the influence of Adams as a writer is evident.

4.14 *Anthony Ward as "Jack" in "Jack And Jill — A Postscript" — a Phillip Adams-Brian Robinson production.*

It provides a ludicrous situation that offers plenty of scope to provide a satisfactory solution. In *Jack and Jill* there is pathos without sentimentality. The climax is almost brutal. Jack ends up under a mangled bike, leaving a distraught Jill running around headstones in a cemetery. Adams and Robinson wrote, produced, directed, photographed and edited the film. The only additional production assistance came from Peter Best who wrote the music.

Jack and Jill won a Silver Reel Award from the Australian Film Institute, December 1969. Further Awards were Second Prize in the 1970 Perth Festival; the Adelaide Advertiser Award in 1970 for the best Australian film, and a special Award at the Adelaide Film Festival, 1970. Its first commercial screening was at the Melbourne Metro (now the Palace Theatre), 29 October 1970. Jack was Anthony Ward; Jill was Judy Leech. The picture took four years to make.

In October 1969 a 27 year old film maker named Peter Clinton arrived back in Australia with a 16 mm rough proof of *Pop Corn* which had been shot in Australia, India, Britain and America. His partner, Peter Ryan, was due back a little later with a 35 mm print that was being completed in the USA. It featured pop music and a series of vignettes. Australian sequences were a nude scene on a Sydney beach and a mock Western gun fight staged outside Sydney. It had been accepted for showing at the San Francisco Film Festival, and was going to have a commercial release in America.

The remainder of the films for 1969 were documentaries: *This Year Jerusalem* came from Terry Turle; Paul Witzig's surfing film *Evolution;* and *Savage Shadows* from Henri Bource, which showed how he lost a leg when skin diving off the Victorian coast. The outstanding Film Australia contribution was *The Pictures that Moved* which was Part 1 of the story of Australian silent films.

An almost grim reminder of past film achievements, *The Pictures that Moved* won a Silver Award at the Australian Film Awards. In addition it was screened at the 20th International Exhibition of Documentary Films in Venice, 1969. It was also on the same programme as *2000 Weeks* at the Sydney Festival, 8 June 1969. Directed by Alan Anderson, it was photographed by George Alexander and scripted by Joan Long (for which she received the Australian Writers' Awgie Award in 1969). The duration was forty-five minutes.

On 3 December 1969, the Prime Minister (Sir) John Gorton made an announcement that would have an overwhelming impact upon the whole of the Australian Film Industry, and provide the right type of incentive for a resurgence of Australian feature film production. He advised the public that the recommendations in May by the Australian Council for the Arts had been adopted without alteration. Film activities for 1969-70 were covered in the following manner:

> The establishment of an Interim Council of the National Film and Television School, and a grant of $300000 for the experimental and exhibiting funds.

From this beginning came the Australian Film Development Corporation in 1970.

5
New Life: The Seventies

The aura of newly-awakened creativity was rudely shattered on 4 February 1970, when *The Set* finally obtained an Australian release at the Trak Cinema, Toorak (Melbourne). Sydney's Roma Theatre followed on 20 February then the small Star Theatre, Melbourne on 6 March. *The Set* could be nominated as the forerunner of the 'buttocks and beds' cycle.

Billed as Australia's first professional sex-exploitation movie, *The Set* was in fact far from professional from the direction by Frank Brittain to the self-conscious acting (?) of many of the leading players. 'If this is the best our picture industry can offer', wrote one critic, 'it's about time we stopped competing. Maybe the old Dad and Dave and George Wallace comedies were pure Australian corn — but they were healthy.'

The Melbourne *Listener In* (now *Scene*) gave *The Set* a no-star rating because it didn't deserve even one. ('One star' itself meant — 'forget it'.) Elza Jacoby (Elza Stenning in the silent version of *The Devil's Playground*) as a twittering baroness was the only one to incite any interest. Yet *The Set* did a record business. Perhaps like the 'strip joints' of Sydney's Kings Cross, the anticipation of the unexpected added certain intrigue value.

The Set with the possible exception of *Alvin Rides Again* carries the dubious distinction of being one of the worst Australian films ever made. It was a 'sick' picture that spilled itself ungracefully across the screen. *The Set* provided nudes, homosexual frolics, and a dreary story by Roger Ward who has been far more successful as an actor than a writer.

However *The Set* really started something. *The Naked Bunyip* came in on cue at the Melbourne Palais Theatre on 12 November. Phillip Adams was executive producer, John B. Murray, director, and Bruce McNaughton took a 'camera view' of everything. This documentary on sex exploitation had a

5.1 *Rod Mullinar cuts a heroic figure in this still from "The Set" (1970). Yet the film itself depicted everything that was distasteful in a quasi-Bohemian life style.*

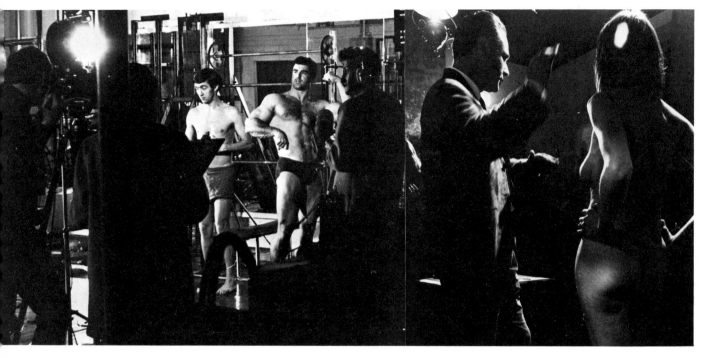

5.2   *Graeme Blundell as a reporter covering the "seamy" side of life, finds that he needs a build up "physically" to keep things moving in "The 'Naked Bunyip". All it lead to was the title role in "Alvin Purple".*

5.3   *Director John Murray shows how he expects a model to react when being questioned by Graeme Blundell for his report in "The Naked Bunyip".*

few censorship problems, but in retrospect, we can ask, was it worth the bother?' It did however serve one amusing purpose. It introduced Graeme Blundell who was given the assignment of conducting the survey, even when he'd rather do one on agriculture.

Christopher Gary who gave up Hollywood to come to Australia made a similar excursion into the field of sex in 1973 with his *Essay on Pornography*. Strangely enough, both documentaries only broke even at the box office in Australia. After the Japanese had departed, there were two further minor invasions from overseas — neither setting standards for the Australians to pattern themselves upon. One was *Adam's Woman* (previously titled *Return of the Boomerang*). It was directed by Philip Leacock and released at Canberra's Center Cinema on 19 March 1970. A pseudo historical story set in the penal colony of New South Wales it had a complete disregard for any but the most slender of factual accuracy, and it was a most disappointing film. One critic likened it to an American Western with some irritatingly platonic folk songs that were included for no other purpose than to entertain. The character of the Governor, Sir Philip McDonald (played by John Mills) was loosely based on that of Lachlan Macquarie and his idealistic system of emancipation. From that point onwards, any similarity between the storyline and historical fact was purely coincidental. The hero (Beau Bridges), an American seaman, is arrested by mistake and transported to New South Wales where the governor wishes to establish a farming settlement of freed convicts. English actress Jane Merrow was cast as a former inhabitant of the Female Factory at Parramatta. There are two totally different forces opposing the farming settlement — a tyrant of a magistrate (portrayed by Australian Peter O'Shaughnessy) who covets the land, and on the other side, a strong gang of bushrangers sworn to destroy it. Finally the bushrangers attack and are driven off. In the face of such adversity, the hero and heroine find solace in each other's company. Katy Wild, Peter Collingwood, Helen Morse and Clarissa Kaye were other players to appear.

The second overseas film was a curious failure. It was an English version of the familiar Australian story of *Ned Kelly* directed by Tony Richardson. It had everything behind the scenes but not so much going for it on the screen. Accidents on the set were attributed to 'the curse of the Kellys'. Then there was the 'original' script by Ian Jones — a recognised authority on the Kelly exploits. Richardson altered it here and there, then others followed, right down to Alex Buzo — resulting in a complete hotch-potch. Behind the cameras, actors like Colin McEwan were screaming about the poor rates of pay. Mick Jagger played a swaggering Ned Kelly with a North of England cum Irish accent that really needed sub-titles in English.

One should not overlook the famous Kelly 'helmet shot'. The clang of bullets, deflected by the armour, gave the dull 'ping' of iron, yet it publicised that Jagger's protective suit was made from aluminium. Of course, a highlight was Jagger's wheezing breath that seemed to signify an attack of asthma. *Ned Kelly* had its first Australian showing in the Glenrowan Memorial Hall on 28 July 1970.

Exit Goldsworthy, Enter More Co-productions

Although the second Goldsworthy Production *Colour Me Dead* was screened at the Metro Theatre, Melbourne on 5 March 1970, the slowing down at the production house must have been apparent before that. As Phillip Adams recalls 'the theatre didn't appear to have much faith in the film *Colour Me Dead*, as on opening night it advertised the following Thursday's attraction even before the box office response could be measured.'

Colour Me Dead was a remake of the American film *Dead on Arrival*. It centres around a young lawyer (Tom Tryon) who has been mysteriously poisoned and has only two days to discover who administered the fatal dose. Australian Tony Ward (now a current affairs commentator) played an excellent role as the villain who figured prominently in a savage fight scene in the hold of a ship, in which he kicked Tryon in the head after he fell. This sequence had been described as excessively violent, and had to be cut. It was this tangle with the censor that had delayed the release of the picture for four months. Others in the cast were Carolyn Jones, Rick Jason, and Australians Penny Sugg, Sandy Harbutt, Suzy Kendall, and Lyndal Moor (who in 1970 was voted Australian model of the year).

As Goldsworthy Productions faded from the scene, the second co-production company NLT-Group W came forward with its first film *Squeeze a Flower*. Released in Brisbane and Sydney simultaneously on 13 February 1970, it was directed by American Marc Daniels. In direct contrast to *The Set*, it possessed a charm seldom seen these days. It starred Walter Chiari in the role of Brother George from the Italian Abbey of Remani, a far different role to that in *They're a Weird Mob*.

Brother George is the only one who knew the secret formula for the making of a famous liqueur. Feeling that the monastery is not receiving fair returns for its product, he leaves Italy for Australia where he becomes George

5.4 *On the set of "Squeeze A Flower". In the background — Jack Albertson (L) and Dave Allen. This depicts grapes being tipped into crushers, with the production crew in the foreground.*

Brothers. He blends *Bel Fiore* (Beautiful Flower) for the Brazzi Wine Company in the Hunter Valley. Meanwhile the Abbot at the Remani Monastery hears of *Bel Fiore* and sends Brother James to investigate. The 'missing monk' is located — but the Brazzi Company and the European distributor for the Abbey of Remani's liqueur cannot agree on a compromise price, so George Brothers, through the business sense he has gained in Australia, demands 75 per cent from both parties. When everything is in order for him to return to Italy, he falls and hits his head. When he regains consciousness, he has forgotten the magic formula. The film ends on an hilarious note and he wears two Brothers out physically as they follow him in the monastery grounds, ready to write down the ingredients as he tries to recall them. Overseas members of the cast included Dave Allen and Jack Albertson. Australian players were Rowena Wallace, Kirrily Nolan, Michael Laurence, Sandy Harbutt and Jeff Ashby.

Distribution Troubles

While Australia was clearly demonstrating that its film front was becoming buoyant again, it still revealed flaws in that troublesome area — distribution. The perfect example of this was *Beyond Reason*, an independent fully Australian colour feature.

Earlier, Mike Bellinger, Canadian writer-producer-actor, had stated:

I think the Government should put a very high tariff on imported films. That's what Canada did in the early 1950s, when I was still working around the home. For the first year the home stuff was terrible, but through necessity it improved.

5.5 *Louise Hall and John Gauci in "Beyond Reason" directed by Giorgio Mangiamele.*

Beyond Reason, directed by Giorgio Mangiamele, was the perfect example of injustice. This film presented a frightening look at the madness in the world today. It could not obtain a city release and had to be content with its premiere at the Sandringham Drive-In and Forest Hill Theatre in the Melbourne suburbs on 21 May 1970.

One Melbourne critic expressed his annoyance with Australian distributors and exhibitors for relegating a rare event — an all-Australian feature — to a second-class release. He did not rate *Beyond Reason* a masterpiece, but as an almost unique product at the time, it deserved a better fate. It was considered a better effort than the previous all-Australian efforts, *Clay* and *99 Per cent* and was the equal of Mangiamene's 16 mm production *Spag*. The director of *Beyond Reason* showed more professionalism in the handling of the performers and in the dialogue. George Dixon as the head doctor was the most experienced and competent, and Maggie Copeland as a nurse gained stature as the film progressed. Louise Hall received honourable mention.

One of the most interesting documentaries of 1970 was the 26-minute 16 mm production *Digger Rig* from Kestrel Films. It received an Honourable Mention in the 1970 Australian Film Institute Awards, and in the same year at the Television Society's Awards, received the $2000 Shell Award for the best TV documentary. It showed the working of an oil rig in Bass Strait with Andy Wilkinson as a typical 'rough neck'. It was scripted and directed by John Richardson, photographed by Alan D. Arnold, and featured a special song by Hans Poulsen. It was screened on HSV 7, Melbourne.

Federal Government Support

Nineteen seventy was to prove how ineffectual the forecast of some critics could be. Many had felt Australians should simply give up trying to compete in the film industry. But one ardent supporter of the new breed of directors felt that the future of Australian films looked exceedingly bright with such knowledgeable men as Warwick Freeman to plot the course of action. Warwick at the time headed his own company and was directing *The Demonstrator*.

Kit Denton, the writer of the screenplay, sent a letter to the *Australian* on 9 November 1970 stating that a number in the Australian film and TV business were able to produce programme material at an acceptable international level. He went on to state that the production of such material needed capital, and that he was 'getting pretty damned sick of listening to the act that's pouted about building an Australian film industry.' Denton desired to make a 90-minute programme for Cook's bi-centenary year that would cost approximately $50 000 but he could not obtain the finance. He concluded his letter by posing the question: 'if you really believe in Australian production in film and television, why not do something about it? Or are you truly the mealy-mouthed, gutless wonders you appear to be?'

The Federal Government had done something. It had set up the Australian Film Development Corporation in 1970. Although Warwick Freeman was nominated as one of the new breed of directors, a certain outsider was not mentioned — Peter Weir. He came out of nowhere and ended up with films like *Picnic at Hanging Rock* and *The Last Wave*.

Weir won his battle spurs in the 1970 Australian Film Institute Awards, with the Grand Prix for *Michael,* one of a trilogy of stories in *3 to Go* produced by Film Australia. Written and directed by Peter Weir, it was photographed by Kerry Brown. It concerned itself with the restlessness of youth that resulted in a revolt against the Establishment, turning Sydney's Circular Quay into a battleground. Matthew Burton was *Michael*, and in the cast was Grahame Bond who later became better known as *Aunty Jack* on ABC television. *Michael* received a Silver Medallion for photography. The

5.6 *Beyond Reason.*

5.7 *"Michael" in the Film Australia triology "3 To Go" was originally conceived as a story of student unrest in Sydney, that turned the ferry terminal at Circular Quay into a battleground. Peter Weir started his Award-winning run with this segment in 1970, being awarded the Grand Prix in the Australian Film Institute Awards. What Weir did not realize was that this story of unrest would have a counterpart in the reaction of the critics, to his win.*

trilogy received a Silver Award, and went on to win First Prize in the Adelaide *Advertiser* Awards as the best Australian film.

Yet Peter Weir wasn't without his critics after the announcement of the AFI Awards. Michael Thornhill, then a newspaper critic, wrote that Brian Hannant, director of another film in the trilogy, was not a genius, but he'd be around making good movies when Peter Weir's type of razzle-dazzle was on the scrap heap of movie history.*

Year of Awards

Two children's features were produced at Artransa Park (Sydney) in 1970 for Mazbrown Productions, America. Both were shown at the Astor Cinema, Mt Lawley (WA) on 11 May 1970 and later released in Melbourne suburban theatres. Both were directed by American Mende Brown and photographed by Australian Brendon Brown. The first was *Strange Holiday* which was based on a Jules Verne story and was shot entirely in Sydney. The second, *Jungle Boy,* used locations in Sydney and Singapore. Unusual casting had Michael Pate as a sultan and Noel Ferrier as a padre.

The AFI Awards in 1970 also revealed that Nigel Buesst, following his *The Rise and Fall of Squizzy Taylor,* won a Silver Award for *Dead Easy.* Top cameraman Vince Monton did an excellent job on this production. *Dead Easy* also shared the $1500 Alan Stout Award. The main characters, a student and a professor, go back in time to seek information about Melbourne's mass murders. The idea for the film germinated after a visit to

---

* *Cinema Papers,* January 1974.

Madame Taussaud's Waxworks in London. In the Chamber of Horrors stands Frederick Deeming, the infamous mass murderer from Melbourne. Players were Peter Carmody as a post-graduate criminology student; Kurt Beimel as a visiting Uruguayan professor; Bruce Spence, Brian Davies, Anna Raknes, Peter Cummins and Alan Finney. In 16 mm colour, the running time was 53 minutes.

One of the biggest award winners for Film Australia was the 9-minute colour short *The Gallery*. A tribute to the Melbourne National Gallery, it won top honours at film festivals in Cork, Brussels, San Francisco, Chicago and Melbourne, and was given the Silver Southern Cross in The *Advertiser* Awards in Adelaide. It received awards in Greece, Sri Lanka, Canada, and in Sydney as well.

The Leyland Brothers, now a household word in television, had literally 'shot' their way to film fame in 1967 by way of the big screen with *Wheels Across the Wilderness*. They followed this in 1970 with *Open Boat to Adventure*, a photographic record of adventure in a 5.5 m boat from Darwin to Sydney.

5.8 *"The Gallery" was a prize winning short directed by Philip Mark Law and photographed by Kerry Brown for Film Australia.*

Disappointments Follow

Nineteen seventy-one was a lack-lustre year. Goldsworthy had learnt only too well in 1970 the disaster of co-production, and NLT was to take its dose of castor oil in 1971. Strangely enough, both companies folded after the second production, although Goldsworthy did make a third film which was never released.

The first Australian release for 1971 was in April. It was *The Demonstrator* and it was shown at Sydney's Town Theatre on the 15th. *The Demonstrator* failed at the box office, yet John McLean won the 1971 award for his cinematography. Interesting characterisations came from Noel Ferrier as the Australian governor-general, and Slim de Grey as the prime minister. Perhaps the real reason for the picture's failure was the timing. During this period most people were heartily sick of demonstrations and the violence that sometimes accompanied them.

The storyline of *The Demonstrator* at least provided the airing of opposing points of view — that of a university student (Gerard Maguire) and of his father, a Federal cabinet minister (Joe James). The older man had

5.9 *The banquet scene from "The Demonstrator", at which the Asian delegates are welcomed to Canberra. Seated in the centre of the far table, parallel to the stage, are Noel Ferrier and Slim de Grey.*

arranged an important international conference to which his son was politically antagonistic. He organised a series of demonstrations at the RAAF base, at a banquet tended by the prime minister for the visiting delegation, and outside the Academy of Science. Hong Kong actor Kenneth Tsang portrayed an Asian delegate, and character actress Irene Inescort was the wife of the cabinet minister.

Nickel Queen was the next Australian film for 1971. It premiered in Perth

5.10   *The production crew setting up a shot for "Nickel Queen".*

in April and enjoyed a record season, but it was not very successful in the other capital cities. In it, a 'hippie' (John Laws) and a prospector (Ed Devereaux) pursue a barmaid (Googie Withers) who overnight becomes rich through nickel. American actor Alfred Sandor plays a smooth-tongued 'confidence' man. Locations were a ghost-town forty kilometres from Kalgoorlie and Perth itself. Direction was by John McCallum, with John Williams, complete with Digger's hat, on camera. *Nickel Queen* was slow moving and devoted far too much footage to the transient 'hippie' colony and their cavorting in a town so small that it didn't warrant a 'stop-over' in the first place. They lived in a deserted railway station.

Two films, both shot in Australia were entered in the Cannes Film Festival of 1971. One was Australian, the other was English. *Walkabout,* the English production, was directed and photographed by Nicholas Roeg. It was the story of two schoolchildren lost in the desert, and of a young Aborigine who befriends them. The Aborigine was David Gumpilil — today Australians know him as David Gulpilil, or simply Gulpilil as billed in *Storm Boy.*

5.11   *David Gulpilil, who as an adult has changed simply to Gulpilil, is seen here in a scene from "Walkabout" in 1971. His companions are Jenny Agutter and Lucien John (in the foreground). The setting is the Australian desert country.*

End of Co-productions

The NLT-Group W feature *Wake in Fright* did go one better than Goldsworthy Productions by making a film based on a novel by the Australian author Kenneth Cook. Retitled *Outback* for overseas distribution, it was described by Alexander Walker in The *Evening Standard* as: 'The year of the kangaroo is how 1971 will be remembered. A relief to see bedrock Australia after the legend of Ned Kelly.' It was the savagery of the kangaroo shooting sequence that horrified many Australians. The protest was so loud that it was heard at the box office. Yet it is reported that it enjoyed a long run in Paris in 1972.

Ken Hall in his autobiography *Directed by Ken G. Hall* wrote a passage that is applicable to the choice of *Wake in Fright* as a screen vehicle.

> The determination of the subject you are to produce is the producer's decision. The people who write it, direct it, star in it, are of course vitally important. But none of them, individually or in the sum total, transcend the critical choice of the subject. Wrong decisions are continually being made. Such a film may win awards, be praised by critics — but if it is the wrong subject, no matter how well-written, directed and acted, it will go into the theatres and oblivion.

Such a film was *Wake in Fright*. The sheer vandalism by male adults that took place after the kangaroo shoot had to be seen to be believed.

Ken G. Hall makes these personal observations:

> The glaring instance of an extremely well-made film that failed utterly, was *Wake in Fright*. Australian critics raved, buffs of film societies cheered, but these things alone do not ensure a film's success. *Wake in Fright* should never have been made.
>
>   The title was meaningless and had no immediate relation to the subject. The advertising behind it was poor. There was practically no woman-interest in the film, unless you happen to believe women would be thrilled to watch the town nymphomaniac lying in a dusty paddock, being made love to by a sweating, beer-sodden man who rolls off her body to vomit.
>
>   You do not build a film industry with masterpeices sitting up on a lonely shelf.

5.12   *Donald Pleasence as the beer swilling doctor who enjoys sucking animal blood in "Wake In Fright".*

The story in brief was of a schoolteacher (Gary Bond) who sets off on a holiday from his one-man school to enjoy a vacation in Sydney (which he does not reach). At Bundanyabba he meets the local policeman and an alcoholic doctor, (Donald Pleasence). In an atmosphere of gambling and constant beer swilling he looses all his money and attempts to commit suicide. Finally he returns to his school a sadder, and we hope, a wiser man.

With the complete failure of co-production, Australia was left to its own resources, and unfortunately could supply only *Country Town* which had a country premiere in Mildura (Victoria) on 19 June 1971. It also enjoyed seasons in Queensland, Tasmania, and South Australia. Photographed by Bruce McNaughton on 16 mm it was later blown up to 35 mm. It was directed by Peter Maxwell and starred most of the cast from the ABC TV series *Bellbird*.

A reporter (Gerard Maguire) arrives in the drought-stricken town of

Bellbird. Rain is badly needed to save the inhabitants from ruin. The reporter is writing a series of articles titled *Death of a Town*. The tension mounts as bankruptcy looms, and long-term jealousies of various families become apparent. Finally they get together to stage a morale-boosting trotting gymkhana to attract visitors and their money to Bellbird. Celebrations at the local hotel after a successful meeting give way to shouts of glee and dancing in the streets as overdue rain arrives. Leading players were Gary Gray, Terry McDermott, Carl Bleazby, Maurie Fields, Frank Rich, Rosie Sturgess, Moira Carleton and Stella Lamond. *Country Town* was made on a modest budget and it never aimed for great heights. The sole purpose was to provide wholesome family entertainment.

5.13 *Actor Carl Bleazby, and director Peter Maxwell on the set of "Country Town" (1971).*

5.14 *"Country Town" location setting — Lake Victoria Station near Wentworth (N.S.W.) (Stills by courtesy of Gary Gray.)*

Commercial Successes

By way of a complete contrast was *The Coming of Stork* David Williamson's first play performed at the La Mama Theatre, Melbourne. Tim Burstall, still licking his wounds after *2 000 Weeks,* saw in it the theme for a film. Williamson at a later stage recalled that originally *Stork* made his appearance in the seventh scene of his play, not realising that he was to be the central character. Yet when the film arrived, only 25 per cent of the stage version was used. The writer felt that Bruce Spence had been directed by Burstall a little bigger than he (Williamson) would have liked, and a few off-hand lines were punched out as heavy gags.

Overall *Stork* was in poor taste in its speech and in many of the situations. For example, Stork's demonstration of abstract painting was utterly revolting. The gangling Stork (Bruce Spence) is a hypochondriac who lives a Walter Mitty existence — being everything from a match-winning footballer and a farmer who drags his own plough to an Antarctic explorer. Jan Friedl tries to seduce him and Jacki Weaver endeavours to understand

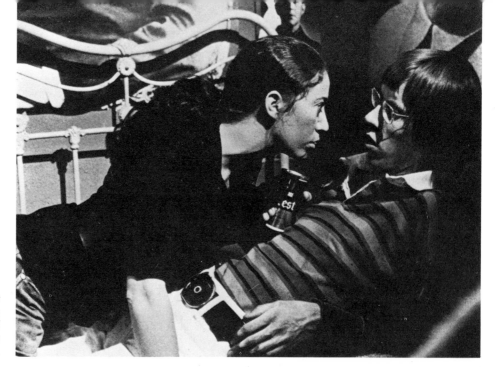

5.15 *Jan Friedl and Bruce Spence in "Stork" directed by Tim Burstall. This was a financial success — a complete reverse to the disastrous "2000 Weeks".*

him, but he remains the same aggressive Stork. He talks himself out of a job and lands on the doorstep of a house conducted by 'free-thinkers', three men and a girl (Jacki Weaver). Finally the girl becomes pregnant and marries one of the group. However at the open air wedding reception, Stork and a member of the quartette, Graeme Blundell, arrive with a fire engine and break up the party. Minor roles were played by Peter Cummins and Terry Norris.

After its premiere at the Palais Theatre, St Kilda on 27 December 1971, and after subsequent showings at the Balwyn and Metro Theatres, Melbourne, *Stork* grossed $150 000. Since then it has been rated by the Australian Film Commission as one of the commercial successes in local films in the 1970s. After it was blown up from 16 mm to 35 mm Roadshow took over its distribution and *Stork* was later sold to the Classic Cinema Chain in England.

In the 1972 Australian Film Awards, *Stork* won the Golden Reel Award, and the producers — Burstall, Bilcock and Copping — received the new Australian Film Development Corporation prize of $5 000. In addition, Tim Burstall was awarded $1 000 from the City Cinemas-Village Theatres Group for best direction; and Jacki Weaver and Bruce Spence shared the Hoyts $500 prize for best performances.

An Acting First

Another 16 mm production blown up to 35 mm for theatre release was *A City's Child* which won a Bronze Medal from the Australian Film Institute in 1971. The leading actress, Monica Maughan, was voted as giving the best performance of the year. This was the first time an acting achievement was acknowledged in the AFL Awards.

A City's Child was a dramatic treatment of the problem of loneliness in a large city. It is told through the eyes of an unloved spinster (Monica Maughan) who is approaching middle-age. A demanding mother (Moira Carleton) is forever mocking her daughter's ugliness, and complaining of her misfortune in being bedridden. After her mother's death, her failure to rejoin the ranks of human society caused her to enter an unreal world where dolls are her sole companions. She places a male and female doll in bed together. Rather surprisingly a baby doll arrives and neighbours raise their eyebrows when napkins appear on the clothes line. A young man (Sean Scully) enters

5.16 *Monica Maughan in "A City's Child" directed by Brian Kavanagh. She won the "performer of the year" Award from the Australian Film Institute in 1971.*

her life, taking her out of her dream world. Then one morning he leaves her never to return. To her horror she learns that she is pregnant. She drifts back into the world of fantasy, when she pulls the head of the mother doll and cradles the baby doll to her. The doll kingdom has claimed her.

It was a one-woman's show — Monica Maughan's. Other characters, with the possible exception of Moira Carleton as the mother, were without depth. Even then, the older woman's role was mere window dressing, as she dies before the titles came up.

A City's Child gained the distinction of being the first Australian film to be screened in the 15th London Film Festival in 1971 as a 'London Festival Choice' on 20 November, and re-screened one week later. It was shown in the Melbourne University's Union Theatre on 8 November 1971. In 1972 *A City's Child,* at the Adealide Film Festival, received The *Advertiser's Gold* Southern Cross Award as the best Australian film of the year. Overseas it was invited to be screened at the 1971 Chicago Film Festival; the 1972 Edinburgh Film Festival; Montreal Film Festival, 1972. In 1973 it was distributed by British Empire Films (now GUO) and opened at Sydney's Roseville Cinema on 23 May 1973, and had a season at the Playbox Theatre, Melbourne on 31 October 1974. In 1976 it was contracted to Rita Jarvis Ltd, for release in England, commencing with the new Electric Cinema, Covent Garden, in April 1977. The budget was $60 000 of which the Experimental Film Fund contributed $6 000.

Opinions of various critics were:

> Although *A City's Child* remains too plot-bound to be absolutely convincing, there can be no mistaking Brian Kavanagh's exceptional talent as a director. Throughout, the precision of his camera placements, the flow of movement within the frame, the exacting performances, serve perfectly the underlying ambiguity of events and produce a masterpiece in miniature.
>
> *Ken Quinnell*

> Brian Kavanagh should be encouraged to keep making films. He is the first Australian director to take his time and examine people's faces. An expressive face can convey a hundred words of dialogue. Linger on Brian Kavanagh. We need your insight, your compassion.
>
> *Edward Rosser*

> Apart from *Homesdale* — the finest home-grown Australian film of our time.
>
> *Bob Ellis*

> Brian Kavanagh's intense view of a lonely spinster finding kinky consolation in the collection of dolls — creates an eerie atmosphere which remains long after most of the Festival's other films have been and gone.
>
> *Eric Shorter on London Film Festival 1971*

Two Awards in a Row

Peter Weir with his *Homesdale* was again to the fore and on 16 mm won the Australian Film Institute's Grand Prix Award for the second year in succession. In addition Peter Weir again became the best director despite certain critics' forecasts. *Homesdale* is an expensive private guesthouse on a remote island near Sydney, where the guests are encouraged to live out their fantasies. Mr Malfrey, having his first vocation on the island, emerges as the odd man out. Weir has become noted for his fascination of gadgets. For

5.17 *"Brake Fluid" directed by Brian Davies won the 1971 Benson & Hedges Award, and gained second prize at the Perth Film Makers Festival in the same year. This still taken in the La Mama Theatre, Melbourne in 1970 shows from left to right — Bill Garner, John Duigan, Linzee Smith and Geoff Gardiner.*
(Still supplied by John Duigan.)

Homesdale he came up with a bizarre sound effect for Grahame Bond igniting an enormous gas cigarette lighter. Anthony Wallis was chief cameraman; Peter Gailey was in charge of lighting, and Ken Hammond looked after sound. The cast included Kate Fitzpatrick, Geoffrey Malone, Doreen Warburton, Phil Noyce, Richard Brennan and Peter Weir.

In the 1971 Benson & Hedges Award *Brake Fluid* narrowly beat *Homesdale. Brake Fluid,* a 16 mm production, was directed by Brian Davies of *The Pudding Thieves.* This story of a young man who could make his admiration for a certain young woman known to everyone but the girl herself, went on to gain second prize of $500 at the Perth Film Makers' Festival in 1971.

One 16 mm production that was the centre of a stormy debate in Federal Parliament is *Stockade.* This film was denounced as 'immoral' and strong exception was taken to the brothel and seduction scenes in the Eureka Hotel conducted by 'Ma' Bentley.* Director Hans Pomeranz in reply stated that the censor had made no 'cuts' and that *Stockade* had an 'M' rating.

Columbia Pictures retorted that Australia had not yet produced a picture that the public would endorse and held up as the prime example *The Demonstrator.* Here one must harken back to the advice given by Ken Hall about the choice of subject. The stand at the Eureka stockade was not in itself the most exciting event in Australian history: it was after all, all over in a matter of minutes. Only the events leading up to the resistance by the miners contained any element of drama and tension. Even the burning of the Eureka Hotel was far from spectacular. Harry Watt, with sweeping cameras, extracted all the action that could be associated with the storming of the stockade, and Jack Fegan as Timothy Hayes the agitating Irishman, did inject some of the rebelliousness that prompted the uprising of the miners. Rod Mullinar played Lalor but he was not convincing. Lalor was essentially a learned and gentle man, a dreamer more than a soldier of fortune. He was forced into assuming leadership of an ill-equipped army of diggers. Consequently there was light and shade in his character — a factor not wholly understood by the actor. Perhaps the real fault with *Stockade* was that it was based on a stage play by Kenneth Cook, and the film production did not explore beyond the confinements that the backdrops of the theatre had imposed.

The premiere of Stockade took place on 5 December, 1971, (the anniversary of the Eureka Stockade.) It was held appropriately enough in Ballarat. During the Christmas period of the same year it was released at the Mecca Theatre in Kogarah, and the Mandala Theatre, Paddington, Sydney.

* This has since been viewed by the Film Exhibition Review Committee of the NSW Education Department and approved for screening to secondary school students undertaking courses in junior history, and all students of drama and film appreciation.

5.18   *The futility of the miners' rebellion at Ballarat — dead bodies and wreckage in*
"Stockade".

5.19   *Rod Mullinar (in Doorway) as "Lalor" meets outraged miners and their wives, prior to*
the erecting of the Eureka stockade in "Stockade" directed by Hans Pomeranz.

More 16 mm Productions of the 70s

Sixteen mm productions in 1971 kept popping up like mushrooms. Just as the Salvation Army was the backbone of the early Australian film industry, so did the 16 mm film makers keep the industry alive during the two decades when the feature film side of it needed an undertaker more than a doctor. Government aid had been urgently required in this area, yet paradoxically enough, the government supported the efforts of Film Australia — also mainly on 16 mm — to sustain the industry in producing documentaries. But during the early 70s, Australia needed to extend the realm of creativity beyond local and international Film Festivals to the world's theatre screens themselves. Everyone in the industry knew that it was the rekindling of feature film making that the country needed to bring about a strong and secure Australian film industry. Yet the government ranks were themselves divided. In October 1971, the government under (Sir) William McMahon deferred for 12 months any action on the recommended National Film and Television School. This led to ex-Prime Minister Gorton publicly hinting that he believed the project had been abandoned. Small wonder prospective feature film makers were uncertain as to the future, even though the Australian Film Development Corporation was supplying some financial backing.

A 16 mm production, *Sympathy in Summer,* has an interesting background. Originally filmed in Sydney and Melbourne in 1968, it was an inopportune time for an outsider to attempt to compete on the Australian film scene. *Sympathy in Summer* was conceived, written and directed by Antony Ginnane as a mini-feature for 1968 release. His budget was $2000. At the time it was titled *We are None of us Perfect,* The project mushroomed to a $7000 production, but editing and sound recording restrained its release until 1971, when it was blown up to 35 mm. *Sympathy in Summer* was finally screened at the Grand Cinema, Footscray (Melbourne) on 15 March 1971, and Carlton Theatre, 18 March. In the same month it was shown at the Dental Hospital

5.20   *Connie Simmons and Vincent Griffith in "Sympathy In Summer" directed by Antony Ginnane. (The previous film title was "We Are None Of Us Perfect".)*

Auditorium, Melbourne, It had a return season at the Grand and Carlton Theatres, and it was shown on 25 March at the Prince Philip Theatre, Melbourne University. The running time was sixty-two minutes.

Sympathy in Summer was the story of a young couple, Len and Anne (Vincent Griffith and Connie Simmons). After a typical Australian party they embark upon a self-destructive relationship. After Anne leaves him, Len drifts through life without any purpose. He begins to probe into his past, secretly questioning everything — his girlfriend, himself, and the world generally. Anne does not return, but instead goes to live with a man she once knew (Tony Horler). Len seeks the companionship of two women, Robin Wells and Pam McAllister. Still not benefiting from his mistakes, his mental collapse continues.

One critic wrote: 'The film has a lot of visual beauty and the music is pleasant, even though it is too loud. Some of the scenes end too abruptly, and the sound is muffled at times. Ginnane had to overcome a lot of technical problems on a small budget, but the mistakes he made are negligible considering the sincerity and originality of the whole film'.

Nigel Buesst photographed *Sympathy in Summer* and he had a second contribution to 1971, this time as producer and director. This film was titled *Bonjour Balwyn* and it was based on a script by John Duigan, John Romeril and Buesst. Buesst shared the editing with Peter Tammer. The photography was handled by Tom Cowan. In *Bonjour Balwyn,* Kevin Agar (John Duigan) starts publishing a new magazine as a form of escape from the family business. The publication is not a success and he goes to work for a petty thief (Peter Cummins). Kevin then helps to repossess television sets. Here he appreciates the conflicts and ethics of Melbourne's middle-class society. Others in the cast were John Romeril, Camilla Rountree, and Barbara Stephens. Antony Ginnane classified the film as 'technically flawless, with Buesst's editing being especially effective.' *Bonjour Balwyn* received special mention in the 1971 AFI Awards, and was screened in the Hawthorn Art Gallery, Melbourne, on 19 October 1972.

A 16 mm production to receive honourable mention in the 1971 Australian Film Institute Awards was *And the Word was made Flesh.* Dusan Marek was a one-man production crew, producer; director; photographer and editor. The cast included David Stocker, Christine Pearce, and David Tilly. In sixty-five minutes it told the story of an anthropologist who found a cocoon and fell in love with it. In his imagination his ideal woman materialises from the chrysalis.

Brian Robinson who was associated with Phillip Adams on *Jack and Jill — A Postscript,* was the director of *Some Regrets* which was also photographed on 16 mm, with a running time of twenty minutes. It related the unfortunate plight of Freddy, who lives a lonely existence in a poorly furnished room. He has three diversions — the newspaper, television, and the pursuit of cleanliness. Seeking escape he dreams of Eden and of love — only to have death intervene. Even in heaven he is dogged by regrets.

Some Regrets won the Silver citation and the prize for creativity in the 1971 Australian Film Awards. It shared first prize in the Alan Stout Awards, and was a finalist in the Benson & Hedges Awards in 1971. It was screened at the Adelaide and Melbourne Film Festivals in 1972.

Paddington Lace

It is fitting to close the entries for 1971 with a tribute to Film Australia, and to one of its most successful productions, the twenty-four minute comedy-drama Paddington Lace. Joan Long, a future producer, was associated with it as scripter and it was directed by Chris McCullogh. *Paddington Lace* was a delightful comedy, a satire on inner-suburban rehabilitation, told through the story of some young people living in the old Sydney suburb. For Joan Long it meant the Awgie Award of 1971 for the script.

The Festival Awards for *Paddington Lace* were very impressive. At the 16th Cork International Film Festival, 1971, *Paddington Lace* received the St Finbarr Statuette for best short fiction and it also received the Irish Film Society Award. It won third prize at London's Festival of Best Sponsored Films, 1971; it received the Golden Reel Award, fiction category in the Australian Film Awards, 1971; and it received a Certificate of Merit in the Kodak Color Awards. It was given the Gold Camera Award in the US Industrial Film Festival in Chicago, 1972 and it received the Certificate of Honourable Mention in the International Film Review in Sri Lanka, 1972. In both 16 mm and 35 mm, this film was later distributed by Columbia Pictures. It was screened throughout Australia, the United Kingdom and the U.S.A. It is the only Australian film to have been screened on a North American Network — CBC — coast to coast in prime time.

These awards reveal the strength that Australian short films had achieved, with credit due to the inspired work from Film Australia.

Beer and Footy

In 1972, the Australian film industry was still awaiting the mythical Phoenix to arise with new vigour. What the industry actually acquired was a loud-mouthed, beer-swilling 'Bazza' McKenzie. Sylvia Lawson in *Nation Review* on 26 May 1977 sums up the situation in this vitriolic manner;

> *The Adventures of Barry McKenzie, Stork,* and *Alvin Purple* all concentrated on those beer-and-footy aspects of Australian society which are summed up in the local parlance as 'ockerism'. They combine a broad, vaudeville sort of titillation with indulgent satire on what ordinary Australian lives and concerns are supposed to be all about. They are deliberately pornographic on Leagues' Club floor-show level, and deliberately anti-intellectual.

Barry McKenzie and Aunty Edna's adventures in London were as subtle as a truckies' picnic barbecue. Samples of Bazza's dialogue are: 'I'm as full as a State school', and 'I hope all your chooks turn to emus and peck your dunny down.' The film was based on Barry Humphries' cartoon strip in a London publication. One critic described it as 'a first for local industry — a technicolour yawn in glorious Eastmancolor.'

There was a sneak preview in August 1972 at Sydney University's Union Theatre, and in the same month it was premiered at the Perth Film Festival. Barry Humphries felt that the name Longford Productions (a memory of director Raymond Longford) would be associated with the English Lord Longford, the famous opponent of pornography.

'Bazza' with an outsize brimmed hat and a double-breasted suit arrives in London by plane, only to be taken for a ride by a London taxi driver; taken for his money by Spike Milligan as the landlord of the Kangaroo Valley Hotel; and taken for his pants by Caroline Thighs (Maria O'Brien). Australian Dick Bentley portrays a member of the vice squad.

The Adventures of Barry McKenzie opened at the Melbourne Capitol Theatre on 12 October 1972, and one year later (11 October 1973) at the Columbia Theatre, London, where at the end of the month it had broken every box office record in the history of the theatre since it began in 1958. In fact only two films in the West End made money at the time and 'Bazza' was one of them. Columbia Pictures stated: 'It's become a cult picture for the young', and one newspaper critic headed his review: 'Oh what a lovely lark.' The same production was banned from television in Australia on 21 June 1975, yet in the battle for the ratings, Channel 7 Sydney and Melbourne screened it on 26 October 1975. Only two scenes were deleted, and the network paid $50 000 for it.

New Attempts at 35 mm Productions

In 1972 Terry Bourke returned to Australia and became involved with the direction of a TV series which included episodes of the popular *Spyforce* starring Jack Thompson and Peter Sumner. In an attempt to be more bizarre than Alfred Hitchcock, and as a follow-up to a statement by Rod Serling that 'Americans loved to be frightened', Terry made a pilot of a horror series for the ABC called *Night of Fear*. This was a gruesome tale of a hermit and his rats. A sexually vulnerable blonde (Carla Hoogeveen) uses the bushland to foster an illicit love affair. In that same tree-bound setting she is destroyed by the hermit (Norman Yemm) and his carnivorous rodents. The 'horse girl' (Briony Behets) is another victim. First the horse is killed for food for the hermit's pets and after a profane ceremony she too is left bound to a table to allow the rats to devour her. Two interesting aspects of *Night of Fear* were the complete absence of dialogue, and the fact that despite police investigation, the hermit was not charged with any crime. It was edited by Ray Alchin and Peter Hendry of the ABC headed the cameramen.

The pilot was rejected by the ABC and *Night of Fear* became a theatrical release. It was first screened commercially at the Bairnsdale Drive-In (Victoria) on 4 November 1972. This showing took place before the Commonwealth Film Censor ban had been proclaimed. In December, the Film Board of Review granted a reprieve without 'cuts', but the film was

5.21 *Norman Yemm as the crazy hermit about to make another "kill" in the Terry Bourke film "Night Of Fear".*

5.22 *A scene from "Sunstruck" showing (from right) Bobby Limb, Harry Secombe, and Norm Erskine opposite John Meillon (behind the bar).*

classified as 'R'. The Penthouse Theatre, Kings Cross, released it on 16 March 1973. In Melbourne it was limited to the Village Drive-Ins.

A disappointing year in 35 mm production ended with a low-key feature *Sunstruck* produced by Jack Neary (of NLT Productions) and James Grafton. In this film a Welsh schoolteacher (Harry Secombe) after an unhappy love affair, decides to take up the same profession in Australia. He is posted to 'Kookaburra Springs' in western NSW — a small bushtown comprising an old pub (the 'Mayfair Hotel') and a ramshackle schoolhouse. The teacher to his horror learns that there are sixteen scholars, ranging from seven to fifteen. The school hasn't had a headmaster for three months, following the sudden departure of the previous one. The new teacher meets the proprietors of the Mayfair Hotel — John Meillon and Dawn Lake — and their screen son Stevie (Dennis Jordan). The youngster is a 'horror'. He lets mosquitoes loose in the schoolteacher's room, places laxatives in his tea, and slips a snake in his desk at the school. The teacher meets a down-to-earth Amazon farmer (Maggie Fitzgibbon) who tosses bags of produce around as easily as if they were filled with foam rubber. She has a brother (Peter Whittle) who has no intention of losing a good housekeeper, and gives the newcomer a rugged time, until his sister persuades him to desist, by taking 'pot shots' at him with a rifle. The schoolteacher marries the 'Amazon'

5.23 *Dawn Lake administers first aid to Harry Secombe in the Jack Neary-James Grafton production "Sunstruck".*

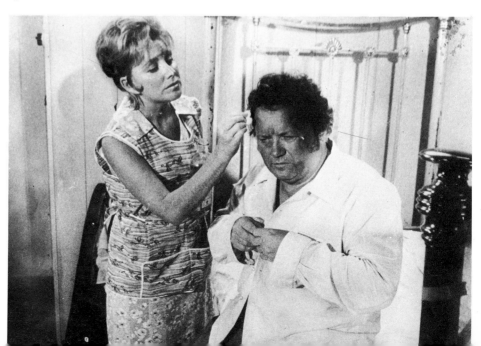

farmer, and as the bridal couple await the arrival of the plane to depart for their honeymoon, the replacement teacher arrives. He is Derek Nimmo — very correct, and so very, very English.

Sunstruck premiered in England, and was screened at the Odeon Theatre, Melbourne on 22 December 1972. It was a modest, but entertaining picture. Brian West was director of photography, and John McLean was camera operator.

16 mm Still in Front

In 1972, the 16 mm production again greatly exceeded the output on 35 mm and many showed more promise than those made exclusively for theatres. Film Australia was responsible for two productions that were worthy of note. Both were in colour. The first, a documentary titled *Gentle Strangers* was directed by Cecil Holmes and scripted by Cecil Holmes. It ran for fifty eight minutes. Photographers included Kerry Brown, Bruce Hillyard, Don McAlpine and David Sanderson.

Gentle Strangers made the point that 12 000 overseas students are training and studying in Australia. For many, the Australian way of life meant a new language, unfamiliar food, and different social habits. The cast included Yee Choo Koo, Clem Chow, Rick Lay, Jennifer West and Lyn Murphy. It received a Bronze Award in the 1972 Australian Film Awards.

5.24 *Preeyah, played by Yee Choo Koo is Lawrence's girlfriend and female lead in "Gentle Strangers". This was directed by Cecil Holmes for Film Australia.*

5.25 *Clem Chow, playing the part of Lawrence, at the degree conferring ceremony which culminates his studies in Australia. A scene from "Gentle Strangers" that won a Bronze Award for Film Australia at the 1972 Australian Films Awards.*

Flashpoint, the second production from Film Australia, was produced by Gil Brealey and directed by Brian Hannant. It was a feature of fifty-five minutes based on a script by Harold Lander and director Brian Hannant. Kerry Brown was in charge of photography. In this production, David (Serge Lazareff) is a new worker in a Western Australian iron ore mine. He learns that a friend, Foxy (Wyn Roberts) although outwardly confident and self-reliant, is in fact insecure and uncertain about his relationship with his attractive wife Vicky (Jan Kingsbury). Fifty-odd miners in an isolated town constitute an explosive force. Vicky, provides the fuse. Many men are wary of igniting a very delicate situation, but David unwittingly provides the spark.

5.26 *Harry Lawrence and Wyn Roberts in a scene from "Flashpoint" produced by Film Australia.*

5.27 *Jan Kingsbury, female lead in "Flashpoint" directed by Brian Hannant.*

Shirley Thompson versus the Aliens, a 16 mm production which didn't make it commercially, is more notable for the people associated with its making than for the film itself. Kolossal Piktures had Matt Carroll as producer, and Jim Sharman as director. With designer Brian Thompson and writer Helmut Bakaitis, Kolossal aimed to produce 'B' grade movies. *Shirley Thompson* was filmed by David Sanderson and featured black and white for domestic scenes, under-exposed white for the asylum sequences, and colour for flights into fantasy.

Shirley Thompson (Jane Harders) is a 1950 'widgee' who rebels against the stultifying suburbanism of her home. She has a nagging mother (Marion Johns) who wishes her to marry that 'nice young man' Harold (Helmut Bakaitis), and a father (John Llewellyn) who has a self-satisfying smugness about life in general. With a crowd of young people, Shirley visits Luna Park and becomes lost in a sideshow. Ron Haddrick as a wax model of the Duke of Edinburgh, comes to life and becomes the spokesman for mysterious aliens who plan to take over the world. For the next ten years she tries to convince people of what she saw, but slowly goes insane, as they refuse to believe her. The story is told in flashbacks as Shirley, in an asylum, is being questioned by the matron and a psychiatrist.

Variety on 22 June 1972, classifies the production as a 'Festival film with little hope of commercial distribution'. The classification proved correct. It was screened in 1972 at the Sydney and London Film Festivals, and in 1973, featured at the Brisbane Film Festival.

A more important 16 mm production was *The Hands of Cormac Joyce* from Crawford Productions. Hector Crawford won the contract to make the film here from a strong field of international production houses. It was a proud achievement for Crawford and Australia generally. Unfortunately its script writer, producer and director were all American and it had many overseas stars. Only in photography did Australia fly the flag, with John McLean and Vince Monton on camera. Made for the American *Hallmark of Fame* TV series, it was produced by Fred Engel, directed by Fielder Cook, and had overseas stars Stephen Boyd, Cyril Cusack, Colleen Dewhurst, and Dominic Guard. Australian actors were Lynette Floyd, Enid Lorimer, and Deryck Barnes.

A little slow-moving, *The Hands of Cormac Joyce* depicts an Irish fishing village which is living under a threat of extinction. When the storm eventually arrives the violence and the fury of the wind and lashing waters are brilliantly captured by the Australian cameramen. It was seen on HSV 7 Melbourne on 24 June 1973. On 21 October 1973, it was screened at the Australian Cinematographers' Festival, Windsor Theatre, Brisbane.

Private Collection another 16 mm production, this time from Keisal-Bonza Films, had a very checkered career. Directed by Keith Salvat, it was screened at the Sydney Film Festival on 31 May 1972. Village Theatres became interested, but held it for eight months before releasing it at the Australia Cinema, Melbourne on 12 April 1973. Even then it was only a fill-in.

Private Collection centres around Henry Phillips (Peter Reynolds), a retired business man, who, because of a heart condition, becomes an avid collector of way out *objets d'art*. His most prized possession is a young wife Mary Ann (Pamela Stephenson). Joseph Tibbsworth another collector (Brian Blain) sends a small-time crook (Grahame Bond) to rob Phillips. The thief loses a finger in a guillotine burglar alarm. Instead of turning him over to the police, Phillips blackmails him into stealing a stuffed eagle from Tibbsworth. Meanwhile a very bored wife retreats into a world of fantasy that becomes one of terror.

Because Salvat did not have a budget that warranted retakes, cameraman David Gribble had to be satisfied with a first take every time. Described as a 'black comedy', it was an ambitious attempt to get the feature film front moving — yet it never quite came off. However one Melbourne critic did claim that it was one of the most interesting Australian films he had seen for several years. He enjoyed the plot and the humour, despite the strange jerky progression of the scenes.

1972 Film Awards

The most creative entries in the 1972 Australian Film Awards were the 16 mm productions: Victor Kay Jnr entered *Magic Camera Film 2;* George Miller gave his *Violence in the Cinema Part 1* and *Jackpot Town* came from Roger Whittaker. These three men shared first prize in the Alan Stout Awards, with third prize of $350 going to Anthony Airey for his *After Image*. In addition *Magic Camera* and *Violence in the Cinema* won Silver Awards. *After Image* received a Bronze Award. *Jackpot Town*, produced by Jeff Carter, not only won a Golden Reel but the Department of the Interior Award as well. With directing and editing by Roger Whittaker, and camerawork by Jeff Carter, it covered in twenty-eight minutes, the frontier-style living in the opal town of Coober Pedy. It reveals how men and women survive in a hostile environment, merely for the opportunity of striking it rich.

Magic Camera Film 2 was filmed in both 35 mm and 16 mm. It shows in ten minutes a series of images with a background of music played on a portable gramophone. These include narrow white trees moving rapidly past the camera; clouds curling past a branch of eerie white leaves; a motor bike plunging into a red landscape; and girls in whirling cloaks on the seashore. It was classified as the 'modified use of the camera in conjunction with unusual editing to transform commonplace everyday reality'. Direction, editing and photography were by Victor Kay.

Violence in the Cinema Part 1 ran four minutes longer than *Magic Camera* and endeavoured to examine violence in the cinema, in which the lecturer, cast and audience become victims of or witnesses to violent assault on themselves or on their emotions. In the cast were Arthur Dignam, Victoria Anoux, Karl Avis, and the Havoc stunt team. It was directed by George Miller and photographed by Byron Kennedy.

After Image ran for only four minutes, and had background music by Bach. It was an exercise in fast editing. Parts 1 and 2 synthesised colour, and Part 3 related percussion qualities of music to abstract images.

Of much longer duration were the entries called *The Hairy Nosed Wombat* (sixty-two minutes) and *The Money Game* (fifty minutes). The former won a Bronze and 'Jedda' Awards, the latter a Silver Award.

The unique Hairy Nosed Wombat is found in South Australia. The film covers its life history, and reveals its importance to different groups of people. Direction, script, editing and photography were handled by Douglas B. Steen. The narrator was Roger Cardwell.

The Money Game, directed by Michel Pearce for the Australian Broadcasting Commission, was a satire on the world of economics. The money game is depicted as a sporting event played by six contestants — the employer, under-developer, financier etc., seated at an economic machine of wheels and levers. No player becomes the winner. The script was by Bruce Petty (the cartoonist who was associated with the short, *Leisure*, that won a Hollywood Oscar in 1977). The photographer was Tony Wilson, and the players included Alfred Sandor (seen in *Nickel Queen*), John Cheung, Nat Leveson, Alistair Duncan and Chris Haywood.

In the 1972 Film Awards, *Upon Reflection* photographed by Gert Kirshener and Diane Nettlefold, won a bronze medallion for colour photography. On 16 mm with a running time of forty minutes, the storyline relates how two music students are driven from their homes because their respective families complain of the noise. The pair meet in a park and a musical relationship develops. The boy is frivolous; the girl is shy and awkward. Just as their relationship develops they are separated by sudden tragedy. The main players are Mary Krisp and Keith Crellin. It was directed by Diane Nettlefold.

As well as awards there was heartache in the 16 mm department. Late in 1972 a Magma Film Corporation production *About Love* directed by Ernest George Schwartz was hawked to a number of distributors, but it was refused a release. However the Penthouse Cinema, Sydney did offer to screen it at a cost of $1000 per week. Even this deal fell through, as the cinema management had been informed by the Chief Secretary that the screening of a 16 mm film in a 35 mm theatre was not permissible. (Yet the Australia Cinema, Melbourne did this in the case of *Private Collection*.)

About Love consisted of five episodes over a ninety minute study of female moods. The photography was by Grant Mudford. *Possum*, a thirty minute segment from *About Love*, is available through the Vincent Library. It tells of a dissatisfied wife who seeks fulfilment in fantasy.

Talent but no Appreciation

Finally 1972 revealed an incredible lack of appreciation of talent. Eric Porter's *Marco Polo Jnr versus the Red Dragon* was an excellent example of this outstanding cartoonist's work. This eighty-three minute colour cartoon was considered the equal, and often better than any of Walt Disney's work. Even though *Marco Polo* was praised by the critics, it was ignored by the public at a time when it should have succeeded. Take Melbourne as a typical example. It opened on 26 December 1972 (the ideal time), but closed on 4 January 1973 — as big a disaster as was *2000 Weeks*. Yet it was sold overseas, and in the 1973 Australian Film Awards, Eric Porter received the $1000 Award from City Cinemas-Village Theatres for best direction. The film itself gained the Gold Award.

At the Tariff Board Inquiry in late 1972, Eric Porter stated that *Marco Polo Jnr versus the Red Dragon* was being distributed by British Empire Films. Although he was pleased with the deal, he could not get it screened at night, not even for one week. Yet other children's films like *Pinocchio* and *Tales of Beatrix Potter* were shown in the evening. This is just another example of unfair distribution that overseas companies inflicted upon local films.

Distribution and Exhibition Costs

On the other hand, one of the heartening aspects of 1972 transpired in April when the Federal Government, rather surprisingly, announced that it would build the controversial National Film and Television School. However the size and cost would be greatly reduced from that in the original recommendation. Yet the scales were unbalanced: on one side, future film makers would be trained, but fair distribution was not being taken into account.

This is an opportune time to mention distribution and exhibition costs. The figures submitted to the Tariff Board Inquiry by Phillip Adams concerning *The Adventures of Barry McKenzie* in late November 1972, prove exceedingly interesting.

Theatre	Box Office	Producer's Net	
ASCOT, Sydney			
First week	$24129	$ 9773	(after heavy initial publicity and press screening)
Second week	$23493	$12818	
Third week	$21031	$11208	

CAPITOL, Melbourne

First week	$21 446	$ 9 464	(after initial expenses)
Second week	$19 351	$10 192	
Third week	$15 597	$ 7 490	
Fourth week	$16 346	$ 8 029	

METRO, Brisbane

First week	$11 705	$ 4 110
Second week	$13 096	$ 6 019
Third week	$10 541	$ 4 180

WARNER, Adelaide

First week	$ 6 126	$ 1 031
Second week	$ 5 848	$ 1 978

KENSINGTON, Newcastle

First week	$ 5 651	$ 2 204

Phillip Adams notes that the above figures reveal the initial box office results, which in Sydney and Melbourne at least, represent approximately 50 per cent of the box office gross, compared to an average of 20 per cent returned to the producer, if he employs a commercial distributor. Mr Adams went on to explain some of the problems he had with the distribution of *The Adventures of Barry McKenzie*. In Sydney, the Ascot was only available for eight weeks. The proprietors had booked *The Tales of Beatrix Potter* over Christmas. He then approached the distributors of the *Potter* film, and suggested that as it was a children's picture, it could be shown at the Ascot in the daytime and the *Barry McKenzie* film be screened at night in the interests of the Australian film industry. The distributor turned it down. Yet this same distributor (BEF) restricted *Marco Polo Jnr versus the Red Dragon* to 'daytime only' exhibition. If this is not a case of restrictive trade practices — then the real example must be a little beauty.

In mid-1977 both Roadshow and GUO were approached for details of exhibition and distribution costs. Only the latter replied:

The company name BEF (Film Distributors) Pty Ltd, was changed to GUO Film Distributors Pty Ltd, in August 1976.

GUO Film Distributors is not a production company. However they do invest money in Australian feature films, and such feature films are distributed in Australia by GUO Film Distributors Pty Ltd. This does not mean that screenings will be limited to GUO theatres, as GUO distributors supply all major circuits throughout Australia.

But it is their reference to costs that are of the utmost importance.

> Distribution fees are resolved after discussion between the producer and distribution company, who will be selling a particular film.* With regard to negotiations between the distributor and exhibitor, this is dependent upon quality and earning potential of a film, which governs the scale of return which a distributor may earn from the exhibition of such film. The film hire of any film is dependent upon the success or otherwise at the box office, which of course is gauged upon public acceptance from first release in key centres.

Phillip Adams explained that the initial results of *The Adventures of Barry McKenzie* gave Australian producers good reason for considering independent distribution. *They're a Weird Mob* retained about 16 per cent of the box office gross and *Stork* since its distribution with Roadshow, was keeping about 20 per cent of the box office.

At the Tariff Board Inquiry in late 1972, Dr H.C. Coombs, chairman of the Arts Council, had stated that the Australian Film Corporation since its inception in 1970, in a broadly written charter, gave encouragement to the making and distribution of Australian films with emphasis on high artistic and technical standards. He explained that the profitability factor was introduced by the prime minister in his second speech but that this emphasis was not written into the Act. Dr Coombs went on to advise that the difficulties of financing production was due to the failure of the distribution section of the industry to invest in Australian production, along with the caution of the banks and other financial institutions in providing finance for films. (Since this statement GUO as already stated, Roadshow, Hoyts and the Victorian and New South Wales Film Commissions, have invested in the production of Australian films.) Dr Coombs pointed out that there was no provision in the Film Development Corporation Act for it to provide marketing facilities. He suggested that the AFDC could establish an agency to service Australian makers of film and television programmes.

Mr Michael Thornhill added more fuel to the fire with regard to distribution, by stating that Australian productions were unlikely to achieve distribution billings greater than 33 per cent of the box office gross, whereas according to Mr R. Kirby of Warner Brothers-Roadshow, *Clockwork Orange* was then returning to the distributors 67 per cent in Sydney and 64 per cent in Melbourne of box office gross. Mr Thornhill argued against an 'open door' to foreign productions. He claimed that writers and directors are not trained or assisted by continually standing around watching other people do their thing.

---

*   Those words 'particular film' hold more significance than at first realised. But the rest is mere jargon that gives no indication of what a producer may expect in returns — and in the first instance, it has to be determined whether the film is good, bad or indifferent in the distributor's eyes. This, according to the statement, determines the earnings. Yet all this preamble gets us no further than square one, as the bad or indifferent films won't be accepted for distribution in the first place.

Mr Hans Pomeranz appeared on behalf of Spectrum Films. He advised that *Stockade* had come in for a lot of criticism because of its alleged poor quality. He highlighted the difficulty he experienced in finding suitable theatres for the screening of his film on 16 mm due to the licensing legislation in New South Wales. Mr Pomeranz hoped that the approval by the NSW Education Department for screening in secondary schools, would offset some of the production costs.

Paul Witzig who had made surfing films, told of his problems in NSW and Queensland over the showing of his productions. He complained of rising costs in theatre rentals. The Avalon Theatre, Sydney, a few years prior to the hearing, was $50-$60 per night. Now that same theatre was $200-$300 per night. In January 1972 theatres in Bundaberg, Rockhampton and Maryborough (Queensland) had screened his films. The picture took $1 639, but 70 per cent of the box office was taken for theatre rentals. Witzig claimed that in America, specialist films were shown in civic and high school auditoriums, and he would like to see this situation in Australia.

Richard Brennan, then director of the Australian Film Institute, gave further figures on the distribution-exhibition costs. He referred to John McCallum and *Nickel Queen*. According to evidence submitted at the Tariff Board Inquiry, Fauna Productions-TVW 7, received nearly 40 per cent of gross takings when handled by them in Western Australia, where it grossed $207 783 — the producers received $83 312. In the Eastern States it was a different story. When handled by BEF, the film grossed $122 189 — of which distributor-exhibitor costs took $116 745. After allowing for publicity this was reduced to $80 000. However the producers' return was $5 444. (At the State Theatre, Sydney, Fauna claimed that a four weeks season actually meant a loss of approximately $5 000.)

A Fair Deal for Australians

Problems in the industry regarding a better deal for Australian producers were not new — and were just as noticeable in the past as they are today. In 1973, following recommendations by the NSW Theatres and Films Commission, it was decided to alter quotas fixed under the Cinematograph Films Act. As from 1 January 1974, a distributor was required to acquire and make available for distribution, a 4 per cent quota of Australian Films. (This had been raised to 5 per cent.) Under the same Act an exhibitor was required to show a quota of 3 per cent per annum (an additional 0.5 per cent). The Commission advised that seven Australian films were registered for quota purposes in NSW during the year ending 30 June 1973 — the second highest since the Act came into force. Under the same Act, British films fared badly. The required quota was reduced from 15 per cent to 5 per cent as from 1 July 1974. The reason for the reduction was that Australian films ceased to receive the benefits of a quota in the United Kingdom after Britain joined the European Common Market on 1 January 1973.

Seeing that the states were reluctant to transfer their powers over film requirements to the Commonwealth Government, the premiers who are so anxious to call conferences at the drop of a hat, should decide without delay to back New South Wales, and pass similar quota requirements.

Feature Films Compete

Nineteen seventy three seemed a little dazed over the activity in the 16 mm ranks, and it wasn't until April that the feature film section of the industry displayed any initiative — and then it took four Australian directors to make one picture — *Libido*.

Produced by the Producers and Directors Guild of Australia, *Libido* arrived at the Rapallo Theatre, Melbourne on 6 April 1973, and Sydney's Gala Theatre on 13 April. The four directors were Tim Burstall, Fred Schepisi, David Baker and John B. Murray. Each handled a story by a different Australian author — Hal Porter, Thomas Keneally, David Williamson and Craig McGregor.

Undoubtedly *The Child* was the outstanding episode, for which director Tim Burstall wrote the screenplay, backed by superb photography from Robin Copping. John Williams was brilliant as 'the child' who sees the adult world through a boy's eyes. He is left to his own bored devices as a merry-widow mother (Jill Forster) becomes attracted to a prospective second husband. Finally a young governess arrives and the boy falls in love with her. He receives a shock when he discovers that the governess (Judy Morris) has 'other' interests. *The Child* won a Golden Reel in the Australian Film Awards in 1974. In addition Judy Morris received the Hoyts' prize for the best actress and Jill Forster received an Honourable Mention. Robin Copping was awarded a Bronze Medallion from Kodak for his photographic contribution to *The Child*.

5.28 *John Williams as "The Child" in the Producers and Directors Guild of Australia's production "Libido". "The Child" was based on a story by Hal Porter, and directed by Tim Burstall.*

Another episode of *Libido* called *The Priest* won a Silver Reel in the 1974 Australian Film Awards. *The Priest* contained a great deal of interest apart from the story itself: Fred Schepisi, the director, was poised on the threshold of his own future and his making of *The Devil's Playground*. In this segment of *Libido* he was showing the promise that would mark him as a director to watch. In *The Priest*, Arthur Digman (previously seen in *Violence in the Cinema*) portrayed Father Byrne, a disillusioned man of the cloth who fell in love with a nun (Robyn Nevin). This causes great emotional and spiritual distress to Sister Caroline, resulting in a nervous breakdown.

The Family Man, the third episode of *Libido,* received an Honourable Mention for Jack Thompson's acting. The story centres around a man (Jack Thompson) who is annoyed when his wife gives birth to a third daughter instead of a son. During a stag night celebration, Thompson with Max Gillies picks up a couple of 'birds' and they spend an evening dancing, smoking 'pot' and 'guzzling'. The whole episode is treated with a heavy hand by director David Baker and when the girls strip at a beach house the film fizzles like a damp cracker. The girls as actresses weren't competent enough to handle the demands of the David Williamson script.

The only non-starter award-wise in the *Libido* production was *The Husband* which combined lack-lustre direction with a trite script. A jealous husband (Byron Williams) indulges in fantasies about his attractive wife's infidelities. This even extends to Elke Neidhardt stripping solely to make a phone call notifying her lover that the coast is clear for their romantic tryst.

Libido was originally shot on 16 mm and later blown up to 35 mm. In the original processing, a great deal of disappointment was expressed at the

5.29   The "Rape sequence" in "The Husband" directed by John Murray for the four-in-one production "Libido".

5.30   Byron Williams (standing) and Elke Neidhardt (right), Mark Albiston is R, in "The Husband" sequence in "Libido". The grain visible in the still is due to the poor quality of the original 16 mm negative.

quality of the film, particularly with regard to grain. This is very evident in one of the stills from *The Husband*.

March 1973 was an interesting month for features for at least two reasons. *The Adventures of Barry McKenzie* was banned in New Zealand because it was contrary to public order and decency, and undesirable in the public interests. It was stated that the censor was prepared to accept it if one 'cut' was made — from 'the beginning to the end'.*

In that same month of March Tom Cowan's *The Office Picnic* was screened at the Center Cinema, Canberra. Tom Cowan could be compared to W. Franklyn Barrett of the silent film days — he is an excellent photographer who often took on the additional duty of director. These two responsible duties are not easily combined on the one set at the same time. In *The Office Picnic* however, it was Michael Edols who handled the photography and did it exceedingly well. *The Office Picnic* revolves around a typical clerk and his own shallow emotional experiences, including what he intends to do to a fluffy blonde at the picnic. During office hours, he makes a joke of the way the mail boy pursues a new and sexy switchgirl. *The Office Picnic* was savagely witty in places, a little crude in others but it did display desire on the part of Cowan to put Australia back in the feature film field. Despite such an earnest wish, this picture never really got going. It became, on the whole, another Festival film. Following the Canberra screening, it came to the Sydney University Union Theatre on 21 May 1973, and was featured at the Moscow Film Festival in the same year. Leading players were John Wood, Ben Gabriel, Kate Fitzpatrick, Patricia Kennedy, and Philip Deamer.

On 19 February 1975, when *The Office Picnic* reached Melbourne and was exhibited at the Playbox Theatre, Tom Cowan admitted that although the film had not been a financial success, it had been made as a non-commercial production.

One critic compared *The Office Picnic* to *Stork*, stating that the story was inferior to *Stork* but that the direction was better. He ranked it with Brian Kavanagh's *A City's Child* and Nigel Buesst's *Bonjour Balwyn* as one of those engrossing, cheaply-budgeted films. In another review the same critic hits the strength, right on target: 'Visually it is one of the most remarkable films to come out of Australia.' That word 'visually' is the keyword.

Another young director determined to 'break all the rules' was Bert Deling. His *Dalmas* for Apogee Film Productions became a 'cult' film in 1973. Shot on 16 mm by Sasha Trikojus, it ran for approximately two hours. *Dalmas* has been described as the film that 'freaked out'. It contained one of the most horrifying heroin-jabbing sequences that could ever be visualised. The picture was a definite 'two-parter' with Deling having some control over the first half. However Part 2 became 'murky' with overtones of mass hysteria when Dalmas after an acid trip, comes close to turning on his ex-director, Bert Deling, with an axe.

One critic wrote: 'It seems unfortunate that Deling could not have surrendered his film to people with more feeling for the cinema, and fewer half-digested concepts were borrowed from media gobbledygook.' Yet

* NZ censors felt that they were more liberal than their Australian counterparts in passing sex and violence, but they drew the line at Australian colloquialisms. Just how far down the NZ social scale were 'ockerisms'?

5.31   *John Wood in Tom Cowan's "The Office Picnic". Screened in 1973 at the Perth and Moscow Festivals, the film had to wait until 19 February 1975 to be shown at the Playbox Theatre, Melbourne.*

5.32   *In "Dalmas" directed by Bert Deling, Peter Whittle portrays a tough policeman investigating the death of his partner.*

another critic took an entirely different view of the picture and found it 'exciting and inventive with probably the most original use of colour and camera yet found in an Australian movie.'

Rejected by the Sydney Film Festival Committee, it opened at the Sydney Filmmakers' Cinema, Darlinghurst, on 25 May 1973. At the Perth Film Festival in 1973 *Dalmas* sold out. *Dalmas* had a further screening at the Schonell Theatre, Brisbane, on 3 September 1973.

A favourite 16 mm production for 1973 was *27A*. This film premiered in Perth on 12 August 1973. Robert McDarra plays a middle-aged alcoholic, who under Section '27A' is committed to a hospital for the insane in Queensland. He is not released after completing his sentence, as he has incurred the displeasure of some of the hospital staff, and various excuses are made for not permitting his discharge. An eccentric lawyer learns of the case and threatens to expose the scandal. Ultimately the man is released only to become the victim of ironic fate. Prior to obtaining his freedom the alcoholic's wife dies, and as he sits on her grave, he feels that life, like prison walls, is strangling thoughts of hope and freedom. His only recourse is the bottle that will lead him right back to the very place from which he sought escape. Overall, *27A* was a commendable effort from Hadyn Keenan and Esben Storm — another pair who could trace their filmic beginnings to Swinburne Technical College. A little harrowing at times, the film showed a great deal of promise, but was more at home at Festivals than in the commercial field.

5.33 *Esben Storm writer-director of "27A". This film won a Gold Award in the 1973 Australian Film Awards. Storm has since directed "In Search Of Anna".*

On 2 December 1973 at the Australian Film Institute Awards, *27A* received a Gold Reel, and Robert McDarra, the star, won the Hoyts prize for the best actor. In addition the film won the Australian Film Development Corporation Award. The following year at the 16th Adelaide Film Festival, *27A* was honoured with the Golden Southern Cross, and received a cash

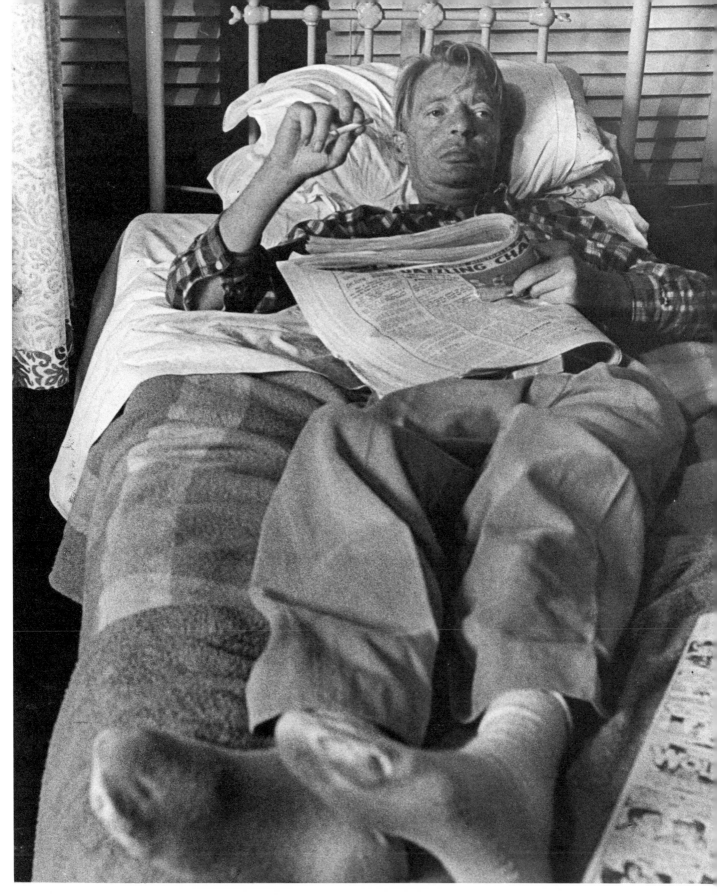

5.34 *Robert McDarra brilliantly portrayed an alcoholic in "27A" for which he was voted top actor for 1973. Placed in a hospital under Act 27A in Queensland, (that has since been rescinded) the authorities had the right to hold him until such times as he could prove his eligibility to be released. This led to many abuses on the part of the hospital authorities — and if the person committed did not become a "vegetable" numerous excuses were put forward to prevent the man from gaining his freedom.*

5.35 *On location for the ABC-TV series "Seven Little Australians". Elizabeth Alexander who plays "Esther", converses with director Ron Way.*

award of $600 as the best Australian film of the year. Its first commercial showing was at the Playbox Theatre, Melbourne on 24 July 1974.

In 1973 there was a feeling of activity in a number of quarters of the film and television industries with praiseworthy efforts from the Australian Broadcasting Commission.

Avengers of the Reef was the first children's feature film produced in Australia for a number of years. It told the story of an Australian boy, Tim, who, accompanied by a Fijian friend, attempts to locate his father, a scientist visiting Fiji. Tim's father had arrived to help prevent the Crown of Thorns starfish from destroying coral reefs. It was produced by Noel Ferrier, directed by Christopher McCullogh, and photographed by Peter James. In the cast were Simon Drake, Bui Kawara, Tim Elliot and Noel Ferrier.

Avengers of the Reef was premiered in the Music Room of the Sydney Opera House on 21 October 1973, and repeated on 28 October and 4 November as part of the Festivities associated with the opening of the Opera House and with the Sydney Waratah Festival. During the screening on the first night Queen Elizabeth II paid a surprise visit.

Another surprise, this time in Brisbane, occurred in August 1973. It was a 35 mm production called *Wheels of Fire* on drag car racing, and was shown at the Alhambra hardtop Theatre, Stone's Corner. It was produced and directed by Gary Young who made *Cosy Cool* which was shown in Sydney in 1977. A Film Factory Production, it was presented by Garron International.

Successful 35 mm Features for 1973

The 1973 tribute to the Arts was *Don Quixote* directed by Rudolf Nureyev and Sir Robert Helpmann. Photography was handled by Geoffrey

5.36 *The children's feature "Avengers Of The Reef" was directed by Chris McCullugh. Tim Elliot is the featured player.*

Unsworth and the art director was William Hutchinson who designed such a magnificent set later for Tim Burstall's *End Play*. The two directors headed the cast, with the Australian Ballet Company providing the back-up. Sir Robert Helpmann portrayed 'Don Quixote' and Nureyev was Basilio the young and romantic barber. *Don Quixote* was premiered at the Sydney Opera House on 19 July 1973, and began its Melbourne season two days later. This International Arts Inc. Production was presented by the Walter Reade Organisation. The shooting was done in an old hangar at Essendon Airport in Melbourne.

The last 35 mm feature for the year was Tim Burstall's financially successful *Alvin Purple* with Graeme Blundell in the title role. It took to the 'buttocks and bed' theme with an obvious relish, giving the full treatment to frontal nudes. In it, Alvin discovers in his schooldays that girls and women

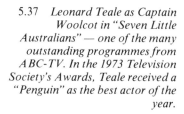

5.37   Leonard Teale as Captain Woolcot in "Seven Little Australians" — one of the many outstanding programmes from ABC-TV. In the 1973 Television Society's Awards, Teale received a "Penguin" as the best actor of the year.

5.38   Five of the "Seven Little Australians" — "Bunty (Mark Shields Brown), "Pip" (Mark Clark), "Nell" (Anna Hruby), their teacher Brenda Starr and seated — "Baby" (Tania Falla) and "Judy" (Jennifer Cluff).

can't resist him. Even the wife of a schoolteacher (Jill Forster) finds Alvin irresistible, and provides one of the amusing highlights of the film. When she sees Alvin on a bicycle pursued by eager schoolgirls, she opens the garage door, lets him in, and promptly closes it behind him. Naturally she expects Alvin 'to come across'. After many 'on bed' encounters during the installation of water beds, Alvin consults psychiatrist Dr Liz Sort (Penne Hackforth-Jones). She takes him on a tour of art galleries where he can consult nudes at close range. However instead of curing Alvin, she demands a 'slice of the action'. A delightful character study is supplied by Noel Ferrier as the Judge on the bench when Dr Sort takes action against her ex-client for his carrying on, and has film to prove it. *Alvin Purple* began its record run at Hoyts Cinema Centre, Melbourne on 20 December 1973. However one critic in the now defunct *Lumière* wrote that *Alvin Purple* was less successful than *Stork*, and aesthetically inferior to *The Child*.

ABC Drama

On 26 August 1973, the ABC-TV commenced a very professional production of ten thirty minute episodes of *Seven Little Australians* by Ethel Turner. Charles Russell, a distinguished American producer, was in charge, but happily, the director of the series was Australian Ron Way. Adaptation was by Eleanor Witcombe and the editor was Ray Alchin. It was superior in every way to the 1939 film production directed by Arthur Collins. The background was Sydney during the 1890s. The seven little Australians ranged from Meg, the eldest, to the Little General. Throughout the story, the father, Captain Woolcot, a straightlaced English officer in the NSW Regiment, shows his inability to communicate with his children. Leonard Teale was tailor-made for the role of the Captain. His second wife, Esther, an Australian, was

5.39   *Graeme Blundell and Shara Berriman get into "hunting gear" in this scene from "Alvin Purple" — another financial success for Tim Burstall, and of course, Hexagon.*

portrayed by Elizabeth Alexander. Barbara Llewellyn played Meg, and Jennifer Cluff was the tragic Judy. Well-known players like Ruth Cracknell, Brendon Lunney, Brian James, Nigel Lovell, and June Salter, made brief but telling appearances.

Seven Little Australians became the fourth top rating programme in Sweden, and Peter Hendry received a Bronze Medallion from Kodak for his colour photography in the 1973 Australian Film Awards. In the same Awards, *Seven Little Australians* received special awards for art direction (Quentin Hole) and music (Bruce Smeaton). In the 1973 Television Awards, the production took 'Penguins' for both the best drama and best children's series. Leonard Teale was named as best actor and Ruth Cracknell, the best supporting actress.

1973 Australian Film Awards

The 1973 Australian Film Awards raised high hopes that talent would be available to our future film front — but for the most part, such hopes were fruitless.

5.40 *Graeme Blundell and one of his schoolgirl admirers, Dina Mann, in "Alvin Purple".*

The documentary *Tidikawa and Friends* won a Gold Reel; a special award for sound (Jef Doring); and a Silver Medallion from Kodak for colour photography (Michael Edols and Jack Bellamy). In the 1973 American Film Festival the film added a Blue Ribbon to its prize list.

In the Silver Awards were *Moving On* and *Scars*. Bronze Awards went to *One Hundred a Day*, *The Passionate Industry*, *Ten Minutes* and the *Incredible Floridas*. *One Hundred a Day* gained an additional Silver Medallion from Kodak for black and white photography by Ross King. Later King was awarded a Golden Tripod for his work on Film Australia's *Viewpoint on Brisbane* in the ACS Awards in 1975. Re-shooting of certain scenes for *One Hundred a Day* were handled by Bill Constable. The featurette gained further distinction with the Film Editors' Guild of Australia Award.

A special citation for ethnographic film went to *Towards Baruya Manhood* directed by Ian Dunlop for Film Australia. Bruce Hillyard was on camera. Its Australian premiere was at the Sydney Film Festival on 9 June 1973, followed by screenings at Flinders University in July 1973, when it took three nights to show the entire film.

An honourable mention went to *Reflections* in the fiction category, while first prize in the Alan Stout Awards for 1973 was shared by *Scars*, *Ten Minutes* and *Reflections*.

Although *The Stuntmen*, which was scripted produced and directed by Brian Trenchard Smith, did not rate more than an honourable mention from the Film Editors' Guild of Australia in the AFI Awards, it did receive special commendation from the Television Society in 1973, plus the Shell Award of $500. *The Stuntmen* gained even greater distinction by winning the documentary section of the Benson and Hedges Awards in the same year.

A brief coverage of the Award winners begins with *Tidikawa and Friends*. Produced and directed by Su and Jef Doring, it was a study of the Biami people of the Great Plateau region of Papua-New Guinea. With *Libido* and *Violence in the Cinema* it was selected by Australia as an official entry for the

Cannes Film Festival. *Tidikawa* was screened at the Sydney Film Festival in 1973, and after taking first prize in the Anthropology/Ethnology section at New York's 15th American Film Festival the BBC purchased the rights of a fifty minute version of the film.

Towards Baruya Manhood also had New Guinea as a background — but its running time was a record seven hours. The Baruya of the Agna group of tribes (formerly known as the Kukukuku of the Eastern Highlands) had a notorious warlike reputation. Every two years or so, they would gather to display their strength and unity. The Baruya came under the influence of the Australian administration in 1960.

The 16 mm production *Moving On* was directed by Richard Mason for Film Australia. Running for fifty-seven minutes, it told of a family faced with near bankruptcy after several seasons of drought and falling prices. A big decision is made to take up a new way of life in a regional city. Ewen Solon, Kay Taylor, and Ken Shorter were in the cast. The scripters, Anne Brooksbank and Cliff Green, won an Awgie from the Australian Writers' Guild for the best feature film screenplay in 1973.

Another Awgie winner in 1973 was Joan Long for the best documentary script for *The Passionate Industry* which she also directed. Produced by Film Australia on 16 mm and 35 mm, it was a sixty minute sequel to *Pictures That Moved* which told the story of the earlier years of Australian film production.

Scars from Paul Winkler, with *Office Picnic* and *Violence in the Cinema* was selected for the 1973 Film Festival in Moscow. In sixteen minutes *Scars* told of the sight, sound, and feelings of lonely city trees depressed by multi-storied office blocks and the hellish roar and acrid fumes of motor vehicles. It was shown at other Festivals including Brisbane in July 1973; Oberhausen Short Film Festival, Germany; and Perth, August 1973.

One Hundred a Day was directed by Gillian Armstrong, who seems to be dedicated to making films with women as the central characters, such as *The Singer and the Dancer*. Both films, strangely enough, were based on short stories by a man Alan Marshall. *One Hundred a Day* is set in the 1930s and concerns a girl who struggles to survive a day in a shoe factory after a backyard abortion. Miss Armstrong was a member of the interim training scheme at the Film and Television School, Sydney. She made *One Hundred a Day* as part of the course. The featurette was screened at the Filmmakers' Cinema, Sydney, on 30 July 1973, with *Reflections* and *Ten Minutes* on the same programme. Sharmill Films took over distribution of *One Hundred a Day,* and on the 10 April 1974, it was featured in a programme of Australian women film makers at the Melbourne University Ewing Gallery. Five days later it was a supporting short at the Palais Theatre, St Kilda (Melbourne).

Ten Minutes directed by David Stocker, actually ran for twenty-six minutes. Stocker was another member of the Interim Training Scheme. Since then he has written a script for Humphrey B. Bear, directed a stage show, and has handled farm management films for the South Australian Film Corporation.

Yet another member of the interim training scheme was James Ricketson who directed *Reflections*. Of twenty-two minutes duration, it concerned a film director in his mid-thirties who doubted his ability to make films and maintain his relationship with his wife.

Incredible Floridas a ten minute short feature, is perhaps better known for its director Peter Weir than for the film's content. It was a study of the composer Richard Meale and of one of his most famous works, which is a homage to the poet Arthur Rimbaud. Other Awards it won were a Silver Medal at the 7th Annual Atlanta International Film Festival (USA) in 1974; cited for special Jury Award at the San Francisco 'Film-as-communication' Competition, 1973; and a Certificate of Honourable Mention at the International Film Review, Sri Lanka, in 1973.

An entry for the 1973 Awards was *Sabbat of the Black Cat* produced and directed by Ralph Marsden. Based on a story by Edgar Allan Poe, this seventy-five minute feature achieved tension by the use of long, dimly lit corridors, a dark stair case and through Marsden's brooding performance. There are flashes of witches and warlocks participating in a forest orgy and of prostitutes and thieves cavorting in murky taverns. A young writer and his wife take up residence in a new house. A weird ritual that the author witnesses in a forest shatters his self-confidence, and the sudden appearance of a mysterious black cat changes his whole life. Ridding

5.41   *Making a blue movie "Split Second" in "An Essay In Pornography" directed by American Christopher Cary (1973).*

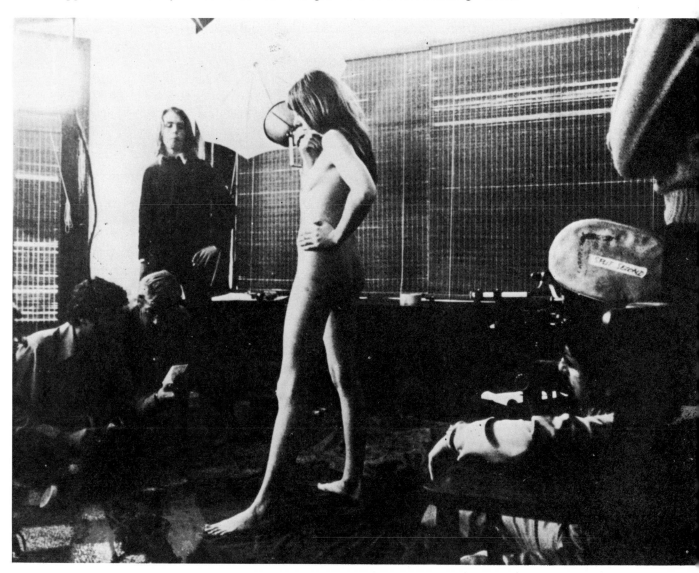

himself of the cat destroys his home, work, and marriage. Murder and madness dictate his ultimate fate. *Sabbat of the Black Cat* had a short season at the Melbourne Filmmakers' Co-operative Theatre on 10 May 1973.

In mid-1973 *An Essay on Pornography* was screened at the small Albany Theatre, Melbourne and at the Village Drive-Ins. It was directed by American Christopher Cary who quit Hollywood to come to Australia. Channel 7 Network contributed half of the budget of $30 000. *Essay* deals with the life of a struggling actress who is eventually cast for a role in a blue movie. Helen Mason was the actress, and the 'blue movie' director was Glen Johnson. It was another entry for 1973.

Nigel Buesst's *Come Out Fighting* cannot be overlooked in this record of 1973. *Come Out Fighting* had a championship record, being joint winner of the fiction section of the 1973 Benson & Hedges Awards. Shown at the Melbourne Pram Factory on 20 July 1973, and as a supporting featurette at the Melbourne Swanston Cinema on 26 December, *Come Out Fighting* was 'patchy' with good acting from some and 'hammy' performances from others. The sound was not first class. This however could be the fault of the speakers in the theatre, as often a good quality soundtrack is incompatible with a less sensitive amplifier. On the other hand, the fighting scenes were exceptionally well handled, when one could almost smell the perspiring bodies. The star was Michael Karpaney, cast as an Aboriginal welter-weight whose prowess as a boxer is noticeable, as is the fact that he is not an actor. He becomes involved with a number of trendy students and his concentration lapses. Lonely and dispirited he deserts the ring to take up a new life-style. A member of the cast was Peter Adams.

Inquiry Outcome

As a result of the 1972 Tariff Board Inquiry, it was recommended that the Australian Film Authority should take over the role of the Australian Film Development Corporation, with a film branch to act as a distributor for Film Australia; and an export agency for Australian films. Another function was to subsidise exhibition outlets for films with special marketing problems. A further recommendation was that exhibition and distribution interests in Australia should be divorced — and a proposal was made for a film authority.

John Bushelle, president of the Film Council stated that it was useless to produce films for theatrical release, unless those films could be screened in Australian picture houses. The Tariff Board recognised that the only way to break the control exercised by overseas producers and distributors on the exhibition of films was through Australian government legislation.

Hector Crawford was not entirely satisfied with the report from the Tariff Board. He did not think that the Board realised the need for increasing Australian content on Australian screens. The worry seemed to be that the demand for Australian content would prove detrimental to the local film industry. Here they missed the point. The world-wide trend was to underwrite feature films with television programmes.

Joan Long, president of the Australian Writers' Guild, claimed that one no longer hears that old catchcry that Australian writers 'aren't good enough'.

Now the excuse is, 'there are not enough of them'. The shortage is the result of the past strangulation of the industry that has channelled many good writers into other occupations.

Quality Features Emerge

South Australia was one state that already had assessed the situation and on 20 April 1972, an Act was passed for the establishment of the South Australian Film Corporation. This Act was amended on 20 November 1975. The Corporation began humbly enough by producing a number of quality shorts. In 1974 *Kangaroo Island* was made for the SA Tourist Commission. It won a Gold Medal at the International Film Festival of Tourism and Folklore in Brussels.

Nineteen seventy-four was noted for the emergence of the Australian feature film as a viable commodity for the picture houses. The 16 mm movie makers regressed a little in importance — but didn't accept defeat completely. If anything, it gave them an incentive to explore other venues of film making. But it wasn't until May that the real action commenced in earnest. Then the gloves were off!

It's a pity that the opener, *Number 96,* wasn't worthy of the occasion. A film version of the then popular TV series, *Number 96* was shot on 16 mm, and was no screen decoration when blown up to 35 mm. It was nothing more than a 'cashable' bonus for Cash-Harmon. The colour was bad, the lighting was flat, and the players as a whole were allowed to amble about without any particular sense of direction. There were too many sub-plots, there was too big a cast, and the alleged humour of the marital squabbles between Dorrie Evans (Pat McDonald) and her long suffering husband, Herb (Ron Shand), would have been 'hot stuff' in *Schoolgirl's Own.* Eventually there was the ruby wedding anniversary party at which Dorrie received some of the 'goodies' right in the face. (This was hilarious when Mack Sennett first thought of it, approximately six decades previously.) The only thing *Number 96* achieved was to show the players from the TV series in colour before the small screen assumed the hues of the rainbow. And it did supply a film for the school holidays, if that can be counted as an asset. It was shown at the Sydney Regent Theatre on 5 May 1974. Strangely enough *Number 96* was a financial success. According to the Australian Film Commission, it was one of the eighteen commercial successes of the 1970s.

Stone was another success of the seventies. It was a film with a 'bikie' background, with shades of ASIO activity that would have gone down well in 1978, when the 'secret files' episode and the sacking of the South Australian Police Commissioner by Don Dunstan, the then SA Premier, would have held real significance. It begins with the assassination of a politician in the Sydney Domain by Ballini (Lex Mitchell) that has a Mafia-like touch. The assassin is observed by a member of 'The Grave Diggers' — a bikie gang. Ballini decides to have the entire group eliminated. The violent deaths of three of them look like precipitating a gang warfare, and an undercover drug squad policeman named Stone is planted among the Grave Diggers to investigate the killings. Stone manages to convince the leader of the Grave Diggers, appropriately named The

Undertaker (played by director Sandy Harbutt) that he is what he claims to be. However he nearly unmasks himself when Toad (Hugh Keays-Byrne) manhandles a young man in a bar, and he intervenes to prevent an unpleasant situation. Yet even here, the real conflict that should have been an essential part of the plot was avoided. Eventually the case is solved, more by good fortune than by clever deduction. Stone is left with a decision to make — a choice between loyalty to the force, or to the bikies with whom he has become associated.

The political overtones and the subject of questionable land deals (this time à la Victoria, 1978) are never clearly defined. There was a positive feeling however that for once here was a film that was being 'directed'. Shots of bikies riding along the Gosford Expressway were graphic and atmospheric (due to the good work of Graham Lind on camera). For the bikie's 'funeral' sequence at St Leonard's cemetery, some 400 cycle enthusiasts turned up from all over New South Wales. The script was under-developed in certain areas, but the glaring weakness was the miscasting of Ken Shorter as 'Stone'. His appearance, his approach to his superiors, and his relationship with the gang, were contrary to the tough, relentless character that 'Stone' was presumably supposed to be — a cop with a job to do and the strength of will and undaunted courage to see it through to the end. Helen Morse, who was later to reach greater dramatic heights in the not-so-distant future in *Picnic at Hanging Rock* and *Caddie,* played a minor role as Stone's beautiful, headstrong, society-minded girlfriend. An even smaller part was that of Ros Spiers as a prostitute. She will be remembered for roles in *The Man from Hong Kong* and the ABC-TV series *Power without Glory*. The bikies 'molls' included Susan Lloyd as Tart; Victoria Anoux as Flossie; and Rosalind

5.43   *The clash of rival "bikie" gangs in "Stone". In this action-packed sequence, "The Grave Diggers" led by Sandy Harbutt (who directed the film) vanquish "The Black Hawks".*

5.42   *Pat McDonald as "Dorrie Evans" in the TV series "Number 96" won TV Week "Logies" in 1974 and 1976. In the former year she appeared in the film of the same name. In this still, she is on the receiving end of a Mack Sennett sequence at her own ruby anniversary celebrations.*

5.44 *Ken Shorter as 'Stone' — a policeman who joins a bikie gang, 'The Grave Diggers' to solve a number of murders. When the murderer is discovered, 'Stone' remembers that he is a policeman first, and prevents the bikies from taking revenge.*

Talamini was Sunshine. Dewey Hungerford, an ex-Texan, played Septic the oldest bikie.

Stone was shown at the Sydney Forum Theatre on 28 June 1974. The film editor was Ian Barry.

Australian Film Industry Totters Again

In the midst of the feature film expansion, it came as a shock to learn that in August 1974, Fauna Productions closed its doors. This was one of the first companies to make the 'big-time' abroad during the re-birth of the industry. The company had produced ninety-one episodes of the highly successful *Skippy* and of more recent times, had filmed the highly commended TV series *Boney* starring Arthur Upfield, the part-Aboriginal detective called Napoleon Bonaparte. While Australian production was recovering from the shock of Fauna's collapse, on 15 October 1974, the Australian Film Development Corporation came out with this statement: 'The Australian Film Industry's problems in re-establishing itself were far from being solved.' The Corporation took a grim step backwards. It warned that it may have to impose tighter controls on film development: 'Any film disaster at this stage of the industry's development may well jeopardise availability of finance for further films.'

When the Minister for the Media, Senator McClelland, tabled the annual report, he advised that the 1973-74 period had seen a 'considerable upswing' in feature film production. Nine full-length features had gone before the cameras during the year, with the Corporation's help. He noted that: 'Revaluation and rising costs of production locally, are making it harder to produce world-standard films in Australia, on budgets which have a good chance of recoupment.'

Unfortunately, Australia was to produce at least three features in 1974 that were financially unsuccessful. In June Australia received a jolt when the English reception of *Alvin Purple* did not augur well for the earning capacity of Australian productions overseas. *The Daily Mail* regarded this production as a sex story with the finesse of a rugby team's booze-up! The *Evening Standard* recommended *Alvin Purple* only to Australians living in London who were old enough to be reminded of home or to Londoners who are not old enough to remember the 1960s when English films had its male swinger forever bedding the birds. The *Sunday Express* stated less in its brief praise. The critic saw it as a sex romp of some freshness and vigour.

The poor image of *Alvin* and of Australian films remained in London as *Between Wars* discovered when it was screened at the Notting Hall Gate Theatre in April 1976. The British public screamed to take it off. They didn't want any 'Bazza' or 'Alvin' films in their country. Despite praise from the English, critics 'John Bull' and his wife 'Britannia' shot first and asked questions afterwards. They forgot that alleged English comedians from George Robey to Benny Hill threw lavatory English at us like empty herring tins.

Between Wars was made in 1974 by Michael Thornhill who must be congratulated on breaking away from the *Alvin Purple* tradition just as Peter Weir had done one month earlier with *The Cars that Ate Paris*. Unfortunately, in both cases, the directors' efforts did not prove popular with the public.

The story of *Between Wars* is of Edward Trenbow (Corin Redgrave) a

5.45 *Corin Redgrave as Dr. Edward Trenbow, and Judy Morris portraying Deborah Trenbow in "Between Wars" — a feature film that created a stir when screened in England. ("Between Wars" stills by courtesy of 'Cinema Papers').*

young Australian doctor who was in constant conflict with the concepts of the time. The period is around 1918. During World War I he is assigned to a mental hospital. There he meets two men who later exercise a great influence over his life — Dr. Peter Avante (Arthur Dignam), and a German prisoner of war, Dr. Karl Schneider (Gunter Mesiner) who acquaints him with the controversial theories of Sigmund Freud. After his return from the war, Trenbow marries Deborah (Judy Morris) and continues psychiatric work in a mental institution. Here, Avante is responsible for the death of a patient. Dr. Schneider had arrived in Australia shortly before the inquest into the demise of the hospital inmate. He gives evidence in support of Avante, but reveals that Trenbow is a believer in Freud. This is the beginning of Trenbow's problems with the medical establishment. Disillusioned, he takes up a practice in the country and becomes a near alcoholic. He meets man-crazy Marguerite Chapman (Patricia Leehy). The pair help set up the Fishermen/Farmers Co-operative to obtain better repayments for primary producers. For this he is branded a Communist, and is victimised by the New Guard. He returns to Sydney and in 1941 endeavours to secure the release of Dr. Schneider who has been interned as an enemy alien. He is branded a traitor by his own son. The climax comes when the son departs to fight in the Second World War.

5.46 *The front line in World War I as depicted in "Between Wars" — an Edgecliff Films production.*

There were many interesting 'bit' players in *Between Wars*, who would become well known in later productions: among them was Peter Cummins of *Storm Boy;* Melissa Jaffer who was in *Caddie;* Robert Quilter who was the hunted murderer in *Inn of the Damned;* Reg Gorman who became prominent in the TV series *The Sullivans;* and Martin Vaughan who was John West in the ABC-TV version of *Power without Glory* which won so many Awards.

Cinema Papers classified *Between Wars* as 'not great cinema', but a 'nice solid little picture'. But they added: 'and it's about time we started making them in this country.' Yet the ultimate box office rating of *Between Wars* would make many producer a little hesitant at accepting such advice.

Between Wars received a Bronze Award in the 1974-75 Australian Film Awards. (There were no separate Awards in 1974.)

Films of the Mid-Seventies

The Cars that Ate Paris did not fare as well as *Between Wars*. Only Bruce Smeaton received a mention in the Australian Film Awards. He was given the Filmways' Prize for the best original music, not only for *The Cars* but for *The Great Macarthy* as well. Its releases were not encouraging. Shown at the Cannes Film Festival, May 1974, and the Melbourne Film Festival 17 June 1974, *The Cars that Ate Paris* had its first commercial screening at the Australia Cinema, Melbourne on 10 October 1974. A fortnight later it was in

5.47   *The Mayor of "Paris" (John Meillon, centre) offers Terry Camilerri the job of parking superintendent in "The Cars That Ate Paris".*

Brisbane, but it had to wait until 19 March 1976 for its initial Sydney screening — and then it was shown only at the Double Bay and Mosman Village Drive-Ins. At the Melbourne festival, the violent climax was hissed at by the audience. The *Sun* however, stated that at last a film had been produced of which Australia could be proud. It found fault with only the editing. One Sydney critic considered *The Cars that Ate Paris* the 'most unusual and original film to come out of Australia'.

John Meillon was cast as the mayor of a tiny hamlet in New South Wales. Like a benevolent dictator he controls the storekeepers, workers and wild young men of Paris. These young men speed around in super-charged cars, the parts of which come from the deliberate wrecking of vehicles that ventured along the steep, rough road to the area. Arthur (Terry Camilleri) is an unlikely hero who blames himself for two killings — the second, that of his brother on the outskirts of Paris. He is given the job of checking parking infringements. He books two 'hot rodders' whose cars are promptly destroyed by order of the mayor. This action is responsible for the violent climax when the hot rod gang, with its porcupine Volkswagen, advances upon the town of 'carefully concealed evil'. Kevin Miles plays a surgeon in Paris whose ward is filled with 'vegies' — hopeless survivors of accidents 'staged' regularly in and around the town.

At the time of the Melbourne Festival screening, Peter Weir related how he, and producers Jim and Hal McElroy had 'conned' the visitors to Cannes into seeing the film by driving around in the horned monster from the picture.

5.48   Peter Weir is noted for the "gadgets" he introduces into the films he directs. "The Cars That Ate Paris" was no exception. Peter Armstrong defends the town from a horned "hot rod".

Cinema Papers summed up the failure of *The Cars that Ate Paris* to 'the inability to tie up the loose ends. This provided one of the characteristic embarrassments of watching an ingenue at work in a sophisticated genre'. However, years later, Peter Weir gave the explanation in much simpler language: 'It was a black film that was too vicious.'

5.49 *Terry Camilerri (extreme R) and John Meillon (on Terry's right) attend the funeral of Terry's "film" brother, in "The Cars That Ate Paris".*

Petersen directed by Tim Burstall, was one film of the mid-seventies which was very successful. It arrived in November. Jack Thompson as *Peterson* was almost a carbon copy of *The Family Man* in the *Libido* series. The screenplay was again written by David Williamson. This time Thompson is married to Jacki Weaver. She is a typical suburban housewife who never fits into his grandiose plans. Peterson is an electrician who decides to do an Arts Course at the university. That a man should turn his back on a lucrative trade merely to improve his mind is understandable. It is even more understandable if the man is an inspired idealist, which Petersen is not. In fact he spends his time living with the professor's wife (Wendy Hughes). After she turns her back on him, he fails his examination and returns to being a TV repairman who glibly quotes Shakespeare. Like 'Alvin' he avails himself of the carnal possibilities open to him during working hours.

One reviewer headed his critique with 'Petersen is great', but another stated that Burstall was hampered with a script that leapt from one idea to another with 'nerveless vivacity'. Perhaps the secret of Petersen's success at the box office was that it didn't make you think. You knew scores of blokes

5.50 *Jack Thompson in "Petersen". He goes back to University to study, only to "finish his thesis" by taking time off to seduce the professor's wife.*

just like him. After a preview at the Melbourne University Union Theatre, it was screened at the Odeon Theatre on 1 November 1974.

Of the feature films for 1974 in the 1974-75 Australian Film Awards, *Petersen* gained the greatest distinction — a Silver Award with Jack Thompson sharing the Hoyts Prize for the best male performer for his roles in *Petersen* and *Sunday Too Far Away*. David Williamson gained the Greater Union Award for the best screenplay. Only one 1974 show did better — the ABC-TV production *Billy and Percy*.

How *Alvin Rides Again* clicked at the box office is one of the great wonders of the mid-seventies film industry. This sequel to *Alvin Purple* was definitely 'cashing in' on the success of its predecessor. It lacked any form of subtlety and was completely devoid of humour. The leads acted poorly and the actors capable of good performances were in throw-away roles mouthing inane dialogue that even a hack writer wouldn't admit to producing. Frank Thring was dressed as if he hadn't changed from his last cigarette commercial. The crudeness of the picture even extended to the *double entendre* in association with people's names — there was 'Balls McGee' and a girl called 'Boobs'. The story on a herring bone was that 'Alvin' had to impersonate a gangster double.

5.51   *Forced to take the place of gangster Balls McGee, Alvin discovers that it's necessary to duplicate Balls' very distinctive facial scar. Graeme Blundell in "Alvin Rides Again".*

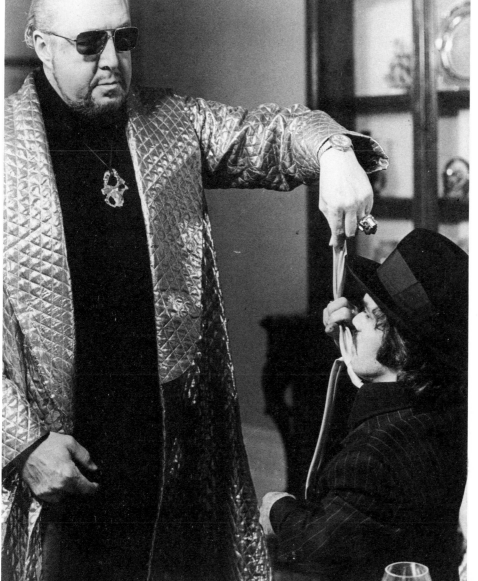

5.52   *Frank Thring (son of F.W. Thring) appeared in "King Of Kings", "The Vikings" and "El Cid" overseas before appearing before Australian cameras. In this scene from "Alvin Rides Again" Thring is a gangster. Note the padded dressing gown and large ring on the finger. Ross Bova is on the receiving end.*

5.53   *"Bazza" (Barry Crocker centre) looks a little wide-eyed in "Barry McKenzie Holds His Own". Who wouldn't be when surrounded by Little Nell and Fiona Richmond.*

5.54   *Michael Newman, Ed Devereaux, Barry Crocker and Clive James are ready for action in "Barry McKenzie Holds His Own".*

Alvin Rides Again opened simultaneously in Sydney and Melbourne on 9 December.

'Bazza' thought he'd try a sequel too, hence *Barry McKenzie Holds his Own*. This opened simultaneously in Sydney and Melbourne one week earlier than *Alvin Rides Again*. It was the same old 'Bazza' — loud-mouthed and beer-swilling. This time, with several other Australians, he endeavours to rescue Aunt Edna from the clutches of Count Plasma, a bloodsucking nobleman from Transylvania.

For some unknown reason audiences accepted the second adventure of 'Alvin' but turned their backs on 'Bazza'. Phillip Adams must have shrewdly assessed the market, for he was associated with the first 'McKenzie' film but not with the second.

ABC Productions in Mid-Seventies

In 1974 the ABC-TV seemed to provide most of the winners. A series called *Marion* as well as *Billy and Percy* earned them not only awards but the highest of praise.

Marion, a four-part drama, was set in a rural area during the 1940s. Location shots were photographed in the Kinglake-St Andrews area, north-east of Melbourne. Scripter Cliff Green called upon his background as a teacher in the Mallee and at Torrumbarry on the Murray for a great deal of the material for *Marion*. Even the writing on the blackboard was done by Green, using the script and layout set down by the Education Department at the time. Helen Morse who had played a minor role in *Stone* was the principal character as the schoolteacher named Marion.

The series gained most of the awards from the Television Society of Australia in 1974. A Penguin was awarded to Helen Morse as the best actress; to Clifford Green for the best drama script; and to David Zweck as the best drama producer. In addition the Australian Film Development Corporation Award for Adult Drama was shared by *Marion* and *Billy and Percy*. Harold Hopkins in the latter show won a Penguin as the best supporting actor. John Power who wrote and directed *Billy and Percy* had won two earlier awards for productions on the ABC — *Like a Summer Storm,* the story of the

5.55 *"Marion" shown on ABC-TV in March 1974, won a number of Awards — and was worthy of every one of them. Here, Helen Morse (as Marion) is shown with one of her pupils Paul Petrie.*

5.56 *Cliff Green, at one time a teacher himself, wrote the TV script for "Marion". Helen Morse is seen with Paul Petrie, Martin Fields, and Martin Foot.*

downfall of Dr H.V. Evatt, and *Escape from Singapore* covering the last years in the life of Lt-General Gordon Bennett.

Billy and Percy covered the period when William Morris Hughes was prime minister. This turbulent man went through 300 secretaries like a 'Puffing Billy'. One was Morris West who became the talented novelist. But Percy Dean was one who could cope with the tantrums of Australia's most fiery and controversial heads of government. Percy was a prolific letter writer, and his widow kept most of them. Those letters provided the basis of the John Power script. *Billy and Percy* won a Golden Reel under general category; and Martin Vaughan as Billy of *Billy and Percy* shared the best actor's prize with Jack Thompson. John Power took out the Village Prize for the best direction, and Geoff Burton received a Bronze Medallion from Kodak for the photography.

But the ABC-TV Awards never ended there. During the 1974 Television Society's Awards, Frank Wilson received a Penguin as the best leading actor (J.J. Forbes) in *And the Big Men Fly* — a six-part series from the stage play written by Alan Hopgood and adapted for television by the author.

The Shell Award went to the ABC documentary series *A Big Country,* and a special commendation, the Film Development Corporation Award for children's drama, went to the ABC's *A Taste for Blue Ribbons.*

More Awards: '74-'75

The South Australian Film Corporation's *Who Killed Jenny Langby?* received a Bronze Award in the short fiction category in the 1974-75 Australian Film Awards. It was directed by Don Crombie and photographed by Peter James.

The central figure of the film is a thirty-two year old housewife whose life becomes unbearable. Her husband is unemployed and insensitive; her children are a problem. She finally throws herself under a train. A television newscaster reporting her death, recalls that Jenny had attempted to commit suicide previously by taking an overdose of sleeping pills. The reporter journeys to Adelaide to investigate. She learns that the husband has left home; the eldest daughter is pregnant; and a teenage son is up on a charge of breaking and entering. A social worker persuades the husband that he should try to cope with the situation and take care of the family. With this thought in mind she finds employment for him, but when asked what the husband's chances were of succeeding, she replied 'about 30 per cent'. Julie Dawson portrayed Jenny Langby; Peter Cummins was her husband; and Anne Deveson, the reporter. In the 1974-75 Australian Film Awards, Julie Dawson was named the best actress for her role in *Who Killed Jenny Langby?*

In the same Awards *Wokabout Bilong Tonten* received a special citation for the first feature film shot in Papua New Guinea. This film had a completely indigenous cast. *Wokabout Bilong Tonten* was a ninety minute drama produced by Film Australia. In 16 mm colour, it was directed by Oliver Howes and photographed by John Hosking. Screened at the Cannes Film Festival in 1975, it was blown up to 35 mm for the occasion, and sub-titled in French. The storyline introduces Tonten, a coastal man whose wife dies in childbirth. She returns as a spirit and tells Tonten to search for her brother who

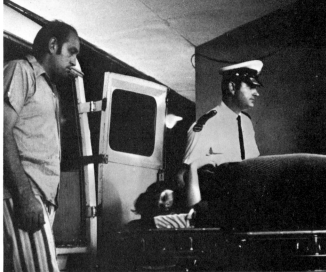

5.57   Jenny Langby (Julie Dawson) with her two children on one of her many visits to hospital for treatment of the youngsters' asthma. The tragedy in Julie's life is the basis of the film title "Who Killed Jenny Langby?"

5.58   Frank Langby (Peter Cummins) looks bewildered as his wife Jenny (Julie Dawson) is taken to hospital after an attempted suicide. A scene from the South Australian Film Corporation production, "Who Killed Jenny Langby?" (1974).

5.59   In "Who Killed Jenny Langby?" there is a complete lack of communication between husband and wife, even on one of their rare nights out. Julie Dawson and Peter Cummins are the players.

5.62   "Wokabout Bilong Tonten" from Film Australia, that in the 1974-75 Australian Film Awards, received a special citation for the first feature film shot in Papua New Guinea with an indigenous cast.

5.61   Photographed by John Hosking with direction and script by Oliver Howes, "Wokabout Bilong Toten" was originally shot in 16 mm colour but was blown up to 35 mm for screening at the Cannes Film Festival 1975. It was sub-titled in French for the occasion.

has disappeared from the village. On his way to Port Moresby Tonten meets a Chimbu girl in the highlands. He locates his brother-in-law, marries the girl and returns to his village.

Mr Symbol Man, which received a Golden Reel in the documentary class, was directed by Bruce Moir and Bob Kingsbury for Film Australia and the National Board of Canada. Photographers were Michael Edols and Barry Perles. On 16 mm it ran for forty-nine minutes. *Mr Symbol Man* is Charles Bliss, a Rumanian refugee who takes up residence in Australia in the late 1940s. He struggles to obtain world recognition of a symbolic language which is made up of 100 basic symbols. These can be built upon to make words and sentences. Bliss's symbols are now being used successfully at a centre for children with cerebral palsy in Canada, and in other countries of the world.

Stirring, the documentary which won the Silver Award was directed by Jane Oehr, with photography once again by Michael Edols. It was a Film Australia production for the Australian Department of Education, and went into the issue of corporal punishment in a New South Wales Boys' High School. The duration was sixty minutes.

Matchless — a 16 mm fifty-five minute production from John Papadopoulos, photographed by Russell Boyd, was judged the best amateur film at the ABU-Shiraz Film Festival of Youth, held in Teheran in August 1974 by the Asian Broadcasting Union. Then in the 1974-75 Australian Film Awards it received a Bronze in the short fiction category, and won the first prize of $500 in the Alan Stout Awards. In the Sally Blake script Victor, an aging alcoholic, takes up residence in a run-down house with Annie an aggressive young woman and Cynthia, a dreamy epileptic. They shun society, but there is conflict when the authorities discover that the derelict house is occupied. They cannot appreciate the fact that all the trio required was to be left alone.

An interesting featurette from a young film maker was Chris Noonan's *Bulls* which shared second prize in the Alan Stout Awards in 1974-75. It was considered one of the best short subjects at the 1975 Melbourne Film Festival. Chris Noonan was a member of the Interim Training Scheme of 1973-74.

Bulls was an eighteen minute film based on yet another short story by Alan Marshall. It told of a lonely eight year old girl on a dairy farm and of her father's greater attachment to his animals than to her. The population of Kerang, a Victorian dairying centre, got behind the production and loaned and handled cattle for the picture as well as converting an old unused farmhouse into a dairy of the 1930s. Those taking part were Kevin Thamm, Gabrielle Bulle, and Beryl Pleasance. *Bulls* had its premiere in Kerang on 27 September 1974.

The final 16 mm entry for 1974 is *Yaketty Yak.* In this eighty minute film, director David Jones also plays the role of Maurice the movie director who states, 'keep the cameras rolling, I'm throwing away the script.' Gordon Glenn kept the camera in action, and Lloyd Carrick and Peter Beilby (one of the editors of *Cinema Papers)* took it all down on tape. It is hard to determine who had the idea of tossing the script away first — David Jones or Bert Deling with *Dalmas*? Naturally, it was a story about film making, with the director moving from behind the camera to participate in the action. Mad characters appeared, such as Socrates — and for no reason at all, Jerzy Teoplitz (head of the Film and Television School) was on the set before he knew it. People popped up like Bing Crosby in a Bob Hope movie. Blood was spattered by various absurd murders; the remainder of the cast and crew became rebellious. The director seized the spotlight by threatening to commit suicide, and when that ruse didn't work, he, supported by Caroline (Peggy Cole) held everyone up at gun point. This crazy, mixed-up film was screened in English, Spanish and Swedish film institutes before it had its premiere season at the Filmmakers' Cinema, Sydney, on 15 October 1974.

Better Quality Sought in Features

In 1975 feature film production was really at its peak, yet the ABC-TV still held its own in face of such stiff opposition. In this year the South Australian Film Corporation and Homestead Films proved that locally produced commercial TV features could still command ratings.

But Australian films in general were still having teething problems. In May 1974, the Festival of Light committee demanded that the Federal Government withdraw its investment in the film based on the bawdy ballad *Eskimo Nell*. The film producers admitted that it would be a 'hot' film.

> The Festival of Light objects to the use of taxpayers' money to finance pornographic films. We demand that the Federal treasury immediately cancel this amazing grant.

But in 1975 it appeared that the 'Alvin' image was here to stay.

All the 'hoo hah' about Canada's 'Nell' did not prevent *The True Story of Eskimo Nell* being the 'first' for 1975 on the Australian billboards. On 27 March it was screened at Hoyts Cinema Centre, Melbourne.

Melbourne film critic Denbeigh Salter described *Eskimo Nell* as 'a bawdy bewdy. The Australian film version of that vulgar poem has the lot — brothels, brawls, and bare boobs. There's swearing, cursing, torrid love scenes and a mine collapse. Backgrounds were Sovereign Hill, Ballarat, Falls Creek and Canada. Perhaps the Australian Film Development Corporation should

5.62   *Serge Lazareff (as Mexico Pete), Max Gillies (Deadeye Dick) and Graham Bond (previously seen as "Aunty Jack" on T.V.) are nominations for the Rogues' Gallery in "The True Story Of Eskimo Nell".*

have listened to the Festival of Light: *Nell* has been classified as a financial disaster by the Australian Film Commission. The direction, editing, music (by Brian May) and Vince Monton's photography were all creditable, with Max Gillies trying his best to rescue the film with a verve that received little response from the laconic Serge Lazareff. But it was the script, once again that let the picture down badly. It should have contained more substance and less juvenile humour. Build up or cut the footage should have been the yardstick used.

The True Story of Eskimo Nell fared much better in the 1974-75 Australian Film Awards than at the box office. Vince Monton received a Silver Medallion plus $500 from Kodak for cinematography. In addition it received an Honourable Mention as a feature film.

5.63 Max Gillies as "Deadeye Dick" in "The True Story of Eskimo Nell." Looks as if he is doing a little "panning" as a side line at Sovereign Hill, Ballarat.

Emphasis on Sex

The Australian premiere of the John Lamond documentary *Australia after Dark* was held at the Melbourne Swanston Theatre on 26 December 1975. It was written by Dennis Bascoigne and edited by Russell Hurley. Photographed by Gary Wapshott, it cashed in (and handsomely) on the pornographic trend — and in its advertising claimed to reveal 'an exotic world of eroticism, witchcraft, masochism, and strange secret places. It takes you behind the bright lights and strip clubs in a very different Australia.' Originally shot on 16 mm, it was blown up to 35 mm for theatre release. It transferred in Melbourne from the Swanston to the Roma Theatre on 19 February 1976. It made the headlines, and unlike *Eskimo Nell* it was one of Australia's commercial successes.

5.64 *Producer-director John Lamond and cameraman Gary Wapshott cover a sequence for the highly successful documentary "Australia After Dark". The girl in the mud bath looks like someone emerging from the "underworld".*

Made at a cost of $64 000, *Australia after Dark* had grossed $1 250 000 by October 1977. The content featured such sequences as a restaurant that served cooked snake and witchety grubs; and there was a segment in which three female witches take part in a white witchcraft ceremony. All shed their clothing to help them release their inhibitions.

In January 1976, Brisbane took a dim view of *Australia after Dark*. One critic stated that it gained no credit for the producer-director. He felt that it was a blight on the new and bustling Australian film industry. The reviewer felt that when this country could produce a work of genuine art like *Picnic at Hanging Rock,* this tripe had no place in our cinemas. Another stated that the photography wasn't bad, but otherwise 'it's a piece of rubbish'. A third described it as 'a plastic bucket of celluloid swill'. In the Sydney *Sunday Mirror* on 22 February 1976, Kate Morgan, the stunning Melbourne model in

5.65 *Nudists enjoy the sun on Daydream Island (Queensland) in "Australia After Dark" — a Roadshow release.*

Australia after Dark stated that she wanted nothing more to do with the film. She refused to be interviewed or pose for publicity shots for the production that was breaking box office records all over Australia. She was the one featured in the advertisement munching an apple. But Terry Herlihy who was photographed rolling in the mud thought that the movie was a lot of fun. Which raises an interesting question: how does one view pornographic films — from a box office point of view that is? *Eskimo Nell* didn't make it — *Australia after Dark* did.

The TV series called *The Box* also placed the accent on sex when it began on Channel 0, Melbourne on 4 February 1974. The film made later of *The Box* was a development of the TV series with the usual characters appearing — Sir Henry Usher (the late Fred Betts), Paul Donovan (George Mallaby), Max Knight (Barrie Barkla), Tony Wild (Ken James), Kay Webster (Belinda Giblin), Lee Whiteman (Paul Karo) and Vicki Stafford (Judy Nunn). Guest spots were filled by Cornelia Francis, Robin Ramsay and Graham Kennedy. It commenced its run in Brisbane on 8 August 1975. Yet unlike *Australia after Dark,* this film was a commercial failure.

The storyline concerned the making of a feature film called *Manhunt* starring Tony Wild. Sir Henry Usher and Paul Donovan hope to sell the picture overseas to boost the ailing finances of Channel 12. With Tony getting into wild scrapes, and Lee Whiteman directing, film making becomes disastrous. Cornelia Francis enters the picture as an efficiency expert with

Robin Ramsay as her assistant. In the midst of it all, Graham Kennedy arrives to compere Channel 12's *Big Night Out*. A scene never to be forgotten is Max Knight the general manager, wearing a leopard skin, Tarzan style. Added comedy spots were a wild car chase and a speedboat sequence on Lake Eildon. (Memories of George Wallace and *Let George Do It.*)

Another movie with an emphasis on sexual exploits was *Plugg*. Like *Nickel Queen*. It was made in Western Australia. A Sydney-based magazine stated that the film crew walked out on the first day's shooting in Perth because it was a pornographic film. Peter McNamara, one of the partners of the Perth-based Romac Productions retorted that this was merely 'paper talk'. The film was not pornographic; they were hoping to get it an 'M' rating. *Plugg* had as much chance of getting the 'M' rating as Deadeye Dick had of seducing Eskimo Nell. Scripter-director Terry Bourke climbed on the band wagon and claimed that *Plugg* would get an 'M' rating without cuts: 'And everyone will have a big belly laugh,' added Terry. But somehow it remained a very 'un'-funny year.

Plugg (Peter Thompson) plays an over-the-hill detective who has been engaged to gain evidence to force the closure of the 'Pussy Cat' Club. Cheryl Rixon is Kelli Kelly, one of the prized 'pussies'. 'Plugg' hides himself in hotel corridors and bathing pools, but finds himself constantly pursued by the police (Norman Yemm and Reg Groman). The end is a complete 'send-up' with marching girls; life savers; a parachutist; call girls arriving for 'client

5.66 *UCV Channel 12 is problem land in "The Box". This scene from the feature film shows Paul Karo in the hustle of things. Chaos behind the little box — that's what "The Box" is all about.*

5.67 *The Junk Dealer (David Vallon) in "Plugg" — the tale of an over the hill detective who is engaged to close down a "bunny" club.*

calls' at the 'Pussy Cat' Club; a monk from a religious order walking along the footpath, and in the final *mêlee,* the technical crew join in. Other members of the cast included Vynka Lee-Steere, Joseph Furst and Edgar Metcalfe. The Reade family created something of an Australian film record in *Plugg.* Eric (this author) and Christina (his wife) appeared in the court room sequences which were shot in an actual courthouse in Perth. Son Anthony played a call boy at a top hotel, and was also a member of the technical crew.

After the WA producers in their wisdom (?) took out their scissors, the 'send-up' scene was deleted in its entirety. Other scenes were left on the cutting room floor as well, resulting in a very bad film that was impossible to follow.

Australian Character Needed

After Sandy Harbutt returned from the 1975 Cannes Film Festival where he had exhibited his own film *Stone,* he advised that to be more successful overseas, Australian films should be more Australian in character. Sandy Harbutt went on to state that *Sunday Too Far Away* had had a tremendous impact, and had been the most successful Australian film at the Festival. It had been accepted for the Directors' Fortnight, and had reached the final three in judging. It was seen later at the 1975 Sydney Film Festival. In the 1974-75 Australian Film Awards, *Sunday Too Far Away* received the Golden Reel and the Australian Film Development Corporation Award. The Department of the Media Award went to Ken Hannam, for his direction of this film. As well as the Film Awards, writer John Dingwall received the 1975 Awgie Award for the best cinema script. Finally came the Golden Charybdis Award at the International Movie Festival in Taormina, Sicily. With *Sunday Too Far Away,* the South Australian Film Corporation did make a major breakthrough for Australian films. The film demonstrated quite clearly that although the story was about shearing, Australia no longer lived off the sheep's back, just as it did not require pornography to ensure survival of the film industry. It took genuine guts to arrive at such a decision, but the reception it was given and the Awards it received, made the gamble worthwhile.

Originally *Sunday Too Far Away* was to be based on the 1956 shearers' strike, but in the finished film, this became a secondary issue. The main

5.68　*John Ewart and Robert Bruning in "Sunday Too Far Away" voted Australia's top film for 1974/75. Bruning has since been directing a series of tele-cine dramas.*

5.69　*Jack Thompson and his bottle of Beenleigh Rum in "Sunday Too Far Away". Here he depicts the shearer's lot of a Sunday — solid drinking after washing his clothes.*

character was an itinerant shearer, Foley (Jack Thompson). He returns to shearing after threatening to give the game away for life. He meets up with old mates John Ewart (playing a well-sustained role), Robert Bruning and Jerry Thomas. They are inveigled by a shearing contractor (Max Cullen) into accepting another shearing job, while they are waiting for the one they have been originally engaged for to eventuate. Here the loneliness of the shearer's life becomes evident; after his work is finished, he has precious little to do but to take to the bottle. There is a mad cook who turns out atrociously bad meals, until Foley laces his 'medicine' with alcohol and when inebriated, he beats the cook up and sends him on his way. But the real troubles come in the form of the mysterious and sullen Arthur Black (a nice characterisation by Peter Cummins). Foley, who has always been regarded as 'top gun', finds that Black's shearing tally for the day is uncomfortably close to his own. Out of veiled hostility comes a grim and dogged 'head-on' encounter for top honours. The tense concentration of Thompson and Cummins is well depicted, as is the noticeable physical strain behind the undeclared war. Finally the honour of being 'top gun' goes to Cummins.

5.70　*In the South Australian Film Corporation production "Sunday Far Too Far Away", the loneliness, the wrangling, the petty jealousies of shearers, are vividly depicted. In front (L) Jerry Thomas and John Ewart — and behind (L) Sean Scully and Graeme Smith portray the itinerant shearers.*

Two things prevented *Sunday Too Far Away* from being a masterpiece —
the flat, uninspired photography (unusual in an Australian film) and the
shortcoming of a script that wound it all up with a voice-over-scene of
deserted shearing sheds: 'The strike lasted for nine months, but the shearers
won.'

No Problems with Photography

Terry Bourke's *Inn of the Damned* brought a new dimension to colour when
he shot in warm amber to flashing red for the murder scene. *Inn of the
Damned* is a sinister lodging house brooding in a haze of evil. Presided over
by Dame Judith Anderson and Joseph Furst, visitors arrive but never leave
the following morning. Michael Craig portrays a wealthy farmer who is
highly suspicious of the Inn, and Tony Bonner is a young trooper who comes
to investigate, but never lives to hand in his report. Alex Cord, stridently
American, is the bounty hunter who looks as if he expects a band of Apaches
to jump out of the bush. He is seeking the murderer Robert Quilter, dead or
alive. He eventually takes him in — dead. John Meillon is a pathetic, petty
thief who genuinely loves his 'stolen' dog, and experiences the torment of the
damned because of it. Unhappily he met up with Quilter. Unfortunately,
according to the Australian Film Commission, this too was a financial
disaster. Two of the main deficiencies were the script and the acting of
American Alex Cord as the 'bounty hunter'. On the other hand, Dame Judith
Anderson and John Meillon provided outstanding character studies. Brian
Probyn was also outstanding in his direction of photography.

5.71 *Trooper Brian Hinselwood
guards the two proprietors of
Terry Bourke's "Inn Of The
Damned" — Dame Judith
Anderson and Joseph Furst.*

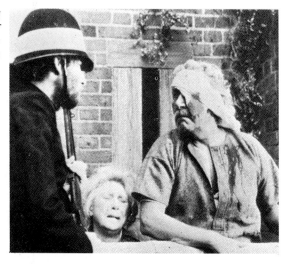

Dubbed by the Melbourne *Sun* as 'Hitchcock on Horseback' and a
'Macabre-like Gothic horror', the critique also said *Inn of the Damned* was
'well worth the wait'. The *Sun's* reviewer went on to state that the film
provided the professional breakthrough the Australian Film Industry needed.
Brian Probyn did receive a Bronze Award from Kodak for photography in
the 1974-75 Australian Film Awards — a distinction so richly deserved. *Inn
of the Damned* was screened at the 1975 Cannes Film Festival before its
Australian season which commenced on 10 October in Adelaide.

Picnic At Hanging Rock

To the surprise of everyone, the South Australian Film Corporation figured prominently as the second winner for 1975 with the unforgettable *Picnic at Hanging Rock,* directed by Peter Weir, produced by Pat Lovell and Hal and Jim McElroy. If ever the camera assumed the role of storyteller, it did in *Picnic.* Under the guidance of Russell Boyd and operated by John Steele, the camera captured the old world atmosphere of St Valentine's Day 1900, painting the scenery in warm pastel tonings to add a joyousness to the memorable occasion of a picnic for the girls of Appleyard College. There is an air of freshness and innocence to starched dresses then the camera sweeps upwards to the towering and ever sinister Hanging Rock of Mt Macedon. Even after the mysterious disappearance of the girls, the photography does not let us down and we watch the mists with wispy, spidery fingers of moist nothingness gyrate around the barren peak like steam from a witches' cauldron. David Williamson is credited with stating that Joan Lindsay's novel had the instant visual appeal for a good screenplay, yet it was Cliff Green who provided the framework for one of Australia's most successful pictures.

5.72   In this scene from "Picnic At Hanging Rock" — a South Aust. Film Corporation feature, the girls of Appleyard College drink their annual toast to St Valentine. The time — St Valentine's Day, 1900. Anne Lambert (extreme right) was selected to appear in the TV series "The Box" in 1976.

The storyline of *Picnic* is interesting: in this period of undoubted class distinction, Dominic Guard portrays Michael Fitzhubert, an English aristocrat who is enchanted with the sight of the beautiful Miranda (Anne Lambert) as she with three other people cross a creek. The four continue their exploration but eventually one turns back in terror, and a second is found unconscious by the groomsman, Albert (John Jarratt). She cannot explain what took place. When a teacher goes to search for the two missing girls, she too vanishes. Michael is also found by Albert, after he too has sought the answer to the disappearance. Strangely enough, Michael has succumbed to the same mental collapse as that of the schoolgirl. He is found clutching a fragment of a white dress, but how it came to be in his hand remains as much a mystery as the fate of the three people who vanish. This mystery is never solved. A local myth says that when Hanging Rock topples, it will give up its secrets.

Rachel Roberts who played the headmistress, stepped into the role on two days' notice, after fellow British actress, Vivien Merchant who was originally signed for the role, fell ill in Hong Kong on her way to Australia. Rachel Roberts was superb as Mrs Appleyard, whose main concern after the girls' disappearance, was whether the tragedy would bring disrepute upon her college. Martindale Hall in Mintaro, South Australia, a Georgian style mansion, became Appleyard College. Helen Morse was well groomed and serenely poised as the French Mistress — but the real stars of the picture were the camera and the director, Peter Weir.

5.73   *Helen Morse as the French Mistress in "Picnic At Hanging Rock" from the South Australian Film Corporation. Later she played the title role in "Caddie".*

Two minor faults in an otherwise outstanding production were the fact that the film was too long, and that the Jacki Weaver in-and-out-of-bed sequences struck a jarring note. When questioned about the inclusion of these scenes, Cliff Green defended them by stating that in his opinion, the maid and the handyman (Tony Llewellyn Jones) were the only two real people in a realm of fantasy. But do fact and fantasy make ideal bed fellows?

Picnic won the Grand Prix at the 7th Festival of the Nations in Sicily in August, 1976, but awards for this film in Australia, at least, were not as plentiful as with other films. *Movie News* in March 1976 gave the South Australian Film Corporation full recognition of its ability to produce first class pictures by naming *Picnic at Hanging Rock* as the 'best Australian film of the year'. It gave *Sunday Too Far Away* second position.

Picnic at Hanging Rock opened at the Hindley Theatre, Adelaide on 7 August 1975. When it arrived in Melbourne, The Listener In-TV (now *Scene*) paid this tribute — 'At last, an Australian film that achieves the elusive double — artistic quality and wide popular appeal.' In 1976, the film had a successful eleven week season in London's West End, then moved to sixteen cinemas around the city. The *Evening Standard* described it as 'an Australian ghost story wholly original, and assured proof of the new cinema Down Under.' *Picnic at Hanging Rock* had a return season at the West End in January 1977 and continued to attract huge audiences. Many Australians visiting London at the time found to their surprise that they had to book some considerable time ahead to obtain a seat to view the picture. It was listed among the ten best films shown in London in 1976.

On 7 October 1976 at the Sydney Opera House, rather belated praise for *Picnic at Hanging Rock* came during the Sammy Awards organised by TV Times in conjunction with the Channel 7 Network. *Picnic* was voted the best Australian film of the year. Helen Morse received a Golden Sammy for the best actress for her performances in *Picnic at Hanging Rock* and in *Caddie*. Dominic Guard received Second Best Actor Award as did Rachel Roberts for their roles in *Picnic*. Peter Weir was in top position for direction. It was left to the English *Films Illustrated* when writing on Australian features at Cannes in 1977 to state that in 1976, Australia had been a major force at the Festival. The article went on to note that the films at the 1977 Festival weren't up to the standard of the two mentioned.

Australian Film Commission

An important change to the structuring of the Australian film industry took place on 8 July, 1975. On that date the Australian Film Commission assumed all responsibilities for the Australian Film Development Corporation.
Its function was:
1   To provide assistance, including financial help, to private producers to make, promote, distribute, and exhibit Australian films.
2   The production of films for the Australian Government and allied authorities, including films of general interest. In addition it assumed responsibility for the funding and future functioning of Film Australia.

Change in Pace

Producers began a cycle in 1975 which we can call the 'action' film. This included *Sidecar Racers, Scobie Malone,* and *The Great Macarthy.* None was wildly successful, and the last two were financial disasters in Australia. American distribution rights to another action film, *The Man from Hong Kong* had been sold before the Australian release, and herein lies the pitfall that many an Australian producer has to face: when this picture opened simultaneously in twelve Paris cinemas, it was publicised as an 'American' film. That is enough stuffing for all the turkeys on Thanksgiving Day.

Sidecar Racers was a joint Australian-American picture made by Universal Pictures and produced by Richard Irving. It was directed by Earl Bellamy, and was based on a screenplay by Jon Cleary. It had a simultaneous Sydney-Melbourne release on 1 May 1975. *Sidecar Races* featured scenes on the Amaroo scramble track and the Bathurst road-racing circuit. Australian riders and stuntmen splashed and scrambled on bush tracks, and burnt the rubber on the road circuits. There was a battle for the honour of being selected as the 'sidecar racers' to represent Australia in Europe.

The advertising described *Sidecar Racers* as the film 'from the land Down Under, where bikes burn the track, and there's always a girl or two.' Ben Murphy plays Jeff Rayburn, a young American living in Australia. He meets a girl, Lynn Carson (Wendy Hughes) whose father (Peter Graves) is an executive in a tyre company. Ocker Harvey (John Meillon) run a spare parts and accessories shop, and Jeff breaks up a fight between the proprietor and a group of belligerent bikies. An employee of Ocker's is Dave Ferguson (John Clayton), a dedicated sidecar racer. Eventually Jeff and Dave win the race that will take them to Europe. Surprisingly, they turn the chance down, being perfectly satisfied with their sense of victory. An added incentive is that Lynn was in the grandstand cheering them both. This provides a very awkward situation. Sooner or later either Jeff or Dave would be the odd man out. Who wins is anyone's guess.

As a picture it didn't warrant much enthusiasm, anyway. The fault was with the script. It could not keep pace with the roar of the bikes, the excitement of speed, and the strained faces of the riders trying to obtain that extra burst of engine power.

Scobie Malone another 'action' film didn't rate much higher than *Sidecar Racers* even though it did star Jack Thompson. By a strange coincidence this too featured Jon Cleary in the credits since the story was based on his novel *Helga's Web*. This film also had an American association: Casey Robinson, co-scriptwriter and producer, had after sixty major Hollywood productions, retired to Australia. Approximately two years later he came out with *Scobie*.

It is claimed that Robinson discovered Errol Flynn playing a 'corpse' in an American production, and manoeuvred him into the title role of 'Captain Blood' where he made corpses, not played them. With Thompson, Robinson had proven material to work upon, and he publicly stated that he would make the actor 'Australia's biggest international star since Flynn'. (He apparently had not heard of Rod Taylor.) If Mr. Robinson had the idea of promoting another Flynn, he should have selected a better script than the one provided for *Scobie*. Judy Morris, who plays Helga Brand, an old girlfriend of Scobie's, is murdered in the Sydney Opera House, and he looks for clues to pinpoint the killer. The script from Casey Robinson and Graham Lockwood merely places Thompson in another 'family man' setting where he is surrounded with

5.74 *Ben Murphy and Peter Gwynn in "Sidecar Racers" written by Jon Cleary and produced by Richard Irving.*

5.75 *Wendy Hughes and Peter Graves discuss the forthcoming European trip for the winner of the Bathurst Gold Cup. A scene from "Sidecar Racers" — a Universal Pictures release.*

5.76 *"Sidecar Racers" was directed in Australia by Earl Bellamy. Here, the starters line-up for the important Gold Cup race at Bathurst.*

5.77   *Judy Morris and Jack Thompson in "Scobie Malone". The sign behind — "one way" — was like the film itself — "out" in box office takings.*

5.78   *Cul Cullen with an atmospheric background of Sydney Harbour and Bridge in "Scobie Malone".*

5.79   *Everybody's in the act — John Jarratt doing the "superman" stint; Barry Humphries trying his best to forget "Dame Edna" by reading the "Financial Review"; Kate Fitzpatrick trying to make her companion aware that there are other "types of figures", and actors as "make believe" Australian Rules footballers.*

breast-bared women and beer cans — or is that the 'beds and buttocks' formula that has wandered in by mistake? As an honest NSW cop, 'Scobie' is one up on Sherlock Holmes: he can solve the crime from the bedroom. Shane Porteous is Malone's offsider, and Noel Ferrier plays a kingpin of crime, with Cul Cullen giving one of the best performances in the film as his henchman. The only time excitement is sparked off is when a chase takes place in the internal structure of the Opera House. One critic labelled *Scobie* a 'bomb', another called it 'Thompson's turkey'.

David Baker's contribution to the 'action' cycle that never came off was *The Great Macarthy*. The script was at fault and the uncertain direction didn't help either. Barry Oakley, writer of the novel upon which this film was based, was so incensed with the finished product that he said he did not wish to be part of it and added that he would look more closely at any future film contracts.

Macarthy the third 'action' film, along with *Scobie Malone*, had a relatively short run in Melbourne, despite the fact that the 'Garden City' is the Mecca of Australian Rules football. *Macarthy* opened at the Athenaeum Theatre, Melbourne on 7 August 1975,. It did not reach the Sydney Rivoli Theatre until March 1976. 'Its particularly Melbournian atmosphere,' noted one critic, 'made it difficult to sell in other states and overseas.' A football writer in the Melbourne *Sun* advised that *The Great Macarthy* wasn't 'the best football picture he had viewed'. Yet he felt that the poor reviews it had received were penned by people who weren't sports orientated — their tastes actually ran to 'croquet and claret'. (On the other hand the general public didn't run to see it either.) The writer of the screenplay admitted that the jokes didn't come off, and that the film contained unnecessary smut. Added to this there was a fair serving of weak and unpalatable material in *Macarthy*. But in the 1974-75 Australian Film Awards *The Great Macarthy* received an Honourable Mention in the feature film category, and Barry Humphries who portrayed the president of the club, was given a similar mention.

The Man from Hong Kong was a tongue-in-cheek, knee-in-groin, *kung fu* romp that had a three-city release at the Melbourne Rapallo, Adelaide State, and Brisbane Albert Complex on 5 September 1975. It had been shown at the Cannes Film Festival in May of the same year. This was an action film in every sense of the word — action constituted approximately 95 per cent of the total footage. In this film Brian Trenchard Smith comes into his own as a worthy successor to Charles Chauvel, the 'action director'. After the Cannes screening, Trenchard Smith received nine offers for co-productions.

Jimmy Wang Yu as Inspector Fang of the Hong Kong police, distended his nostrils impressively before going into action, even though he couldn't act for rice paper. His voice, according to *Cinema Papers* was dubbed for the English soundtrack, yet his fatal Asiatic charm was good enough to obtain intimate interludes with Ros Spiers and Rebecca Gilling. In the story, Fang meets Inspector Taylor (Roger Ward) of the Federal Narcotics Bureau, and Sergeant Norrie Gross (Hugh Keays-Byrne), Taylor's offisder. A courier for the drug traffic is intercepted near Ayers Rock but he is killed by order of Mr Big (George Lazenby). This is merely a curtain raiser to a hang-glider flight by Fang over Sydney Harbour; a perilous ascent on to a ten storey building

5.80   *Jimmy Wang Yu and Ros Spiers in "The Man From Hong Kong".*

5.81   *In "The Man From Hong Kong" (a Golden Harvest-Movie Company co-production) the police capture a drug courier at Ayers Rock. Actors in this scene — Roger Ward and Hung Kam Po.*

5.82   *Directed by Brian Trenchard Smith, "The Man From Hong Kong" (played by Jimmy Wang Yu) guides his kite over Sydney Harbour.*

by way of a drain pipe; and a *kung fu* battle royal between Lazenby and Jimmy Wang Yu. An outstanding aspect of the picture was the excellent photography from Russell Boyd and David Gribble , the same team that did the camera work for *Between Wars*.

The Removalists

Australia witnessed another film failure with *The Removalists,* produced by Margaret Fink and directed by Tom Jeffrey. Once again it was clearly demonstrated that a successful play cannot easily be transplanted in another medium. The reason isn't hard to find: when action is stage-bound, dialogue has to compensate for any limitations of action. Consequently when a stage play is transferred in its entirety, and is blandly exposed in a studio in front of a camera, the performance of the players appears restricted.

The Removalists centres around a husband whose wife was leaving him. She is goaded into action by her interfering sister; the removalist around whom the drama pivots; a lecherous police sergeant and a young and inexperienced police constable. It depicts everyday life and is completely devoid of any excitement. It seems to have its roots firmly embedded in brutality and violence. In terms of the cinema, *The Removalists* had little to offer although it was a successful play. Granted that playwright David Williamson is a keen observer of human behaviour — but the question that arises is: does one go to the theatre to be entertained, or is one expected to leave the theatre completely disenchanted with life? The box office in this case voted in favour of entertainment.

Poor lighting in *The Removalists,* uninspired photography, and the TV-style direction contributed to the lack of force and strength in the transference of the play to the screen. *The Removalists* had its world premiere at Hoyts Cinema Centre, Melbourne on 1 October 1975.

5.83   *Martin Harris and John Hargreaves in the film version of the David Williamson play "The Removalists".*

Children's Shows

After *The Removalists* the release of children's features in December 1975 provided welcome relief. The Walt Disney, Australian-produced *Ride a Wild Pony* was released in Brisbane, Sydney, Melbourne and Adelaide on 26 December. It was directed by Don Chaffey, and had the now well-known juvenile actor Robert Bettles in one of the leading roles. A Sydney critic made the point that it's a pity children's pictures as good as this *Ride a Wild Pony* don't appear from local film makers. The story centres around Scott (Robert Bettles) who loves the Australian bush. He requires a pony for the seven mile journey to school. Scott lives with his parents, Alfred Bell and Melissa Jaffer, on a farm that isn't self-supporting. He makes the acquaintance of a well-to-do farmer, Michael Craig and his wife, Lorraine Bayly and is allowed to ride one of the wild Welsh ponies. When Scott doesn't attend school, a police sergeant serves a summons on his parents. The father engages a lawyer (John Meillon) who by devious means, forces the police prosecutor to drop the charges. Scott is offered one of the Welsh ponies as a gift, but his father insists on paying for it. The pony, Taff disappears, and returns to the wealthy farming property where it pulls the crippled daughter's pony cart. Eventually there is a court case over the ownership of the horse, and it is agreed that the animal must pick its own master or mistress. Taff finally returns to Scott, and the crippled girl and the boy became firm friends.

The Lost Islands, another children's feature, premiered as a TV series on 28 February 1976 on ATV Channel 0, Melbourne. It is the story of five teenagers who survive a typhoon, but are shipwrecked on an island that still retains the customs of the eighteenth century. Twenty-six episodes were made for the 0-10 Network and Paramount Pictures at a cost of $500 000. It had been running successfully in Canada for six weeks prior to the Australian launching, and had been sold to Japan and Europe. Amanda Ma (who had migrated from Hong Kong to live in Melbourne), Tony Hughes, Robert Edgington, Jane Wallis and Chris Benaud were the five youngsters in the series. It was produced by Roger Mirams and directed by Bill Hughes. The pilot was shown as a children's film at the Capital, Sydney and the National Theatre, St Kilda, Melbourne as the second Christmas feature for 1975. It reached the Sherwood Theatre, Brisbane on 19 January 1976.

6
Ups and Downs

A Mixed Year: 1975

On the television scene in 1975, one of the major disasters was the termination of the Crawford Productions, *Matlock Police*, *Division 4*, and *Homicide*. This meant large-scale reduction in staff, resulting in confusion and uncertainty in the industry. Crawfords took some time to recover.

On the film front *Angel Gear* which has been listed as a 1975 film, was never completed. *The Understudy* is another film listed for 1975, but nothing is known about it, beyond what is in *Cinema Papers*, in November 1975.

Leaving the realm of uncertainty behind, we look at Award winning documentaries, featurettes, and drama for both film and television. *A Steam Train Passes* received a Silver Award in the documentary section of the 1974-1975 Film Awards, and Dean Semler was honoured with a Bronze Medallion from Kodak for photography. Yet another gem from Film Australia, the film covers a twenty-one minute journey in a huge steam locomotive from Sydney to the country in the early dawn. It was one of the last journeys of this C38 class engine. On 16 mm *A Steam Train Passes* continued on its award-winning way with a Special Citation from the 1975 Melbourne Film Festival; the Golden Tripod to Dean Semler for photography in the 1975 ACS Awards; the Statuette of St Finbarr at the 20th Cork Film International, 1975; and a special Jury Award, 19th Annual San Francisco Film Festival, 1975.

In the 1975 Television Society of Australia Awards, John Power as writer-director won a 'Penguin' for adult drama with *They Don't Clap Losers* produced by the ABC. In this, Martin Vaughan was far more impressive than in *Power without Glory;* he was right in character as the story opens with him walking his greyhound, which he feels sure will win him a packet one day. His mother (superbly played by Pat Evison) won't allow the dog into the house. She accuses her son of not caring for anyone. He queries her right to criticise. She had seen very little of him as a child as she was always on the road with her husband and his tent show — a boxing troupe. Meanwhile, the

6.1 *Frank Wilson and Martin Vaughan in the ABC-TV production "Power Without Glory". It was based on the controversial book by Frank Hardy.*

grandson, with a friend, is brought before a magistrate for breaking windows in a vacant Housing Commission flat, and for setting fire to a number of items. The friend's mother accompanies her son to court. The magistrate acquits the two boys, but places the onus on the parents to keep them out of further trouble. One of the conditions of acquittal is that the two boys must be kept apart. This low-key drama was excellently directed by John Power, with some brilliant shots from cameraman Geoff Burton.

The ABC received further bouquets in 1975 for its three-episode drama *The Fourth Wish* which will be covered fully later with the film version of the same drama. John Meillon received a Penguin as the best actor of the year and Michael Craig was named the best drama scriptwriter — both in association with *The Fourth Wish*. But it was *Rush* that was the real ABC success story for 1975. A twelve-part saga of the Victorian goldfields, it was set in Crocker's Gully. The actual location was on the outskirts of Melbourne, and the 'gold mining' set was fashioned on the Bendigo diggings of 1851-52. Some forty tatty tents and bark humpies were erected. The one fault about an otherwise excellent series was that it was not in colour. Episode 1 of *Rush* (first series) was 100 minutes, but the ensuing episodes were of 50 minute duration. Into this setting came Olivia Hamnett, an attractive widow, John Waters, a mysterious and often surly Sergeant McKellar and Brendon Lunney who was well cast as the elegant Gold Commissioner. Peter Fleet played a doctor and Max Meldrum was George Williams, a digger. Writers included Cliff Green, Howard Griffiths, and Sonia Borg. Directors were Oscar Whitbread, David Zweck, Keith Wilkes and Douglas Sharp. Guest artists were Gerard Kennedy, Mike Preston, Brian James, Martin Harris (the husband in *The Removalists*) Alwyn Kurts, and Terry Donovan. In the 1975

TV Awards, Oscar Whitbread received a Penguin for the best producer of drama, for *Rush;* George Dreyfus received a Penguin for the best original theme music; Olivia Hamnett for the best actress; and John Waters received a Certificate of Commendation as the leading actor. All these awards related to *Rush.*

Other TV Awards went to the ABC for *Wildlife in Papua, New Guinea — Bird of The Volcanoes*, a documentary photographed and directed by David Parer. This film was the recipient of a Penguin. Penguins were awarded to: Gary McDonald for *The Norman Gunston Show*; Richard Carleton for the best current affairs interviewer, *This Day Tonight*; Geoff Raymond for the best national newsreader; and for *The Dreamtime* — an educational programme.

In the Certificates of Commendation, the ABC again figured prominently. June Salter received a Certificate for leading actress in *Certain Women*; Terry Norris and Moira Carleton got Certificates for their supporting roles in *Bellbird*. By contrast, commercial stations were only represented in the Certificates of Commendation by one show — the Crawford Production called *The Box*. The named players were supporting actress, Judy Nunn, and supporting actor, Paul Karo. In the Australian Film Commission Awards administered by the Television Society of Australia Crawford Productions reaped a rich harvest — and for two shows that had been terminated — an ironic touch. First prize went to *Gary* an episode of *Matlock Police* and second prize to *The Graduation of Tony Walker* from *Homicide.*

6.2 *Oscar Whitbread who produced "Marion" and the later "Rush" also directed one of the quartette of plays in the former series, for ABC-TV.*

A co-production called *Ben Hall* was responsible for a less successful venture by the ABC in 1975. A joint series with BBC-TV and 20th Century Fox, it had Englishmen Jon Finch and John Castle portraying Australian bushrangers Ben Hall and Frank 'Darkie' Gardiner. It was premiered in England on 6 July 1975, and was greeted by *The Express* with such archaic Australian vernacular as 'Well, shiver my billabong, the BBC has struck gold by discovering the wild west in darkest Australia. I can tell you, cobbers . . . .'. (Enough of that!)

The only thing wrong with *Ben Hall* was the whole thirteen dreary episodes. Historically inaccurate, it tried to paint 'Ben' as lily white until he was hounded into joining the bushrangers out of sheer defence. In actual fact Ben Hall was a cattle duffer when 'Darkie' Gardiner ran a 'discount' butcher's shop on the Lambing Flat goldfield. When police questioned the source of Gardiner's meat supply, the 'butcher' went bushranging in Ben Hall country, and included friend Ben in the gang. When Gardiner escaped to Queensland, Hall assumed command. Then there was Ben's 'loyal' wife. She had run off with a former policeman, years ago. Australian folk songs attest to that. The ABC unfortunately would never learn the valuable lesson that it could make better programmes under its own banner.

16 mm Films of 1975

Cash & Co from Homestead Films commenced transmission from the Channel 7 Network early in 1975. This was more in the nature of an American western, the spirit of which was retained in the spin-off film *Raw*

Deal. Shot at Emu Bottom, Victoria, *Cash & Co* was the story of two outlaws (or bushrangers or whatever) trying to reform. They are given shelter by a widow. She, poor soul, manages to run an extensive holding with practically no assistance. Yet the main chore of the 'boys' appears to be the chopping of wood, so that the widow can supply them with an outstanding range of food from farm fresh eggs to freshly baked bread. Quite a remarkable woman in the Elizabeth Macarthur mould! *Cash & Co* proved popular with viewers and in the 1976 TV Week Logies, it received an Award as the best new drama series. High ratings could probably be attributable to the personality of the stars Penne Hackforth Jones, Gus Mercurio, and Serge Lazareff. London Weekend Television was the first to purchase the series, and it was screened in London before Australia. The same television company bought thirteen episodes of the show's successor *Tandarra*.

On the Track of Unknown Animals was a 16 mm documentary that was premiered in Horsham (Victoria) on 16 July 1975. Produced and directed by Gordon Glenn and Keith Robertson, with photography by Glenn, it explored the possibility of the existence of a large unknown striped animal in the Victorian Otway Ranges. Running for fifty-five minutes, it was narrated by Terry Norris.

The final line-up of films for 1975 covers *The Firm Man*, *The Golden Cage* and *Double Dealer*. All were 16 mm productions.

The Firm Man was produced, directed and written by John Duigan with photography by Sasha Trikojus. Basically a Festival film, it was originally screened at the Playbox Theatre, Melbourne, on 9 April 1975. A further showing was a week's season at the Sydney Filmmakers' Cinema on 17 June 1975. The lead is an anti-hero, Gerald (Peter Cummins) who is suddenly elevated to the top ranks of a bizarre organisation headed by a pink-suited tycoon (Max Gillies) who leads his executives in singing choruses of business policy. Gerald is indoctrinated by a loony section chief (Don Gunner), and becomes the envy of his best mate, Barry (Peter Carmody), who is left to answer all the phones. *The Firm Man's* wife (Eileen Chapman) is at first flattered by her husband's good fortune, but then the family relationship deteriorates, and Gerald finds himself not only at variance with his wife, but with Barry as well.

Variety saw the performances of Peter Cummins and Eileen Chapman as 'adequate', but the others rose 'little above amateur level'. It did not consider *The Firm Man* a commercial prospect, but noted that the film could attract attention at Festivals.

The Golden Cage was scripted and directed by Ayten Kuyululu and photographed by Russell Boyd. The players were not well-known. The only Australian was Kate Sheil. The other leads were Ilhan Kuyululu, Sail Memisoglu, and Cesar Rozerio. It was the story of two young Turkish men who migrate to Australia, but find it difficult to throw off the traditions of their native country. One meets an Australian girl and becomes interested in her. He demands that she become a Moslem. She is not prepared to make such a drastic change. She disappears, and when he locates her again, she is pregnant. He proposes, but to his amazement, the girl refuses to marry him.

The cine-drama *Double Dealer* didn't make such heavy going. A great deal of this film was shot in the same area in Sydney as was the silent film *The*

6.3   *Eric Reade as a Police Inspector in the Phil Avalon T.V. drama "Double Dealer". It is awaiting release.*

Devil's Playground. It is the story of a vice king who deals in white slavery and drugs. An undercover policeman obtains a position in a model agency that is a front for the criminal activities. A small-time confidence man is placed in charge of the agency but through a girl's love, he tries to 'go straight'. But his associates will not permit it. This leaves him with one alternative — to murder the vice king. At the wrong moment, the police spring the trap. One of the outstanding features of *Double Dealer* is a unique camera shot: the vice king is standing in the lounge of his home; behind him is a mirror on which the head of a girl is engraved. It is an old-time mirrored advertisement. As the vice king is shot in the throat, a backview is seen in the glass. As the shot rings out, red liquid is squirted on to the throat of the drawing, and oozes down the glass. This shot gives added realism to the sequence.

6.4   *Phil Avalon and Bob Lee as policemen at the showdown in "Double Dealer" when an underworld leader is shot. This scene was photographed at Bilgola Beach.*

Double Dealer was a Phillip Avalon production directed by Allan Dickes and photographed by Rick Bradley. The cast included David Calcott, Phil Avalon, Guy Peniston Bird, Bob Lee, Sharyn Smith, Sue Church and Eric Reade (this author) as a police inspector.

1976 — An Interesting Year

Nineteen seventy-six was a beehive of film activity. It was to introduce pictures that would make merry at the box office — *Caddie*, *The Devil's Playground* and *Don's Party*. It would look a little startled at *Eliza Fraser* one of Australia's biggest budgets, a film which would make headlines on and off the screen. ABC-TV revealed that it still retained the power to produce outstanding drama, with their musical version of *The Sentimental Bloke* and their production of *Power without Glory*. And of course there would be howls of protest against its TV series *Alvin Purple*. Even American TV came to Australia, but with disastrous results.

Finally, the Australian film industry replied to the often repeated request: why can't we have decent films at Christmas time? Pictures that are typically Australian? In 1976 two films answered this request, only to be rebuffed at the box office: the kids apparently preferred to see a remake of an American 'oldie' like *King Kong* or yet another revival of a Walt Disney production than sit through Australian films. The trouble here was with the theatre management. Australian films for children were shown as 'matinée only' features. Cartoons — and excellent ones at that — never reached the night market. Even *Dot and the Kangaroo* in 1977 received a matinée Christmas.

End Play was first off the assembly line. It arrived on New Year's Day in Sydney, Melbourne and Adelaide. Tim Burstall had been rather quiet on the film front for a short period, and confounded everyone by featuring dead bodies instead of live ones. He'd changed from pornography to post mortem. This change of pattern however, was not in the best financial interests of Hexagon. *Alvin Purple* and *Petersen* were monetary successes, but *End Play* did not click even at a time when the general public claimed that it did not want pornographic films.

In *Movie News* Awards in March 1976 *End Play* occupied third place in three separate sections. It shared third position with Trenchard Smith's *The Man from Hong Kong* for best Australian film section. For best actress,

Belinda Giblin was placed third for her performances in *End Play* and *The Box*; and for best actor, George Mallaby and John Waters (the two leads in *End Play*) tied for third place. In the 1976 Australian Film Awards, as well as in the 'Sammy' awards Edward Macqueen-Mason was credited with the best film editing for the year for his work on *End Play*.

One of the amazing omissions for the 1976 Awards was Bill Hutchinson who designed such a magnificent and compact set for *End Play*. It was tastefully furnished throughout, and even contained a view of an outside garden. It was erected in the lower studio of Channel 0, Melbourne.

When shown on TV on 25 September 1977, *End Play* was described as a 'stretched out "homicide"-type story'. Yet the poster stated, 'The last chilling piece falls into place in *End Play*. It's a heart-stopping experience in the Hitchcock tradition.' Unfortunately it didn't quite fit into the Hitchcock image as the action was confined with most of it taking place indoors. This was governed by the fact that George Mallaby played a paraplegic. The suspects too were limited — two step-brothers portrayed by Mallaby and John Waters with everything pointing to the latter. When the body of Delvene Delaney is left in the Rex film theatre, the heavy-handed police Inspector (Ken Goodlet) takes over. He looks with contempt upon a more scientific approach to the investigation, and considers the advanced methods of police detection as advocated by Sergeant Robinson (Robert Hewett) with utter contempt. It is the wordiness in the police interviews that slows the pace of the film. The only tension that was built up was when Mallaby revealed a sadistic streak and pursued Waters through the house with a bow and arrow. In fact he puts one shaft through the leg of Waters. The acting of both men in

6.5   *George Mallaby played a paraplegic in "End Play". This required a skill in archery, and the manipulation of a wheel chair.*

6.6   *Delvene Delaney (the victim) and John Waters in the Tim Burstall feature "End Play", that by way of a change, featured "bodies" of another type.*

this sequence placed them in line for performing honours for the year. Belinda Giblin supplied one of the few decorative touches to the film, although romantic interludes of course do not figure prominently in a story of a mysterious man who picks up female hitch-hikers, murders them, and leaves their bodies strewn over the countryside. There were some excellent photographic shots, especially in the opening of the picture, but the real fault of *End Play* was in a wordy and rather lifeless script.

Robin Copping was director of photography and Dan Burstall was the camera operator. The screenplay by Tim Burstall was based on the novel by Russell Braddon.

The critic for the Brisbane *Sunday Mail* found *End Play* claustrophobic in its intensity, with a story that tended to be too wordy. The Melbourne *Sun* stated that 'despite the occasional lapses, *End Play* was entertaining, and was carefully put together with an attractive set.' Kevin Miles as a physiotherapist and Charles Tingwell as a doctor, were worthy of mention!

6.7 *Arthur Digman as "The Doctor" who tries to revive the past in the Australian science-fiction thriller "Summer of Secrets".*

Australia produced a second thriller in 1976 called *Summer of Secrets* that was even less successful than *End Play*, and certainly more forgettable. Like Tim Burstall with *Eliza Fraser*, director Jim Sharman seemed unsure of the mood he wished to sustain in *Summer of Secrets*. From mystery through to the point where Arthur Digman seemed to carry on from where he left off in *Between Wars*, the mixture that resulted ranged from 'ari scari' to 'sci fi'. With Mike Thornhill as producer it is easy to understand the *Between Wars* touch.

Summer of Secrets opened at the Rapallo, Sydney on 24 December 1976, but did not reach the Rapallo, Melbourne until 10 June 1977. It closed there on 23 June even though it was the winner of both the Jury and the Critics' Prize at the Festival of Science Fiction and Fantasy Films in Paris.

Variety dubbed it as a 'peculiar film' and went on to say that 'had it been made in a foreign language with English sub-titles it might have impressed with its profound obscurantism'. In the Sydney *Sunday Telegraph* it was called a 'horror with a clumsy look — an Australian movie directed in a clumsy, ponderous manner by Jim Sharman'. The Melbourne *Herald* called it a 'mishmash'. Russell Boyd as director of photography, did a remarkable job in trying to save the film visually, but where the writing didn't falter, the acting did.

6.8 *Andre Sharp as a young medical student in the GUO Film release "Summer Of Secrets". This Australian film won the Prix du Jury and the Prix de la Critique at the 1977 Paris Festival of Fantastic and Science Fiction films.*

Summer of Secrets begins with a young man, Steve, taking his girlfriend Kym, to a remote beach to have a picnic and spend some hours alone. He is on a sentimental journey, trying to re-capture a dream associated with an idyllic past. Whilst Steve and Kym swim ashore from a small yacht, they are observed by a tall, sinister blackman. Here, an ambitious film runs off the rails. On the same island is a kinky doctor (Arthur Dignam) who is obsessed with the manipulation of complicated machinery. He and Bob (the blackman) then indulge in wordy dialogue about memory and the brain. A straightforward mystery now develops shadowy shapes of Frankenstein, or perhaps it could be Dr Jekyll with Mr Hyde at his elbow. It appears that the aging Marcus Welby wishes to get away from suburbia and its implications, and in the evening dons a tuxedo, has dinner and then watches flickering films of his late wife Rachel doing Apache dances in a South American nightclub. (What a switch!) Far from burying his beloved, he keeps her on ice

6.9 *Rufus Collins as the mystery figure, Bob, in Australian science-fiction thriller "Summer of Secrets".*

— in fact she was deep frozen on her death. At the back of the dear doctor's mind is the thought of revolutionary brain surgery to restore her to life. The operation is performed while Rachel is being defrosted. Meanwhile Kym has been kidnapped by Bob and taken to the doctor's house. There she is tissied up like the doc's old flame, while Rachel recovers from a bout of pneumonia, or something equally as inconvenient. Steve comes to the rescue, and here the picture becomes a real frost. The doddery doctor and the lovers become friends, and actually go on a picnic together. The walking ghost (the resurrected Rachel) goes along for the ride — but when her husband indulges in another diatribe about the shortcomings of medical science, Rachel shrewishly rebukes him. It's a wonder she didn't find herself back in cool storage. Bob is played by Rufus Collins; Kate Fitzpatrick is Rachel; and the lovers are Nell Campbell and Andrew Sharp.

It is hard to imagine that *Caddie* belongs to the same year — 1976. It is so superior to the other two that it does not seem a product of the same period and country. *Caddie* was produced by Anthony Buckley, directed by Donald Crombie, with screenplay by Joan Long. The leading role was played by Helen Morse. Jack Thompson's S.P. Bookie, after displaying some ruthlessness in wishing to switch houses in pursuit of other *de facto* relationships, gave significance to the film title by nicknaming Helen Morse 'Caddie' because she had class like his Cadillac. John Ewart played a sympathetic part as an S.P. bookie friend in need to 'Caddie.' Melissa Jaffer and Jacki Weaver play barmaid friends, with Ron Blanchard and Drew Forsythe as rabbit-os who befriend 'Caddie' at a time when she is seriously ill and unemployed.

In recreating the period of the 1930s the sure hand of the art director is noticeable, especially in the sequence where the bleak outline of a hall is wedded to harsh electric light on one cheerless side where a notice board reveals the positions available. Some slink out of the darkness, peer hopefully down the list of vacancies, then shuffle off, their shoulders hunched. Their only means of sustenance is a bowl of thin soup from a hand-out kitchen. Nostalgia was well to the fore with an old Sydney tram, a horse-drawn

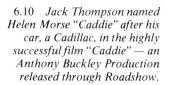

6.10 *Jack Thompson named Helen Morse "Caddie" after his car, a Cadillac, in the highly successful film "Caddie" — an Anthony Buckley Production released through Roadshow.*

brewery waggon, a Rugby car, and a rabbit-o hawking his wares in a sulky.

Caddie was a heart-warming film without being sickly sentimental. The elimination of the first scene which featured some very bad tennis players would have helped the picture, as it had no bearing on the story, nor was it required as a setting — the house and Caddie's dress would have done that quite satisfactorily. As a contribution to International Women's Year, *Caddie* was a notable milestone. It wasn't fiercely feminine, even though it was essentially a record of woman's role in the world. It would be seen as the female contribution to a film industry that in the past had been dominated by the male of the species — 'Alvin Purple' and 'Barry McKenzie'. More important it revealed that a woman's film could make money for its backers as easily as the male role films.

Direction remained taut throughout and it was very imaginative at times, as in the scene where Caddie, after leaving her philandering husband, seeks shelter for herself and two children. As she discusses the formalities with the boarding house proprietress, the young son, completely bewildered by the changes going on around him peers up at the two women. His face portrays what scores of words could not have done with equal success, and this scene is a tribute to the director's skill. In complete contrast was the smoky atmosphere and the noisy babble of voices in the bar room during the notorious 'six o'clock swill'. Scores of men try to consume as much liquor as time and uncivilised drinking laws would permit. Character studies by nameless actors gave a new dimension to the way some new Australian directors can add the Cecil B. DeMille touch. Complete revulsion is evoked in one incredible shot where a drinker vomits on the floor. It is so real that one instinctively reaches for the soap and towel. The same realism however is not applied to Caddie's make-up and overall appearance. Possibly a poetic licence has been taken to keep Caddie remarkably attractive despite the hard times that she experiences.

Caddie eventually meets a well-to-do Greek businessman, spends intimate moments with him, and then eagerly awaits his return from his native country where he goes to obtain a divorce. Here unfortunately comes the *Sunday Too Far Away* touch: the whole film is wound up with a caption advising that the Greek lover is killed in an accident on his way back to her, and that Caddie herself died many years later. What a way to end a film that had so much going for it, including a good script by Joan Long based on an almost forgotten autobiography of a barmaid; excellent direction by Donald Crombie; first-class acting; and clever photography in the hands of Peter James and camera operator John Seale. (This caption was removed for overseas versions, and the ending apparently worked well without it.)

Caddie enjoyed long runs in various Australian cities and received plaudits overseas. This film certainly added distinction to the Australian movies' record for 1976. The picture opened at the Pitt Cinema Centre on 9 April 1976, and took over from *Picnic at Hanging Rock* at the Bercy, in Melbourne on 10 June 1976.

The Awards for *Caddie* were fully justified. At the 'Sammy' Awards in October 1976, Helen Morse took out top honours and Jacki Weaver was voted the best supporting actress. In addition, Judith Dorsman won an award for the best costume designer (films). In the Australian Film Awards of the

6.11 *Melissa Jaffer and Helen Morse as barmaids in the film "Caddie" directed by Donald Crombie.*

6.12   *Misty Rowe as the young Marilyn Monroe in "Goodbye Norma Jean" — an Australian-American production.*

same year Helen Morse was again honoured as the actress of the year for her performance in *Caddie*. Drew Forsythe took out the best supporting actor award, and Melissa Jaffer and Jacki Weaver tied as best supporting actresses. Last but by no means the least, the Mille Award went to *Caddie* for the best cinematography. In October 1976 *Caddie* was the first foreign film not financed by America, to head the San Francisco Film Festival and was officially invited to the Teheran Festival. Helen Morse attended the San Sebastian Festival, Spain, where she was acclaimed as the best actress and the Special Jury Award went to *Caddie* as the best picture. From there she journeyed to San Francisco.

Caddie was sold to a British company, and it opened in London in October, 1978, to rave reviews. 'The biggest film of the week is *Valentino,* and the best is *Caddie'*, wrote David Robinson in *The Times*. He said the outstanding attraction of the film was 'a fierce honesty which is communicated to all the performances'. Alexander Walker wrote in the *Evening Standard:* '*Caddie* is a film that puts you in touch with what cinema used to be all about — namely emotion . . . *Caddie* is a marvellous picture — one you should travel far to see'. Helen Morse was called 'an actress of star quality', and 'the face of the seventies'.

Another film that fitted into Women's Year, but not so snugly, was the Aust-American Production *Goodbye Norma Jean*. The film was shot in America. Star Misty Rowe visited Australia for this country's premiere on 21 May 1976 at the Bryson Theatre, Melbourne and Ascot, Sydney. In Melbourne it transferred to the East End Cinema on 2 July. It was first screened in Atlanta (USA) in 1975. The opinion of the critics was far from flattering. *Scene* in Melbourne wrote:

> Poor Norma Jean Baker. If this film bears any resemblance to the way she was transformed into Marilyn Monroe, then it was hardly worth the effort. If this is the truth she had to put up with the greatest bores in showbusiness. It's not the greatest film in town, but it could keep you out of the rain for a couple of hours.

6.13   *Misty Rowe reveals a more relaxed Norma Jean Baker before a dream takes her to Hollywood, as the much publicised, neurotic Marilyn Monroe. "Goodbye Norma Jean" was released through Filmways.*

Another Melbourne critic headed the review 'Sugar 'n' Spice and not very nice.' It was felt that the picture was hampered by 'bad editing, poor lighting and a banal script. From it all emerged a hard, neurotic bitch!' (Strong words for a film dedicated to the girl with a waggle.)

In Sydney *Goodbye Norma Jean* was labelled a 'shabby unconvincing picture with a sloppy story-line typical of cheap girly pictures, containing lots of pointless undressed-to-panties scenes. It was filmed in a tawdry, grubby way'.

It appears that Norma Jean Baker had only one dream — to be adored as a movie star. On her way to work at a war plant, she is booked for speeding. The police officer tears up her ticket, but keeps her address. That night he visits her and rapes her. She accepts the friendship of a young army photographer who helps launch her on her career as a model. On the way to the screen she appears to have met more than her quota of lecherous producers and second-rate agents *ad nauseum*. Finally she makes contact with a retired movie mogul who grooms her into the Marilyn Monroe image. *Goodbye Norma Jean* was one of the two unofficial Australian pictures shown at the 1976 Cannes Film Festival. (The other film was *Fantasm*.)

No More Outback

On 1 March 1976 a letter from a female in San Mateo, California, was published in a Melbourne newspaper. She stated that she had lived in Australia for a number of years and had seen many beauty spots here. However the films she saw in America of Australia mostly depicted the outback, with 'odd kangaroos hopping along'. She went on to say:

> I would suggest to those concerned that they should not overlook those really beautiful places. It would pay dividends.

Photographer Russell Boyd seemed to answer her request in *The Singer and the Dancer*, where he made full use of scenery. This was a film not only about women, but produced and directed by a woman — Gillian Armstrong. The picture won the Fiction Prize in the Greater Union Awards for Australian short films, in 1976. It was highlighted at the Sydney Film Festival. In the 1977 Australian Film Awards *The Singer and the Dancer* received a Silver Award. The production was also the recipient of a Special Award at the Mannheim Festival, Germany. Ruth Cracknell received a Sammy in 1977 as the best actress, adding this award to her 1973 Penguin for her role in *Seven Little Australians* from ABC-TV.

Columbia Pictures took over *The Singer and the Dancer's* release in 1977, and it was blown up from 16 mm to 35 mm. It opened at the Australia Cinema, Melbourne on 21 April 1977 and closed a fortnight later. At the Sydney Filmmakers' Cinema it was screened at 5 pm in September 1977.

Basically *The Singer and the Dancer* does not qualify as a feature film as it runs fifty-four minutes, but it has been listed, as it marks the real beginning of a film career for Gillian Armstrong. Based on a short story by Alan Marshall, Mrs Bilson (Ruth Cracknell) an eccentric, lives in a country town with a nagging daughter (Jude Kuring). Her favourite escape is a beautiful river with clear running water. It winds picturesquely amidst huge formations of volcanic rock. Here she listens to her radio and the race broadcasts. Charlie, a young woman, and her philandering boyfriend Pete move into an old house nearby. Charlie and Mrs Bilson meet by the river — the

6.14 *Ruth Cracknell as Mrs Bilson in "The Singer And The Dancer". This 54 minute film was produced and directed by Gillian Armstrong — one of the younger school of film makers. A winner of many awards, "The Singer And The Dancer" was released through Columbia Pictures. Unfortunately the quality of the still is not first class, but has been included for a visual record.*

6.15 *Reg Livermore as Betty
Blokk-Buster in "The Betty
Blockk-Buster Follies", the stage
revue that became a film.*

peacefulness of which Charlie also appreciates. Here they discuss at length the faithless nature of men. But if the women are larger than life in this film, the male characters are merely cardboard cut-outs. Their development is incomplete — more like a line drawing than a completed canvas. They lacked penetrative depth. Even the reliable Gerry Duggan, as a doctor, functions solely as a means of transport for Mrs Bilson from house to river. Only one male comes out of it a clear winner — Russell Boyd on camera. Once again he ably demonstrates the beauty of the Australian countryside.

More Films About Women

An unexpected entrant in the 1976 film field was *The Betty Blokk-Buster Follies.* It appeared at the Roma Theatre, Melbourne, on 5 August. Starring Reg Livermore (perhaps one of the most talented performers on the Australian stage in the 1970s), the backing was supplied by the Baxter Funt Band and The Reginas. This film followed a successful 'live' season at Melbourne's Princess Theatre. Prior to that, the 'live' show had enjoyed a big success story in Sydney when it was often booked out three months ahead and bus loads from as far afield as Newcastle came to see the show.

In this show all the well-known Livermore characterisations were included — Betty Blokk-Buster, the German maid who wears nothing but a muslin apron and cap and waggles her bare bottom at the audience; Australia's leading male prima ballerina, Vaseline Amalnitrate; Tara, the female lion tamer; and Captain Jack. One sketch followed another almost as rapidly as machine gun fire, involving a complete change or wardrobe — yet Livermore managed to keep up such a breathless pace. The only exteriors were 'front of house'; the show's title in lights; and the arrival of the audience. Then Livermore was seen making up for the night's entertainment. Other than that, the actual revue was a close-up. In this way most of the stage 'business' was completely lost. The film did not click like the stage version, and it came and went without making screen history.

Although *Promised Woman* was ready for release in early 1975, and a coverage of the picture was given on the now defunct ABC-TV series *Flicks* it did not receive a commercial release in this country until 3 December 1976 at the Village Cinema Centre, Sydney. Even then it did not reach the Longford Theatre, Melbourne until 15 December 1977 — and then only as a support to *Love Letters from Teralba Road.* The Sydney *Sun Herald* assessed *Promised Woman* as 'belonging to that class of Australian films that although not successful would be remembered'. Based upon a play *Throw away your Harmonica* by Theo Patrikareas, it was scripted, directed and photographed by Tom Cowan.

The promised woman was Antigone (played by Yugoslav actress Yelena Zigon). She leaves her village in Greece to come to Australia to marry Telis (Nikos Gerassimou) whom she has never seen. When she arrives, she is rejected by Telis who feels he has been tricked about her age. Antigone is resentful of her treatment and indulges in dreams of a lost love affair (the lover being played by Jean-Claude Petit) that made her feel unworthy of the customary dowry that Telis had waived. Telis is more interested in building a

new block of flats in Sydney, but his older brother Manolis (Takis Emmanuel) feels that he should settle the question of his marriage first. Meanwhile Antigone meets a friendly Australian barmaid Marge (Kate Fitzpatrick) but is unable to accept her sympathy. There is a bitter fight between the two brothers — and finally Manolis proposes marriage. Antigone is forced to examine her dreams and eventually is able to disassociate herself from the past and emerge free to decide her own future.

6.16   *Yelina Zigon in "Promised Woman", Yelina later played a minor role in "The Picture Show Man".*

6.17   *Yelina Zigon, star of "Promised Woman" with the man who plagues her dream-life. (played by Jean-Claude Petit).*

Interesting associations with *Promised Woman* were Takis Emmanuel (who played the Greek lover in *Caddie*) and Gillian Armstrong (mentioned earlier with *The Singer and the Dancer*) who was production designer and played a minor role as a nurse.

On the whole, *Promised Woman* was an honest and sincere attempt to depict a migrant's problems in a new country that has a different life-style. It was a story that had to be told, but as the commentator in *Flicks* remarked — 'what a pity the film wasn't equal to the occasion'. It lacked the professional touch of *Caddie* and *The Devil's Playground*. The direction and script were a little crude at times, and the action was stiffly handled. The acting was adequate, but the short exchanges of dialogue did not allow for character development. Somehow Yelena Zigon and Takis Emmanuel looked like synthetic substitutes for genuine players. The editing, too, was a little patchy. Yet Tom Cowan must be given credit for tackling such a complex situation with courage and determination. At the very least, it did present the Greek side of the Australian story.

The final entry in the women's cycle is *Eliza Fraser*. This was the film with the biggest budget Australia had produced to date, being estimated at between $1.2 and $1.5 million to produce. Like *2000 Weeks* also by Tim Burstall, *Eliza* didn't make the expected impact on the local film front.

Released in Brisbane, Sydney, Melbourne and Adelaide on 16 December 1976, it did take $1 million in the first seven weeks of screenings, but it would have had to do much better than that to come out even, let alone make a profit.

Theatre Australia (May 1977) claimed that *Eliza Fraser* represented two of the most boring hours spent in a cinema. The review described the picture as a 'dud', and ended with: 'It's not that *Eliza Fraser* is bad — it's boring.' Brisbane's *Sunday Mail* headed its critique: 'A Tom Jones Down Under' and the Melbourne *Sun* called *Eliza Do Little*. Yet another critic dubbed it *Eliza Purple*.

The one thing that *Eliza Fraser* did prove was that David Williamson was out of his depth in period drama (or should it be farce?). It also seems that Tim Burstall (who from all appearances really wishes to direct a *great* Australian film) could not determine the pace of this one —whether farce, fantasy or factual!

But how could any picture recover from such an opening splurge as: 'a faithful narrative of the capture, sufferings and miraculous escape of Eliza Fraser'? Act one depicts Eliza as a hussy with actors John Castle and John Waters finding her bed-style invitations impossible to resist. Act two is a switch to high drama that doesn't succeed. The disclosure that Captain Foster Fyans, Commandant of the Moreton Bay prison, is a homosexual, provides another shock. Not being content with his selected convict stripping and warming his bed, he demands that he remain for his personal pleasure. Convict John Waters, not appreciating the Captain's interest, makes his escape minus clothing. (If it was cold enough to have the bed warmed, then it must have been a chilling experience for the said Mr Waters!) A rather

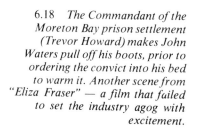

6.18   *The Commandant of the Moreton Bay prison settlement (Trevor Howard) makes John Waters pull off his boots, prior to ordering the convict into his bed to warm it. Another scene from "Eliza Fraser" — a film that failed to set the industry agog with excitement.*

unconvincing shipwreck follows, when Captain and Eliza Fraser are tossed on the rocks on Fraser Island, where the remainder of the crew slaughter one another for food. Up to this point Noel Ferrier as the captain portrays his pompous role with conviction, but when he is seen wearing a *lap lap*, a ludicrous touch is introduced. The leader of the natives who has not a Christian bone in his body (he much prefers missionary meat) decides that Eliza would make a good wife and has her prepared for the big occasion. In the process she loses clothing and is daubed with red ochre. But those natives look as fearsome as ladies on a croquet lawn. Finally Fyans' Filibusters arrive and rescue Mrs F., but not before Captain F. is speared right in the middle of the rescue operations, by one of the Commandant's cohorts.

Act three provides 'doings in a tent show' when Eliza tells of her experiences to paying customers. Eliza plays up her horrible and heinous happenings in those savage and satanic surroundings. Finally ex-convict David Bracefull, who had located Eliza, unbelievably appears as a man of considerable means, and sails with her on his own boat, mark you, into a New Zealand sunrise.

Susannah York sums up the film best as 'a pudding' — a bit of everything. On the credit side was Robin Copping's photography and the music by Bruce Smeaton.

6.19   *Noel Ferrier as the captain of the clipper "Stirling Castle" that was wrecked on Fraser Island (Queensland). A scene from the film "Eliza Fraser" directed by Tim Burstall.*

6.20   *The Aboriginal tribe on Fraser Island prepares for the marriage of their chief to Eliza Fraser. He claims her despite the fact that her husband is the captain of the wrecked "Stirling Castle". A scene from the Hexagon production "Eliza Fraser".*

Action Cycle for 1976

Mad Dog Morgan is one of the films qualifying as an 'action' picture for 1976. It is hard to justify its making. Australian film makers in the past had been obsessed with the idea of depicting the exploits of our various

6.21 *David Gulpilil and Dennis Hopper in a scene from "Mad Dog Morgan", directed by Philippe Mora. It was screened at the Cannes and Sydney Film Festivals in 1976.*

bushrangers. Then right in the middle of our film resurgence comes *Mad Dog.* The main reaction by theatre audiences to this film was: 'What beautiful scenery'. That is damning a film with faint praise. However top marks must go to cameraman Mike Molloy for his artistic treatment of Australian bush scenery. The only actor to show any promise was David Gulpilil as Morgan's offsider, Billy. Michael Pate and Jack Thompson were not up to standard. This could be attributed to director Mora not exercising enough control over his actors.

Mora is quoted as stating that *Mad Dog* was 90 per cent factual. In that case the remaining 10 per cent is well worth investigation. First, the recreation of the Lambing Flat Gold Riots of 1861 was very poorly done. It was implied that this area was bushranger Morgan's hunting ground. In actual fact this was the Darkie Gardiner-Ben Hall stomping ground. Morgan terrorised the lower part of New South Wales, in the Albury region. Mora depicted Morgan (Dennis Hopper) as an Irishman — a member of an oppressed race — who fought bitterly against the injustice of the Colonial Establishment with a vicious contempt for the rights of its fellow men. Yet according to a number of reliable sources, Morgan was born at Campbelltown (NSW). He was an illegitimate son of a Sydney prostitute and a former London barrow boy. After escaping from Pentridge Gaol (Melbourne) he robbed people in the Wagga and Deniliquin districts, and he shot a station hand in the back (his own ultimate fate).

6.22 *Dennis Hopper is the crazed "Mad Dog Morgan" — one of the most blood thirsty bushrangers in Australia. Still by Angus Forbes.*

This picture was shown at the Cannes Film Festival in 1976, but not in the official Australian theatre, The Regent. *Mad Dog Morgan* was screened in Australia at the Sydney Pitt Centre on 9 July 1976.

The Sydney *Sun Herald* advised that the characters were commonplace cut-outs. Even attention to small detail had been sacrificed in an effort to provide action — and more action.

Deathcheaters, a second action film for 1976, once again revealed that Brian Trenchard-Smith excelled as an action director, but had no flair for comedy.

In *Deathcheaters* ex-commandos John Hargreaves and Grant Page set up a stuntman agency for film and television work. Into this field of activity steps a kind of ASIO agent, Mr Culpepper (Noel Ferrier — but this time with his clothes on) who tempts the pair of ex-commandos to penetrate an industrial complex in the Philippines which is headed by an international gangster called Hernandez. Culpepper requires incriminating plans and papers. To get to Hernandez Hideaway, the ex-commandos climb tall cliffs and buildings, and to effect their escape, rig a sling-shot that catapults their two-man hang glider into the air and over the sea where they are picked up by submarine. After all that, Steve, one of the stuntmen, advises in Walter Mitty style that 'it's a living'. It is when the film delves into the private lives of the two men that Grant Page, although good at his job, reveals that as a Casanova he is no Tony Curtis.

On 5 December 1976 in Brisbane, Brian Trenchard Smith stated that *Deathcheaters* was completed in twelve weeks. Once again it was aimed at providing non-stop action for both juvenile and adult audiences, and also provided a spoof of a super hero, like James Bond. In February the following year Trenchard Smith received offers for the exhibition of the picture in the United Kingdom, Germany, Italy, Spain, France and Venezuela. He was pleased to learn that at long last, overseas buyers were looking to the Australian film industry with greater interest.

Deathcheaters opened in Sydney on 16 December 1976, and in Melbourne one week later. However in the Awards for 1976 *Deathcheaters* did not receive a mention. Neither did *Mad Dog Morgan.*

6.23 *Action is the keynote of "Death-cheaters" directed by Brian Trenchard Smith and released through Roadshow.*

Experiments — 1976

July and August provided a rather different cycle on the local film front. Two films were in the realm of fantasy: *The Fourth Wish* and *Oz. Fantasm,* another strange picture, covered sex-ploitation, while a fourth called *The Trespassers* dealt with authorities trespassing on an individual's rights to refuse to fight in Vietnam.

The Fourth Wish was one film that marred the good record of the South Australian Film Corporation. This time short seasons in Sydney and Melbourne did not signify the standard of the picture. The ranks of the critics were divided, with some calling it 'wishy-washy' and others 'a film too good to miss'. The Melbourne *Scene* was right in its assessment when the reviewer wrote that 'John Meillon and Robert Bettles were in line for further acting awards'. Meillon was voted actor of the year for his role in *The Fourth Wish* in the 1977 Australian Film Awards, and Robert Bettles received a Sammy in the 1976 Awards.

Perhaps one of the main reasons for its failure was that it followed too closely upon the TV series (for which Meillon picked up yet another acting award). Meillon with his great capacity for inflection, gave new meaning to such an ordinary line as: 'I don't give a stuff whether you or the whole AMA says he's going to die. He's my son and he's not going to die.' His flexible face added strength to his outburst. In fact, there wasn't a bad performance in the whole film.

Abandoned by his wife (Robyn Nevin), Casey (John Meillon) attempts to raise his son Sean (Robert Bettles) but to his horror discovers that the boy has leukemia. He asks Sean to name three wishes. The granting of those requests, will test the ingenuity of the father. Sean wants a dog, a visit from his mother, and a handshake with Queen Elizabeth II. The dog, a lovable, scruffy type, is the easiest wish to grant. He is located in a dog pound. But the canine causes the first problem — the landlord of the flat in which father and son dwell — will not permit a tenant to have an animal on the premises. Casey is told to leave. He decides to fight fire with fire and engages a lawyer MP to fight the

6.24 *John Meillon gives Robert Bettles some good fatherly advice in "The Fourth Wish" — a South Australian Film Corporation Production.*

case, telling him bluntly: 'I bloody well voted for you'.

The granting of Sean's second wish poses a far greater hurdle. Casey's wife, an alcoholic, is working in a sleezy night club and has forgotten the existence of her son. Casey literally bullies her into at least seeing Sean. In a pitiful and emotional scene she struggles to spruce herself up for the occasion. But after a day with paddle boats on the Torrens, she drifts back to her old way of life, stating that business will take her away from Adelaide. The one chance photographer Geoff Burton has of introducing a lyrical sense of beauty into the story is when the father takes his son for an outing in the country which includes boating on a tranquil waterway. The granting of the third wish is very well done with the Royal car arriving at Government House, and a back view of an actress dressed to represent the Queen. The first obstacle that Casey has to overcome is the policeman (Gordon McDougal) on duty at the gate.

Even the eventual death of Sean does not allow pathos to develop into sickly sentimentality. The realisation of his son's imminent death liberates a new flow of strength within Casey and promotes a capacity for action that is ultimate salvation.

6.25   *The first of four wishes — the dog "Roger" is greeted by John Meillon and Robert Bettles in "The Fourth Wish".*

The Fourth Wish opened at Adelaide's Hindley Theatre on 16 July 1976, after being one of the official Australian entries the previous May at Cannes.

Oz the third experiment for 1976, was a poor man's version of *The Wizard of Oz*. This rock and roll updated story pleased youngsters but horrified those who remembered the Judy Garland classic. Although not in the same class as *The Devil's Playground* or *Sunday Too Far Away*, at least it was Australian. The characters of *The Wizard of Oz* are basically still there — there is Dorothy; the Cowardly Lion becomes the Bikie who didn't wish to fight; the Scarecrow with no brains is a Surfie without a beach; and the Tin Man without a heart emerges as a mechanic who interferes with distributor caps on cars. Robin Ramsay is the Good Fairy.

6.26 *In "Oz" Bruce Spence of "Stork" fame is the Bass player and "Surfie" and Joy Dunstan is 'Dorothy'. This Australian musical was written and directed by Chris Lofven.*

In the storyline of *Oz* Dorothy goes in search of her popstar idol, the Wizard. Bruce Spence (who is 'Stork') is outstanding as 'the Surfie' and some of the camerawork is imaginative, especially the exterior shots. One of the main faults with *Oz* is that bursts of dialogue are broken up with scenic images accompanied by explosive music featuring obscure lyrics. Dorothy was played by Joy Dunstan; the Bikie (Gary Waddell); the Mechanic (Michael Carman); and the Wizard (Graham Matters). As one critic wrote: 'It's a long 105 minutes filled with forgettable music.' And there is a lot of film wastage in the rather dusty version of The Yellow Brick Road: 'It took the gee-whiz out of fantasy replacing it with a very jaded so-what', wrote another critic.

6.28 *Gary Waddell as the Guitarist and 'The Bikie' and Michael Carman, The Drummer and "The Mechanic" in "Oz".*

Written and directed by Chris Lofven, *Oz* opened in Brisbane and Melbourne on 30 July 1976, and in Sydney one month later.

On 5 January 1977 it was reported that *Oz* (financed by the Australian Film Commission and Greater Union) had been sold to American distributors. The sale involved a substantial cash guarantee plus a share of the box office.

Oz did not receive many bouquets in Australia, nor was it a commercial success in this country. Then came the startling revelation. On 4 April 1978 the Australian Film Commission advised that *Oz* was 'currently showing to very good audiences in more than twenty cinemas in the United States of America, and has been sold to a number of European countries.' This is one example of an Australian film being a financial success thanks to overseas rather than Australian sales.

Fantasm — A TLN Film Production released through Filmways — was another 'different' film for 1976. Mainly shot in America, it had some secondary footage from Australia. Although not an official Australian entrant, it was screened at Cannes in May 1976. Australian International Films was set up in late 1975 to market the picture. The world premiere of *Fantasm* was scheduled for a Brisbane suburban theatre, The Capri, in East Brisbane. Contrary to general belief it was shown on Friday 16 July 1976, and was not viewed by the local Board of Review until the following Monday, 19 July. It was banned the following morning. The Capri was closed on the Tuesday night, as the management did not have time to warn patrons and cancel advertising. The chairman of the Board stated that *Fantasm* was: 'a lot stronger in obscenity content than some other films. In *Fantasm* male and female frontal nudes, masochism, and almost every conceivable sexual fantasy is depicted. One local critic felt that it would have been just another skin flick, had it not been for the Queensland ban. 'The wobbling bottoms, sagging breasts, and inane incantations', continued the writer, 'was almost enough to make one consider emigrating to Queensland.' Screened at the Melbourne Dendy Theatre immediately following Brisbane closure on 22 July, it had a record run. In early January 1977, two critics in New Delhi were outspoken in their condemnation of *Fantasm* on the eve of an International Film Festival in that country, calling it 'filth'. Antony Ginnane replied: 'The Indian Government and associated officialdom, is well known for repressive policies.'

The Trespassers, directed and written by John Duigan, was yet another experiment in this cycle of 'different' films. It dealt with another aspect of war that by 1978 had become a further page in our history books — the struggle in Vietnam. An official entry at the 1976 Cannes Film Festival, *The Trespassers* commenced its world premiere at Melbourne's Longford cinema. Conducted by the Australian Film Institute, this cinema perpetuates the name of Raymond Longford. *The Trespassers* had its gala night on 17 August 1976. On 29 July 1977 it was the support at the Centre Twin Cinema, Melbourne.

Set in Melbourne in 1970, the backdrop of *The Trespassers* is one of turbulent moratoriums and draft dodgers on the run. Into this setting is placed Richard (John Derum) a radical journalist participating in anti-Vietnam War demonstrations. He lives with Penny (Briony Behets), an aspiring writer. Richard has another female interest, Dee (Judy Morris) an actress who is fiercely independent. The two women meet by chance when they attend a secret television interview with draft-resisters. The pair decide to spend a few days at the seaside. Penny shows Dee one of her plays, and the latter states that she would like to produce it. When Dee decides to spend the afternoon with a farmer (Chris Haywood) whom she has befriended, Penny feels let down and goes to bed with a man she met in the pub. Richard arrives home unexpectedly to find the women together. Penny is cool and distant, but Dee is openly hostile. Richard for the first time feels insecure, and he becomes aware of the fact that a personal re-assessment of the position has suddenly become important.

6.30 *Celeste as Shayne in "Fantasm" — a TLN Film Production produced by Antony I. Ginnane and directed by Richard Bruce. "Fantasm" was banned in Queensland.*

Vince Monton, photographer on *Fantasm* again took the camera in *The Trespassers* to reproduce the lush South Gippsland countryside and to capture the chilly grey of a wintery sky and sea. Although some critics headed their reviews, 'Forgive Us Our Trespassers' or, 'A neat triangle — but what's the angle?', the acting of Briony Behets and Judy Morris was praised. It was felt however that the script did not develop the early promise of conflict or the issues associated with the war in Vietnam. Critics generally agreed that John Derum did all that was required of him, but that he looked too young and unwordly to hold the interests of Judy and Briony. The Melbourne *Herald* did see *The Trespassers* as an indication of the growing maturity of the Australian cinema. *Cinema Papers* summed up the film as 'exciting — the work of a young film maker who is honest, mature, and serious. It is also, unless you want hang gliding, entertaining.'

Nineteen seventy-six was a memorable year for Australia at Cannes. At the Regent Cinema, 4 Rue Florian, Cannes from 13-28 May the following features were screened at least three times each: *The Trespassers; Caddie; The Fourth Wish; Picnic at Hanging Rock* and *Let the Balloon Go.* One screening each was allocated to *Sunday Too Far Away; End Play* and *Between Wars.* In addition, *Mad Dog Morgan, Fantasm* and *Goodbye Norma Jean*, the unofficial Australian entries, were projected elsewhere. The campaign, hosted by the Australian Film Commissioner, was captioned 'Australia's Beautiful Surprise'. Approximately $200 000 was spent on the promotion.

Award Winners for Mid-Seventies

The following two pictures won Awards in 1976 and 1977: *The Devil's Playground* (the second Australian film of this name), and *Don's Party.*

The Devil's Playground was produced and directed by Fred Schepisi. It was considered to be an un-commercial film, but it had considerable success with Schepisi handling the film's distribution himself. Set in a college monastery which prepares boys for religious orders, *The Devil's Playground* brought forcibly to the screen the problems of body-conscious youths who experience the trauma of pubescence. In this atmosphere of sexual unreality, the brothers too, under vows of celibacy, had to conquer their own temptations and wordly desires. The story shocked many, but it was told with sincerity by Fred Schepisi, a man who had drawn upon his own boyhood experiences. Critics were generally full of superlatives with many stating that the film was deserving of the Awards it had won, and that as a frank and serious picture, it would be hard to beat.

Simon Burke was ideally cast as Tom Allen, the bed-wetting boy who was always late for service because he had been hurriedly washing his bed clothes after nymphs had tormented him in his dreams. Nick Tate, is a rebel brother who is willing to accept life in a monastery providing it does not interfere with his drinking and spectator sports. A quick drink at a bar after viewing such outdoor activity often brought inviting offers from females in hotels that had to be subtly side-stepped. Only Arthur Dignam, somewhat out of place in this film, is the odd man out — the fake — a man of starchy stiffness without any sense of humour, and without the merest suggestion of mirth in his eyes. He is

6.31 *From Fred Schepisi's first full length feature "The Devil's Playground". From left to right, Charles McCallum, John Frawley, Arthur Dignam, Peter Cox and Nick Tate.*

constantly staring — under bathing booth doors, and into the shower rooms where the boys are acquiring that state that is next to godliness. Overall, the acting is outstanding, with the possible exception of the visiting priest who conducts the retreat for the teenage novitiates. During the three-day retreat when complete silence is demanded, Tom Allen who is extremely bored, throws a pebble into a nearby stream. It breaks the solemnity with a musical 'plop'. A second and a third stone follows. There is a titter, then a laugh as other boys follow Tom's example. Eventually there is a loud roar as one of the boys falls into the water. After the retreat, a special party is given, at which the boys really break the 'sound' barrier.

Ian Baker's superb photography, already demonstrated in *The Priest* segment of *Libido*, must come in for high praise. It was carefully studied symmetry throughout, with outdoor shots of sheer beauty. *The Devil's Playground* was selected for the Director's Fortnight at Cannes Festival in 1976.

In the 1976 Australian Film Awards, *The Devil's Playground* dominated the prize charts. It won best film of the year and gained the Jury Prize for a feature film. Simon Burke and Nick Tate shared the best actor award and Ian Baker took out the Kodak Award as the best cinematographer. In 1977 Nick Tate received a Sammy for his role. TV Times also voted *The Devil's Playground* as top film and in 1977 Sammys went to Fred Schepisi as best feature film writer and director. In addition it was the most popular film of the 1976 Sydney Festival. *The Devil's Playground* began its commercial season in Melbourne on 13 August 1976.

6.32 *Ray Barrett, John Hargreaves (as Don) and Graham Kennedy in "Don's Party". Written by David Williamson, it was directed by Bruce Beresford and produced by Phillip Adams.*

Don's Party, an award winning film for 1977, took David Williamson out of his ill-fitting historian's coat and placed him back in his own environment — scandalous, sexy suburbia. *Don's Party* merely offered another excuse to portray another boozo — and to get 'respectable' husbands into bed with their mate's wives. It is the type of party symbolising the so-called Ocker way of life. People had their hang-ups, just as the morning after provided its let-down. Graham Kennedy, rather surprisingly, came up well as the insecure photographer who obtained his kicks from taking shots of friends making love to his wife. But his humour was crude which emphasises the earthiness of playwright Williamson's dialogue. But when condensed to fit the lens of a camera, even though it may be exploded later on the wide screen, the dialogue retains its shades of blue, which seems to indicate that Williamson's material is better for stage than for film.

Theatre Australia (June 1977) describes *Don's Party* as:

... a play I love, but the film seems to have forsaken much of its scatalogical humour, to concentrate on those tiresome yobbo Ockers. I have very little patience with the film which I find tiresome and plodding... Harold Hopkins is too hip and good-looking as the womanising Cooley. I longed for the cheeky exuberance of John Ewart ... We all know people who behave like guests at *Don's Party* ... I found it a bloody bore and could hardly wait for it to be over.

Graeme Blundell directed the stage play when it was first performed at the Melbourne Pram Factory on 11 August 1971. In the film Graeme was able to cast aside his 'Alvin Purple' image and portray Simon, the nervy Liberal voter at a party to celebrate a Labor victory at the Federal elections. He was one of the few 'straight' characters in the picture, and he gave an outstanding performance. Pipe-smoking and even-tempered, he was out of place in the gathering of Don's loud-mouthed, bed-crawling, beer-swilling guests at these premature victory celebrations. (Labor lost).

Cinema Papers felt that:

> The men's roles are meatier than the women's, which is just as well since, apart from Pat Bishop (as Ray Barrett's wife, Jenny), their performances are below par. One can only regard them as adequate, competent, and sometimes even amateurish. For those who have not seen the stage version, the film will probably be satisfying; others who have, are likely to be disappointed.

A Sydney critic advised that by the time the big flagons were being broached, the party had disintegrated, and a bunch of immature, backbiting no-hopers were revealed. But Bruce Beresford did receive praise for the way he built up and changed the mood of the party with masterly control. *Scene* on 2 April 1977 saw *Don's Party* this way:

> Director Bruce Beresford has lost nothing in translating David Williamson's hit play to the screen. It is a faster, funnier, more stunning think-piece than the stage version.

Shown at the 1977 Cannes Film Festival, the picture was chosen to compete in the Berlin Film Festival. It was screened in Canberra in November 1976, and in Sydney on 3 December.

In the 1977 Australian Film Awards, *Don's Party* gave an award-winning performance. Pat Bishop was selected as best actress; Veronica Lang as supporting actress; Bruce Beresford for direction; David Williamson for the best screenplay; and William Anderson for achievement in editing and a similar award for sound editing.

Storm Boy

Storm Boy arrived out of the blue at the Fair Lady Theatre, Adelaide on 18 November 1976. It swept all records before it, both in awards and as a financial success. The unlikely star 'Mr Percival' the pelican, receives good human competition from Greg Rowe as 'Mike' — a boy growing up with 'Hideaway Tom' (Peter Cummins) his gruff, secretive father. Mike receives no affection or understanding from his mother either. David Gulpilil (or just plain Gulpilil as he prefers to be known) is 'Fingerbone', a young Aborigine wise in the ways of animals and birds. This young man from *Walkabout* reveals that he is fast becoming a very talented actor.

Storm Boy is a charming and sensitive film with Geoff Burton's camera capturing the sheer loveliness of the coastal wilderness that is the Coorong of South Australia. Produced by Matt Carroll and directed by Henri Safran, this is a film of which Australia could be justifiably proud. Most people who have seen it have thoroughly enjoyed it.

In *Storm Boy* there are no lengthy or impassioned speeches, there is no brilliant dialogue, and the camera sets the mood into which the players are neatly dovetailed. From the tranquility of the Coorong and its picturesque surroundings to the savage fury of a storm, the camera is there to portray it all — and brilliantly. One discordant note is struck when beach buggies with telescopic lights intrude upon the setting, and in an unbelievable display of sheer vandalism, destroy Hideaway Tom's shack and nearly kill young Mike. There is no need for this sequence. A storm could destroy the tranquility of the setting far more effectively than any beach buggy.

The second flaw in a nearly-perfect film was the shipwreck scene in which Mr Percival the pelican flies out a lifeline to the men on board the doomed vessel. This lacked the necessary tension that could have been built up. The situation was there — but the direction wasn't! One leaves with a feeling of slight disappointment: why can't birds win 'Oscars', 'Logies' or more appropriately still, 'Penguins'?

Successful at Cannes in 1977, *Storm Boy* went to the Moscow Film Festival where it won the Grand Prix in the children's division and the International Youth Prize awarded by a children's jury.

When top Russian film director Stanislav Rostotsky arrived in Melbourne on 4 November 1977, he stated that a programme of Australian films would be shown in Moscow and Leningrad in December and later in Odessa. Those to be screened were *Storm Boy, The Getting of Wisdom, The Picture Show Man* and *Sunday Too Far Away*. On 16 December, newspapers reported that *Storm Boy* opened the Australian Cinematography Premiere in Moscow where thousands of Soviet film fans welcomed the picture back after its triumph in July at the International Film Festival.

Storm Boy made a triumphant entry to Melbourne on 28 July 1977 at East End and Rivoli (Camberwell) Theatres, and to Sydney on 4 August at Cinema City. On 21 January 1978 it was revealed that *Storm Boy* rated third to *Star Wars* and *The Spy who Loved Me* in Australian cinemas during the 1977 Christmas holidays — a mighty performance for an Australian film. In addition, American David Soul recorded the ballad *Storm Boy* which was based on the picture. In Adelaide during the 1976 Christmas holidays the film was second only to *King Kong*. It is encouraging to note that *Kong* was given a run for his money by at least one Australian production.

For once, critics were unstinted in their praise and even looked up special superlatives to use in their critiques. In many papers *Storm Boy* received a four star grading.

Storm Boy in the 1977 Australian Film Awards was voted the best film of the year, and in addition received the Jury Prize for a feature film. The third honour was the Jedda Award from Australian National Travel. Sonia Borg in the 1977 Awgie Awards won the best film screenplay award for *Storm Boy*. In the 1977 TV Times Sammy Awards, Geoff Burton took top honours for cinematography for his work on this film.

After the let-down with *The Fourth Wish*, *Storm Boy* more than replenished the coffers of the South Australian Film Corporation, and added to its prestige in the annals of Australian showbusiness. Author Colin Thiele did very nicely too, with numerous reprints, some of which were very lavishly illustrated. *Blue Fin*, Thiele's second work is being filmed, again under the South Australian film Corporation banner with producer Matt Carroll and scripter Sonia Borg teamed once more. 'Blue Fin' is a tuna fishing boat and the location is Port Lincoln.

From Success to Flops

In the closing stages of commercial films for 1976, two production units heeded the cry for local Christmas attractions — D.S. Waddington Productions and Film Australia. Waddington produced *Barney* and Film Australia did *Let the Balloon Go*. Full responsibility for their failure must be laid at the door of the many parents who preferred to let their children see a remake of *King Kong,* rather than some new Australian films. In Melbourne as an example, Hoyts Cinema Centre started off *Barney* as an all-sessions feature, but it soon became like *Dot and the Kangaroo* did in 1977, a matinée-only picture. It began on 16 December, but by the 6 January 1977 it was advertised for the suburban Hoyts Malvern and Camberwell theatres. In the city *Barney* was replaced with *Let the Balloon Go* also for matinées only.

6.33 *Brett Maxworthy (holding "Amanda" the Wombat), Sean Kramer, and Mike Preston (extreme right) in "Barney". Directed by David Waddington, it was released through Columbia Pictures.*

This relegation to matinées is really infuriating to those people who wish to see Australian-made films accepted in their own country. This will neither help nor encourage further production of Australian features for children. It has been stated that *Barney* was 'sickly sentimental and lacked any appeal for adults'. On the other hand critics agreed that *Let the Balloon Go* did possess adult interest. Yet the film was still restricted to matinée showings.

The wreck of a sailing ship in 1880, while travelling between Sydney and Melbourne was one of the highlights of *Barney*. It was cleverly engineered by director David Waddington. Barney Dawson (Brett Maxworthy) and Rafe Duggan (Sean Kramer) a roguish Irishman, are the only known survivors of the shipwreck. Of course one must not overlook Barney's pet wombat, Amanda. Rafe has a price on his head, but a tender heart, and helps the boy on his overland trip to Ballarat to locate his father. On the way they meet a hawker (Spike Milligan) who hides them from the troopers pursuing Rafe. This time the Irishman is wanted on a charge of horse stealing, of which, for once, he is innocent. Three bushrangers, one of whom is O'Shaughnessy played by Mike Preston, bail up a coach. Barney and Rafe arrive and O'Shaughnessy recognises the Rafe. In the coach is Charles Dawson (Lionel Long) who is Barney's father. He grabs a rifle, but is quickly subdued. Barney looks around for the would-be hero, and sees his father for the first time. Troopers appear and the bushrangers speed off. Rafe sees a riderless horse and leaves hurriedly.

Columbia Pictures partially backed the production and guaranteed world distribution. *Barney* was the first Australian film this American company had had an interest in since *Smithy*. Columbia executives, on viewing the completed picture, advised that *Barney* was the most commercial film to come out of Australia in thirty years.

According to David Waddington, *Barney* was due for release in New Zealand and twelve other countries during Christmas 1976. It was to be shown in America in June 1977. What a pity it was labelled a commercial failure in the land of its origin. Referring to *Barney* the Melbourne *Sun* pointed out that any Australian movie was a significant event, but that a children's film adults can enjoy too was of special significance. Melbourne *Scene* on 4 December 1976 wrote of *Barney:*

> The wombat's a winner. This is a delightful Australian surprise in which 'Barney', a twelve year old, is played well and without cuteness by Brett Maxworthy. The convict Rafe Duggan, is portrayed by Sydney club entertainer, Sean Kramer. I see this as a long and successful career from the tiny Irishman. He's very, very funny, and very, very good. Spike Milligan without the usual Milligan twitches, shows a side that I hope to see again. It could start a whole craze for wombat pictures.

Unlike Waddington, Film Australia did not look for overseas backing for *Let the Balloon Go*. It was however sold to America for a six-figure sum on 10 August 1976. It was stated that this figure would go a long way towards recouping the initial production cost of just under $400 000.

The world premiere of *Balloon* was in Los Angeles, California, on 8 December 1976. Australian screenings were on 16 December at the Town Cinema, Sydney and at the Valley Twin Theatre, Brisbane. A gala charity night was held in Orange at the Australian Theatre, on 15 December.

Let the Balloon Go was filmed in the NSW town of Carcoar — which is remembered historically as the place where the Australian bushranger 'Darkie' Gardiner lived on parole before he became a discount butcher on the Lambing Flat goldfield. 'A balloon is not a balloon until the string is cut and it is allowed to float freely' is the thought which provides the inspiration for this film which was adapted from Ivan Southall's novel. The talented Robert Bettles plays the crippled boy, John Summer. In the background of this delightful story is Bruce Spence as the inept acting fire chief (a far cry from his roles in *Stork* and *Oz)*. He and his red-painted, brass-adorned fire truck

6.34 *Robert Bettles in "Let The Balloon Go". Robert was a popular young actor whose other roles were in "Ride A Wild Pony" and "The Fourth Wish".*

(which is seldom operative) are the butt of caustic comment from the townspeople. Then there is Ken Goodlet as the tipsy Major Fairleigh who encourages John to overcome his frustrations and limitations. John Ewart is excellent as the overbearing police constable who tries to organise untrained citizens into a home guard. However the military exercise at Bennett's Bridge becomes a shambles when the children of the town intervene with fire hoses and flour bombs.

John is over-protected by his parents (Jan Kingsbury and Ben Gabriel) and dreams of running away, and climbing, effortlessly, the tall tree outside his bedroom window. Like the balloon, he wishes to climb and feel liberated from the restrictions placed upon him. As a dramatic, if not defiant gesture, he decides to climb the tree. Like the balloon he wants to 'do his thing'.

Directed by Oliver Howes with photography handled by top notch Dean Semler, this was a film worthy of greater support than it received. The Mayfair Theatre in Melbourne considered it good enough to re-present on 7 April 1977, during the Easter holidays.

Like *Barney* the picture had a mixed reception from Australian critics who often slate the local production and over-rate overseas films. *Scene* on the 22 January 1977 was sympathetic:

> Undaunted by the failure of the charming Australian family film *Barney* which should have been a hit, Hoyts have tried again in the family film trade with *Let the Balloon Go*. It's a great little movie about a crippled kid who wants to do what other kids do — climb trees. Robert Bettles plays the boy and is surrounded by actors who are really great. It's a simple, moving film with lots of fun. I hate to use the cliché, but it really is a picture for the whole family.

6.35   *From the Film Australia production "Let The Balloon Go". L-R. Ray Barrett, Jan Kingsbury, Robert Bettles and Ben Gabriel. The location for the film was Carcoar, the town in which "Darkie" Gardiner was released on parole.*

In contrast, Sydney's *Sunday Telegraph* on 2 January 1977 felt that it was 'impossible to be unkind about this admirably intentioned movie. It had the right sentiments and was strikingly beautiful!' Then came the blunt axe: the critic felt that 'equally, it was impossible to work up any enthusiasm about it'.

Let the Balloon Go won two of America's top awards. The first was Hollywood's Award for Excellence by the International Film Advisory Board that endorses family films of the highest quality. (Even that didn't encourage Australian parents to send their children to see it.) The second honour was a Silver Medal at the 9th Annual Festival of the Americas for an outstanding children's feature film. Surely the answer to this standard of excellence isn't a remake of *King Kong*?

16 mm Productions for 1976

On 28 March 1977 it was reported in the newspapers that a new film was being shot in North Queensland called *The Irishman*. It was claimed to be the first to be photographed in that state since *Sons of Matthew*. In actual fact *The Irishman* comes third to *Surrender in Paradise* screened on 4 October 1976 and *The Mango Tree* shown in December 1977.

6.36 *Paddy Doolan is a proud Irish-Australian teamster in North Queensland. This is his team in the new Australian film "The Irishman" produced by Anthony Buckley.*

6.37 *Michael Craig and Jim O'Connor in "The Irishman" — A Forest Home Film based on Elizabeth O'Connor's prize winning novel.*

Surrender in Paradise actually begins the parade of 16 mm productions for 1976. Its world premiere was in October at the Schonell Theatre, St Lucia (Brisbane's university suburb). The supporting feature was Charles Chauvel's silent picture *The Moth of Moonbi* (also shot in Queensland). *Surrender* then commenced one week's season at the Crystal Palace, Windsor (another Brisbane suburb). Directed by Peter Cox and photographed by Don McAlpine (who handled camera for *Don's Party*) *Surrender in Paradise* starred local artists Errol O'Neill, Ross Gilbert, Rod Wissler, Bill Reynolds, Carolyn Howard and Gaye Poole. Claimed to be 'the first wholly produced feature film since the days of Charles Chauvel' it was a strange blend of bushranging adventure, a road movie, and a chase picture which covered a period from the past to the present dazzle of Surfers Paradise.

Written and produced by the director, *Surrender in Paradise* could be labelled black comedy. The climax however is termed by some as 'outrageous comedy with real tragedy — the attempt to hang a man with a lifesaver's lifeline as the shallow waves at the beach's edge turn crimson with blood. This is ignored by the happy crowd of holiday makers.' One critic thought the first half was 'flatly paced' and that some of the actors were amateurish.

6.38 *The Queensland produced "Surrender in Paradise". On location at the Rosevale Hotel, director Peter Cox (lower right) talks to cast and crew. Next to Cox is Sound operator Jan Murray, with production asst. Salvatore Esposito looking at camera. In back row from right — Gavin Patterson (actor) and star Errol O'Neill in doorway. Production associate and Australian film historian Chris Collier is third from left.*

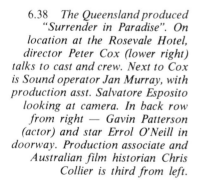

On 23 March 1978 *Surrender in Paradise* was advertised at the Ozone Theatre, Paddington Town Hall Centre, Sydney. It was described as 'an unusual new Australian film — life behind the peanut curtain.'

Illuminations, another 16 mm production which was written, directed and photographed by Paul Cox, is an expressive, almost poetic journey into the indeterminate depths of the mind. 'Man always underestimates the power of the mind and confuses it with is own man-made illusions,' gives one an idea of what the production tried to achieve. It was the type of film one expects to see at a film festival, but not as a commercial venture. In the story, a young couple (Tony Llewellyn Jones and Gabi Trsek) go to live in an old house in the country. The girl's father (Norman Kaye) has died, and the pair endeavour to communicate on a psychic level. The house is guarded by a horse which symbolises evil. In their minds, a church which doesn't exist is presided over by the dead father who tries to incarcerate them in a tomb that the brain has created. They escape from the hallucination, and leave the house that is still guarded by the fiendish horse.

6.39 *Made in Melbourne, "Illuminations" features Gabi Trsek and Tony Llewellyn-Jones. Producer Tabor Markus died shortly after the film was completed.*

The photography in *Illuminations* is brilliant, but audiences, although mindful of the camera work, leave a bit bewildered and a little depressed by the theme. It was premiered at the State Film Theatre, Melbourne on 26 March 1976, and was shown at the Melbourne Filmmakers' Co-operative Theatre in May.

A third 16 mm feature, of 1976 is *Pure S.* This is a production that received an Award for the most creative entry in the 1976 AFI Awards and Tom Cowan received a Silver Medallion for Cinematography from Kodak. One critic described *Pure S* as, 'the most evil he'd even seen'. Melbourne *Scene* on 22 May 1976 quipped, 'with publicity like that, it should make a fortune.'

Director Bert Deling seems to be obsessed with the 'drug' theme and like *Dalmas* traverses the same ground in *Pure S*. One Melbourne critic headed his comments, 'the shoot up — 1976 style', and goes on to advise that the critic's lot is not a happy one when a film like *Pure S* comes up for review. This critique also mentions that Deling cleverly disguises the fact that the cast does not contain actors by using a minimum of dialogue, which is mostly four letter words. 'S' is slang for hard core drugs like heroin and cocaine. To Tom Cowan must go the credit of first-rate photography that glamorises seedy surroundings even if the lenses do linger on such facets as hypodermics and bulging veins.

Pure S leans heavily towards violence. When Gary Waddell and John Laurie hold up a chemist shop in search of drugs, they threaten the owner with a monkey wrench and a knife. A customer intervenes. He wrestles the knife from one and carves the head of one of the would-be hold-up men. This distorted sense of the dramatic is matched only by a discordant sound track on various occasions. Yet the story is well paced. It follows the search for drugs by a few junkies in a battered FJ Holden. Max Gillies appears on the scene as a benevolent, but rather crazy psychiatrist. Ann Hetherington and Carol Porter portray the female partners in the search.

Overall, *Pure S* is an exercise in incoherence. Perhaps the editing by John Scott creates this illusion. A shot of the car travelling along the highway in the late afternoon sunlight suddenly becomes a journey at night, followed by a plunging view of a flight of stairs. A Holden plunges through a gigantic car wash — followed by a dramatic cut to a couple on a bed in a stupor. The aim of *Pure S*, according to Bert Deling, was to present the reality of drug-dependent persons, while not moralising about their position.

Pure S was released at the Playbox Cinema, Melbourne on 7 May; at the Union Theatre, Adelaide, 7 August and at the State Cinema, Hobart on 26 August, 1976.

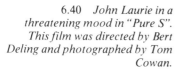

6.40   *John Laurie in a threatening mood in "Pure S". This film was directed by Bert Deling and photographed by Tom Cowan.*

ABC-TV Awards for 1976

ABC-TV in 1976 televised a number of high-standard productions that on many occasions reaped their rewards in Awards.

For *Essington*, directed by Julian Pringle which was telecast in March 1975, Chris Haywood was named the best actor in an individual performance in the 1976 TV Week Logie Awards, and Thomas Keneally was cited the best scriptwriter. This four-part drama came to the small screen unpublicised and almost unnoticed, yet it was comparable with anything produced overseas.

An account of the Royal Marine settlement at Port Essington (Darwin) in the 1840s, it reveals how the township slowly crumbled through fatigue, disease, and madness. Into the area stumbles Bob Squires (Chris Haywood) a convict on the run, who makes himself indispensable to the marines manning the disintegrating garrison. A naval vessel arrives with orders to evacuate the settlement and destroy the fort to prevent it from falling into the hands of a possible enemy. Squires remains in the ruins in the company of a half-witted girl, Pretty Polly (Sandra MacGregor). In the star-studded cast are Wyn Roberts, Michael Craig, Cornelia Frances, Melissa Jaffer, Drew Forsythe,

In *Sally Go Round the Moon,* another ABC-TV production, Jacqui Lochhead (Gordon) acted brilliantly enough to take out a 1976 Logie as the best juvenile performer. This is an absorbing drama about a retarded child. Olivia Hamnett portrays a patient, understanding mother. The father, Kit Taylor, looks upon his daughter as a handicap.

ABC-TV's *A Big Country* continued its Award-winning run by collecting a 1976 TV Week Logie as the best documentary series, as well as a 1976 Penguin from the Television Society of Australia. Then it took the hat trick with a 1976 Sammy.

6.41   *Wyn Roberts in "Essington" from ABC-TV.*

6.42   *"The Big Country" — an excellent ABC-TV documentary series, originated in 1968. A consistent Award Winner, its best year was 1976, when it received a "Penguin" from the Television Society of Australia, and a "Logie" from TV Week for the best documentary series. This still is from "Undermining Control" covering a unique worker-controlled coal mine at Nymboida near Grafton. The man in the foreground is Vane Ross, one of the miners.*

6.43 *The site of "Rush" for the first series — Churchill National Park, in the foothills of the Dandenong Ranges, Victoria.*

Andra, an eight-part children's series costing $98 000 received a Certificate of Special Recognition for imaginative and competent production in the 1976 Penguin awards. This was a science fiction story set in an era some 2000 years from now. It centres around 'Andra' (Lisa Peers) who is given a brain from a rebellious student of the 1980s. The transplant is performed by Bruce Kerr, who was the villainous police sergeant in *Cash & Co.* The town is Sub City One, whose inhabitants live underground after an atomic explosion.

The Melbourne premiere of the second series of *Rush* took place on 1 March 1976. The ABC made a shrewd move in scheduling the series immediately after *Tandarra* had completed its episode for the week on HSV7. The whole appearance is changed. Crocker's Gully has disappeared and in its place is the NSW setting of Turon Springs. Sergeant McKellar's wife, Sarah (Olivia Hamnett) has died and he has found himself a new romantic interest in June Harders who portrays the wife of an influential goldmine owner Captain Farrar (Paul Mason) for whom most of the 'diggers' work. In addition, McKellar has a French police reinforcement (Alain Doutey). This series of *Rush* was a co-production, and it was shown in September 1976 in Scotland and France, with Doutey dubbing his own part in French. England also showed it in September. Episodes of the second series of *Rush* were shown in Cannes in 1976.

Local critics viewed the second series coolly with such captions as, 'Why Rush? There's no hurry!' Yet the second series of *Rush* again proved quite popular. John Waters was named as the best actor in a TV series in the 1976 Penguin and Sammy Awards. In addition, in the best drama series, *Rush* received a commendation from the TV Society's 1976 Penguin Awards.

6.44 *Olivia Hamnett, John Waters, Sydney Conabere, and Brendon Lunney in the first series of "Rush" produced by ABC-TV.*

One episode of *Rush* — *A Shilling a Day* — received a Penguin in 1976 and Hugh Keays-Byrne was awarded a Sammy from TV Times in 1976 for the best actor in a TV performance. Keays-Byrne received a TV Week Logie in 1977 for the same role. Another Sammy in 1976 went to Colin Free as the scriptwriter of *A Shilling a Day*.

Power without Glory was a production that clearly indicated the standard and the fearlessness with which ABC-TV could approach certain works that commercial stations eyed with caution. But as an originator it must accept its share of brickbats as well as bouquets. This so-called fictional drama by Frank Hardy contained a number of names that seemed to be co-incidental with the initials of factual people. John West, Snoopy Tanner and Archbishop Malone could appear to have a certain identification with John Wren, Squizzy Taylor, and Archbishop Mannix. With some imagination Carringbush also could become Collingwood. West begins with an illegal 'bookie' shop and amasses a fortune. He becomes corrupt and manipulates

6.45 *John West has his trouble with the police over his illegal betting shop. Award winning Irene Inescort as Mrs West Senior (L) with Martin Vaughan next to her as her son John West in "Power Without Glory".*

politics, fixes pigeon racing, rigs prize fights, is responsible for underworld killings, and becomes involved in financial scandals.

The ABC has to be congratulated for its courage in tackling such a controversial story and for spending over $2 million on it. The curtailing of ABC's production which began in the late seventies came just when the ABC was demonstrating that given the right material and the money, Australia was capable of producing television features of international standard.

Although *Power without Glory* did get fantastic ratings, especially in Melbourne, and did cause commercial stations to take stock of their own programming, the show ignored one vital rule of the stage — a good entrance and a good exit. The exit was perfect — but that entrance! Martin Vaughan as West was self-conscious; the switch from video-taped interiors to filmed exteriors was so marked that tonal values of the scene were in confused conflict and the episode itself failed to have the life of even the printed word of the script. Both Vaughan and Ros Spiers as John and Nellie West, were miscast, although Vaughan did improve, and was impressive in the last episode when he died. Ros Spiers, on the other hand, did not impress at any time. But what a wonderful array of talent was assembled for the supporting roles — George Mallaby, Frank Wilson, Terry Donovan, Irene Inescourt, Heather Canning, John Wood and Wendy Hughes. In later episodes Michael Pate was excellent as Archbishop Malone.

In the beginning, critics panned the acting of Martin Vaughan, but praised the performance of George Mallaby as Barney Robinson. Melbourne *Scene* on 10 July stated, 'if West's tote got only the small handful of customers as shown on the screen, the next episode should show him facing the Bankruptcy Court.' However facts have a habit of speaking for themselves, and it was a fact that *Power without Glory* did resurrect the West-Wren controversy, and the Wren family in June 1977 released a book by Hugh Buggy disproving any similarity between Hardy's 'John West' and the real John Wren.

It was in the various Awards that *Power without Glory* revealed the power of its impact. In the 1976 Television Society of Australia's Penguin Awards George Mallaby as Barney Robinson was named as the best supporting actor, with Heather Canning (Mrs Moran) receiving a Penguin as the best supporting actress. Irene Inescourt (John West's mother) received a Certificate of Commendation. *Power without Glory* took the top award as the best drama series. Best drama scriptwrites were Cliff Green and Howard Griffiths for episodes of *Power*. In the TV Times Sammy Awards for 1976, the best supporting actor on TV was Michael Aitkens as 'Piggy Lewis', and this time Irene Inescourt received a Sammy as the best supporting TV actress. Again, the best TV drama series was *Power without Glory*. In the 1977 Penguins for the best individual production achievement went to Robert H. Perkins for TV design. But it was in the TV Times 1977 Logie Awards that *Power* took five awards. Logies went to *Power without Glory* as Australia's most popular TV drama series. The two leads, Ros Spiers and Martin Vaughan received the coveted awards as leading actress and actor; and supporting players Wendy Hughes as 'Mary West' and John Wood as 'Sugar Renfrey', also received Logies.

Only One Award for 'Alvin' ...

On 20 October 1975, a NSW Equity Court had ruled that the ABC could proceed with the TV production of *Alvin Purple*, but that the makers of the feature film *Alvin Purple* were entitled to damages since the ABC were attempting to pass off their 'Alvin' as the same character who appeared in the feature.

But problems for the ABC did not end in the Equity Court. The half-hour time slot for *Alvin* was blacked out on 18 September 1976 in New South Wales, because the series *Casanova 73* had been booked to replace the suspended *Alvin* in the time spot of 9.15 p.m. The staff went on strike because of the ban.

Friday the 13th and *Alvin's* thriteen-episode series seemed to be right for each other. The ABC Commissioners barred it from going to air for its premiere performance on the 13th and according to Sir Henry Bland, 'some improvements would have to be made'. The series was deferred until the changes were made. However the producer, Maurice Murphy and the crew refused to adhere to the demands. Then a Melbourne newpaper carried the banner headline, 'Alvin's in the pink after the blue' and reported that the show would be premiered in Melbourne on 19 August.

The critics already had sharpened their scalpels and one of them felt that the ABC had scraped the bottom of the barrel with *Alvin Purple*, especially after revealing that it could produce shows of the calibre of *Power without Glory*. Amidst all the uproar, Graeme Blundell who played 'Alvin', stated that he was finished with *Alvin Purple*, and refused to sign a contract for a third film covering Mr Purple's stud business. When a few episodes of the TV series were taken to England and shown to TV outlets such as London Weekend Television they thought *Alvin* one of the funniest shows they'd seen, but that it was far too dirty for their screens.

Award-wise *Alvin* didn't turn up trumps, and only Chris Haywood as Purple's mate received a Certificate of Commendation for the best supporting actor in the TV Society's Penguin Awards for 1976.

... And No Awards for *The Bloke*

One superb ABC-TV production that was deserving of recognition, but never received it, was the musical version of *The Sentimental Bloke*.

Executive producer Michael Shrimpton used his imagination in the selection of Graeme Blundell as 'The Bloke'. The choice raised a few eyebrows, but his faith was justified. Blundell turned in a mighty performance, making one wonder why he had hidden his talents so long under the 'Alvin' profile. Not a Caruso or even a Barry Crocker, Blundell still managed to put over a number with a certain charm — and did keep in tune. Another pleasant surprise was Jimmy Hannan as Ginger Mick. He had sung before, but his performance was an eye-opener. For excellent measure there was Geraldine Turner (as Doreen), Nancye Hayes and Jon Finlayson (stror 'at 'n' all). One bright and very catchy number was *On Sunday Arvo* sung with verve by Nancye Hayes. Another scene-stealing moment was when Joy Westmore as Doreen's Ma put over *Her Poor Dear Pa*.

The director of *The Sentimental Bloke* was Alan Burke. Although a number of sets were cardboard, and lighting at times looked like a send-up, *The Sentimental Bloke* was really good entertainment. Brian May and the ABC Showband attended to the musical side of things. It was telecast from ABV 2 on 8 July 1976.

Commercial TV in 1976

On the commercial side of the picture in 1976, the TV shows were *Luke's Kingdom;* an Australian episode of *McCloud; Tandarra; Bluey; Solo One; Chopper Squad*, a few that didn't take off, and a dreadful lot of tripe in the so-called one-shot dramas.

Luke's Kingdom took some time to reach the Australian TV screens, and it fared badly in Sydney. Shown on the 9 Network in Sydney and Melbourne on 7 April, the critics in Melbourne could not understand why the first five episodes were scheduled outside the rating period. The answer wasn't far away.

6.46 *Graeme Blundell and Geraldine Turner (as Doreen) in a musical version of "The Sentimental Bloke". It was directed by Alan Burke for ABC-TV.*

Peter Weir, discusses a pose with Luke (Oliver Tobias) on the set at Ingleside, for the TV series "Luke's Kingdom".

While the direction was stylish, and the art direction and outdoor scenery was superb, Luke, as portrayed by Oliver Tobias was heavy-handed, sadistic and sullen. Even his voice was expressionless. Luke was an unsavoury character who tried to take possession of everything within reach including land, an Aboriginal girl, and even his own sister.

It was set in the Blue Mountains in 1813 and cost $1.5 million to make thirteen episodes. Players like James Condon, Gerard Maguire, Elizabeth Crosby, and guest stars Helen Morse, Jack Thompson, John Meillon, Chris Haywood, Katy Wild and John Ewart helped save the show. A tragic association with the show was English executive producer Tony Essex, who died ten days after returning to England.

Luke's Kingdom was dubbed 'Lewd Luke' and 'The Kingdom Lost By Violence'. In the English *Stage and Television Today*, it was described as 'nasty rubbish unworthy of a place on English television'. The critic went on to point out that because it was made in Australia it was a failure. In actual fact, since a great deal of British money was tied up in the series, Tony Essex virtually had total power over the show, and he insisted on violence to give *Luke's Kingdom* 'integrity'. Perhaps the real reason behind some of the remarks in *Stage and Television* was the statement that closed the critique — British folk are not interested in Australian history anyhow. Could one be wrong in believing that many Englishmen made that history for us in the first place?

6.49 *In the American produced T.V. series "McCloud" — an episode "Night of the Shark" was photographed and produced in Sydney. "McCloud" (played by Dennis Weaver) is seen here at the Sydney airport. To provide the right atmosphere, notice the "Arrivals" Board in the background.*

In Australia there were no Logies for Luke; and the so-called overseas know-how didn't do much for the Australian-based episode of *McCloud* either. Filmed in early 1976, this episode titled *Night of the Shark* was screened on Channel 9 Sydney and Melbourne on 26 March. The storyline for the local adventure was so thin that it made a fuse wire look like a Blackwood butt. This time it wasn't the English but the Americans who had a hand in, and one thing the Yanks did introduce into Australia was 'instant' television. The speed at which McCloud travelled on horseback would make even a Sydney taxi driver gasp. He started his chase at Circular Quay, then in a blink of an eye, was at the Alamein Fountain in Kings Cross. A few frames later he was heading for North Sydney via the Bridge, then he arrives at the Showgrounds of all places. According to the book of directions, he must have been travelling backwards to Moore Park!

According to reports at the time, flake was in short supply, but in *Night of the Shark*, the Harbour was packed with them, like sardines in a can. One wonders how the Jap midget subs made it in World War II. The excuse for McCloud to come to Australia was that he witnessed the murder of a young Sydney policeman at Kennedy Airport. It appears that a bunch of American 'hoods' had set up shop in Sydney, and a local cop was obtaining information about them. Good old Uncle Sam McCloud accompanied the body to Sydney then set about cleaning up Crime Incorporated. Gus Mercurio played a Mafia heavy, and the Australians in the cast were Fred and Max Cullen, Grigor Taylor, Jack Fegan, and Alwyn Kurts. Even ex-Australian actress Victoria Shaw came over to be in it.

Panned by the critics, *Night of the Shark* amazingly enough attracted a record rating.

Tandarra from Homestead Films, the successor to *Cash & Co*, began its run on HSV 7 in Melbourne on 9 February 1976. But why did the term 'bounty hunters' have to be used? Gerard Kennedy as 'Rylah' was the so-called bounty hunter. The familiar Gus Mercurio as Joe Brady and Penne Hackforth-Jones, portraying the young widow Jessica Johnson, were there to back up the play of Rylah who first comes to capture Joe, then remains to become one of the team. They overcome bushrangers led by Norman Yemm; foil the wiles of Vicki Hammond whose husband meets with a 'mysterious' accident; and see to it that George Mallaby doesn't purchase the widow's property for the price of wild oats. Perhaps the poor acceptance of *Tandarra* in Sydney made Homestead Films auction everything used in the two series. Thousands flocked to Emu Bottom homestead for the sale on 25 July 1976. Included in the articles were a five-metre high gallows; carts; period furniture and even a 100 year old hearse complete with plumes and a coffin.

In the 1976 Television Society of Australia's Penguin awards, Penne Hackforth Jones was named as the best actress for her role in *Tandarra* and Certificates of Commendation were issued to Gus Mercurio in the best actor category, and to Patrick Edgeworth under the heading of best drama

6.51   *In the Sydney-based episode of "McCloud" released through Universal Television, and screened on the Channel 9 Network, Lloyd Bochner and Australian actress Victoria Shaw (now living in America) bring the "country look" to Sydney. Apparently the second horse wasn't photogenic.*

6.52 *Gerard Kennedy (Ryler) becomes a regular in the Tandarra series. Here he chats with Joe Brady played by Gus Mercurio.*

scriptwriter. In the TV Times Sammy awards, for 1976, Penne Hackforth-Jones was again acclaimed as the best actress in a TV series. In the 1977 TV Week Logie awards, Lyndell Rowe was named as giving the best individual performance by an actress for her role in *Tandarra*.

Crawford Productions in 1976 produced a very mixed bag. *Solo One* began on 18 June 1976. It should have enjoyed greater success than it did. It was a brilliantly conceived programme with a delightful difference. However the television station executives showed a complete lack of foresight in ordering only thirteen episodes. *Solo One* was very well acted and directed.

On the other hand *The Bluestone Boys,* another Crawford Production which began on 15 August, was an utter disaster. Allegedly revealing the 'funny' side of prison life, it was as humorous as a life sentence. Lucky Grills as 'Bluey' looked like the Australian version of 'Cannon'. He portrays a police sergeant with John Diedrich as his offsider. Gerda Nicolson portrays a police woman, Victoria Quilter, who gained prominence in a soft drink commercial, was dropped after thirteen episodes. It was a police drama that hadn't basically altered the pattern of *Division 4* and *Matlock Police*.

6.53 *The star of Solo One, Gary Hogan, played by Paul Cronin. This is a follow up role from 'Matlock Police'. The series received a penguin award from the Television Society in 1976.*

In the 1976 Penguins the *Bluey* gained second prize of $750 awarded by the Australian Film Commission in the limited section. *Solo One* however scooped the pool. In the Australian Film Commission Awards in the 1976 Television Society's Penguins, *Solo One* gained first prize of $3 000 for the episode *Watch out for the Robinsons* starring Brian James. *Goodbye George,* another episode starring Alwyn Kurts, won first prize of $1 000 from the AFC in the children's drama section. The same episode received a Certificate of Merit in the open section. In addition *Solo One* gained a Penguin as the best children's programme. Then in the 1977 TV Week Logie awards Greg Stroud was named for his outstanding performance as a juvenile in the episode called *The Runaway*. A 1976 Penguin went to Mike Brady for the best original music for *Solo One*. So much for the judgement of a certain TV station management.

6.54 *The pilot for "Chopper Squad" that formed the basis for a TV series. In this still Dennis Grosvenor (L) the "Chopper" pilot finds himself in real trouble.*

The pilot for *Chopper Squad* was seen on Channel 10 Sydney on 31 October, and on Channel 0, Melbourne, on 5 November. A Melbourne TV critic urged everyone to tune in, if only to see how bad Australian television could be. His only comparison was the dreadful *McCloud* episode, *Night of the Shark*. Dennis Grosvenor as a helicopter pilot for a surf rescue squad, on his first day frees an escaped prisoner from an over-turned police car and rescues a pregnant woman from a bushfire. He then tries to locate a junior member of the life-saving squad who was lost at sea, only to widen his search when an over-the-hill surf club member paddles his surf board into the horizon, looking for the youngster. Grosvenor was backed up, cast wise at least, by Max Osbiston, Rebecca Gilling and Eric Oldfield. Strangely enough *Chopper Squad* survived that disastrous pilot to go into a series.

Television Goes Downhill

In 1976 when feature films in Australia were improving the television side of the film industry was failing miserably — ABC-TV excluded!

A series of pilots that were lamentably bad along with many so-called one shot dramas were thrust at an unsuspecting public under the guise of promoting Australian-made television film fare. Most ranged from shocking to positively monstrous. These included *Bushranger* from Pedra Films; *Is There Anybody There?* from Gemini; Cash Harmon's *Murcheson Creek*, *Polly Me Love* (Eric Porter); *The Secret Doors* and *The Spiral Bureau* (Roger Mirams); *Paradise* (Robert Bruning); *Rod Cromwell MD* (Screen Gems); *Hotline* (Channel 7 Production) and *McManus MPB*. *The Haunting of Hewie Dowker*, however, is worthy of special attention as it did present a notable contribution to the small screen.

The flurry actually began in April 1976 when the Channel 9 Network in Sydney advised that they had purchased nine Australian movies at a cost of $1 million. It wasn't stated that a quota had to be filled, and no matter how bad the product, sales were virtually assured even if only through 'loaded' time spots. GTV 9 Melbourne was so thrilled with the arrangements that it did not bother to obtain pre-publicity or stills.

The Spiral Bureau from Roger Mirams led the onslaught on 15 April. It possibly set back local production at least ten years. In this show, a trio of psychic researchers are caught up in a nightmare battle with a nameless supernatural source, beginning with the sighting of flying saucers. Peter Sumner, Wendy Hughes, John Derum, John Ewart and Jack Fegan did nothing for their reputation by appearing in such a childish effort.

In *The Bushranger* Leonard Teale gallops over the countryside in a cabbage tree hat, being chased because he has strung up a couple of fellows after they had fired his homestead and ravaged his wife. Then just because he robbed a train and a police inspector who was one of the passengers, he is hotly pursued by a special constable. Kate Fitzpatrick plays a sympathetic pub keeper. The best part of the picture is the location selected by Smoky Dawson. On 26 June 1976 *The Bushranger* was re-cycled and sent back to the faded pages of the history book.

Robert Bruning was associated with *Is There Anybody There?* This was screened on 24 June. It centred around two women who are terrorized in a Sydney block of flats. Wendy Hughes, Tina Grenville, George Lazenby, and Charles 'Bud' Tingwell go along for the thrills. This story of double cross in every frame of the picture highlights Bruning in a brief appearance at the end. *Is There Anybody There?* did receive a Penguin in 1976 as the best one shot drama, and in the same year's Sammy awards, Bob Young was named as composer of the best theme music. These awards probably prove how bad tele-cine films were in 1976.

Channel 0 joined in the banging of Australian drums, and on 19 April telecast *McManus MPB* (Missing Persons Bureau). It should never have reached a film can, let alone a tele-cine room. The daughter of a Russian Consul disappears, and McManus has to find her to avoid awkward questions being asked by Moscow. Peter Sumner, Anna-Maria Winchester, Chantal Contouri, Serge Lazareff, and Pamela Stephenson were cast members. Pamela at least did better for herself by going to England.

Murcheson Creek directed by Terry Bourke, came from Cash Harmon by way of Channel 9, on 25 June. With a story straight from *Poppy's Paper* it centred around young Dr Murcheson who deserts his Macquarie Street practice to help his aged father. When the doctor (Mark Edwards), an accountant, and two girlfriends arrive back from a fishing trip, they discover that the township of Murcheson Creek has been deserted. The mystery is explained when the doctor learns that his father had been buried that day. A diary of names with mysterious implications is discovered by the accountant, but the incriminating evidence is stolen by the housekeeper and handed to the local chemist. It appears that the nice old Doctor Murcheson has been signing false medical certificates and performing abortions to save the good names of various families. Although this was one of the better tele-cine films for 1976, Cash Harmon should have stuck to *Number 96*.

On the same night on Channel 9 was *Polly Me Love* produced by Eric Porter. This was a film in very poor taste that was equalled by extremely bad acting even though it starred Jacki Weaver (with long curls) and Hugh Keays-Byrne. In the tradition of *Luke's Kingdom* (*that* was a poor pattern for a start) it centres around a pub of ill-repute which stables a bevy of fun-seeking girls who provide a haven of love in the hay shed. After 'Madame' tries to turn her own daughter into a harlot, she is saved from 'a fate worse than death' by a woman whose father has been injured by an escaped convict. A convict tries to rape Polly but a second ditto saves her. The troopers arrive and both convicts are escorted back to gaol, leaving Pretty Polly sitting on a window ledge in lieu of a perch. Both Jacki Weaver and Hugh Keays-Byrne were worthy of better roles.

The night of the 25 June is one that Channel 7 would like to forget. It was then that it presented *The Hotline* — a Channel 7 production. The story in a nutshell is that of a newspaper man who has to cope with a broken marriage and a mental breakdown. He comes out of retirement to conduct a 'heartbreak' column. Fred 'Cul' Cullen and Max Cullen were in the credits.

Secret Doors from South Pacific Films was telecast on 19 June — again through Channel 9. This was obviously a pilot as the ending left one high and dry, like driftwood on an ebb tide. Every known cliché was employed, and sex was the central link from caravan park to the back room of a cheap hotel. Gerard Maguire, Rebecca Gilling and Max Osbiston did what they could with a hopeless plot.

The first shall be last applies to *Rod Cromwell MD* which led this forgettable parade on 2 February 1976. Trapped by two gunmen in an abandoned cool storage plant, Cromwell is forced to operate on a badly wounded female accomplice. Those appearing were Jeanie Drynan, Ken Goodlet, Hugh Keays-Byrne and Jenny Duggan. As previously stated *The Haunting of Hewie Dowker* was one tele-cine film that was different in every way to all these other productions just mentioned. Roger Mirams had delved into psychic phenonema before in *The Spiral Bureau*, but without success. This time he came up with a winner. It was set in an eerie world of unexplainable happenings that extended from ESP (extra sensory percep-

6.55 *John Waters as "Hewie Dowker", a detective, finds that he possesses psychic powers that can be used to combat the forces of evil. This brings him into conflict with the followers of the dead man, that are responsible for "The Haunting of Hewie Dowker".*

tion) to the unseen forces of good and evil. It begins in the early days of Australia, when a man is hanged. This scene seems out of context, and only towards the end is its significance manifest. John Waters who had been a colonial policeman in *Rush* steps easily into the role of a modern Sydney cop. He realises that he has psychic powers which have been allowed to become dormant. Slowly he becomes aware of the existence on earth of an alien intelligence. Kate Fitzpatrick and Donald McDonald appear rather mysteriously as forces of good that must work through Dowker to destroy a nightmare world of murder and black magic ruled by Ron Haddrick as Dr Steven Reikel. He is urged to once again develop and use his own peculiar psychic powers. Then it becomes known that the body of the hanged man in the opening sequence had been spirited away and preserved. While that body remains in a living tomb of evil, the alien forces will remain. There is a battle of wills between Reikel and Dowker, in which one seeks to destroy the other.

Dowker in the hands of John Waters becomes real and lifts the story above the mumbo-jumbo of *The Spiral Bureau*. Camilla Rountree supplies the romantic interest and Fred 'Cul' Cullen changes sides for once and is seen as a down-to-earth police detective. Tim Elliot and Walter Sullivan are additional members of the cast. *The Haunting of Howie Dowker* was seen on ATV 0, Melbourne on 6 November 1976, and was the only television feature to hold out any real hope for the future of Australian commercial television production. Tension packed and with excellent background music, it was a genuine thriller in the supernatural vein. *The Haunting* was repeated on ATV 0 on 17 February 1978.

Series Tests

Two TV series began late in the year on Channel 9 to test their acceptance with viewers. One was the story of a Melbourne family in the early 1940s called *The Sullivans*. It was produced by Crawford. This series was an instant success, and received ratings from surveys conducted privately which equalled those of *Power without Glory*. *The Sullivans* went from strength to strength. In the 1977 TV Times Sammy awards, Lorraine Bayly was voted the best lead actress in a TV series, and Andrew McFarlane, the best supporting actor. Then in the 1977 TV Week Logie awards, *The Sullivans* was named the best new drama series and in the same awards in 1978, the show scooped the pool. Logies went to *The Sullivans* as the best drama series; to Paul Cronin as the best leading actor; to Lorraine Bayly again as the best actress; to Michael Caton as the best supporting actor; to Vivean Gray as the best supporting actress. Yet Frank Thring was to state later that *The Sullivans* showed what a dreary place Melbourne was in wartime.

The second series Channel 9 ran for testing was *The Young Doctors*. This was axed in December, 1976, but it was later granted a reprieve.

More Co-productions For ABC

The ABC once again came up with a co-production plan. In a deal with Trans Atlantic Enterprises eighteen TV movies were agreed upon. The Americans were to contribute $9 million ($500000 for each production). Out of this, Trans Atlantic paid for American lead players and Australian supports. The ABC supplied facilities plus $1 million for extra technical staff. In late September 1976, cameras started turning on the first picture. Then financial cuts and huge costs in overtime severely curtailed the programme — and six only were to be made. By this time, marks from West Germany had been poured into the project.

Hunted, the first of these co-productions, was re-titled *No Room to Run* and was seen on ABC-TV on 18 May 1977. It was fifth rate, with the entire footage fit only for the cutting room floor. The Sydney Opera House and international intrigue played 50-50 parts in this exciting(?) film fare. From storyline and acting to general production, *No Room to Run* was weak and did not leave one with the feeling of wanting more.

The second of the films was *Fuzzy* (later changed to *Barnaby and Me*) and starred Sid Caesar and Juliet Mills who were both worried about being upstaged by a talking koala named Higgins. James Franciscus arrived to make the third co-production called *Puzzle*. Australian born Victoria Shaw took another *McCloud* journey to appear in the fourth *Surf* with Beau and Lloyd Bridges. The film written by Australian Colin Free, called *She'll Be Sweet*, made Sally Kellerman take the plunge Down Under. Finally Jack Thompson appears with Karen Black in *Because He's My Friend*.

Australian TV was in a disastrous state by the end of 1976. On 2 November 1976 Senator Button in Federal Parliament stated that the Australian content had dropped from 43 per cent to 34 per cent. 'Creative talent is being lost to the industry,' he stated. In March 1977 a Sydney newspaper had already posed the question as to whether Australia hadn't become the 51st State of the USA. In the top twenty programmes, three commercial news services, two current affair programmes (*Willesee* and *A Current Affair*), and *This is your Life* were the only Australian contributions. Not a dramatic or comedy series was mentioned. In June 1976 even Actors Equity was complaining of the drop in local content. Then in another Sydney newspaper on 31 October 1976, this clanger was dropped: 'The Australian motion picture industry, despite recent successes, is facing disaster.' The reporter went on to advise that unless this country can crack the overseas market in a big way, the movie business would be bankrupt within two years.

Film Australia Holds Up Standards

Australia's greatest triumph for 1976 was when *Leisure* won an Academy Award in America on 29 March 1977. This was Australia's second Academy Award; the first was for Damien Parer's classic newsreel reporting in New Guinea in 1942. *Leisure* from Film Australia was produced by Suzanne Baker and directed by Bruce Petty. David Deen handled the animation and Michael Carlos co-ordinated the music. The commentary was by Alexander Archdale.

Leisure failed to qualify for the Australian Film Awards in 1976, but it did win the Grand Prix for short films at the Melbourne Festival. After the Academy Award win, *Leisure* was immediately programmed with *Break of*

6.56 *A drawing from the Academy Award winning Australian short "Leisure". This cartoon with Alexander Archdale as commentator, is a Film Australia production.*

6.57 *Producer Suzanne Baker and Bruce Petty political cartoonist, who designed and scripted the film, read congratulatory telegrams after "Leisure" won an American Academy Award in 1977.*

Day on 1 April 1977 at the Bercy Cinema, Melbourne and Pitt Centre, Sydney. The Oscar itself, by the way, did not arrive in Sydney until 27 May 1977, due to an air strike in New York. Congratulatory telegrams were sent by the Prime Minister, Malcolm Fraser, by Gough Whitlam (then Leader of the Opposition), by NSW Premier Neville Wran, and by Al Grassby of Community Relations.

Leisure thoroughly deserved its Oscar. This brilliant animated featurette depicted man's everlasting quest for ways to enjoy the time that sits unevenly between his working and sleeping hours.

Greater Union Awards For 16 mm

Outstanding 16 mm films that figured prominently in the Greater Union Awards and which were featured at the 1976 Sydney Film Festival were *Lalai Dreamtime,* winner of the Rouben Mamoullan Award; *Sunrise Awakening,* top film in the documentary section; and *Red Church* in the general category.

Lalai Dreamtime was produced and directed by well-known cameraman Mike Edols. This was an earnest attempt to understand the Aboriginal society and culture. *Lalai* introduced a pre-colonial Australia, a myth from the spiritual tradition of the Aboriginal people. *Lalai Dreamtime* received a Bronze Award in the documentary section of the 1976 Australian Film Awards.

Sunrise Awakening from André Reese was billed as 'a black view of the first urbane threatre-training programme held at the Black Theatre for six weeks in 1975.' It was designed to give black people a sense of pride and accomplishment — to express their joy and creativity! This was seen at the Sydney Filmmakers' Cinema on 15 July.

One week later in the same theatre was Paul Winkler's *Red Church.* This attempted to create a build-up of tension through the re-photographing of still and moving objects, providing yet another type of kinetic image.

More Successful 16 mm Productions

Another film at the Sydney Film Festival in Sydney on 8 July 1976 was *Queensland.* This received a Bronze Award in the short fiction section of the 1976 Australian Film Awards. It was neither a travelogue nor a satire on the Sunshine State. Rather, it represented an ideal for Doug (John Flaus), a factory worker who has broken with his *de facto* wife Marge, and who boards with an invalid friend, Aub (Bob Karl). Directed by John Ruane and photographed by Ellery Ryan, many of the scenes seemed more pre-arranged than spontaneous, and the small-time drama appeared to reach a point where the whole spirit of it seemed to say — what the hell! Doug drifts back to Marge, then off again. Of the three who agreed to make the break — Doug, Aub and Marge — only Doug eventually sets off — and in a badly battered Holden that would be lucky to make the highway, let alone reach Queensland. Alison Bird and Gary Metcalfe were other members of the cast.

Made in 1975 by Kestrel Films another 16 mm production called *The Birders* won the Jedda Award in the 1976 Australian Film Awards. This was produced and directed by John Richardson. The theme was the muttonbird industry of Furneaux Islands in Bass Strait. Research into the life of the short-tailed shearwater (muttonbird) is one of the interesting aspects of this first-class documentary.

One of the most absorbing documentaries of the 1970s was *Journey to a Legend*. It clearly demonstrated that Sydney and Melbourne could expect strong opposition from Martin Williams Films in Brisbane. Of forty-eight minutes duration, this film showed every interesting aspect of the recovery of the skeleton of the *Southern Cross Minor*, a plane that came down in the Sahara Desert. The pilot's skeleton was also discovered beside the plane. In the diary found, Captain William Lancaster, the pilot, writes of how a small bird came from nowhere, landed on the fuselage, and flew off again. The dying man appreciated its company, if only for a short time. When filming the skeleton of the plane, yet another bird arrived. When questioned later, producer-director John Stainton was emphatic about the incident not being faked. It added a poignant touch to a really remarkable film. The script was written by Garrett Russell and photography was handled by Richard Marks. Camera assistant was David Rankin. Director John Stainton was in charge of sound, and Mark Moffatt handled the music. The narration was by Ray Barrett.

Journey to a Legend received well-deserved recognition from the Television Society of Australia in its 1976 Penguin awards. John Stainton was the recipient of a Certificate of Special Recognition for excellence in sound. The documentary received a Penguin in the open section, in addition to the Shell prize of $2000 in the limited section.

In the same Penguin awards, the Australian cartoon *Ivanhoe* from Air Programs International won second prize of $250 from the Australian Film Commission, in the limited section of children's drama. This one-hour film was sold to the CBS Network, USA; to Channel 7 Network, Australia; and to Hong Kong, New Zealand, the Middle East, and the United Kingdom.

Early 1977 — Box Office Downturn

Early 1977 saw a serious downturn in the local box office for all films, Australian and imported. The drop was estimated in the trade to be as much as 40 per cent, and was ascribed to the heavy inroads of colour television. Although the box office picked up slightly in 1978, few Australian films would be destined again to reach the box office heights of *Alvin Purple, Picnic at Hanging Rock* and *Caddie*.

Raw Deal was the first Australian film to open the 1977 record and one of the first to suffer from the downturn. Screened in Sydney and Melbourne on 4 February, it was a 'meat pie' Western with a pace at times slower than a snail smitten with gout. From Homestead Films, this carry over from *Tandarra* was not representative of any aspect of the Australian way of life. Opening at the Odeon Theatre in Melbourne, it transferred exactly one month later to the Australia Cinema. The original advertising read: 'They fought . . . they loved . . . they laughed, but the joke was on them.' One month later the American influence was even more apparent: 'Australia's answer to the Magnificent Seven. The hearse-robbing, women-chasing, trigger-happy five.' In the display the review from the *Nation Review* was quoted: 'At last an Australian film that entertains.' Just to counterbalance such a claim, the Melbourne *Sun* dubbed it: 'The worst of the west.'

Singer Margret Roadknight alleges to have seen *Raw Deal* three times. She agreed that it was never meant to be an art film, but disagreed with most critics who dismissed is as a cheap American Western imitation. She went on to capitalise on her statement by recording the title song of the film. The tune was written by Ron Edgeworth, husband of Judith Durham, the former Seeker's lead.

Once again the objectionable reference to 'scalp hunters' was made — but this time to all five of them — Gerard Kennedy, Gus Mercurio, Rod Mullinar, Hu Pryce, and Christopher Pate. Some crooked politicians offer a reward to seek out and destroy a gang of revolutionaries. The revolutionaries led by Norman Yemm, are Irish Catholics. It's about time racial and religious prejudices were buried in Australia, not brought back like Lazarus from the dead. Shades of homosexuality were rampant when Hu Pryce is freed from prison. They steal a horse-driven hearse, fill it with dynamite, and set out on a long dreary trip across the desert. One isn't sure whether it is the Painted Desert or Death Valley — or then again it could have been the Simpson. On the way, Christopher Pate who claims that he is a 'devil' with the women, raises a smirk from the others, and he is left overnight with a certain 'Madame' and her bevy of stunning harlots. Eventually they blow up an almost impregnable fortress manned by the revolutionaries, and return for their money. The politicians who hired them were having a ball at the time — a real one that is — with smartly groomed ladies, and with a background of the most costly set in the whole production. It is here that Noni Wood and Briony Behets, among others, make their first and only appearance ... and briefly at that! The five learn that they are victims of a double cross, and that their friendly neighbourhood politicians have no intention of paying them. Instead they learn that the mansion is surrounded, and the whole place is bristling with guns held by police and militia. In the shoot out, practically the whole army and squads of police are wiped out. Only Kennedy and Mercurio are still able to ride into the sunset: whether they are headed for America or for Italy to make another Western is a matter of little importance. Rod Mullinar as a 'top gun' Lothario cuts a dashing figure, and even finds the time to fight a duel over Melbourne TV weather girl Illona Komesaroff.

Cannes 1977

Although Australia had fourteen films at Cannes in 1977, it was not considered such a good year as the previous one.

John Gillett, the London *Sunday Telegraph* critic at Cannes, wrote:

> The Australians are out again in force, without, perhaps, the really outstanding film one hoped for this year, but with a lively selection which has been drawing substantial crowds. So far the best has been John Power's *The Picture Show Man,* another glance backwards, this time to the touring movie shows of the 1920's, with rival showmen fighting it out in little towns and trying to find suitable pianists for their one-night stands. Apart from some weak acting (a current problem with Australian cinema) it contains a good deal of charm and sharp observation.

The Picture Show Man premiered in Sydney on 5 May. It had an opening
worthy of the title: George Street was closed temporarily for the premiere at the
Village Cinema Centre. It was the first feature film of former television director
John Power, and was written and produced by Joan Long. It was inspired by
an unpublished manuscript of true reminiscence by Lyle Penn.

It had a lukewarm reception from the local critics, but the *Sydney Sun*
called it, 'an Australian film with charm ... lacking the forced vulgarity and
contrived box office pretensions of so much recent Australian production'.

Overseas critics have been warmer. London critic David Robinson
described it in *The Times* as 'irresistible ... This casual artless picaresque
overflows with fun, nostalgia and sheer good nature, with well-tuned comic
performances from John Ewart, John Meillon, Rod Taylor and Patrick
Cargill'. The American critic William K. Everson wrote in the U.S. journal
Films in Review: 'Although I know it's a very broad statement, *The Picture
Show Man* is both the best and the most enjoyable new film I've seen in years'.

The film is a comedy based on the adventures of a little team of showmen

6.58   *Rainbeaux Smith in
"Fantasm Comes Again" directed
by Colin Eggleston.*

6.59   *Lisa Peers, Diana Fuller, Nell Campbell and Jude Kuring in "Journey Among Women".
It is the story of dangerous female prisoners who escape from an isolated penal colony in the
18th Century.*

6.60   *Helenka Link in "Journey Among Women" directed and photographed by Tom Cowan.
This was screened at the 1977 Cannes Film Festival.*

who travel from one small town to another providing the people with movie
entertainment — father, son and a pianist. The father — Pop, played by John
Meillon — is a flamboyant showman who resists progress in the shape of
electric generators, motor vans and talking pictures. His shy son, played by
Harold Hopkins, chafes under his father's dominating personality. Their
pianist, played with cheeky charm by John Ewart, tries to keep the peace
between them. The film follows their adventures with the women they meet on
the way, with horses, motor vans, with the technical revolution of sound, and
especially with a rival showman, an American played by Rod Taylor, who
invades their territory and threatens their livelihood. The films drags a little at
times, but it is a story of the easy-going type of existence of a bygone era.

John Meillon's performance was highly praised, but overseas he seemed to
be everybody but Meillon. The *London Times* dubbed him a W.C. Fields, the

American Films in Review saw him as Charles Laughton, and the *English Cosmopolitan* settled for 'Australia's answer to Walter Matthau'. John is said to have stated that he studied the work of at least five actors, including one no critic spotted, Peter Ustinov.

The cast also included Jeannie Drynan as the charming widow seduced by Freddie the pianist (John Ewart), Sally Conabere as a squatter's daughter the son falls in love with, and Judy Morris as an Isadora Duncan-type dancing teacher. Patrick Cargill and Yelena Zigon are a pair of aging vaudeville artists stranded in the backblocks.

The Picture Show Man was another Australian film to suffer from the box office downturn, although its performance appears good compared with some later releases. It ran for five months in the Village Centre in Sydney. It has been successful in overseas sales, and is one of the tiny handful of Australian films to have been sold to America.

At the Festival of Comedy Films, Chamrousse, France, in March 1978, it won the popular vote Dauphin d'Or. It was a popular hit at the London Film Festival, December 1977, and at the Telluride Festival, U.S.A. in September 1977. Following its screening at the latter it was screened for the National Board of Review in New York, and was selected for their ten best list for 1977 — a first for an Australian film.

Local honours for *The Picture Show Man* began with the 1977 Australian Film Awards: John Ewart was declared the best supporting actor; Peter Best scored for the best original music; and David Copping took an award for the best achievement in costume design. Judith Dorsman followed with the best achievement in dress design. John Ewart collected a Sammy in TV Times 1977 Awards for the best supporting actor for his role in *The Picture Show Man*. Upon receiving this award, he remarked, 'Australia has its twenty-first birthday in television. Now that we have the key of the door, why don't we kick the bloody thing open?'

Possibly the best memory of *The Picture Show Man* is the catchy musical number 'Tap Tap' performed by John Meillon and John Ewart.

Another film at Cannes in 1977 was *Break of Day*, produced by Pat Lovell, and directed by Ken Hannam. It also suffered from the box office downturn, and from the local critics who were beginning to attack the preponderance of period films being made here.

Russell Boyd won the best achievement in photography in the 1977 Australian Film Awards sponsored by Kodak. His award was richly deserved. Many of the shots in *Break of Day* were sheer poetry, especially towards the end when dawn breaks. The sunlight edging a tree top; the splash of warm light on a man's face, giving external evidence of an inward glow of self-satisfaction; the sky losing its golden tinge and turning to blue. This constant change of tonal values is captured for theatre audiences to enjoy and to appreciate.

Cliff Green's storyline was a little thin — more an interlude than a well-developed plot. Yet it did convey the limited horizon of an Australian country

6.61   *John Meillon as the travelling "Picture Show Man" and John Ewart as the silent film pianist. Together they presented the breezy number "Tap Tap on my Window" in the film.*

town of the 1920s. Just after the First World War, many men returned to their home towns to be fêted as heroes. They married, raised children, and died without wishing to journey into the sunrise or sunset. At the end of the main street, in most country towns there was the same off-white memorial, bleak and inartistic which listed the names of the fallen sons. In *Break of Day* Tom, one of the 'heroes' returns from the War with a limp. He becomes the central figure of the community as the editor of the local paper. Andrew McFarlane as Tom, is a good-looking juvenile lead who has become well known through the TV series *The Sullivans*. He has a future in films, but in *Break of Day* he had not acquired the dramatic ability to be entirely convincing in some tension-packed scenes that the story contained. Ingrid Mason portrayed Beth, the country lass whom Tom married. Most of the time she looked petulant in her pregnancy. Then along comes Alice, an artist from the big city. In next to no time she becomes emotionally involved with Tom. But when her noisy friends arrive in an open tourer, Tom is uncertain of his position with Alice. There is a local cricket match in which Tom becomes a hero once more. This and a ding-dong free-for-all in which the visitors participate are some of the riotous highlights of the film. It is after the match and during a drunken spree at the artist's shack that the real reason for Tom not wishing to discuss his war experiences becomes apparent. One of the male visitors starts singing and Tom tells him to shut up. The singer replies rather pointedly that he is no war hero, but neither did he have a yellow streak or receive white feathers (a popular symbol of cowardice in World War 1). He then resumes his singing. The expected confrontation does not take place. The scene dies in the picture. On the way home, a flashback with an irritating coupling of images in the town recreates the war. In the battle sequences the film fails badly. Like life in a country town, they are too localised or too restricted. A broad canvas such as the landing at Gallipoli is depicted by having one boat land on a Victorian beach. The battle itself is in miniature, and suggests frenzied action rather than depicting it. A few soldiers are shown clinging to the side of a sand dune, looking upwards to where the enemy is supposed to be entrenched. Sound effects work overtime in this battle on a mini budget. Then comes the big climax. Tom is no hero after all. He shoots himself through the foot in order to be invalided back to Australia. One point that is not explained is why Tom chases rabbits with traps and gun. He does not require food, yet seems to gain sadistic pleasure from their destruction. The film wraps itself up when Tom finds Alice in bed with one of her friends from town. Then comes the dawn, and Tom returns to his wife.

Break of Day just misses being a little gem of a picture. The picture received a special invitation to the San Sebastian International Festival in September 1977. Qantas purchased it for in-flight screening to passengers travelling across the world. It is believed to be the first Australian picture to be shown by an international airline. *Break of Day* was first screened in Melbourne at the Bercy, 31 December, 1976.

6.62 *John Ewart feels that this is not the time to turn stunt man. Harold Hopkins looks on apprehensively in a scene from "The Picture Show Man" written and produced by Joan Long and released through Roadshow.*

6.63   *Tony Llewellyn-Jones adds a literal significance to the title of the film in which he appears "Inside Looking Out".*

Change of Diet

F.J. Holden provides a startling change of mood from *Between Wars* for Mike Thornhill. Shown in Sydney and Melbourne on 29 April 1977, the Melbourne *Scene* on 14 May heads its review — 'This F.J.'s a Lemon.'

> It's about a boy and a girl and his F.J. Holden. It's also about the same dreary sameness of a lot of suburban living — the aimlessness and boredom. The director made us feel these emotions by boring us to slumber with monotonous and no-story dialogue. The cast is largely unknown and as they are mostly untalented, shall probably remain that way. The film rambles on and on, and the second last scene can be described only as the greatest bit of self-indulgent twaddle I've ever seen. Two youths are seen drinking beer, throwing bottles and mumbling incoherently for what seems a lifetime, Maybe the *F.J. Holden* will grab them at the drive-ins. Frankly I don't think it would ever get a roadworthy certificate.

That just about sums up the whole picture.

The *Sun Herald* Sydney, of 1 May was kinder. It claimed that *F.J.* did for Sydney's flat, low-rise suburbs what *Don's Party* did for the pseudo-intellectuals ... the 'North Shore set'. The write-up ended with the statement that 'the picture joins the increasing number of Australian productions that are right on target.'

The Melbourne *Herald* on 3 May noted that Michael Thornhill had in *F.J. Holden* effectively answered one major criticism of Australian film makers: he had overcome his obsession for the past, as in *Between Wars* and had come up with a poetically-photographed study of teenagers in a modern working-class suburb. There were no villains: the young people were inherently nice guys and deep down inside them there is untold good! In the background, one can almost hear 'Glory Alleluia!

From Brisbane came the news that when the *F.J. Holden* began its showing there on 20 May and it carried an 'R' rating (similar to that in South Australia, Western Australia, and Tasmania). Yet in NSW and Victoria it was classified as 'M'. Somewhere along the track, the Holden seems to have gone off the road.

Mike Thornhill saw the film as a gutsy story, presenting life in the raw and honestly. In one of the stills, the NSW number plate carries the prefix 'BAD'. No further comment appears necessary. The summing up in *Scene* was after all closer to the truth than all the other publications. *F.J. Holden* was a disaster in the theatres, but a success in drive-ins: at the film's opening at the Chullora Drive-in all drivers of F.J. and F.X. Holdens were admitted free!

High Rolling another drive-in variety, began rather unobstrusively at the small Swanston Theatre, Melbourne on 4 August, but it did graduate to a bigger theatre later. Director Igor Auzins forgot that a 35 mm film is more expansive than 16 mm, and this apparently made him overlook the scanning of his backgrounds closely. In addition he should have read Cecil B. de Mille's autobiography to study the technique of handling crowd scenes. Unlike the bar room sequence in *Caddie* where faces were expressive and reactions were spontaneous, Mr Auzins' extras were flat-footed, open-mouthed, and camera-conscious. They were distracting onlookers — not members of the cast of a film.

In *High Rolling* Tex (Joe Bottoms) an American, and Alby (Grigor Taylor) an Australian, become 'drifting' mates. At the time the story begins, Alby is with a boxing troupe, and Tex is conducting a shooting gallery. The American is sacked because he pays too much attention to a female customer, and Alby finds that a large local opponent is almost too much to handle. The pair set out for the bright lights of Surfers Paradise. They eventually get a lift from Arnold, who reveals himself as a homosexual after arranging accommodation for the night at a motel. Alby and Tex decide to borrow Arnold's car after discovering a large quantity of marijuana in the boot, and money and a gun in the glove box. On the way to the Gold Coast they pick up Lyn (Judy Davis) a sixteen year old. At Surfers they blame their untidy images for not making an impression with the girls. They purchase two very loud outfits and visit a night spot where Tex tries to date two singers (Wendy Hughes and Sandra McGregor). For his trouble Tex is beaten up by the bouncer (Gus Mercurio). He heads for the beach, clutching a bottle of whisky. Lyn discovers him there. Alby however meets with more success than Tex, and escorts the two singers to his apartment, where they help him to spend Arnold's money.

6.64 *Sydney's Western Suburbs' teenagers as portrayed by Karlene Rogerson and Gary Waddell in the controversial "F.J. Holden" released by GUO Film Distributors.*

Meanwhile Robert Hewett and Roger Ward, two friends of Arnold, arrive to search for the stolen car, marijuana, gun, and money. They force a description of Tex and Alby from two terrified nightclub singers. Short of money, Alby and Tex decide to hold up a busload of tourists with an unloaded gun. The plan misfires because of the unexpected arrival of a carload of police closely followed by the two thugs. As usual, Tex, Alby and Lyn prove to be born losers, and the end finds them doing what they know best — walking — and headed for no place in particular.

The Melbourne *Herald* classified it as a rather pointless little film, and the Melbourne *Age Weekender* summed it up as 'disappointing and pointless and shot with the verve of a lavatory paper TV ad.' In the Melbourne *Sun* it was mentioned that producer Tim Burstall's budget of $400 000 obviously wasn't enough. The Sydney *Sun Herald* found it 'the easy, popular way to make a road comedy', but that the 'world of illusion in this picture had neither charm nor reality'. This was considered a pity, as it was 'a well-made film'.

A Breakthrough

On 19 August, 1977 took an important step forward to consolidate the position already attained in the film world with pictures like *Caddie, Sunday Too Far Away* and the biggest success of them all, *Picnic at Hanging Rock*. (In March 1978 it was estimated that *Picnic* had taken $6.3 million, of which the Australian public had contributed $6 million.) The milestone was *The Getting of Wisdom* which opened in Sydney, and Melbourne simultaneously.

It has been stated that when the novel was first published in 1910, the name of the authoress Ethel Henrietta Richardson, better known as Henry Handel Richardson was removed from the honour board of the Melbourne Presbyterian Ladies' College. *The Getting of Wisdom* provided the framework for the excellent film script by Eleanor Witcombe, and for a superb film produced by Phillip Adams. Directed by Bruce Beresford, with skilful camerawork from Don McAlpine, the carefully chosen locations were the Methodist Ladies' College for the exteriors of the school in the film, and the Catholic Mandeville Hall, Melbourne, for interiors. For the lush outdoor scenery, the Ballarat Gardens doubled for the Fitzroy Gardens, and the tiny country town of 'Warrenega' in the book was Eddington outside Bendigo.

Laura Tweedle Rambotham (Susannah Fowle), a defiant, independent, and talented girl leaves Warrenega to continue her study at a Melbourne boarding school. Her mother (Kay Eklund) has made garish clothing for her to wear, including a dress with a series of frills and flounces, and an unsightly bonnet with fluted brim. Wilful in many respects, Laura soon learns that life is what you make it. The girls at the school make fun of her clothes, her background (many of the boarders came from wealthy homes) and her name. This only makes her even more rebellious. The teachers come in a variety of temperaments. One (Candy Raymond) is romantically inclined; another (Jan Friedl) is cynical. The lady superintendent (Sheila Helpmann) is austere and haughty, yet the deputy headmistress (Patricia Kennedy) shows kindness and understanding. Barry Humphries as Rev. Strachey, the headmaster divorces himself completely from the 'Edna Everage' image to give an outstanding performance. Laura at a musical afternoon, defies convention and plays a

6.65 *Barry Humphries in his more famous disguise ... as "Dame Edna Everage" in "Barry McKenzie Holds His Own".*

tasteless piece of music that disgusts Strachey. Endeavouring to be the envy of the other girls, Laura pretends that the new curate, the Rev. Shepherd (John Waters) and she are having a secret romance. She has tea with the curate only to find him rude and demanding. His sister (Julia Blake) has to give immediate attention to even his slightest wish.

A girlfriend Chinky (Alix Longman) steals money to purchase a ring so that Laura can elope with the minister. The theft is discovered, and Chinky is dramatically expelled. Laura, as a result, is ostracised by the school. Only an older girl (Hilary Ryan) remains her friend, and Laura develops a crush on her. (Something that certainly would cause the good ladies of the PLC to reach for smelling salts.) The older girl leaves and Laura feels rejected. Laura finds her only escape in study — something that she had neglected for months. Even though she cheats in the final history examination, she wins both the coveted literary prize and the musical scholarship overseas. The Rev. Strachey at prize giving, states that the music prize belongs not to Laura alone, but to the whole school. Still defiant and independent, she leaves the school. Throwing her bag and hat aside, she demonstrates her newly won freedom by going for a triumphant run across the park.

The Australian on 20 August 1977 noted that *The Getting of Wisdom* was a low-key film made with love, resulting in a rich and amusing portrait of an imaginative young girl. It was felt that director and writer had handled the story sensitively and that the external photography had a strong 'Australian feel' about it. Faults were — too episodic a script; and the irony of the book didn't quite come off in the picture. But the closing of the critique contained a sense of patriotism and genuine feeling for the future of the Australian film industry:

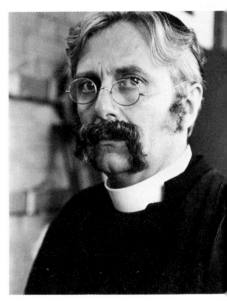

6.66 *Barry Humphries departs from his "Dame Edna" image to give a portrayal of the austere Rev. Strachey, in "The Getting Of Wisdom". Produced by Southern Cross films, the story is set in 1897. Many exteriors were shot on location such as the Ballarat Gardens, and the small Victorian town of Eddington.*

> *Wisdom* has a fine spirit about it. A spirit that is Australian — wild, imaginative, defiant and proud.

The Melbourne *Sun* contained these words of praise: 'If the State Government ever doubted the wisdom of its decision to establish the Victorian Film Corporation *The Getting of Wisdom* should allay those doubts.' Praise was given to the scripter Eleanor Witcombe (who previously adapted *The Seven Little Australians* for ABC-TV). The critic also praised the imaginative photography of Don McAlpine, and most of the cast — Susannah Fowle, Barry Humphries, Sheila Helpmann, Patricia Kennedy, Jan Friedl, Monica Maughan, Candy Raymond, and Kim Deacon as the bitchy Lilith.

The Sydney *Sun Herald* was of the opinion that *The Getting of Wisdom* was a beautifully complete and satisfying film: 'The characters came to life with all their faults.' It was felt that Bruce Beresford and Phillip Adams had done honour to one of Australia's classic women writers.

A Let-Down

By contrast *Summerfield* was something of a let-down. It premiered in Sydney at Pitt Centre on 29 September 1977, and was shown at the Bercy, Melbourne on 14 October. It wasn't the fault of cameraman Mike Molloy that the film failed to take off. Although often his camera was confined to verandas and interiors, he handled the shots well and gave an impressive dignity to the scenic exteriors.

Summerfield was produced by Pat Lovell, and directed by Ken Hannam. In his screenplay, Cliff Green tried to create a sense of brooding malevolence through furtive faces; the superimposition of heads over a peaked rock; a hub cap in a swirling eddy of foaming water trickling through rocky recesses; and

6.67   *Michelle Jarman and Nick Tate in "Summerfield" — A GUO Film Distributors release — directed by Ken Hannam, and produced by Patricia Lovell.*

6.68 *Nick Tate (as a schoolteacher who tries to trace his predecessor), John Waters and Elizabeth Alexander (as parents of Michelle Jarman who was very fond of the missing schoolteacher). This is a scene from "Summerfield" — a mystery story by Cliff Green.*

the surge of some mysterious cadence. Yet the sinister disappearance of a schoolteacher on which the story hinged provided a lack-lustre anti-climax. The script provided not enough opportunity for character definition. The dialogue lacked sparkle, substance, or significance. Charles 'Bud' Tingwell tried desperately to create the illusion of someone who could provide the key to all the mumbo jumbo that transpired in front of the camera, but the script forgot him.

One thing that came out of *Summerfield* was the natural ability of Michelle Jarman as the child in the gloomy house. But that sickening scene of violence, where the new teacher (Nick Tate) learns of the licentious sexual intercourse between brother and sister (played by John Waters and Elizabeth Alexander) which results in the brother murdering his sister and his ultimate suicide, did nothing for box office returns.

This film once again raised the question of sound. When the voice was compressed (supposedly issuing from the radio amplifier), it is clear and distinct — yet voices in a crowd scene for example, are muffled and lack clarity. Sound *is* important. Far too often the Australian accent is blamed for the rejection of the film overseas, whereas the real cause is that not enough attention has been given to the sound track. Like Henry Kendall's poem about bellbirds in the gorges, every word must be as sharp as the tinkle of a bell. The words count — not the accent.

The Sydney *Sun Herald* opened its attack on *Summerfield* with the statement that suspense mystery movies seldom supply what they promise. The result is often an anti-climax. The Melbourne *Herald* labelled it a 'secret of sorts'. The critic felt that the competent cast did reasonably well with the

6.69 *Agnetha signs autographs for enthusiastic fans, closely watched by ABBA's bodyguard (played by Australian, Tom Oliver). A still from the Reg Grundy Production "Abba — The Movie"*

rather trite material. The Melbourne *Sun* noted that the patrons' comments as they left the Bercy Theatre indicated dislike, even revulsion, at the horror they had seen. The Melbourne *Scene* wrote:

> In spite of some good performances and an attractive setting, *Summerfield* is rather thin on entertainment, slowly paced, and fatally lacking tension.

Abba — The Movie, did not lay claim to making an outstanding contribution to the local film output. It was based on the activities of the Swedish singing group. It opened on 15 December 1977 at the Regent Theatre, Sydney; at The Astra in Parramatta; and the Palace, Melbourne. *Abba — The Movie* was produced by the Reg Grundy Organisation and most of the footage was shot in Australia during the Abba concert tour in March 1977. The remainder was filmed in Stockholm. The script was by Australian Bob Caswell, and it was directed by Lasse Hallstrom. It revolves around a lightweight story of an Australian Country and Western disc jockey (Robert Hughes) who wishes to obtain an exclusive interview with the group. Other Australians in the cast are Tom Oliver as Abba's personal bodyguard, and Bruce Barry who portrays a radio station manager.

A film critic wrote that the picture did not provide an intellectual experience, nor did it tell you more about Abba than the fan magazines and newspapers had already supplied. The girls belted out the words, then settled for wiggling and waving their posteriors at the audience. The blonde as often as not was decked out in skin-tight white slacks to give her admirers a better view of what has been hailed as the sexiest bottom in Europe.

6.70 *Left to Right: Bjorn, Ashley the D.J. (played by Robert Hughes), and Benny, in a scene from the dream sequence in "Abba — The Movie".*

Cosy Cool, a Film Factory Production released through Garron International, crept into Sydney silently in early September 1977 at the Town Theatre. Directed by T.C. Fields, and photographed by James Davis, it starred Gary Young and John Wilson. The storyline was that 'Cosy Cool' and 'Gracious Grytt' were two bikies who set out to prove that the rest of the world was wrong and they were right. According to the splurge it contained great music, great bikies and some blood.

The sequel to *Fantasm* called *Fantasm Comes Again* was a 1977 Boxing Day present at the Dendy Theatre, Collins Street, Melbourne. Remarks passed by producer Antony Ginnane about the local film industry are more interesting than the pornographic pic itself. He stated that no other film industry outside the European socialist countries had government finance to the extent that Australia has. Mr Ginnane likened it to a *de facto* nationalised film front.

Fantasm Comes Again was written by Ross Dimsey, and directed by Colin Eggleston. Unfortunately it was a waste of Vincent Monton's time photographing it. Melbourne film critic Denbeigh Salter summed up the show succinctly with, 'this new Australian-American co-production is a pornographic jigsaw with some of the bits missing.' Perhaps those 'bits' met their fate in the hands of the censor's scissors. *Fantasm Comes Again* did not do the record business in Melbourne that *Fantasm* had done and closed on 16 March 1977.

A little more sensational but still rated 'R' was Tom Cowan's *Journey among Women.* The theme of this film was one of savagery and brutality, with many explosive and often repulsive scenes of sheer violence. Set in a similar period to that of *Luke's Kingdom,* the opening centred on female prisoners in a British penal colony in Australia. Then it becomes Sydney in the late eighteenth century. In *Journey among Women* there appear to be more redcoats guarding a handful of women that one would have thought necessary. These women without hope appear to be there for one purpose only — to satisfy the insatiable lust of the soldiers. No doubt that explains the reason for the breakout: the women aren't being paid overtime rates. The aristocratic Judge Advocate's daughter, Elizabeth Harrington (Jeune Pritchard) discovers her fiancé Captain McEuen (Martin Phelan) raping a woman convict. Piqued, she assists ten female prisoners to escape, and goes with them. The women, products of a sadistic environment, cannot master their bestial instincts and fall victim to the very system that condemned them. They become beasts of the jungle, discard their clothing that shackled them to civilisation, and savagely attack and murder any unfortunate male who invades their domain. The ending, like the opening, contains a spirit of helplessness that does not supply even a vestige of hope for the survivor in the story. The germ of a very good idea was present, but it somehow became hidden in the telling. (As a point of interest were hair slides the 'in' thing in the late eighteenth century?)

Journey among Women was made on a small budget of $200 000. A great deal of the outdoor scenery was shot at Berowra Waters in the Hawkesbury River area. Cowan as a photographer has provided and still is providing proof of his outstanding ability with a camera. As a director however, he has a lot to learn. The screenplay was lumbering, and at times — banal. The pace was tiresomely slow with the exception of the bloodthirsty ending. Tim Elliott in a minor role, was the sole player to give any credence to the dialogue. He portrayed a doctor. In general, as in *The Singer and the Dancer*, the male characters came up little more than cardboard cutouts.

It has been stated in various publications that *Journey among Women* attracted attention at Cannes, and had been sold to Italy, Canada, and Belgium.

Journey among Women was not hailed with delight by the critics. One referred to it as 'The Balmain Girl Guides' Day Out'. In Melbourne, a critique stated that other contributors to the Australian film revival had been far more accessible, better acted, and more entertaining. But none had been as thought provoking. Sydney attacked it viciously. One report was that neither the script nor the movie worked. Problems were in the acting and script — both of which were amateurish. However Tom Cowan received full marks for his photography. Another critic noted that rape, frontal nudity, violence and murder in blood-stained close up were the main ingredients of the film. The critic went on to advise that since Australian films had achieved such high standards, this picture was an unacceptable step backwards to the earlier era of fumbling immaturity.

Journey among Women was screened at the Sydney Rapallo 18 August 1977, and Melbourne in October. In the 1977 Australian Film Awards, *Journey among Women* received a special award for creativity.

Inside Looking Out is another film for 1977 which was made on a low budget. Featured players were Briony Behets, Tony Llewellyn Jones, Elke Neidhart, and Norman Kaye. It was directed by Paul Cox. who commented that we live in an 'instant' world where a lack of patience ruins many marriages. *Inside Looking Out* deals with a marital break-up. To accompany the promotional material, Paul Cox wrote that 'only sometimes do we come across a ray of light, falling through a narrow window, or a dark hole above. Suddenly a light speaks to us, and for a moment lifts the dark veil from our fragmented existence.' 'Marriage in a cage' was the basic theme of the Paul Cox production. A young couple played by Briony Behets and Tony Llewellyn Jones live in a trendy terrace house. They suffer from a complete lack of communication. The reason for the break-up is never made clear. Phrases like being an 'emotional cripple', and 'we can no longer talk to each other', do not provide that 'shaft of light' Paul Cox referred to. Like *Journey among Women* the photography is often graphic, and always well done. If one look is worth a thousand words, then perhaps the still of Tony Llewellyn peering out sums the film up more neatly than the script. *Inside Looking Out* was first screened at the Melbourne film festival in June, 1977.

The Last Wave

Peter Weir turned to mystery in 1977 — and when Weir's name is associated with a film, one looks for something different. This talented director again obliged, and came up with a 'sci-fi'-cum Aboriginal Dreamtime fantasy called *The Last Wave*. Shown in Glenelg, South Australia in December 1977, it then transferred to Sydney and Melbourne.

In *The Last Wave* we have Richard Chamberlain, the lawyer, who is driven by a force over which he has no control. He comes in contact with an Aboriginal tribal killing and tries to arrive at a solution through Aboriginal mysticism. Even resistance from the Aborigines does not deter him. After the tribal killing a number of Aborigines are arrested and charged with murder. Chris (Gulpilil) who is the leader of the younger Aborigines is not included in the group charged. David Burton, the lawyer, claims that it was a 'tribal killing', but a member of the Justice Department ridicules the idea, because 'there was no tribe in Sydney'. David meets Chris and invites him to dinner, so that he can discuss the background to the killing. Chris brings an uninvited guest, a tribal elder, Charlie (Nadjiwarra Amagula) who denies any knowledge of English. The older man looks at the lawyer strangely during the evening, as if recognising in him something that sets him apart from other white men. The meeting does not supply the answers that Burton requires. Later he learns that there is a Sydney tribe of Aborigines and that Chris and Charlie are members of it. Freakish rainstorms meanwhile flood the city. Chris takes David to sewers deep beneath Sydney to reveal the secrets that the Aborigines had defended with murder. When the lawyer asks the Aborigine whether he will be there when he returns, Chris states that he has broken the law by taking him to this place, and that he must return to the Dreamtime.

In the cave David discovers a mask facially identical to his own — it is a death mask. Then he notices strange markings on the wall similar to those in a photograph of his own great grandfather that Charlie recognises when he perused it. The strange point is that his forefather was a South American. In the same cave are paintings similar to those in Egyptian tombs, and stone images similar to those on Easter Island. (Perhaps Peter Weir in some way was trying to make Aboriginal mysticism part of the post-psychoanalytic phase that embraced the Yucatan Indians and the Yaqui!)

Burton finally sends his wife and children away because he fears a catastrophe. A huge tidal wave is suggested at the end, and we see the lawyer kneeling on the sand.

Does that wave sweep him into eternity, or does it send him forth into another world, thus perpetuating eternal life? Throughout the film, one notes that David Burton has some strange affinity with water in all forms, whether it is torrential rain, giant hailstones, or the black mud that bespatters his car. This water imagery makes one think of the eternal life theme, which is picked up at the end with the 'last wave'.

There was excellent acting from (David) Gulpilil and a dignified character study by Nadjiwarra Amagula. The sound effects were violent, startling, and thunderously loud, yet as in *Summerfield*, the dialogue is quite often almost inaudible. But there is no doubt as to Peter Weir's directional ability, and Russell Boyd is a master craftsman with the camera.

Screened at the Paris Film Festival on 5 November 1977 and then at the Teheran Festival, *The Last Wave* really hit the headlines in 1978, when a London newspaper ran the story, 'The Year The Aboriginals Hit West Germany'. This story was the result of the 1978 Berlin Film Festival, where eight films about Aborigines were screened including *The Last Wave*, Phil Noyce's *Backroads* and Michael Edols' *Lalai Dreamtime*.

These films on 'Black Australia' proved so successful and impressed director Werner Herzog so much that he arranged for the films to be exhibited in Munich. Further plans were to screen them at the various festivals in Cannes, Paris, and the United States. Australia itself wasn't overlooked and the 'Black Australia' productions were screened for a three weeks season at the Sydney Film Co-operative from 1 April 1978. *Storm Boy*, *The Last Wave* and Fred Schepisi's *The Chant of Jimmie Blacksmith* were Australia's biggest draw cards in 1978. The Aboriginal influence was extended to the Asian Film Festival in Sydney in October 1978. With an Aboriginal motif as the logo, awards were in the form of individual hand-carved Aboriginal sculpture. Gulpilil was booked for opening night.

In the Paris Film Festival on 5 November 1977 *The Last Wave* was voted into number one spot by a press delegation of some 500 journalists. On 12 November Peter Weir arrived back in Australia with a Special Award created by the Jury for a film that drew rave notices from Paris critics. This was followed by the Golden Winged Ibex at the Teheran International Film Festival. In February 1978 *The Last Wave* won the Jury prize at the Sci-Fi Festival at Avoriaz (a similar award to that won by *Summer of Secrets*. *Wave* however was the far superior film). On 16 May 1978, Jim McElroy returned to Sydney from the USA with a $250 000 contract for the distribution of *Picnic at Hanging Rock* and *The Last Wave*. This amount was only an advance, and returns would be increased if the productions were successful.

Denbeigh Salter, Melbourne film critic, felt that with *The Last Wave* the Australian film industry took another encouraging step forward: 'This brilliant Australian movie should win International Awards for its originality and craftsmanship,' he wrote.

The Australian provided a mixed comment. It agreed that Peter Weir had made the film with intelligence, integrity, and a fine professionalism. It undoubtedly provided a breakthrough for Australian pictures. On the debit side was the limp ending; the critic felt that tension fell away into confusion, which deprived the climax of dramatic punch. The Melbourne *Herald* felt that in the dramatic torrent of imagination, disbelief is 'not only suspended — it's temporarily converted'. This may or may not be the great Australian movie, but, the *Herald* noted, it 'was great film making by any standard. It confirmed Peter Weir as our best and most original director'. The *Herald* in its ten best films for 1977 placed *The Last Wave* third, *Storm Boy* sixth, and *The Getting of Wisdom* seventh. The critic from the Melbourne *Sun* classified

The Last Wave as the most 'atmospheric and threatening film yet made in Australia'. It was a 'powerful experience', and a picture that 'the Australian industry would be proud to claim'.

The final summing up is left to the Melbourne *Scene*:

> Peter Weir's *The Last Wave* is further exciting evidence of a major talent working in our newly re-born film industry. The tensions raised in this film have to be experienced to be believed. Individual sequences have a seat-edge quality which one experiences only rarely in the cinema, and rarer still in films that are not out-and-out thrillers.
>
> Technically, from Russell Boyd's masterful photography on down, *The Last Wave* is stunningly good. Let us hope our audiences will see in this film the unique qualities it possesses.
>
> It deserves every support — it is quite an exciting event in the Australia cinema.

Profits

In September 1977, Jim and Hal McElroy revealed that *Picnic at Hanging Rock* to that date had made 170 per cent profit on investment. But once again that hoary bugbear of every Australian producer raised its ugly head: exhibition and distribution used up approximately 75 per cent of the takings. The point must be stressed that the Australian government, if it does honestly and sincerely believe in a prosperous, indigenous film industry, must view the financial aspect of film making with more than a nodding concern. It must act to provide protection for the local film industry, which after all, has reached the stage of being an export.

The McElroy Brothers took a hard keen look at their latest venture *The Last Wave*, and came up with a 45 per cent return instead of the usual 25 per cent-30 per cent. United Artists did not invest in the picture but paid $350 000 for Australian, New Zealand, English and South African release rights. Janus Films of Germany paid $50 000 for German, Austrian, and Swiss rights. This meant that at long last an Australian producer had arrived at the point where there's a chance to make a solid profit. With Richard Chamberlain in the lead *The Last Wave* stands a reasonable chance of cracking the worthwhile American market.

6.71 *"The Last Wave" produced by Hal and Jim McElroy and directed by Peter Weir is a psychic thriller. Richard Chamberlain (as a lawyer) invites Chris (Gulpilil) to dinner to discuss a tribal murder. Chris (left) brings an uninvited guest, his tribal elder, Charlie (Nandjiwarra Amagula).*

Rose-coloured Nostalgia

The Mango Tree scripted and produced by Michael Pate and directed by Kevin Dobson had its world premiere at the Crest Theatre, Bundaberg, Queensland, on 13 December 1977. Six hundred tickets were sold at $12 a head, and the theatre was sold out in two and a half hours after the bookings had opened. Many people from outside Bundaberg came in especially to book seats but had to be refused. Tempers rose and even the manager of the theatre missed out on a seat.

The Bundaberg Sugar Company invested in the film, which accounts for a number of shots of tall green-topped cane with red paths through the plantation providing a contrast in colour. The whole film was geared to accommodate a time when bicycles and curved-bonneted, stiff-backed, well-

6.72 *Richard Chamberlain is dumbfounded to find his likeness in an ancient death mask in a vault in an underground cave in Sydney. "The Last Wave" is another film in which the South Australian Film Corporation has an interest. It is released through United Artists.*

ventilated cars took in the scenery at a leisurely pace. Christopher Pate as the seventeen-year old youth practically opened and certainly closed the film — beginning with a ride down a country road, and ending on his leaving the town by train — destination not stated. Young Pate was a greatly improved actor since his appearance in *Raw Deal* early in the year, but it was Geraldine Fitzgerald who stole the show with a polished and subtle inflection as in the scene where she visits the headmaster's office and persuasively suggests that it would be unwise to expel her grandson just because he intervened when a teacher lost control and savagely attacked a truant with a cane. The headmaster was played by Terry McDermott; the teacher was Ben Gabriel.

Overacting, especially in the beginning, was very noticeable, from Grandma Carr's housekeeper to the schoolteacher. The housekeeper improved as did Sir Robert Helpmann as the remittance man, who after having been nursed back to health after heavy drinking bouts, was at first, very theatrical both in speech and movement. Later he delivered his lines with dignity and assurance. Brian Probyn's photography came up well — especially in the interiors of Grandma Carr's home, where there was a glow and warmth for which this talented lighting-cameraman has no peer on the Australian film front.

Jamie's coming of age was handled delicately. He goes to Miss Pringle's house to receive tuition in French. After a number of lessons, a physical attraction develops, until the night she invites him in, her hair down and carefully brushed, her clothing loose and easily shed. Miss Pringle (Diane Craig) encourages Jamie to realise that he has reached the age of manhood. Afterwards she finds that she is in love with Jamie, and leaves the town, after professing her love in a tender note to him. She also tells him that by her remaining, life would become impossible. Slow patches in the film, like a trio cycling, were given interest by music composed by Marc Wilkinson.

The script provided only one opportunity for a tension-packed, nerve-tingling sequence but despite the ingredients, the scene was as flat as a plateau. Preacher Jones (Gerard Kennedy) becomes a Bible-quoting, maniacal murderer. He shoots the sergeant of police (Gerry Duggan) and is holed up in a sugar mill. Armed with a heavy rifle Jones pins his pursuers down with screaming hot lead. A sniper who had just returned from the First World War is sent for. He waits patiently for the preacher to expose himself, then shoots him down like 'a mad dog'. It was a knockout with the referee already counting. One had to admit that in *The Mango Tree* the mortality rate was high.

In the Sydney *Daily Telegraph* on 28 June 1977, Sir Robert Helpmann was associated with one of the most senseless and misleading pieces of publicity ever associated with a film. The newspaper carried the banner headline on Page 1, 'Who is this Man?' and showed the actor re-enacting the role of the 'professor' in *The Mango Tree*. It was revealed on another page that Helpmann was putting the finishing touches to the picture by rolling in a Woolloomooloo gutter after swigging cheap wine. Why resort to this make-believe when his 'drinking' sequences had been shot in Gayndah? Then followed this unbelievable piece of gaff: Sir Robert is alleged to have stated that the most exciting scene in the picture was when he fought a minister of religion in the main street of Gayndah. The story as reported advised that there wasn't much of the town to start with, but by the time the professor and the parson had finished, they had almost destroyed what remained. Anyone who saw *The Mango Tree* would wonder whether the censor had been at work — all that remained of that particular scene was that after arguing with the minister of religion, the good man threatened to club the professor with his Bible. The sergeant of police intervened, and the terrific fight that was supposed to have taken place, never eventuated.

The Melbourne *Herald* called *The Mango Tree* 'rose-coloured nostalgia'. It was thought that the episodic events overshadowed the essential theme of life changing dramatically for a youth on the threshold of manhood. The critique went on to advise that the basis for the title was not made clear in the film. It also noted that Hinkler's plane as shown was years ahead of its time. This critic thought Hollywood veteran Geraldine Fitzgerald magnificent, and noted that behind a 'gently mocking smile was a character of pure steel'.

The Melbourne *Sun* reported that drawn-out thinking and dreaming could be important with a book, but that in a film events shown on the screen convey the message in an instant, leaving its imprint on the memory of the viewer. The *Sun* thought that this was what *The Mango Tree* did quite beautifully. *The Australian* took a much harsher look at *The Mango Tree*. Christopher Pate's 'lessons in love did not get anywhere, or cover much on the way'. Gerard Kennedy 'went screaming around as a mad parson'. His make up was 'atrocious'. Worst of all it was felt that the script was disjointed and sometimes gauche. On the other hand, the cinematography of Brian Probyn; the costuming by Pat Forster; the brilliant sets by Leslie Binns and the superb acting of Geraldine Fitzgerald received the highest praise. The critic also gave full marks to the one who thought up the business of having Geraldine Fitzgerald twiddling and changing her earrings. It was felt that this was the best idea in the whole movie. *The Australian* concluded with the view that *The Mango Tree* had to be made, but 'let's not do it again'.

On 25 March 1978, *The Mango Tree* transferred from the Bercy, Melbourne to the Eastend Cinema, which shows the interest that still remained in the picture in that city.

Aussie Films Take Second Place

It is amazing how American films can have many an Australian production relegated to daytime only showings even though picture theatres need Australian money at the box office to keep them in existence. What is more amazing still is that the Australian film is quite often far superior to the American. Take *Dot and the Kangaroo* from the Yoram Gross Studio for example. This was judged to be the best feature film by a Children's International Jury at the Teheran International Film Festival. But when *Dot and the Kangaroo* was released through Hoyts on 15 December 1977, it was screened only in the morning sessions. It is enough to provoke the remark, 'to hell with Walt Disney!' This would only be a similar outburst to that made by Glenn Ford a few years ago at a TV Week Logie award night when he stated that he would 'defend the right of Americans to make films to the bitter end, and would not stand by and see fellow actors thrown out of work'. In Australia's case, it is this country's right to occupy a fair share of the screen in its own domain at least.

Dot and the Kangaroo was snapped up by overseas distributors at Cannes in 1977, even when the local scene remained basically unimpressed. The Melbourne *Sun* recalled that Walt Disney had a world monopoly on animated cartoons, but that *Dot and the Kangaroo* was animated well and that the bush settings looked real. The Sydney *Sun Herald* felt that while the superimposition of cartoon figures over genuine backgrounds gave the film a two-dimensional look, it led to some confusion. The critic hoped that in future productions Yoram Gross would produce only wholly animated features. The *Sun* thought adults as well as children would appreciate *Dot and the Kangaroo* whereas the *Sun Herald* recommended it for only youngsters.

Based on Ethel Pedley's book released in 1899, *Dot and the Kangaroo* relates the story of 'Dot' who lives on the edge of the Australian bush. One day she penetrates too deeply into the thick trees and becomes lost. She is adopted by a kangaroo whose joey has been killed. Dot meets the Platypus who knows everything, and the Willy Wagtail who eventually leads her back to her own farm. There are catchy tunes to make the bushland enjoyable rather than frightening. Voices belonged to a number of well-known performers, including Lola Brooks, Ron Haddrick, Ross Higgins, June Salter and Spike Milligan.

Dot took a second bow in Melbourne at the Swanston for the school holidays on 15 May 1978, as well as at many suburban theatres. It was only a matinée feature.

Small Budget Features in 1977

Backroads, one of the 'Black Australia' movies so popular overseas, was a 16 mm release. Screened at the Union Theatre, Sydney, on 30 May 1977, it transferred to the Melbourne Longford on 30 June. Then followed a season at the State Theatre, Hobart, commencing 4 August. Made on a bedrock budget of $23 000 funds would not often permit retakes. With Lloyd Carrick on sound, it was scripted by John Emery and featured Russell Boyd on camera, who contributed graphic and unforgettable shots of a dusty wasteland. The film was directed by Phil Noyce.

This advertisement sets the story — 'Outback New South Wales. Two Aborigines and a white man in a stolen car, on the road to nowhere.' Gary (Gary Foley), a young Aborigine living on a reserve, meets up with Jack King (Bill Hunter) a loud-mouthed, hard-drinking white man. The pair steal a Pontiac Parisienne and make for the coast. On the way they pick up an older Aborigine, Joe (Zac Martin), a young French hitch-hiker, Jean-Claude (Terry Camilleri), and Anna (Julie McGregor) a petrol pump attendant, who goes along for the ride. They race truckies and confront hostile storekeepers. The biggest loser on the trip is Gary who learns from Jack how to live life violently — with a gun.

6.73 *Zac Martin in "Backroads" directed by Phil Noyce. Although an older Aborigine he comes to learn that living in a white man's society can cometimes mean being behind a gun.*

6.74   *Sir Robert Helpmann and Gloria Dawn in "The Mango Tree" produced by Michael Pate. It is set in a small Queensland town (and photographed in and around Bundaberg).*

6.75   *Geraldine Fitzgerald and Christopher Pate in "The Mango Tree" — A GUO release, directed by Kevin Dobson.*

The Melbourne *Sun* critic mentions the fact that Russell Boyd fills the screen with sunburnt Australian outback landscapes. He notes that this is the land that the white man took from the Aborigines ... once a proud race that has degenerated to a 'life of idleness, a humpy and a flagon of cheap wine'. *Backroads* however, depicts several whites in a state of comparable degeneration. The critique concludes with the thought that with a bigger budget *Backroads* could have been the 'most important social document made in Australia — and certainly would have gained commercial release through one of the major exhibitors'.

A kind of documentary record of the last days in the life of a 'wino' gave painful truthfulness to *Listen to the Lion* another low-budget film which was directed by Henri Safran who is remembered for his work in *Storm Boy*. Shown at Cannes in 1977 and the winner of two awards at the 1977 Sydney Film Festival, it has been sold for distribution in the United States. Grouped with *Queensland* on a programme at the Sydney Union Theatre on 10 September 1977, it was transferred to the Filmmakers' Cinema, Darlinghurst, five days later.

Listen to the Lion follows a derelict from rubbish tip to cheap pub, from a park bench to a rubbish-strewn lane. The 'wino' takes constant swigs from the always visible bottle, and he often shares the contents with nameless, tattered mates. As a contrast to Wyn Robert's role of the derelict who waits for death to relieve him of his misery, is Barry Lovett's portrayal of a grim-faced, one-legged down-and-out who clings fiercely to his freedom. Comedian Syd Heylen was another member of the cast.

Love Letters from Teralba Road a third low-budget film came into prominence in the 1977 Australian Film Awards. That year there were two Special Awards for Creativity. One went to Tom Cowan for *Journey among Women,* the other to Stephen Wallace for his *Love Letters*. *Love Letters* also won a Gold Award in the Special Fiction Section.

On 6 August 1977 it was recorded in *The Australian* that *Love Letters from Teralba Road* and *The Singer and the Dancer* rang up Sydney's fourth biggest box office takings for one week. The two films, both shot on 16 mm, grossed $10 000 for a six day, two sessions daily week at the Union Theatre. *Love Letters* (with *Promised Woman* as the supporting feature) was also exhibited at the Melbourne Longford Theatre on 15 December 1977. In addition it was selected for screening at the 1977 Teheran Film Festival.

Love Letters was produced by Richard Brennan, directed and scripted by Stephen Wallace, and starred Bryan Brown, (Len) Kris McQuade, (Barbara) Joy Hruby, and Kevin Leslie. The story begins with the finding of a bundle of love letters in a run-down house. In flashback Len beats up his wife Barbara because he thinks she has been unfaithful. She leaves Newcastle and goes to live with her father and sister in Sydney. In desperation Len writes a series of love letters to Barbara in an attempt to bring about a reconciliation. The letters link scenes of Len at work in the warehouse and at home with his mother. Barbara is revealed talking to a friend in the local pub, and at home with her father and sister. Barbara finally agrees to meet Len in Sydney. They try to sort out their problems, but Barbara remains suspicious of her husband. Len returns to Newcastle and starts planning for his move to Sydney. He finds that he can't save money and becomes unpopular at work. Barbara realises

6.76 *This scene in "Listen To The Lion" (1977) shows the permanent chess tables in Sydney's Hyde Park. Directed by Henri Safron, the two derelicts are Syd Heylen, and Wyn Roberts.*

the hopelessness of it all, and the film ends with Len's last letter. Whether they eventually come together again is left to the imagination of the picture-goer.

A Melbourne film critic saw it as being far from a pretty film that probed the problem of patching up a weak marriage. The critic pointed out that the film neither dressed up the couple nor degraded them, it merely treated them as ordinary people in none too attractive circumstances.

Television on an Upswing

On the television side of the picture in 1977, there was a great deal of creativity. One Film Australia production, *Do I Have to Kill my Child?* won a Bronze Award in the Special Fiction Section of the 1977 Australian Film Awards. It also received mention in the 1978 TV Week Logie Awards when Jacki Weaver won recognition for giving the best individual performance by an actress.

It is hard to classify *Do I Have to Kill my Child?* It actually falls between a documentary and a feature. The opening is a self-conscious monologue to cover Dianne's family background. Dianne's own mother once broke a broom handle over her back, and she appears to remain dominated by this oppressed feeling. She finds she can't cope with her domestic responsibilities. She promises things to her children, then causes problems for herself by forgetting those promises. She chews tranquillizers like lollies and doesn't care whether the new baby she is carrying lives or dies. When the baby is born, she looks upon it as a wizened up little red thing — like a fetus in a bottle. Dianne becomes tense all the time and angry. When baby Jamie cries, she hates him to the point of wanting to murder him. Her husband (Brendon Lunney) wanted a son. She didn't! The breaking point arrives when the baby cries. She rocks him faster and faster until she fractures his skull. The husband is alarmed and tells her that he requires a responsible person to look after his children. The film deals with a problem that actually exists — but a solution isn't there. Yet the ending still packs a punch: Dianne turns despairingly to her husband and says: 'Do I have to kill my child before anyone understands?'

Directed by Donald Crombie (who also directed *The Irishman*), and scripted by the director and Anne Deveson, it was jointly funded by an International Women's Year grant and Film Australia. Screened in Cannes on 21 May 1977, it was telecast by Channel 9 two days prior to its European showing. A repeat screening followed in Melbourne on 10 May.

The Melbourne *Sun's* TV critic had always thought of Jacki Weaver as a dumb blonde, always good for a light comedy role. But after viewing her in *Do I Have to Kill my Child?* added Jacki's name to two others whom he considered gave outstanding performances on television — Martin Vaughan in *Billy and Percy* and Olivia Hamnett at the distraught mother in *Sally Go Round the Moon*.

Surprisingly, ABC-TV presented yet another version of the Kelly saga in *The Trial of Ned Kelly* with John Waters playing a magnificent role as the ill-fated bushranger. Telecast on 12 September 1977, it provided a new angle to the case heard before Judge Barry (played by John Frawley) and the subsequent sentence to be hanged. Alan Hopgood sat in on the trial in modern dress and pointed out certain developments that should have been followed up by the defence which would have thereby altered the whole course of the trial. This technique added a new dimension to a familiar story, although at times it was distracting.

First, Ned was defended by a barrister with only ten months' experience who consequently failed to recognise certain weaknesses in the case for the prosecution. It was also unfortunate that it was Melbourne Cup week, and Justice Barry would not allow any case to interfere with his sporting activities. Finally there was His Honour's summing up that was tantamount to an ultimatum: self-defence would not be accepted; Kelly had to be found guilty of the murder of the policeman or acquitted.

6.77   *The central figure is John Derum in "Listen to The Lion". When screened at the Longford, Melbourne on 6 April 1978, one critic said that it was a pity that at 53 minutes, it was neither a short nor a feature. It was written, designed and produced by Robert Hill. The budget was a mere $36,000.*

Pig in a Poke, an unusual and well-acted series from ABC-TV, was the recipient of numerous awards. In the 1977 Television Society of Australia's Awards, it won a Penguin in the open section for adult drama for *The Ginny Story.* For this same episode scriptwriters John Dingwall and Margaret Kelly received a Penguin as well as a Logie in TV Week's 1978 Awards, as the best drama scriptwriters. Acting honours were — a 1977 Penguin to Arianthe Galani as the best supporting actress in the episode called *Theo's Story* and a 1978 Logie to Neil Fitzpatrick as the best individual performance from an actor in *Lisa's Story.* The story of Dr Reynolds (Paul Mason) and the various cases in which he is involved form the basis for a parade of heartbreak, tragedy, and human relationships between various ethnic groups. Most of his work is done in the name of 'sweet tragedy' in an under-privileged inner suburb of Sydney.

Tele-cine Films in 1977

In 1976, some of the worst tele-cine films ever made in Australia were featured. But in 1977, Robert Bruning, after weathering financial problems and a few poor productions, hit the jackpot.

Productions became smoother, the acting was better, and the critics sat up and took notice (always a heartening sign). Finally — the awards came for a job well done.

Gemini Productions (now backed by the Reg Grundy Organisation) made three tele-cine dramas for the Channel 7 network, prior to the amalgamation taking place. Bruning began in excellent style with *The Alternative,* quickly followed this with *Mama's Gone A-hunting* and then ended with *Gone to Ground* — all of which warranted rave notices everywhere.

The Alternative gained most of the awards. In the 1977 Television Society's Penguin awards Peter Adams and Wendy Hughes won the best actor and actress awards, and Alwyn Kurts received a Penguin for the best supporting actor. The Australian Film Commission's $3 000 award went to *The Alternative* itself. In the 1977 TV Times Sammy awards, Tony Bonner was judged the best actor in a single TV performance, and finally in the 1978 TV Week Logie awards, *The Alternative* was named as the best single dramatic production.

The Alternative was photographed by Russell Boyd and directed by Paul Eddey. Robert Bruning was producer and editor of *The Alternative* and he wrote the story line and the song, and played a small role as well. Wendy Hughes portrays Melanie, the editor of a women's magazine, and Alwyn Kurts is her boss. She has to take time off to have a baby and then must raise it as a single parent. Her parents are unsympathetic, and a housekeeper she engages is partially deaf and remains glued to the TV set all day. Meanwhile she is having problems with Peter (Tony Bonner) the violent father of the child, who demands to see the child. At work she has her problems too when she is instructed to let the firm's white haired boy (Peter Adams) assist her in running the magazine and helping to boost circulation. A romance blossoms between Melanie and her assistant, Noel Denning, to which Peter objects. One of the most realistic fight scenes on Australian TV erupts between Peter and Noel.

Peter is warned off by the management and Melanie is instructed to keep her private life out of the office. Noel proposes marriage and says that he will

6.78   *Bryan Brown and Kris McQuade in "Love Letters from Teralba Road." In the 1977 Australian Film Awards, this picture won Awards for creativity, cinematography (by Tom Cowan) and in the special fiction category.*

take up freelance writing. But when Melanie states that she will remain in her job until he is established, he does not agree. He informs her that he intends to be the breadwinner. It is Melanie's turn to reject the idea. Noel storms out stating that she doesn't want a husband but a wife. Linda (Carla Hoogeveen) who has worked with Melanie asks to remain at home with the baby — and the ending suggests a lesbian relationship with Linda attending to Melanie's needs when she arrives home from the office.

Mama's Gone A-Hunting followed *The Alternative.* One critic said that this film proclaimed the fact that Gerard Kennedy was one of the best horror characters in the country, and that Judy Morris was one of our best actresses.

Judy Morris plays Tessa the baby sitter, who decides to kidnap the baby she is minding. She is unaware that a psychotic prison escapee, Elliott (Gerard Kennedy) has talked David (Vince Martin) into kidnapping the same baby and holding it for $500 000 ransom. Tessa however has plans to keep the baby herself. A chase ends up at Sydney Central Station. In the search for the baby snatcher, David gets down on the train tracks to learn if Tessa is hiding in one of the empty carriages. He fails to notice an oncoming train and is killed. Tessa leaves the baby with a woman in the tea rooms (Queenie Ashton) while she attempts to elude Elliott. Finally she locates a luggage hauler with engine still running, and pins her pursuer against one of the stone pylons. In an effort to escape, Elliott falls over a parapet to the street below. After all that, Tessa decides to return the baby to the parents. The twist to this picture is that the would-be kidnappers were both killed, while the actual kidnapper gets away with it — for the time being at least, and is rewarded for her crime.

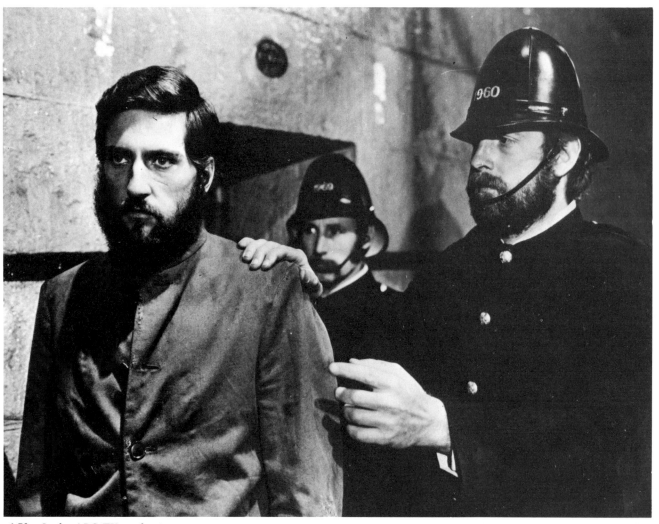

6.79 *In the ABC-TV production "The Trial of Ned Kelly", John Waters played the role of the bushranger. This shows Ned being led to the death cell. The one-hour dramatised reconstruction of the trial, was written by Roger Simpson.*

In the 1977 Sammy awards, Bruce Wishart won the award for the best writer of a TV drama, and *Mama's Gone A-Hunting* won a Sammy for the best TV play, defeating *The Alternative* which was nominated in the same category.

The third tele-movie from Gemini was *Gone to Ground* which was shown on 22 June. Directed by Kevin Dobson (who also directed the feature film *The Mango Tree*) and photographed by Russell Boyd, this TV drama did not receive any awards.

Eric Oldfield is a newly-wed whose wife is Robyn Gibbes. After receiving anonymous death threats, and being beaten up by a gang of hooligans, he gladly accepts an invitation extended by his ex-boss (Charles 'Bud' Tingwell) to a holiday in his weekender. Elaine Lee plays Tingwell's wife. During a weekend of terror, four murders are committed, and most of the holiday group reveal that their past does not warrant close scrutiny. It is Charles Tingwell's show with good support being supplied by Marion Johns, Judy Lynne, and Dennis Grosvenor (from *Chopper Squad* and *Homicide*). Elaine Lee also reveals that she has more talent than was previously revealed in the limited scope of *Number 96*.

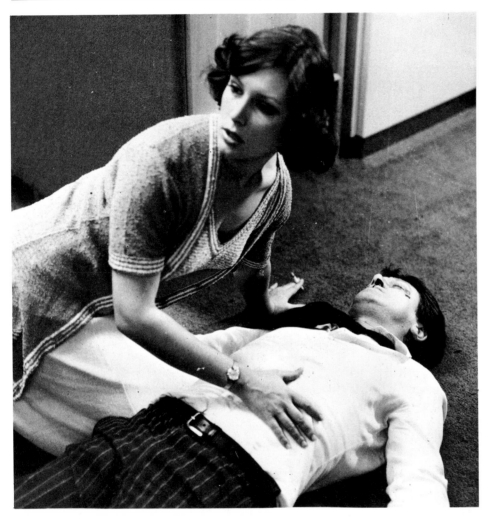

6.80   *In 1977 Robert Bruning and his Gemini Productions were producing top quality telephotoplays. "The Alternative" with Wendy Hughes and Peter Adams won numerous Awards, and firmly established Bruning as a director. This scene follows a fierce fight in an office of a woman's magazine when Tony Bonner floors Adams.*

Further Activity in Television

The Sullivans continued to make excellent progress and win even more awards. Battle scenes from Bardia to Crete were being introduced, and were superbly handled into the bargain. But everything didn't come up chocolates for Crawford Productions. *Bobby Dazzler,* the story of a teenage rock star and his agent manager was captioned 'they've laid another egg'. However in the 1977 Sammy awards, Terry Stapleton was named the best comedy writer for *Bobby Dazzler.*

Another blotted page in the Crawford book was *Hotel Story.* This $1 million TV show was axed after seven episodes. Channel ATV 0, to gain ratings, screened the seven episodes and invited viewers to judge for themselves. Richard Lawson as Conrad, a trouble shooter for an international chain of hotels, was especially imported from America but the results were far from impressive. One of the leads of the show, Terry Donovan, was not at all happy about the collapse of the show, and said so publicly. The irony of it all was that June Salter won a Sammy in 1977 for the best single TV performance by an actress for her role in *Hotel Story.*

However Crawford's were commissioned by Channel 7 for a series titled

Young Ramsay which centred around a veterinary surgeon in a country town. In the 1978 Logie awards, six year old Beau Cox captured the hearts of the audience and viewers when he collected a Logie for an outstanding performance by a juvenile in *Young Ramsay*.

In the 1977 Penguin awards, an unbelievable documentary that was superbly photographed was *The Garden Jungle*. Made by Mantis Wildlife Films and directed by Densey Clyne it won the $2000 Shell award. This film provided a close-up view of minute specimens of insect life that dwelt in an ordinary suburban garden. Densey Clyne also received a Penguin as the best documentary director. In the 1977 Australian Film Awards, *The Garden Jungle* won a special award for macrophotography.

But the best television news of the lot appeared in a Sydney newspaper on 29 May 1977, where it was reported that Air Programs International — an Australian company — had over the past five years sold fourteen cartoon series to the United States. It was further stated that Air'Programs were in fact better known in the USA than in Australia. Movie length classics suitable for general viewing made up the bulk of the sales. The animated version of *A Christmas Carol* had already been shown on the giant NBC Network seven times, reaching an estimated 200 to 300 million viewers. In association with Swiss and German television networks, Air Programs International began filming their first 'live' production in June 1977. This was the latest version of *Heidi* with Ros Spiers in the cast as the aunt. Twenty-six half-hour episodes will be made, and the Channel 7 Network has already purchased the series for Australia.

Stalemate

The big question for 1978 was — where is Australian film production going from this point? In the 1977 Cannes Film Festival, the slogan was 'Down Under Delivers'. It was then stated that until a year ago the world never knew that Australia made pictures. Interest however was soon stimulated with the arrival of *Picnic at Hanging Rock*. From the area of push and shove, hustle and bustle, one overseas reporter urged Australia to get out and promote, and let the product speak for itself. Mike Thornhill showed more caution and described Cannes as the 'greatest freak show on earth'.

Ex-Australian Al Daff in late June 1977 arrived on yet another visit to his home country from America — this time for the launching of Ken Hall's autobiography. Some of his remarks, including those concerning Cannes, are worth noting.

> What the hell are Australian movie makers trying to do — sell cars? Two films, *Caddie* and *F.J. Holden* should have different names for a start. If they'd called the films 'General Motors' they'd have had as much impact. Even the Cannes Film Festival is nothing more than the bargain basement of the industry. If the money that Australia spends on junkets to Cannes was spent on breaking into the American market, perhaps there would be some return on the investment. Anyone with any sense doesn't go to Cannes to sell a movie. He already has a buyer before he goes, if it's any good. As for stories that Australia has sold $2 million worth of films at Cannes, I can't believe it. Just because people say they're interested, doesn't mean they'll take it. Until something is in the bank, you don't have a deal. That's the rules of good business.

6.81   *The second Gemini
Production for 1977 starred Judy
Morris and Gerard Kennedy. This
scene is just prior to Kennedy being
forced over a parapet.*

In those early months of 1978, Australia was not delivering. *Blue Fire Lady, Summer City,* and the *ABC of Love and Sex* comprised an indifferent trio.

Blue Fire Lady opened at the Mayfair Theatre, Melbourne, on 19 January 1978. The story by Robert Maumill was as thin as a wafer. Cathryn Harrison helps run the family farm with her widowed father. He hates horses because one was responsible for his wife's death. When the girl persists in being interested in a neighbour's horses, her father sends her to a boarding school. Eventually she obtains a job as a stable hand for a horse trainer (Peter Cummins). She encounters a number of problems, but when the owner of the stables (John Ewart) arrives with an 'unmanageable horse', he asks that the horse be given a chance, but agrees that if 'Blue Fire Lady' does not show promise as a racehorse he would sell her. Only the girl is able to control the horse. At the Caulfield Race Track, the horse wins despite the fact that the jockey (Roy Higgins) has been instructed to use the whip on her. In succeeding appearances 'Blue Fire Lady' becomes troublesome at the barrier, and is sold. During the progress of the film the girl meets up with Mark Holden — and it is he who persuades the father to purchase the horse. Although it has been disbarred from the racetrack, the girl rides 'Blue Fire Lady' successfully at horse trials.

Cathryn Harrison and Mark Holden were pleasant enough, although they would not win awards for acting. Some of the minor roles however, were poorly portrayed, and Gary Waddell as the top stable hand gave one of the worst performances ever seen in an Australian film. Peter Cummins and John Ewart were completely wasted in the film.

Vincent Monton's photography was the outstanding feature of the picture especially in the countryside scenes, and also with the atmospheric morning shots of horses galloping with vaporised snorts issuing from distended nostrils. The colourful setting at Caulfield and the activity behind every big meeting were interesting enough, if one happened to be a racing enthusiast.

The Melbourne *Scene* on 14 January gave the following impressions of *Blue Fire Lady:*

> Lady lacks fire!
> *Blue Fire Lady* is an extremely lightweight, although attractively photographed story ... Although it singularly lacks tension of any kind, the film is pleasing to look at. Cathryn Harrison, an inexperienced actress, makes a photogenic heroine. Mark Holden is adequate for the requirements of the part. The rest of the cast range from satisfactory to barely adequate. *Blue Fire Lady* is not in the same class as the best of recent Australian films. Indeed at times it reminds one of local productions of twenty years ago, in the unevenness of the acting and the lack of distinctive style. It should appeal to its chosen audience, but it is a pity that it didn't set its sights a little higher.

The Melbourne *Sun* felt that the delight of *Blue Fire Lady* was Marion Edwards as the Italian Momma. She delivered some ordinary lines with a gusto that convulsed the audience. But Cathryn Grayson was the problem. She was haughty and stubborn, and it was hard to assess whether the role was that of a prig, or if that's what Miss Harrison made of it. Her characterisation was devoid of any humour, or of light and shade.

When shown in Sydney's Hoyts Entertainment Centre in the city and at Parramatta in May 1978, one critic felt that everything happened as expected, and that *Blue Fire Lady* had a simple charm reminiscent of the popular horse stories for young people in the 30s and 40s. The photography was imaginative with some inspired moments, and Mike Brady was to be congratulated for his musical theme.

The final opinion of the film comes from Melbourne critic, Denbeigh Salter:

> It was wholesome entertainment for the family — the type of film we don't often see. Aimed at the youth market, *Blue Fire Lady* is one of the best pictures ever made about racing.'

However, like Australian Rules (shades of *The Great Macarthy*) not every one is interested in horse racing.

Blue Fire Lady may have had a larger impact but it wasn't the first film on the scene in 1978. The little publicised Phillip Avalon Production *Summer City* was premiered at the Sydney Century Theatre on 22 December 1977, and was still running when the New Year dawned. It was directed by Christopher Fraser and photographed by Jerry Marek. The Phillip Avalon script was reminiscent of the 'B' features (or supports) from America in the early 1960s.

Robbie (Phil Avalon) and Scallop (Mel Gibson) are happy-go-lucky surfers. On the other hand, Boo (Steve Bisley) is an aggressive 'Ocker' and Sandy (John Jarrat) a rather proper university student. The four journey in Robbie's black Chevrolet to a small coastal town where they attend the local Surf club's stomp. Boo seduces the landlord's daughter, Caroline (Debbie Forman). Robbie and Scallop go surfing, get drunk, and crash the car. They spend the night in the bush and an argument takes place between Boo and Sandy. Meanwhile the landlord searches for Boo, and the climax comes with a fatal shoot out.

On the credit side, the story is action-packed and the players enact their roles with considerable energy. On the debit side, the dance sequence, while well mounted, lacks both direction and good music. It's a pity more time wasn't spent on script and direction. Yet there were some positive signs of sensitivity at times, such as the sequence in which Boo seduces Caroline in a water tank, and the girl returns home, a little frightened and ashamed. Here the photography and acting is of a very high standard.

Pornography for pornography's sake appeared to be the theme of John Lamond's documentary *The ABC of Love and Sex*. This film never aims for subtlety. The *Sun* treated its Melbourne season rather tersely: *ABC's* for the birds.' This headline was followed by the scathing comment, 'the film must create some kind of record for banality.' The report concludes with the profound observation that if this pseudo sex education proves anything, it is that the birds and bees do just the same, the world over.

The ABC of Love and Sex opened at the Swanston Theatre on 2 March, 1978, and transferred to the Roma Theatre, Melbourne on 30 March.

Problems Loom

Nineteen seventy-eight probably will go down in film history as the year that Australia wondered where all the wool had gone. The twelve months were packed solidly with traumatic delusion, frustrating disappointment, and bewildering conflict. The unions were shouting about unemployment, yet appeared hell bent upon making the position chaotic. In the film theatres in Australia in 1978, projectionists fought new advances in the bio box in the same way the workers had done in England over new technology three centuries ago. But progress is one item that even union leaders cannot combat. Curb temporarily — yes; halt permanently — no! These set-backs are all the more amazing, when overseas, the film business was booming, and 'Saturday night at the pictures' was once again becoming the 'in' thing.

A major blow was delivered by the Federal Government, when three weeks after 4 March entry, came a depressing and frustrating report that there would be a $2 to $3 million cut in the next Australian Film Commission's budget. The news was badly timed — it was like urging one's young son up a tree then tackling the trunk with an axe.

To add insult to injury, concurrent with the bad news about the budget, Alexander Walker, a visiting London *Evening Standard* film critic stated: 'The Australian government should be aware of the impact Australian films are having. They are the best things you are sending out of this country in cans.' (The fruit canneries would have appreciated that remark!) This comment is given credibility by the fact that in March 1978, Klaus Helwig of West Germany's Janus Films, a proven champion of Australian films in Europe, was in this country looking for new products to invest in, and distribute. Janus was an investor in *The Last Wave* that it was distributing in Germany. Helwig had been instrumental in setting up a successful season of Australian films at the recent Berlin Film Festival.

Then came the big crunch. On television on 18 April, producer-director Fred Schepisi announced that the Australian Theatrical and Amusement Employees' Union were using heavy-handed standover tactics and had banned screenings of the picture *The Chant of Jimmie Blacksmith* because non-union labour had been used. As *Jimmie* at the time was expected to provide the big breakthrough in the world market, such shortsighted action could have meant that the Union was actually stultifying rather than promoting employment. It appears that seven crew members were not Unionists and eight were not up to date with their dues. As Schepisi pointed out, most were not employees but really sub-contractors who run their own businesses, and were not bound by the Union's rules.

The Producers' and Directors' Guild of Australia warned that investors would boycott the film industry, while doubts remained as to whether producers *or* unions were in charge of productions. On 1 May bans were lifted on *The Chant of Jimmie Blacksmith* after the last member paid his Union dues.

More Trouble

ABC technicians and their union were in the news in September, when a video cassette copy of *Newsfront* was sent to the Governor-General, Sir Zelman Cowen. A member of the Government House staff requested the assistance of the ABC to show the film privately, but the technicians, after seeking the advice of their union in Sydney, refused to co-operate. A rather lame excuse followed: ABC technicians felt that they should not be requested to screen a tape that was not the ABC's.

On 5 October newspapers carried the news that a major industrial dispute was brewing in the cinema industry in Melbourne that could close the picture houses. The trouble was over the manning of multi-theatre complexes. Proprietors wished to reduce the number of projectionists. The row involved the new six-theatre Russell Street complex to be opened at Christmas time. Only three projectionists were required. Once again the Theatrical and Amusement Employees' Union was providing the opposition. The state secretary advised that projectionists throughout Melbourne would cease work immediately if employers tried to introduce the new manning levels.

Theatre owners had their problems during 1978 and drive-ins aren't to be excluded. Drive-in theatre operators probably won't be happy with the news from America that a chain is about to launch a new type of screen. Coated with chrome-covered nodules of pure copper, the containment screen appears black outside the exact peripheral area specified. This will eliminate complaints from nearby neighbours who do not want their children viewing 'R' rated sex movies. This is a long way from the first commercial drive-in which was opened in New Jersey in June 1933 and was a twelve metre screen with loudspeakers mounted above it.

No headache powders were offered to the film industry by David Williams, managing director of Greater Union in August 1978, when he stated that Australian actors lacked star status. 'Australia needs more film actors who are prepared to try for the Hollywood style star status syndrome.' He went on to state that Australian producers should drop their fixation with cracking the US cinema market. They should concentrate on films that would return their investment, and make a profit at home.

There were complaints from Australian actresses too. Judy Morris complained that in Australian films, women were usually placed in one of two categories: 'A sweet appendage to a man, or a woman of the night.' She was pleased however with her role in the 1978 film *In Search of Anna:* "She is interesting because she is both sweet and bitchy; she behaves like a real person.'

Women in the News

Two women producers made the film news in 1978. In September the headlines included 'Oscar winning producer is putting China on film'. Suzanne Baker from Film Australia, whose cartoon short *Leisure* won an American Academy Award, had returned from China after two months. She stated that she was interested in making a comprehensive series of human-interest documentaries. By the end of September it was reported that several television networks were competing for five 30 minute films of aspects of China never seen before by Westerners. The film crew went off the beaten track, covering territory previously 'forbidden'. One film covers a three-day boat trip along the Yangtze River to Chungking.

The other woman who made news was Pat Lovell, who became a part-time member of the Australian Film Commission.

Budget vs Profits

In October one Hollywood producer quipped, 'there seems to be no limit to the amount of money you can make.' Fred Schepisi is one Australian director-producer who is sceptical of such a remark. That budget of $1.2 million for *The Chant of Jimmie Blacksmith* became more formidable as the weeks progressed. Its Melbourne run commenced at Hoyts Cinema Centre on 22 June 1978 and ended on 11 October — a sixteen weeks season. Considering the outlay, that didn't even pay the rent on his premises — Film House.

Despite the costs Australian films were somehow being produced. Alexander Walker in the London *Evening Standard* in late April, described the British film industry as nothing more than a ripple compared with the Australian counterpart. He pointed out that such films as *Picnic at Hanging Rock, Caddie* and *Sunday Too Far Away* were still being screened in and around London. He thought that *The Chant of Jimmie Blacksmith* was the most stunning of an enormously varied, highly individualised bunch of Australian movies. The violence was stunning, he continued, with the bluntness of a confrontation rarely seen on a screen of a continent trying to fit many such outsiders as Jimmie into society without bloodshed. 'Schepisi's use of detail suggests much, much more than it depicts,' the critic wrote. Walker added that his was not the blood-bolstered self-indulgence of a Sam Peckinpah, but more that of the Spartan shocks of Saul Bass.

The Chant of Jimmie Blacksmith

Early in 1978 it seemed that Australia's great 'White Hope' was about to obtain world-wide recognition, and cause a genuine stir at Cannes.

Before the actual judging of *Jimmie* at Cannes, praises for the film were published in various newspapers. The Melbourne *Sun* reported, 'Cannes is wild about our *Chant*' and stated that it was given a standing ovation after being screened. The Sydney *Sunday Telegraph* wrote, 'Jimmie Blacksmith in fine ovation at Cannes', and *The Australian* printed that hysteria came to Cannes as 'judgement day nears'. It advised that Friday 26 May 1978, was the day Australians in Cannes were waiting for. On 29 May Geraldine Pascall of *The Australian* reviewed the world premiere of *The Chant of Jimmie Blacksmith*. She wrote that it was not only the best Australian film made so far, but it was a magnificent, daring and powerful film in general. Fred Schepisi said:

> All I know is, it is a bloody terrific film. It has everything — it is completely involving, powerful, and contains action and pathos.

Neither the film nor the director were successful in winning an award. Instead, Italy scooped the pool with entries that were considered 'cheerful and human'.

Fred Schepisi on his return from the French Festival stated that his film had been canned because it was too violent. One French critic had felt that the continued bloodbath was unbearable, and advised tender-hearted people not to see it.

The Age led the 'post-Cannes' critiques with, 'This Blacksmith hammers home the guilt of the whites', and described it as 'a tragic Australian Western comparable but superior to *Mad Dog Morgan*.' The critic summed up the review with: 'We could not take this kind of thing in the days of the underrated *Wake in Fright*. I wonder if we can take it now?' The Sydney *Sun Herald* compared *The Chant of Jimmie Blacksmith* to those anti-Nazi films in which post-war Germans seem to want to atone for past evils. The critic felt that this film acknowledged an Australian guilt. The Melbourne *Sun* classified the film as, 'when the chant is ended, the violence lingers on.' Then it gets down to the gory details: '"Thunk" goes the axe into the white woman's neck ... "chonk" goes a white child's skull ... "thud" goes the white teacher's breasts.' Although admitting that it was a professional piece of film making, the critic wrote that the picture should have been titled 'The Drone of Jimmie Blacksmith' with the sub-title 'Blood on the Egg'. The Melbourne *Herald* felt that the film was worth making, even though it lacked the subtleties of Schepisi's earlier success *The Devil's Playground.*' It concluded, 'I advise you to see the film,' but admitted that, 'the best Australian film has not been made.' Melbourne *Scene* felt that, 'Jimmie just falls short'. It was the opinion of Ivan Hutchinson that Fred Schepisi showed great promise as a director, but that he is not yet the master of his chosen art. Finally *The Bulletin* summed up the production as, 'Blacksmith's hammer too heavy.'

In reply a special advertisement was inserted in the papers for *The Chant of Jimmie Blacksmith* on 8 July quoting twelve favourable comments on the picture.

6.82   *Another 1977 Gemini Production — "Gone To Ground". This is a story of terror and murder in a weekender. Players from left to right . . . Elaine Lee, Charles "Bud" Tingwell, Eric Oldfield and Robyn Gibbes.*

> The story is set at the turn of the century — but the chant does not end there. Jimmie lives today in Australia, and many, many countries. He has other names, other races, other faces, other environments. But he is still with us, as we are with him. And that is the heart of it.

6.83 *Cathryn Harrison (standing),*
Marion Edwards (left) and Mark
Holden in "Blue Fire Lady".

This is Schepisi's foreword which opens the film.

Jimmie Blacksmith is a half-caste who is educated by a mission superintendent (Jack Thompson) and encouraged to take his rightful place in the white man's world.

He sets out full of hope. His first job is cutting posts and rails for a farmer (Tim Robertson), but he receives less than the sum agreed upon. He leaves, bitter and resentful. In an Aboriginal camp he learns that Harry Edwards (Jack Charles) has killed a white boy. Jimmie helps to bury the victim. Jimmie goes to work for a Scottish farmer (Rob Steele) and is assisted by his half-brother Mort (Freddy Daniels). Once again he is short-changed.

He becomes a tracker for a drunken, Aboriginal-hating Chief Constable (Ray Barrett). He helps arrest Harry Edwards, but is sickened by the sadism

6.84 *Tommy Lewis (Jimmie Blacksmith) has a farewell dinner at the mission house, Jack Thompson (as the Rev. Neville) and his wife (Julie Dawson) are seated at the table with the aboriginal. "The Chant Of Jimmie Blacksmith" is released by Hoyts Theatres.*

of the police officer. Next morning the murderer is found hanged in his cell. But the question is — was it suicide or did the lawman save the hangman a job?

At a shearing shed, Jimmie has his first sexual encounter with a white woman — Gilda, played by Angela Punch. Later she confesses that she is pregnant and Blacksmith marries her. Jimmie finds work at the Newby homestead. The owner (Don Crosby) allows him to live on the property in a shack. Gilda gives birth to a white child! Mrs Newby (Ruth Cracknell) and a schoolteacher (Elizabeth Alexander) are shocked. Then Newby turns nasty. He refuses to pay the money he owes to Jimmie, and orders a number of the half-caste's relations off the property. This is when Blacksmith takes to the women with an axe. Eventually Jimmie is hunted down, and the hangman's services are called upon.

In the final scenes one witnesses the mark Charles Chauvel has left upon the industry. As in *Jedda* audiences are spared the death sequence, and instead see a flock of white cockatoos in flight.

But the important question that arises after one sees *Jimmie* is — does this film represent entertainment? The photography of Ian Baker is sheer poesy at times; the make-up by Deryck de Niese is superb; and the editing by Brian Kavanagh is smooth and professional. But the message becomes very heavy-handed towards the end when the hostage schoolteacher, Peter Carroll, drives home the moral already more subtly made earlier by the director. Glaring faults were a colourless performance by Jack Thompson. whose role, although small, should have been more forceful as it contained the real key to the tragic story of Jimmie Blacksmith. Even his utterance of, 'poor Jimmie' at the finale held no real meaning. Then there was the very vital point of racial discrimination. The whites were shown in a very poor light — but there was no real contrast. The Aborigines were depicted as lazy, beer-swillers, who, when Jimmie tried to resist the drink, forced beer between his lips and poured it over his face. The real acting actually came from the non-professional named Freddy Reynolds. At the end when he knew death was inevitable, even his facial muscles accentuated the mixed emotions he was experiencing.

Are the Golden Days Over?

Now 'the chant' becomes a mournful dirge. In late July actor Jack Charles was gaoled for eight years, on some forty-eight counts of burglary, and for becoming a multiple drug user. On 29 July Fred Schepisi in the Melbourne *Herald* was labelled as being 'embittered', 'sad' and 'angry'. He was quoted as hearing 'the chant of despair'. Schepisi was angry over an article entitled 'The Tall Poppies Fall' written by Terry Bourke under a pseudonym. In it the end of Schepisi was predicted, as well as other big-budget film makers in Australia. Schepisi replied: 'I live for the day when our films are compared with American films, rather than masterpieces of the world.'

On 26 August, *The Australian* reported that it seemed Fred Schepisi's third film would be a co-production with the American Avco Embassy. It could be shot in either San Francisco or Sydney. In the same month the Sydney *Sun Herald* headed an article: 'Aussie Films: Is the Honeymoon Over?' In it *Weekend of Shadows* was listed as one of the recent flops, with more casualties being inevitable. *Solo,* a New Zealand-Australian co-production was listed as another cinema failure of 1978.

Fred Schepisi is quoted as saying, 'I think our golden days are over.' But Greg Coote, general manager of Roadshow was even more caustic: 'The honeymoon was over, two to three years ago. This is a crucial time for the industry — the watershed. I see this as a revitalisation period.' But the disaster continued. On 3 September, the Sydney *Sunday Telegraph* printed that *Jimmie* failed to live up to hopes of the film industry, and that at the time it was playing to half-empty hardtops and drive-ins. Hoyts and the Australian Film Commission were quoted as being 'highly disappointed' at the reception at the box office.

In the Australian Film Awards, for 1978, *The Chant of Jimmie Blacksmith* received three awards, which is nowhere near what Schepisi had won with his first film, *The Devil's Playground*. *Jimmie* won best performance by an actress in a leading role — Angela Punch; best performance by an actor in a supporting role — Ray Barrett; best original music score — Bruce Smeaton. On 14 July Fred Schepisi received an Awgie award from the Australian Writers Guild for his screenplay of *Jimmie* which was based on the novel by Thomas Keneally. Finally in the TV Times Sammy awards on 11 October 1978, Ruth Cracknell received the best supporting actress award and Tommy Lewis was named as the best new talent.

Newsfront is Star of 1978

The 'dark horse' *Newsfront* which had ousted *Jimmie* at Cannes took a total of eight awards at the 1978 Australian Film Awards in Perth in August. They were:

> Best director — Phil Noyce.
> Best actor in a leading role — Bill Hunter.
> Best actress in a supporting role — Angela Punch (her second award for the night).
> Best original screenplay — Bob Ellis, Anne Brooksbank, Phil Noyce.
> Best film editor — John Scott.
> Best production designer — Lissa Coote.
> Best costuming — Norma Moriceau.
> Best film of the year.

In the TV Times Sammy awards, for 1978, *Newsfront* gained the awards for best direction; best screenplay; best film actor in a leading role; and again, best film of the year. The one difference to the AFI Awards was that Chris Haywood received the best supporting film actor. This constitutes thirteen awards from only two sources.

Newsfront had been a virtual 'sleeper' before Cannes. Then it appeared in 'rave' reviews and immediately received invitations to some eight film festivals. It was the 'opener' at the London Film Festival, and the first Australian feature in the New York Festival.

Phil Noyce claimed that *Newsfront* was a 'medium-budget' film ($550 000) and that on 22 August, one-fifth of the budget had been recouped on sales to the BBC and German TV. On 3 October it was reported from New York that 'the kookaburras of the movie newsreel in *Newsfront* were laughing at the storm of praise and money-making interest for young Australian director, Phil Noyce.' Its only major set-back was the language barrier. Some New Yorkers could not understand the Australian accent.

Newsfront wasn't without its problems despite its financial success and all its awards. On 12 August it was stated that Bob Ellis, writer of the original screenplay which had been cut considerably by Phil Noyce, took out a newspaper advertisement to the effect that he 'wishes it known that he will now accept congratulations for *Newsfront*' He acknowledged with surprise that despite all the cuts what is left is a very good film. He added that he would shoot Mr Noyce (the director) and Mr Elfick (the producer) should they ever appear on his lawn.

After Cannes, *Newsfront* visited the Taormina Film Festival, Sicily long enough to pick up awards for 'best film' and 'best direction'. According to Phil Noyce no other picture had even won two top awards before at this exclusive festival.

With such good prospects, Roadshow set about promoting *Newsfront* in the grand manner. They used the 'sneak preview' principle in the various capital cities before the initial release; excellent TV commercials were prepared; top press coverage was given, and a book of the film was issued. The Sydney premiere (at Village Cinema City and Parramatta) was the 27 July and the Melbourne showing began at the Bryson on 24 August.

After its success at the Australian Film Awards, business doubled in Sydney. Over a weekend *Newsfront* was viewed by capacity houses.

Newspapers weren't slow in taking advantage of a good thing either. *The Sun,* Melbourne, on 3 August featured a centre spread headed, 'That was the news that was.' *Toorak Times* (a Melbourne suburban paper) on 29 August carried the heading, 'Putting a Bit of Front on the News', and ended by stating that the 'film was b— good!' *The National Times* carried a salute to *Newsfront* in the issue for the week ending 12 August, and then stated that 'the blemishes are there, but they are part of humanity. The film should make people like their parents a whole lot more.'

The Sydney *Sun Herald* felt that the best feature of the film was the way in which Phillip Noyce had edited actual newsreels into recreated scenes. However the critic considered the plot flabby and as conventional as a soap opera serial. He felt that the newsreel footage could be relied upon to save the film.

Melbourne *Scene* on 2 September advised that *Newsfront* is 'instant nostalgia, a history lesson, a moving salute to the past:

> *Newsfront* is quality ... is entertainment ... is totally ours. Let us continue to make films for the world market, and let us hope we succeed. But it is this film which, more than any other lately, seems to come from the heart of us.

The Australian on 29 July sings the praises of *Newsfront* although the critic thought that the last 10 to 15 minutes were a bit slow because 'no one seemed sure where to end it'. This critic felt that it was a picture of 'great originality and charm'.

The entry in the Sydney *Sun Herald* on 30 July under the headline, 'Those Daring Young Men Who Put it on Newsreel' recalls one inaccuracy that should be corrected: the credits listed 'Bert Nichols' as one of the newsreel men whose work was used. A man of the stature of Bert *Nicholas* deserves better treatment than that. In general, *Newsfront* received excellent support from both capital city and suburban newspapers, which is unique in the history of local films.

Old Newsreels the Real Interest

Len (Bill Hunter) and Frank (Gerard Kennedy) are brothers who stand shoulder to shoulder during the Depression, and proudly boast that they have never been on the 'dole'. They enter the newsreel field together, but whereas

6.85 *Jimmy (Tommy Lewis) goes about his task of fence erecting seriously. Not so Mort (Freddy Reynolds). He manages to laugh most of the time. Film by Fred Schepisi. Released by Hoyts. "The Chant of Jimmie Blacksmith".*

6.86 *An atmospheric shot from "The Chant Of Jimmie Blacksmith" directed by Fred Schepisi and photographed by Ian Baker. In this scene Tommy Lewis as "Jimmie Blacksmith" watches the farmer (Tim Robertson) and his wife (Jane Harders) drive by, after the farmer had stated that he would not be going into the town.*

Len remains staunchly Australian, Frank, like many an Australian before him, sees a future in the film business only in America. Amy (Wendy Hughes) is a convenient lover for Frank, who steers clear of matrimonial ties. Len is a Catholic and a staunch Labor Party supporter — but both the church and politics go sour on him. His wife (Angela Punch) strictly adheres to the doctrine of the Catholic Church, and does not share the liberal views of her husband. This causes their marriage to break up. To add to Len's bitterness, R.G. Menzies is elected prime minister. Amy, saddened by Frank's departure, enters a *de facto* relationship with Len. The climax comes when Len covers the 1956 Olympic Games in Melbourne, and is fortunate enough to film the blood-bath between the Russian and Hungarian water polo teams. Frank, who has arrived back in Australia as an executive for an American company, asks Len to let him have the 'scoop' footage, so that he can sell it to the US for a profit. Len remains loyal to his employer, despite the fact that he knows the newsreel industry has reached a point of no return. The ending provides an air of uncertainty as to the destiny of film in Australia. We also wonder about Len's future. Amy smiles at Frank's look of disbelief, and says, 'he's just a bit old fashioned.' Len freezes at the end of the passage, leaving the viewer wondering whether it leads somewhere, or nowhere!

The old newsreels provide the real interest in this film although Phil Noyce claims that they occupy only ten minutes of actual screening time. The build-up and by-play in the editing room, as well as the circumstances surrounding the taking of every item, make up part of the best footage. The editing of *Newsfront* also provided the opportunity for John Dease (as the voice-over on the newsreel) to air cryptic comments. The story itself is thin, and *Newsfront* is not an actor's picture, despite the awards bestowed upon it.

The successful duplication of the Maitland flood scenes, and the filming of the drowning of Chris Haywood while on a mission of mercy in *Newsfront* provides genuine hope for the Australian film industry.

Other Awards in 1978

Minor award winners at the 1978 Australian Film Awards were: Jury Prize: *Mouth to Mouth;* Best Cinematography: Russell Boyd for *The Last Wave;* Best Sound: Don Connelly, Greg Bell, Phil Judd for *The Last Wave;* Best screenplay adapted from other material: Eleanor Witcombe for *The Getting of Wisdom.*

The Raymond Longford Award for a significant contribution to Australian film making went to the McDonagh Sisters, and was received by Phyllis McDonagh.

In the 1978 Sammy awards the Chips Rafferty Award was received by Ken G. Hall, another film maker of the 1930s. This award was a little ironic as it was Ken Hall who gave Chips his first film role.

Mouth to Mouth was screened at the Melbourne East End Cinema on 20 July 1978, and the Village Cinema City, Sydney on 24 August. Starring four previously unknown performers — Sonia Peat, Kim Krejus, Ian Gilmour,

6.87 *Newsreel cameramen Charlie (John Ewart), Chris (Chris Hayward) and Len (Bill Hunter) in Phil Noyce's "Newsfront" produced by David Elfick. A Roadshow release.*

6.88   *Wendy Hughes as Amy in Roadshow's "Newsfront" directed by Phil Noyce, produced by David Elfick.*

and Serge Frazzetto, it was really a director's picture aided by the skilful photography of John Duigan and Tom Cowan. In the storyline, very little happens, and the action is fragmentary. It centres around Carrie and Jeanie (Kim Krejus and Sonia Peat) who escape from a social welfare training centre for teenage girls, and meet two young men from Wonthaggi, Tim and Serge (Ian Gilmour and Sergio Frazzetto). The males are unemployed and arrive in Melbourne to seek work. The girls share mattresses with them in an old warehouse. When the young women lose their jobs in a cafeteria, they steal food and clothing. This provides one humorous scene in which one girl shoves food beneath her clothing and pretends she is pregnant. A noticeable difference in the natures of the two girls becomes apparent when one, deeply shocked when a derelict is beaten up by a teenage thug goes back to the reformatory to complete her term. The other girl, too interested in obtaining easy money as a call girl, wanders the streets in search of prey.

John Duigan as a director-writer has a bright future in films, and Tom Cowan has the awards to prove his excellence behind camera. But *Mouth to Mouth* does perpetuate one of the glaring mistakes that occur regularly in Australian productions — *acting* versus a *reading* of a part. Players can look right in a role, but they often become robots mouthing dialogue. This makes for a complete lack of involvement on the part of an audience and provides no rapport between player and theatre patron. Another fault is the player who has been seen before playing the same role, whether in *Mouth to Mouth,* or in *Truckies.* He seems to get the parts — but never any awards for acting. Finally there was a nice touch that was completely nullified: Walter Pym as the derelict, living in the same empty, ramshackle warehouse provides a contrast between an unwanted teenager, and a forgotten old man. Yet Pym's role is not developed in the film, and one soon realises that he is there for the sole purpose of being bashed.

In October, it was reported that television networks were chasing the 'small screen' rights to *Mouth to Mouth,* while the film's producer, Jon

6.89 *The main characters in "Mouth To Mouth" as portrayed by Kim Crejus (left), Ian Gilmour, Serge Frazetto, and Sonia Peat. The film is directed by John Duigan.*

Sainken, was thinking of taking the picture to the United States personally to try to effect a sale.

A writer in the Melbourne *Sun* on 24 July found *Mouth to Mouth* a far more subtle and concerned film than the 'bang-wallop-whack of *The Chant of Jimmie Blacksmith* which had been made at ten times the cost'. One critic described the picture, 'as Today as Tomorrow', and classified it as 'a movie that took top marks for effort and compassion, although it lacked consistency of excellence'. Another wrote that '*Mouth to Mouth* was something to shout about, and was rich in insight, wit, and imagination. The film is also fiercely contemporary.'

Strangely enough the Australian Film Award magically opened doors previously closed to *Mouth to Mouth*. At the Toronto Film Festival which commenced on 14 September 1978, twelve recently produced Australian features were screened, including *Mouth to Mouth*. *The Getting of Wisdom*, *Caddie*, *Don's Party*, *The Picture Show Man* and *Picnic at Hanging Rock* were also screened. There was a gala performance of *The Chant of Jimmie Blacksmith* and the documentaries *The Last Tasmanian* and *The Passionate Industry* were also shown.

6.90   *Michael Carman stands over a derelict, Walter Pym, prior to beating him up in "Mouth To Mouth" — a Vega Film Production.*

6.92   *Tom Haydon directing a scene for the controversial documentary "The Last Tasmanian" — a Tasmanian Film Corporation presentation.*

6.91   *A scene from the documentary "The Last Tasmanian". Photography was handled by Geoff Burton.*

Postscript: What of the Future?

At present Australian film making once again seems to stand at the crossroads.

Weekend of Shadows, backed by the South Australian Film Corporation, did not have a good run at the box office and ran for only a fortnight in Sydney. The Melbourne *Herald* compared *Mouth to Mouth* with the more recent film and described the former as 'Australia today', but *Weekend of Shadows* as 'Australia yesterday'. Meanwhile the very basis of the Australian film industry — its financial support — is receiving close scrutiny. While several Government bodies do have the extensive financial capacity required to back film-making in this country, the question of return on investment continues to raise its head.

However, while the Australian industry is having to compete with a seemingly never-ending flow of major American films, like the multi-million dollar epics *Superman, Close Encounters of the Third Kind, Alien* and *Apocalypse Now!* it is also evident that the home-grown product *is* capable of both quality and commercial appeal. Gillian Armstrong's *My Brilliant Career*, Australia's official entry in the 1979 Cannes Festival, is showing every sign at present of emulating the example set internationally by *Picnic at Hanging Rock* and *Caddie*, and the fast moving *Mad Max* — another financial success locally — has been sold to the United States for a considerable sum.

So the next few years will be quite crucial to Australian film-making. It is to be hoped that the encouraging progress achieved in the 1970s will not be scattered to the winds in the coming decade.

Index

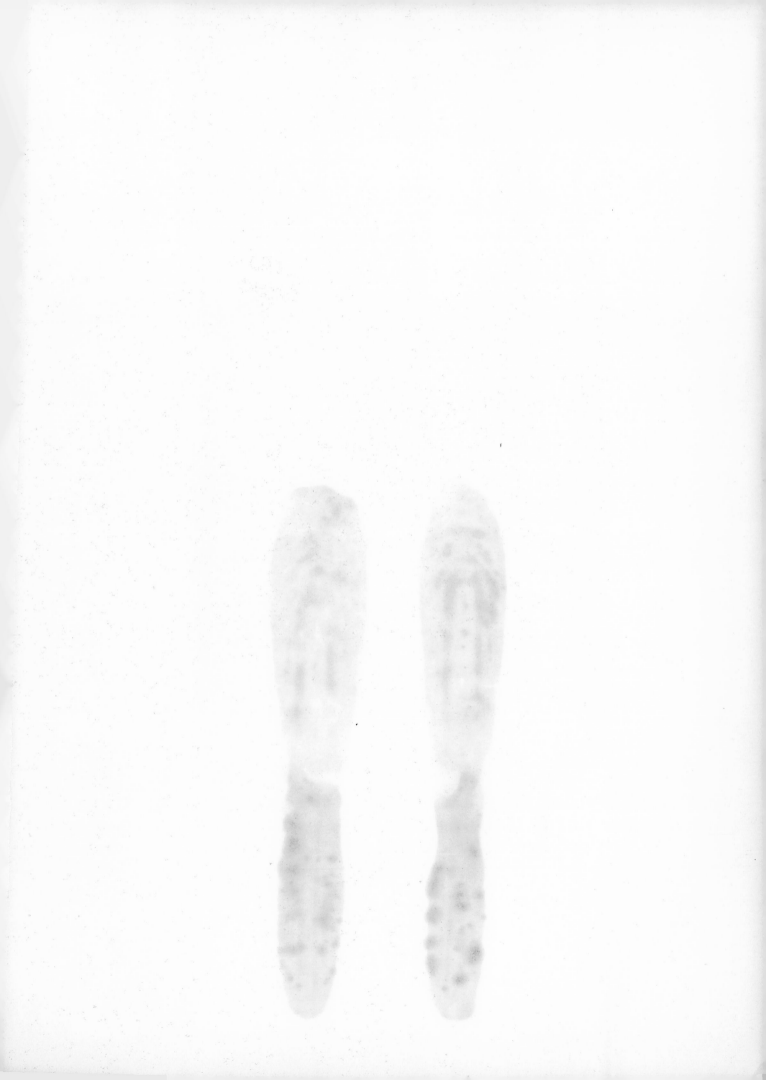